"Allyson May builds on her study of the Old Bailey bar with a marvellous account of the trial of the Swiss valet hanged in 1840 for murdering his employer. The case fascinated early Victorian England. Drawing on an unusually rich prosecution source May shows why, citing class tension and political upheaval."

Douglas C. Hay, *York University, Canada*

"This first-rate study of the Russell murder illuminates the workings of English criminal justice, increasing unease with the death penalty, and the breakdown in the master-servant relationship in which the crime was rooted. It has import, too, for the history of class, gender, and masculinity."

Victor Bailey, *University of Kansas, USA*

Class, Servitude, and the Criminal Justice System in Early Victorian London

This volume draws on the recently discovered and extraordinarily rich scrapbook compiled by prosecuting solicitor Francis Hobler about the 1840 murder of Lord William Russell to consider public engagement with the issues raised from discovery of the murder itself through the ensuing legal processes.

The murder of Russell by his valet François Benjamin Courvoisier was a cause célèbre in its own day by virtue of the fact that the victim was a member of one of England's most prominent political families. For criminal justice historians, the significance of this case lies instead in its timing. In 1840, England had neither an official detective force to investigate the murder nor a public prosecutor to undertake the prosecution. Those accused of felony had only recently (1836) won the right to full legal representation, and the conduct of Courvoisier's defence was controversial. Reaction to Courvoisier's execution was also noteworthy, testifying to a new public unease with capital punishment. The subject of master and servant relations in early Victorian England is another key component of the book: previous studies have not considered the murderer's motivation.

This book will be of interest to students and scholars of criminal justice and law, Victorian England, and microhistory.

Allyson N. May is Associate Professor in the Department of History at the University of Western Ontario, Canada. She is the author of *The Bar and the Old Bailey, 1750–1850* (2003) and *The Fox-Hunting Controversy, 1781–2004: Class and Cruelty* (2013) and co-editor, with David Lemmings, of *Criminal Justice during the Long Eighteenth Century: Theatre, Representation and Emotion* (2019).

Routledge Studies in Modern British History

Networks of Influence and Power
Business, Culture and Identity in Liverpool's Merchant Community, c.1800 to 1914
Edited by Robert Lee

The British Conservative Party
Ideology and Citizenship
Lenon Campos Maschette

The Mystique of Running the Public House in England
Quest for El Dorado, 1840-1939
David W. Gutzke

The Working Men's College and the Tradition of Adult Education
Edited by Tom Schuller and Richard Taylor

Orchestrating Warfighting
A History of the British Army's Corps and Divisions at War since 1914
Edited by Tim Bean, Edward Flint, James E. Kitchen, and Paul Latawski

Sir Ronald Storrs
Personality and Policy in Mandate Palestine, 1917–1926
Christopher Burnham

Britain and the International Civil Service
Empire, Internationalism, and Expertise in the Twentieth Century
Amy Limoncelli

Class, Servitude, and the Criminal Justice System in Early Victorian London
The Russell Murder
Allyson N. May

For more information about this series, please visit: https://www.routledge.com/history/series/RSMBH

Class, Servitude, and the Criminal Justice System in Early Victorian London
The Russell Murder

Allyson N. May

NEW YORK AND LONDON

First published 2025
by Routledge
605 Third Avenue, New York, NY 10158

and by Routledge
4 Park Square, Milton Park, Abingdon, Oxon, OX14 4RN

Routledge is an imprint of the Taylor & Francis Group, an informa business

© 2025 Allyson N. May

The right of Allyson N. May to be identified as author of this work has been asserted in accordance with sections 77 and 78 of the Copyright, Designs and Patents Act 1988.

All rights reserved. No part of this book may be reprinted or reproduced or utilised in any form or by any electronic, mechanical, or other means, now known or hereafter invented, including photocopying and recording, or in any information storage or retrieval system, without permission in writing from the publishers.

Trademark notice: Product or corporate names may be trademarks or registered trademarks, and are used only for identification and explanation without intent to infringe.

Library of Congress Cataloging-in-Publication Data
Names: May, Allyson N. (Allyson Nancy), 1961- author.
Title: Class, servitude, and the criminal justice system in early Victorian London : the Russell murder / Allyson N. May.
Description: Abingdon, Oxon [UK] ; New York, NY : Routledge Taylor & Francis Group, 2025. | Series: Routledge studies in modern British history | Includes bibliographical references and index.
Identifiers: LCCN 2024025448 (print) | LCCN 2024025449 (ebook) | ISBN 9781032771700 (hardback) | ISBN 9781032771731 (paperback) | ISBN 9781003481638 (ebook) | ISBN 9781040133668 (adobe pdf) | ISBN 9781040133675 (epub)
Subjects: LCSH: Criminal justice, Administration of--England--London--History--19th century. | Capital Punishment--England--London--History--19th century. | Criminal investigation--England--London--History--19th century. | Trials (Murder)--England--London--History--19th century. | Courvoisier, François Benjamin, -1840--Trials, litigation, etc. | Russell, William, Lord, 1767-1840. | Slavery--Law and legislation--England--History--19th century.
Classification: LCC KD9085 .M39 2025 (print) | LCC KD9085 (ebook) | DDC 364.152/3092--dc23/eng/20240612
LC record available at https://lccn.loc.gov/2024025448
LC ebook record available at https://lccn.loc.gov/2024025449

ISBN: 978-1-032-77170-0 (hbk)
ISBN: 978-1-032-77173-1 (pbk)
ISBN: 978-1-003-48163-8 (ebk)

DOI: 10.4324/9781003481638

Typeset in Times New Roman
by SPi Technologies India Pvt Ltd (Straive)

**For John Sinclair May
(1929–2015)**

and

**Elizabeth Anne May
(1932–2023)**

Contents

	List of Figures	*xii*
	Preface and Acknowledgements	*xiii*
1	Introduction	1

A murder is announced – and the butler did it 1
Policing and detection 5
The Courvoisier trial 6
Storytelling and voice 8
Execution 9
Master and servant 9
Organization 15
Notes 16

2	14 Norfolk Street, Park Lane: Upstairs and Down	20

Introduction 20
14 Norfolk Street 21
Upstairs: Lord William Russell's 'incomplete household' 23
Downstairs and outside: Russell's 'family' 27
   The female servants: cook and housemaid 30
   Menservants: valet, coachman, and groom 36
   Employment histories: 'place' and home 37
Life below stairs 41
Master and servant relations: unhappy friends? 44
Conclusion 53
Notes 54

3	Inspectors Call: The Investigation	59

The murder discovered 59
Investigating officers 60
The coroner's inquest 62
   The coroner and the new police 62

x   *Contents*

The police investigation 66
Tainted evidence? 72
The chief suspect 75
'The persecution of Sarah Mancer' 76
Public 'assistance' 83
The investigation and the press 91
Conclusion 98
Notes 100

4   The Case for the Prosecution Rests ... with Francis Hobler   106

Introduction 106
'Publick prosecutions' 107
Hobler and Whitehall 110
The pre-trial hearings: Bow Street 113
Briefing the prosecution 118
The Old Bailey trial 121
   Making the case for the prosecution 123
   Counsel for the defence 125
   New evidence 126
   The trial concludes 132
Conclusion 133
Notes 136

5   'Going to See a Man Hanged'   147

Introduction 147
'The old honest way of cutting throats'?: William Russell's
   private execution 148
The victim laid to rest 149
Courvoisier's final days 151
Courvoisier at the scaffold 155
'Constraints on sympathy': class and execution 161
Thackeray and execution 163
Conclusion: 'The household shiver of razors' 165
Notes 166

6   Who Speaks?: Voice, Image, Agency – and Truth   169

Introduction 169
Servants, voice, and history 169
   Servants as storytellers 170
Courvoisier and translated speech 171
Talking heads: servants and portraiture 173
Silence in court: the accused does not *speak 176*
Post-trial confession(s): from anonymity to celebrity 178

Capitalized speech and commercialization 184
  Broadside coverage in the 1830s and 1840s 184
The convict appropriated: The Newgate novels 186
  Servants and reading 187
  Jack Sheppard *190*
Conclusion: 'abominable falsehoods', 'palpable lies', and unreliable narrators 194
Notes 195

7 Explanations and Consequences   199

Explanations: 'Disorder and discontent within the domestic space' 199
  Domestic manhood 205
Immediate consequences: Russell's household 207
Long-term consequences 213
  Courvoisier and the novelists 213
  Policing and detection 214
  The criminal trial 219
A few last words 220
Notes 221

Bibliography   *224*
Index   *237*

Figures

1 The title page of Francis Hobler's scrapbook demonstrates that he clearly envisioned his collection of materials as constituting a 'book'. The text is reproduced on page 7   141
2 A newspaper sketch of the exterior of 14 Norfolk Street, Park Lane. The murder victim's modest house was endlessly described in the newspaper press and subsequently in the Old Bailey courtroom. The sketch establishes that these premises were indeed small, more akin to a middle-class dwelling than one inhabited by an aristocrat   142
3 Another portrait of Lord William Russell, from *The Town*. He looks much younger in this portrait and has all his hair. The two newspaper sketches could easily represent two entirely different men   143
4 Surgeon Robert Blake Overton's explanation of fingerprint evidence. Overton wrote to Lord John Russell on 16 May 1840 saying that fingerprint evidence might be useful in identifying Lord William Russell's murderer   144
5 One of two pencil courtroom sketches of François Benjamin Courvoisier by C.A. Rivers. This sketch was made on the third day of the trial (Saturday 20 June 1840). Solicitor Francis Hobler thought Rivers had made Courvoisier look slightly cross-eyed but was satisfied that it was otherwise an accurate portrayal of the murderer   145
6 A newspaper representation of Courvoisier at the scaffold, 6 July 1840. Such illustrations were a routine feature of execution coverage and tended to be generic   146

Preface and Acknowledgements

This book constitutes a return to a subject I first considered in *The Bar and the Old Bailey* (2003): the trial, in 1840, of François Benjamin Courvoisier for the murder of William Russell. In Chapter 8 of that book, I discussed the impact of Courvoisier's defence on the development of professional standards of conduct in criminal courtrooms, which had been fundamentally altered by the Prisoners' Counsel Act, passed four years earlier, and on the public reputation of England's criminal bar. Here, I explore the case assembled and presented for the prosecution, from the police investigation into Russell's murder through the work done by their solicitor in preparing for trial. I also consider the crime itself and offer an explanation for what might have occasioned it. In doing so, I depart from the prosopographical methodology of my first book; the following study is instead an exercise in microhistory, using the close examination of a particular case to illuminate much larger issues. Any criminal prosecution could of course usefully be examined in this way, but in the case of the Russell murder, the larger issues are large indeed. The documentation that flowed from Russell's violent end sheds light not only on personal tragedy but also on the infancy of modern policing and detection; a transitional moment in the history of the coroner's office; a new focus on murder rather than the violent property crimes which had preoccupied eighteenth-century officials; a pivotal moment in the development of crime fiction; government involvement in an age which had no formal system of public prosecution; changing views on capital punishment, and, last but not least, master and servant relations in early Victorian Britain.

The immediate, contemporary interest generated by the murder of William Russell owed primarily to the social status of the victim. That interest, happily for history and historians, resulted in extensive newspaper coverage of the murder, the police investigation into it, the coroner's inquest and pre-trial hearings of the accused, the criminal trial which resulted, and the execution of the convict. But this particular retelling of the investigation into William Russell's murder and the prosecution of his murderer owes much to a 792-page scrapbook compiled by the solicitor for the prosecution, Francis Hobler. The way in which Hobler's scrapbook came to light constitutes a dramatic story in and of itself.[1] On 6 December 2012 I received an email from Guy Holborn, then librarian at Lincoln's Inn, informing me that he had just noticed in a Sotheby's catalogue an xiv *Preface and Acknowledgements*

item relating to the trial of Courvoisier that was being sold off by the Law Society. Had I been aware of the document? I had not, and to the best of my knowledge, previous historians who have written on the case had likewise been unaware of its existence. Lincoln's Inn was not in a position to purchase the manuscript. Nor was the British Library, despite the valiant efforts of Jonathan Sims, curator, Law and Socio-Legal Studies. Nor was I. I did write to the Law Society suggesting that they rethink the sale, as the item in question is an important part of the historical record. The sale, however, went ahead and on 12 December 'Lot 22' was purchased by an undisclosed buyer described as 'trade'. On 18 December Jon Sims wrote to suggest that 'trade' could mean either a dealer or a cultural institution, but that it seemed likely the manuscript would be sold on. At this point, John Langbein, Sterling Professor of Law and History at Yale, kindly put Yale's rare book librarian, Mike Widener, onto the case. A month later, on 18 January 2013, Ed Nassau Lake emailed to say that the manuscript had been purchased by Jarndyce Antiquarian Booksellers, opposite the British Museum. The asking price was now, understandably, almost trebled, although we were offered first refusal. An institutional purchase was the most desirable outcome and as the item did not fit Yale's purchasing program Widener contacted his counterpart at Harvard, Karen Beck. On 24 January he wrote to say that Harvard was indeed interested, and on 20 March Beck emailed with the happy news that the manuscript had been acquired. Hobler's scrapbook could not have found a better home. I was fortunate to be granted a first viewing before it was catalogued and preserved, but the material was subsequently digitized and has been made available to the public, free of charge.[2] Historians will draw upon it for years to come.

The saga of this paperchase, while exciting in retrospect – and it did enthral my crime and society seminar students as I reported developments week after week – was at the time terrifying, as there seemed to be a very real possibility that the manuscript would fall into private hands and disappear from view. That it did not owes entirely to the efforts of librarians and is a salutary reminder of the importance of their work. Without Guy Holborn's alert I would not have known of its existence. I thank him from the bottom of my heart, and am also extremely grateful for the efforts of Jonathan Sims and Mike Widener, and to Karen Beck for the ultimate purchase of Hobler's scrapbook. In this digital age it is often forgotten that librarians and archivists are the custodians of our history, preserving it for posterity. While their efforts are not entirely unsung, they deserve greater acknowledgement.

As discussed in the introduction, Hobler's primary intent in assembling his 'book' was to document the construction of a criminal prosecution. But in doing so he also created a portrait of an early Victorian household, its inmates, and their neighbours. Hidden behind the wallpaper, so to speak, are a host of individuals who, but for the temporary interest generated by murder, would have vanished entirely from public memory. Hobler's careful preservation of their statements has allowed me to explore master and servant relations in this period as well as the operation of the criminal justice system at a time of transition: the crisis that produced stories which would otherwise have remained

Preface and Acknowledgements xv

untold opens a brief window into what Lena Orlin characterizes as 'underrepresented lives'.[3] In Russell's time peers and their children, who comprised a tiny minority of England's population, attracted enormous attention, while those who toiled to serve them and were legion remained largely invisible and ignored. The study that follows utilizes the investigation into Russell's murder and the trial and execution of Courvoisier not merely to illuminate fundamental changes in the administration of English criminal justice, but to contemplate the lives of those who served the murder victim – including his murderer.

***

As is always the case, my research and writing have been supported by a variety of colleagues. I am grateful to Rachael Griffin for collating and printing out the extensive newspaper coverage of the case during her brief time as my research assistant. Of much greater help, however, was her own research into mid-Victorian detective policing, which resulted in a very fine doctoral thesis.[4] Thank you, Rachael. A very early version of Chapter 3 was presented at the 2012 meeting of the North American Conference on British Studies in Montreal; I also gave a brief overview of the project as a whole at the 2013 meeting of Western's Law and Governance in Britain conference and more recently to the law school's legal history seminar (2024). I'm grateful to Tim Meldrum for discussing servant life with me in the early stages of writing. Victor Bailey, Simon Devereaux, Tom Green, Douglas Hay, and Michael Lobban kindly read and commented on the penultimate version of the manuscript. I hope I have put their suggestions to good use and beg their forgiveness if I have failed to do so. I wish John Beattie had been here to critique the final incarnation and thank him once again for enabling my academic career. My debt to Guy Holborn at Lincoln's Inn has already been acknowledged, but I would like to add thanks to deputy librarian Catherine McArdle, who died of cancer in January 2024. I also thank Roland Nedd: Guy, Catherine, and Roland were a remarkable team and I am extremely lucky to have worked with their support over the years. Thanks to Sarah Wharton at Harvard Law School Library for facilitating access to the illustrations from Hobler's scrapbook. Finally, thanks to commissioning editor Max Novick for his enthusiasm for the project, which was much appreciated, to editorial assistant Louise Ingham for her patience, and to Yassar Arafat for overseeing the production process.

This book is dedicated to the memory of my parents.

Notes

1 This was not Hobler's first scrapbook: he had previously compiled one on the visit of Queen Victoria to the City of London on the Lord Mayor's Day, 1837: London Metropolitan Archives, CLC/521/MS00036.
2 Francis Hobler Scrapbook, HLS MS 4487 (http://nrs.harvard.edu/urn-3:HLS.Libr:12188023).
3 *Locating Privacy in Tudor London*, 14.
4 'Detective Policing and the State'.

1 Introduction

A murder is announced – and the butler did it

On 6 May 1840, the English newspaper press reported a crime that was to preoccupy public attention for months: the murder of 72-year-old William Russell, a younger brother of the Duke of Bedford. The elderly victim's social status, coupled with the fact that he had been killed in his own home, while he slept, generated enormous alarm and guaranteed extensive press coverage. The early Victorian public was enthralled and absorbed by the murder of an aristocrat; the case literally, as we shall see, haunted their dreams. As a detective story, however, there is no element of a 'whodunnit' in this murder: the initial suspect, and the only person to be arrested for it, was Russell's young manservant, François Benjamin Courvoisier, who combined the roles of footman, butler, and valet. Courvoisier did in fact commit the crime and eventually confessed his guilt. He was duly tried and executed. Why then revisit the case? While it continues to attract attention purely on the grounds of sensation,[1] the historical significance of William Russell's violent death rests chiefly on its timing. And that timing is highly significant: in 1840 the criminal justice system was undergoing a radical transformation on a number of fronts. The Metropolitan Police, created in 1829, had as yet no detective division.[2] Russell's murder in fact occurred in a brief vacuum where official detection was concerned: England's 'first detectives', Bow Street's 'runners', had been disbanded in 1839 and Robert Peel's uniformed, preventive force had of necessity to undertake investigation of the case.[3] Prosecution during this period ostensibly remained the responsibility of private individuals, but the new police worked quietly with the Home Office in certain cases, just as Bow Street's magistrates had done.[4] The prosecution of Russell's murderer, although not labelled as such at the time, is very much an instance of public prosecution, and noteworthy for that fact alone. It also took place a mere four years after persons accused of felony had won the legal right to counsel.[5] No professional standards of conduct for defence counsel had been established by the bar, and the origins of those standards can be traced back to Courvoisier's trial.[6] The punishment meted out to the convict was, by contrast, traditional: the death penalty had been removed from the vast majority of criminal offences by 1840, but not for murder, and executions remained public.[7] Public reaction to Courvoisier's execution, however, is commonly acknowledged as demonstrating a new unease with capital punishment. The investigation into Russell's death, and the prosecution and execution of his murderer, thus offer a unique perspective on a criminal justice system undergoing profound change.

Public interest in what was known to contemporaries as 'the Russell murder' also highlights a new preoccupation with lethal violence rather than property crime. In his famous study of the criminal law, Leon Radzinowicz argued that little value had traditionally been attached to human lives, and property crime had been Robert Peel's focus when developing his new police force.[8] But it was the crime of murder that would result in the creation of a detective division within it. Timing is again important. Twenty-nine years earlier, the nation had been gripped by the murders of the Marr and Williamson families in London's docklands. The attacks took place at night in two homes in Wapping, roughly half a mile apart, in December 1811.[9] Linen draper Timothy Marr, his wife Celia, and apprentice James Gowen were battered to death on the 7th and the Marr baby's throat was slashed; 12 days later publican John Williamson, his wife Elizabeth, and their servant Bridget Anna Harrington were killed in equally violent night-time attacks, found with smashed skulls and slit throats. These crimes predated the creation of the Metropolitan Police, let alone a detective force within it, and suggestions that London required such a force were matched by vehement arguments against its implementation. The humble social status of the victims, together with the location of their murders – London's East End – may help to explain why, unlike the Russell murder, no legislative change ensued in the aftermath of these events. John William Ward, the future Earl of Dudley, commented that he was

> inclined to suspect that it is next to impossible to prevent outrages of this sort happening in those parts of the town that are inhabited exclusively by the lowest and most profligate wretches in the nation, except by entrusting the magistrates with powers vastly too extensive to be prudently invested in such hands

and famously continued that he 'had rather half a dozen people's throats should be cut in Ratcliffe Highway every three or four years than be subject to domiciliary visits, spies' and everything else associated with the French system of police.[10] Policing historian David Philips noted that it was 'easy enough' for a man of Ward's class, 'who was unlikely ever to be found – dead or alive – in such an insalubrious neighbourhood as the Ratcliffe Highway, to make this generous offer of other people's throats for the cutting'.[11] William Russell, by contrast, was a member of the aristocracy and had been murdered in the West End. Yet class and location alone do not sufficiently account for the notable change in public attitudes. When a press critical of the Russell investigation indignantly cited earlier policing failures, the murder victims in question included barmaid Eliza Davis and prostitute Eliza Grimwood. The press was also indignant with a perceived privileging of the Russell investigation over that into the murder of John Templeman, an elderly gentleman of more modest means, who lived without servants, only a few months earlier.[12] And the victim in a case two years later, which would prove to be the straw that broke the camel's back where public exasperation with detective policing was concerned, Daniel Good's murder of his common-law wife Jane Jones, was a laundress.[13]

The social class of murder victims was clearly no longer a bar in attracting public interest. But why did the interest in murder become so intense? Famous eighteenth-century criminals included gaol-breakers (Jack Sheppard), thief-takers (Jonathan Wild), and highwaymen (Dick Turpin). And murder, as Rachael Griffin notes,

> only ever made up a fraction of prosecuted crime in London; statistics from the Old Bailey indicate that 480 murders were prosecuted there between 1830 and 1880 out of nearly 83,000 total criminal trials, constituting less than one per cent of prosecutions.[14]

Albert Borowitz suggested the 'relative rarity' of murder as one of the explanations for public interest in this crime.[15] Regardless of the reasons, as Richard Altick declared, 'it was in, or just before, the early Victorian period that homicide first became institutionalized as a popular entertainment, a spectator sport'. One of his own explanations strikes me as somewhat bizarre: 'it does seem likely', Altick argues, 'that the Victorian masses' sustained enthusiasm for murder was in part a product of their intellectually empty and emotionally stunted lives, so tightly confined by economic and social circumstance'.[16] But he also points to the development of the newspaper press and foregrounds the loss of war news, which had preoccupied the newspapers from the French Revolutionary through the Napoleonic wars: after 1815, some new sensation was required to fill pages. '[B]lood', Altick concludes, ultimately proved to be 'an important ingredient in nineteenth-century printers' ink'.[17] This new public fascination is nicely captured in Charles Dickens's Mr Wopsle, a one-time church warden who runs away to London to become an actor. Chapter 18 of *Great Expectations* (1861) describes Wopsle reading aloud a newspaper account of a coroner's inquest:

> A highly popular murder had been committed, and Mr. Wopsle was imbrued in blood to the eyebrows. He gloated over every abhorrent adjective in the description, and identified himself with every witness at the Inquest. He faintly moaned, 'I am done for,' as the victim, and he barbarously bellowed, 'I'll serve you out,' as the murderer. He gave the medical testimony, in pointed imitation of our local practitioner; and he piped and shook, as the aged turnpike-keeper who had heard blows, to an extent so very paralytic as to suggest a doubt regarding the mental competency of that witness. The coroner, in Mr. Wopsle's hands, became

4   *Introduction*

Timon of Athens; the beadle, Coriolanus. He enjoyed himself thoroughly, and we all enjoyed ourselves, and were delightfully comfortable. In this cozy state of mind we came to the verdict Wilful Murder.[18]

The kind of detail newspapers offered to fellow Wopsles can be found much earlier in the nineteenth century. Press coverage in *The Times*, the *Morning Chronicle*, and the *Morning Herald*, among others, of John Thurtell and Joseph Hunt's 'most horrible' murder – and the details of the killing are indeed horrible – of William Weare in 1823–24 is often cited in this regard.[19] A onetime second lieutenant in the Royal Marines, amateur boxer and trainer of pugilists, bankrupt bombazine maker, and failed publican, Thurtell was also a gambler, though not a successful one. By 1823 he was in financial difficulties: a hefty insurance pay-out for a warehouse fire had been withheld pending a fraud indictment as the fire had almost certainly been deliberately set, and he lost £300 to Weare, a gameshark. On 24 October Thurtell, with Joseph Hunt and William Probert, lured Weare to Gill's Hill Lane, near Radlett in Hertfordshire. There Thurtell shot him in the face and, when the bullet failed to penetrate, slit his throat and pushed the pistol into Weare's skull. But he was no more successful as a murderer than he had been in business or at the games table. Both knife and pistol were discovered by labourers, and Hunt directed the authorities to the pond where the body had been dumped. Probert turned king's evidence and was acquitted; Hunt's sentence was commuted from death to transportation; Thurtell was hanged. The Thurtell case has been identified as the first instance of 'trial by newspaper'.[20] By the time of Russell's murder, the public was used to following events from the first reports of the crime through the inquest, investigation, arrests, pre-trial proceedings, and trial to conclusion in an execution.

Precisely who was now responsible for investigating violent deaths is another issue raised by the Russell murder. Traditionally, suspicious deaths had been investigated via a coroner's inquest, but at the time of Russell's death the coroner's office, like the police, was undergoing fundamental revision. A protracted and highly contentious battle between the legal and medical professions with respect to the qualifications appropriate to the position of coroner had raged throughout the 1830s. Should the coroner, as he had been from the Middle Ages, be a lawyer, or, as some now believed more appropriate, a medical man? The contest lay between two warring branches of professional expertise.[21] In Middlesex the medical profession wrested control from attorneys in the year prior to Russell's death; the surgeon who had won the battle, Thomas Wakley, was convinced that 'any intelligent man could in two hours learn all the law required of a competent coroner'.[22] Russell's inquest reveals that this was not strictly true: concerns were raised about Deputy Coroner Thomas Higgs's oversight of the proceedings (Wakley had been ill and unable to attend).[23] The substitution of a deputy was itself novel and had not yet been sanctioned by statute. But Higgs's conduct in the inquest into Russell's death attracted more specific criticism. Key questions had not been raised, discrepancies in the evidence had not been resolved, and the chief suspect's lips had been sealed by what amounted to a warning not to incriminate himself.

Policing and detection

If in Middlesex the war between law and medicine had been concluded by 1840, the working relationship between the coroner's office and the new police remained open to question.[24] The effectiveness of Peel's preventive officers in investigating murder was also criticized. Public attention quickly shifted from inadequacies in the inquest to the activities of the police. None of the myriad officers who descended on 14 Norfolk Street to investigate Russell's violent end were officially recognized as detectives. In 1840, England had no detective force. London, the largest city in Europe as well as Britain, had once been served by a form of detective policing established by Bow Street magistrates Henry and John Fielding, whose 'runners' focused on the investigation and prosecution of felonies. There was an obvious need for a detective force in the capital and Parliament subsidized the Fieldings' private initiative, but parliamentary attention subsequently turned to the preventive policing model. In the decade preceding the Russell murder Bow Street's runners had nonetheless operated as a parallel force to the new Metropolitan Police, and there was a significant overlap in personnel between the two institutions: Inspector Nicholas Pearce, one of the key officers responsible for the Russell investigation, had begun his career as a Bow Street officer. But Bow Street's principal preoccupation had always been property crime; as J.M. Beattie indicates, its officers had rarely been involved in investigating homicide within London. And while in the provinces, local magistrates had called on Bow Street's officers for assistance in murder and attempted murder cases, the cases in question tended to involve larger public order issues, including property damage.[25]

Where murder investigations were concerned, at the time of Russell's death the police were still feeling their way, and they were hampered by the methodology available to them. In the twenty-first century physical evidence linking Courvoisier to the murder of, as well as theft from, his master would quickly have established his guilt. But in 1840 fingerprint and DNA evidence were non-existent. Crime scene photography also lay in the future. The murder weapon – one of the dining room carving knives, casually rinsed and replaced in the sideboard – was never identified by the police. When Courvoisier's trial opened the only evidence the prosecution could offer was circumstantial, and the police almost certainly resorted to the desperate remedy of fabrication. Like so many of the nineteenth-century murder cases that continue to fascinate the twenty-first-century public – the Ratcliffe Highway murders, Constance Kent's murder of her step-brother (1860), the serial killings of 'Jack the Ripper' (1888) – the investigation of Russell's death is an example of policing failure. This prompted reconsideration of similar failures in the immediate past and contributed to public demand for a detective force within the Metropolitan Police: the Detective Department was created two years later.[26] But again we see continuity. Despite the mistakes made, the police commissioners continued to believe in their officers and drafted members of the flawed Russell murder investigation into the new division.

The Courvoisier trial

Until now, academic discussion of the Russell murder has focused on its impact on the development of professional standards of conduct for defence counsel. The issue raised in Courvoisier's trial – the duty owed by counsel to a client he knew to be morally guilty – had not been considered in the parliamentary or professional debate preceding enactment of the Prisoner's Counsel Act (1836). The primary concern had instead been the potential contribution of a professional speech to the jury to the protection of innocence. First in the field on discussion of this subject was American law professor David Mellinkoff, whose remarkable study, *The Conscience of a Lawyer*, was published in 1973. Mellinkoff explored the professional issues inherent in the scandal occasioned by Courvoisier's defence: having privately confessed, mid-trial, his guilt to his solicitor and barristers, Courvoisier refused to change his plea to guilty. His leading counsel, Charles Phillips, chose to continue to argue his client's case. Despite Courvoisier's conviction and execution, when the confession became known, that decision enraged the public and the bar engaged in considerable soul-searching with respect to the duty owed by defence counsel to his client in such circumstances. Contemporary debate played out over some ten years in a variety of published forums, including the newspaper press and lay and professional periodicals. The end result was elaboration of the guidelines which today govern professional practice.[27]

The prosecution of Russell's valet, by contrast, was uncontroversial and generated little public discussion at the time. Where historical enquiry is concerned, sources have been a major issue, as records were thin on the ground. It is difficult to find 'briefs', the written instructions provided by solicitors to the barristers who appeared in court at the Old Bailey. Most were likely destroyed post-trial, when they were no longer needed. Published accounts of pre-trial hearings and trial proceedings sometimes allow a degree of reconstruction of the way in which cases had been assembled, and the names of the solicitors as well as barristers involved, but detail is obscured. This is especially frustrating as solicitors, rather than barristers, were responsible for interviewing witnesses and suggesting strategies later employed in the courtroom. Working behind the scenes and out of the limelight enjoyed by courtroom counsel, they built cases from the ground, handed them on, and usually disappeared from sight – to posterity, at any rate. At the Old Bailey Courvoisier's prosecution was led by John Adolphus, but details regarding how he was briefed, or by whom, or how the case he presented was assembled have only recently come to light in the scrapbook compiled by police solicitor Francis Hobler.[28] Although the briefs themselves – there were two, the first rejected by the Home Office – were not included, the scrapbook reveals in detail how the solicitor prepared the case to be presented. Hobler, a storyteller as well as a magpie, was like the rest of England intrigued from the beginning. The documents he collected and preserved were arranged chronologically and with care, and his 'book' was prefaced with a handwritten title page:

> An Account of the Murder of Lord William Russell on the night of the 5th and 6th May 1840, with the discovery & confession & execution of his murderer. Being a collection of all the Examinations of Witnesses both in private & public, anonymous Letters and Every Document which has passed through my hands relating to the case and assisting in its prosecution – with two portraits of the criminal taken by Mr C.A. Rivers.[29]

Such documentation would be of significance in any case, but it is especially significant here because it reveals what can only be described as a public prosecution. Against David Bentley's assertion that 'Until 1879 the only person who could be described as a public prosecutor was the Attorney-General' must be set, as Bruce Smith has argued, Glanville Williams's recognition that 'a prosecution by a policeman or other official is brought in pursuance of superior orders or under statutory authority and at public expence, so that it is unreal to describe it as a private prosecution'.[30] By 1840 Hobler had acquired the position of solicitor for the new police; like his predecessor John Stafford he worked with the Home Office on cases deemed to involve the public interest, and on reading of Russell's murder he volunteered his services for what promised to be a high-profile case. Hobler's scrapbook allows a rare glimpse into the way in which the newly established Metropolitan Police and the Home Office worked together to pursue prosecutions believed to be too important to be left entirely in private hands.

Hobler was very much aware of the significance of this assemblage:

> This collection of materials from whence the Evidence was drawn that was afterwards presented to the Court is curious & interesting as a legal Document, as it shows the <u>working part</u> of such a case and although to the casual observer it may be only a heterogenous mass full of repetition yet when examined more closely it will shew how a case of mystery is elucidated & put together so as to become a complete piece of machinery tending to one point – The discovery of the Murderer ...[31]

Hobler's compilation of documents helps us to reconstruct the way in which murder was investigated at a time in which formal detective policing did not exist. It reveals relationships between the relatively new Metropolitan Police, the Home Office, and the lower and upper branches of the legal profession. The marked-up statements and depositions and lists of witnesses to be called are there, together with a running commentary that allows us to see Hobler's thought processes. The case eventually argued by barrister John Adolphus at the Old Bailey in late June 1840 was Hobler's creation.

8 *Introduction*

Storytelling and voice

How were the facts of the Russell murder told and understood by contemporaries of the victim and his murderer? Who spoke, under what circumstances, how were their voices communicated, and what uses were made of their speech? The legal records generated by a violent death constitute a unique form of mediated and often reluctant storytelling. Those who speak do not do so voluntarily but are compelled by the state. Police officers, the coroner and his jury, the magistrate taking depositions, solicitors assembling cases to be presented in court, barristers examining and cross-examining witnesses and addressing the trial jury: all solicit narratives in pursuit of specific interests. Francis Hobler's scrapbook was consciously shaped to provide a detailed but unauthorized history of the case as seen from the prosecuting solicitor's perspective.

The victim of course was silent, having no opportunity to relate the circumstances of his death. But the voice of his murderer is also elusive. Courvoisier said little to the police in the house and spoke only briefly at the inquest. His speech was initially reported second-hand by his fellow servants as they were questioned by various officials during the investigation. This second-hand reporting is further complicated by the fact that the discourses in question were later filtered through the press. There is a good deal of repetition amongst the newspaper accounts of the investigation and trial of Courvoisier, but discrepancies can be found as well. Also to be considered is the fact that English was not the Swiss valet's mother tongue. One of his post-trial confessions and a biography were recorded in French and published in translation. And in one key forum – the Old Bailey – Courvoisier's voice was not heard at all. In 1836 Parliament had granted defendants in felony trials the right to full representation by counsel. Many such accused, unable to afford counsel, continued to defend themselves and thus the older form of trial, dubbed by John Langbein as 'the accused speaks' variety, had certainly not disappeared by 1840.[32] But where defence counsel were employed, the defendant, forbidden to testify on oath until the Criminal Evidence Act of 1898, usually remained silent, allowing his barrister to speak on his behalf.[33] With the assistance of public funds, Courvoisier instructed a solicitor, Thomas Flower, and barrister, Charles Phillips, to speak in his place. The loquacious Phillips paid a high price for acting as mouthpiece for this client.[34] Restricted to cross-examination, 'Counsellor O'Garnish' had prospered in England's criminal courts. The closing speech he made in defending Courvoisier would occasion his professional downfall.[35]

Having remained largely silent prior to his conviction, Courvoisier made a number of contradictory confessions before he was hanged. He was in effect courted for them, enjoying a brief notoriety before he was 'turned off'. In at least one of these confessions it seems likely that his voice was appropriated to pursue an agenda not his own. Some of the versions of Courvoisier's story followed a traditional trajectory; capital convicts had for centuries left a record in the form of confessions or 'last dying speeches' and, by Courvoisier's time, broadsides. Such records had always been somewhat suspect, shaped to fulfil an Establishment agenda, warning against the consequences of crime and asserting the justice of state retribution, as well as to entertain. These potted biographies were crafted, and at times totally fabricated, by others. Where Courvoisier had made a simple confession of guilt to his solicitor and barrister during the trial itself, more elaborate confessions were reputedly made post-trial to the prison chaplain and sheriff of London. In one, which became famous in literary history, he was said to have been inspired to commit his crimes by reading William Harrison Ainsworth's 'Newgate' novel, *Jack Sheppard* (1839–40). The horrified novelist wrote immediately to the papers protesting that he could not be blamed for inciting murder, and whether Courvoisier had read the novel in question is open to question.[36] As a servant, and with English as a second language, he would more likely have been familiar with one of the popular stage versions. But moralists had been complaining about the potential impact of works that glamourized criminals on impressionable youth, and they seized on the Russell murder as proof of their concerns.

Execution

The execution of convicted murderers continued in England until 1964 and remained public until 1868. By 1840, however, public hangings were far less common than they had been in the eighteenth century and the early Victorians had become preoccupied with a capital convict's final night. Charles Dickens, a long-term haunter of London's prisons, had imagined the condemned man's experience in *Sketches by Boz* (1836), and returned to the theme in *Oliver Twist*, in a chapter published roughly a year before the Russell murder. Dickens was also among the crowd who assembled to watch the valet hang, but his outrage at Courvoisier's crime and Phillips's conduct of the defence was sufficient to preclude sympathy. William Makepeace Thackeray, however, like Dickens in the early stages of his career and reliant on occasional journalism for an income, accepted a commission to report on the event. The execution proved an unexpected shock and Thackeray's description of it, published in *Fraser's Magazine* as 'On Going to See a Man Hanged', has been cited as marking a radical shift in public attitudes towards capital punishment. The tenor of the article, and Thackeray's reaction to the 'judicial murder' he witnessed, is all the more remarkable given public feeling about Russell's murder and the absence of sympathy for its perpetrator prior to, during, and immediately after the valet's trial. Until the day of his execution Courvoisier had attracted nothing but opprobrium. Yet this article was not Thackeray's last word on the subject of capital punishment, and his opinions appear to have changed over the years.

Master and servant

Courvoisier murdered William Russell after a mere five weeks' employment, which begs a number of questions. Previous academic studies of the Russell murder have not dwelt on the issue of motivation, being more interested in Courvoisier's trial than the crime itself, and the explanations offered by trade accounts are unsatisfactory. Courvoisier, Yseult Bridges argued, 'provides an outstanding example of the cynical young man who, with everything in his favour, deliberately chooses to follow the path of crime'. 'From an early age', Russell's valet 'had shewn an incurable propensity towards falsehood and deceit' which intensified as he grew up, as did 'a dislike of any settled occupation'.[37] Bridges's account is replete with stereotypes about both servants and convicted criminals and is deeply unhelpful. In a more recent study, Claire Harman asked the obvious question: why would Courvoisier 'have risked so much for so little'? She speculates as to a potential sexual motivation.[38] But there is no hint whatsoever in contemporary discussion of the Russell murder of either master or servant being homosexual or engaging in homosexual relations, in a time when such rumours were difficult to suppress. As we will see, the reputation and parliamentary career of Russell's son-in-law, Henry Grey Bennet, was ruined by alleged homosexual relations with a male servant. In William Russell's own case, suspicions were expressed about a potential – and equally unlikely – sexual relationship with his housemaid, but never about a relationship with his valet. Courvoisier's actions might more usefully be seen as an extreme example of a breakdown in master/servant relations caused by social frustration and a sense of injustice. As one broadside put it, in a remarkable understatement, Russell's valet 'was not contented' with his place.[39] Carolyn Steedman reminds us of William Godwin's suggestion 'that depressed footmen might be the first among the labouring population to develop "an inextinguishable abhorrence against the injustice of society", or what would be called by some later historians, class consciousness'.[40] What Bruce Robbins describes as 'the historical pressure of subalternity' seems to me the most persuasive explanation for Courvoisier's extreme act.[41]

Like the criminal justice system, if in more subtle ways, domestic service was undergoing something of a transformation in the early Victorian period.[42] By 1840 many London servants would have been employed by the middle classes and supervised by a mistress rather than a master: the male head of the household was now likely – or at least expected – to go out to work and advice manuals were increasingly directed to women. These manuals, aimed at anxious middle-class Victorian employers of servants, tell only one part of the story. At the same time as such texts were urging strict, verging on draconian, control over domestics, novelists Thackeray and Wilkie Collins were demonstrating troubled consciences and a new sensitivity to the plight of servants, recognizing them as possessing feelings, and equally recognizing that conditions of servitude allowed no sanctioned space for the articulation of those feelings, which had instead to be continually, and inhumanely, repressed.

William Russell was of course not middle class, nor was he a Victorian. As an elderly aristocratic widower of limited financial means his household was anomalous – that fact in itself is a useful reminder of the limitations of advice manuals, with their neat tabulations of incomes and numbers of servants, as reflections of the social order. He would also repeatedly be described as having lived alone. It would be more accurate to say that he was the sole occupant of the main floors of his modest house: working below him and sleeping above were three live-in servants. Exploring the composition of Russell's household and situating his death within the context of early Victorian domesticity reveals details of the more ordinary life that preceded the murder. Prosecution of the extraordinary events of a crime sheds light on the work lives and living circumstances of people who, even if literate, rarely wrote journals or letters, left few if any records behind, and whose stories tended to be extinguished at their death, or following the deaths of those who had remembered them.[43] Again, Hobler's scrapbook proves enormously useful. The solicitor's primary objective in compiling it, as he himself declared, was to create a useful legal record, and there were sound professional reasons for the care with which the solicitor recorded the back stories of servants who, even if not suspects, might be in possession of significant information and possibly called as witnesses at trial. Hobler needed to establish – or not – good character and credibility. But it is clear that he took an indignant personal interest in William Russell's servants as well. His record not only provides insight into their lives prior to engagement within Russell's household and during their employment at 14 Norfolk Street, but enables us to follow them, if briefly, afterwards, and beyond the print record.

Contemporary discussion of the composition of Russell's household speaks to another significant issue: 'family'. This term had once been employed to encompass servants as well as blood relations. By 1840 such usage was archaic but it had not entirely disappeared and its continued employment raises significant questions about relations among those who shared a common physical living space, confounding the public/private divide. From the early eighteenth century complaints had been made that master and servant relations had shifted from affectual to purely monetary, that servants were increasingly insubordinate and utterly lacking in loyalty. Social commentators – Defoe, Swift, Richardson – worried that personal loyalty had been eroded by the cash nexus. Urban service in particular had become a cause of anxiety: the greater autonomy and economic mobility available within an urban labour market, the ease with which servants could communicate with each other, and move from one position to another, were thought to subvert traditional relations between master and servant.

In the public imagination, by the eighteenth century 'the figure of the urban servant … crystallized a greedy self-interestedness and moral degeneracy'. Kristina Straub argues that '[s]ervants with economic mobility become intruders upon the family instead of subordinate members of it'.[44] Is this true? The servants interviewed in the course of the police investigation into Russell's murder, both his own and those of his neighbours, reveal a number of the contradictions inherent in early Victorian service. While by 1840 'establishment' was gradually replacing 'family' in descriptions of the occupants of a household that included servants, most of the servants used the older terminology.

Yet only one of them had been in their current situation for more than three years. There is ample evidence among the police interviews of individuals hoping to better themselves, or simply leaving situations that did not suit, of the economic mobility, that is, that so troubled commentators in the previous century.

Apart from multiple interviews with Russell's own servants, five in number, and two of his previous valets, the police also interviewed the servants of his immediate neighbours and an unemployed friend of Courvoisier. Thirteen individuals by no means constitute a representative sample, but their testimony, which contains more detail than that found in published accounts of the inquest, Bow Street hearings, and the Old Bailey trial, is illuminating nonetheless. Historically, very few instances can be found of servants voluntarily writing their own stories, such as the anonymous *Adventures of a Valet, written by himself* (1752), John Macdonald's *Memoirs of an Eighteenth-Century Footman* (1790), and footman William Tayler's diary for 1837, first published in 1962. Maidservant Hannah Cullwick's 17 diaries cover the years 1854–73. But such accounts are numerically swamped – and that is an understatement – by both literary representations of servants and the exasperated commentary and advice manuals published by those who employed them. E.S. Turner traces 'the servant problem' back to the English Civil War; certainly, by the early eighteenth century, there is ample evidence of vicious criticism such as that found in two pamphlets by Daniel Defoe – *The Great Law of Subordination Considered; or, The Insolence and Unsufferable Behaviour of Servants in England Duly Considered* (1724) and *Every-body's Business is No-body's Business; or, Private Abuses, Publick Grievances: Exemplified in the Pride, Insolence, and Exorbitant Wages of our Women-Servants, Footmen, &c* (1725) – and Jonathan Swift's *Directions to Servants* (1745), which Turner characterizes as 'a painstaking exercise in malice'.[45] This early anti-servant literature had some counterparts in the law,[46] and the opinions voiced in such polemics were also broadcast in eighteenth-century drama, most famously in James Townley's *High Life Below Stairs* (1759). The eighteenth century produced the world's most famous fictional maidservant, Samuel Richardson's Pamela, as well as Henry Fielding's satirical portrait of her brother, Joseph Andrews. Tobias Smollett's Humphrey Clinker is another example of a fictional eighteenth-century footman and servants abound in nineteenth-century fiction as well, including Emily Brontë's *Wuthering Heights* and the novels of Thackeray.[47] These cultural representations, whether savage, comic, or sympathetic, have their uses, but convey little of the economic histories and lived experiences of actual servants. Prescriptive literature in the form of instruction manuals similarly speaks to contemporary ideals, from the employer's perspective, rather than the reality of master and servant relations. Information obtained during police interviews or revealed in courtroom examinations thus provides an important counterbalance when considering servants' lives, providing at least a skeletal outline of birthplace, family, friendships and social life, and employment history. These records too, of course, have limitations. The information is acquired via interrogation, and in the case of police interviews, the questions asked, which provide the overall shape of the stories told, are not recorded. It is also limited to the factual. William Russell's housemaid Sarah Mancer would repeatedly be queried about her precise actions during the course of discovery of her master's murder, but never about her emotional reaction to that discovery or the disastrous effect the murder had on her own life. She was treated by the justice process as a means to an end rather than a person in her own right.

With the exception of the valet who created the crisis, Russell's servants were not remarkable and, but for the murder of their employer, would have remained under the historical radar, their lives ignored as inconsequential. Yet, as noted above, the existence of the servant class was beginning to be recognized in new ways. An empathy not found in the eighteenth century is discernible by the time of Russell's death and Francis Hobler's protective interest, described in the following chapters, in housemaid Sarah Mancer's reputation is indication of a change in public perception where servants were concerned. What might be understood as a democratization of feeling, however, was tempered by a new fear. Thackeray's emotional response to Courvoisier's execution raises 'On Going to See a Man Hanged' above the level of commissioned, hack journalism. But servants, as Bruce Robbins has discussed, would subsequently haunt Thackeray's journalism and fiction.[48] In the eighteenth century, servants had been castigated as greedy, grasping, and insubordinate; now, they constituted a threat to physical safety as well. In 'On a Chalk-Mark on the Door', an essay published in the *Cornhill Magazine* in 1861, reference to footman 'Jeames's dangerous strength, and the edge-tools about his knife-board'[49] suggests the alarmed shadows cast by Courvoisier's murder of William Russell 20 years earlier. It was not merely the valet's execution, but the crime which occasioned it, that caused Thackeray profound and lasting discomfort.

Exploring Russell's domestic circumstances also contributes to an understanding of Courvoisier's actions. Explanations for the murder, I argue, lie in the master and servant relationship per se rather than a purely personal animosity. Legally, by the time of Russell's death the relationship between master and servant had become a matter of contract, and the servant class had acquired at least a degree of agency and independence in choosing 'the family' in which they preferred to be employed.[50] The nature of their service and their relationships with their employers, however, remained intimate. The murder of William Russell is in my view best characterized as a species of domestic murder, one that tends to be overlooked. It is worth reflecting that while household servants were called 'domestics', 'domestic' is also used to describe a particular type of violent affray, one usually restricted to events involving persons related through marriage. Master and servant relationships, however, could and did easily engender similar tensions and resentments. Famous proven instances of lethal attacks by employers on servants include Laurence Shirley, Earl Ferrer's conviction in 1760 for the murder of his steward, and Elizabeth Brownrigg's for the torture and murder of a female servant, Mary Clifford, in 1767.[51] But there were also occasions on which servants, like Courvoisier, resorted to deadly violence. The 'unthankful, discontented hearts' cited by Richard Baxter in the seventeenth century as preventing servants from enjoying 'quieter' lives were found equally in the eighteenth and nineteenth centuries.[52] Such discontent rarely resulted in murder, but there were cases in which it did. Sometimes domestic tensions erupted among the servants themselves: one of Lord Dacre's footmen, Daniel Blake, was hanged in 1763 for murdering the butler.[53] Another lethal affray involving a manservant is less easy to characterize. On 31 May 1810 Joseph Sellis, valet to Ernest Augustus, fifth son of George III and Duke of Cumberland, was found in the duke's apartment at St James's Palace with his throat cut. The duke, who had suffered a serious head wound himself, claimed he had been attacked by Sellis while he slept, and that the valet had subsequently committed suicide. This verdict was accepted by the coroner's inquest, but the motive for such an attack was unclear, much of the evidence presented contradictory, and some believed Sellis had been murdered by the duke.[54]

Carolyn Steedman cites a number of eighteenth-century examples of murders in which servants were the perpetrators rather than victims. Some of the murderers in question were (very) young women who targeted the children they were employed to care for: 15-year-old Elizabeth Morton strangled a noisy, troublesome infant in 1762; Ann Mead (1800), also 15, poisoned a child after her mistress had scolded her for not keeping it clean. Ann Vine (1800) was convicted of manslaughter for having scalded a toddler, who had soiled herself, in a boiling copper. One of the most famous nineteenth-century instances of catastrophic rupture in master and servant relations is found in the case of Eliza Fenning, hanged, despite considerable public support, in 1815 for the attempted poisoning of the family which employed her.[55] An employer's bad disposition seems frequently to have been the trigger for domestic violence: Thomas Armstrong (1777) poisoned his master's wife because of her illtemper. Might such actions not be read, Steedman suggests, as 'crazed reactions' to the class relationship inherent in domestic service?[56] This certainly appears the best explanation for Courvoisier's crime, for the single remaining mystery about his violent attack on Russell is motivation.

> How it was that a good man became criminal, whether suddenly or by premeditation – how it was that an individual of sound mind and untarnished character fell into temptation and committed crime – this was matter for consideration of the jury

barrister John Adolphus indicated in his opening speech for the prosecution.[57] How indeed. Courvoisier had given none of his family, friends, or previous employers cause for concern or alarm. He had never appeared violent or particularly dissatisfied. In purely personal terms, this convict seems something of a cipher, the murder out of the character attested to by family and fellow servants, all of whom were astonished and bewildered as well as horrified by his actions. Courvoisier's violent attack on Russell might usefully be seen as an extreme example of a breakdown in master/servant relations caused by a sense of injustice. 'It is exactly in servant-master relations of dependency', Edward Thompson wrote, 'in which personal contacts are frequent and personal injustices are suffered against which protest is futile, that feelings of resentment or of hatred can be most violent and most personal'.[58] In crime fiction, the identity of the murder victim is usually viewed as equally significant as that of the murderer: 'once you comprehend the life, you comprehend the death'. Victims die because of their unique personal history.[59] In real life, this is not necessarily true. Russell's murder, violent as it was – Courvoisier's victim was almost decapitated – committed after a mere five weeks of acquaintance, seems curiously impersonal, an explosion of anger that arguably originated in the valet's resentment of his general situation in life. Russell died not because of who he was, but what he was.

Organization

In pursuing the various themes and issues described above, this book proceeds chronologically, beginning by describing the household within which the murder was committed, its physical premises and their occupants. Chapter 2 thus explores life at 14 Norfolk Street, above and below stairs. Russell's social background is compared with that of his servants, prescriptive texts and employers' concerns about service in the early Victorian period with the lived reality revealed via police interviews. This comparison, apart from contributing generally to 'history from below', allows consideration both of the murderer's motivation and the circumstances that enabled his crime: a physically frail elderly employer and an absence of supervision. In his previous 'places' Courvoisier had worked in larger households and under older, male servants. At 14 Norfolk Street he was the only male employed indoors and the housemaid's testimony suggests a freedom of behaviour that was unlikely to have been engaged in, or gone unnoticed and unreproved, had he reported to a butler or steward.

With the setting and various characters introduced, Chapter 3 turns to the discovery of the murder, the coroner's inquest, and the police investigation into the crime. It relies heavily on, and quotes liberally from, both Francis Hobler's notebook and newspaper coverage of the investigation. Hobler's collection of documents provides much of the evidence and his voice is as present as my own in this retelling. The police investigation into Russell's murder was extraordinary in a number of ways. One of the commissioners, Richard Mayne, almost immediately replaced Inspector Jarvis of C Division to lead it; Prince Albert and the Duke of Wellington made anxious enquiries as to progress. But there were also constants in the investigative process as it existed at this time, including both the absence of a dedicated detective force and the lack of what we would today consider essential forensic methodology.

Chapter 4 turns to the construction of the case for the prosecution, again relying heavily on Hobler's painstaking accumulation of material that demonstrates, among other things, the working relationship between the upper and lower branches of the legal profession in assembling the case to be presented in court. In exploring the rise of adversarial procedure in the criminal courtroom attention has been focused overwhelmingly on the role of defence counsel.[60] Hobler's annotated scrapbook allows a rare glimpse into the work involved in prosecuting.

Chapter 5 picks up the story post-trial. It begins by contrasting the private 'execution' and public burial of William Russell with the public execution and private interment, in an unmarked grave, of his murderer. It then turns to public reaction to Courvoisier's execution, more specifically, to Thackeray's essay published a few weeks after the fact and to an apparent moderation of the novelist's initial response in subsequent years. It also places Thackeray's views on execution within the broader, and intimately related, context of his views on the servant class. Ultimately, it was not merely Courvoisier's execution that troubled this author: the crime itself haunted Thackeray and echoes of his concern would ripple through his fiction.

Case studies are a form of microhistory and microhistorians, as Keith Wrightson observes, tend to be 'sensitive to the role of imagination, conjecture, and interpretive decisions in the writing of history', to be 'remarkably open with what historians actually *do*'.[61] Microhistory involves analysis not merely of historical events, but of the way in which those events were reported by contemporaries and interpreted by subsequent historians, exploring not merely an individual story but the documentation of that story both initially and over time. Even where there is agreement on a series of facts, their import will be gauged differently as time passes and the events in question are retold for a new audience. 'Voice' is also central to my telling of this story and I have deliberately reproduced the many earlier voices – most notably, those of Hobler and Thackeray, but also those of other novelists (Dickens, Wilkie Collins) as well as a variety of police officers, journalists, and members of the public – who discussed the murder and its aftermath. Most contemporaries had opinions on this case and were eager to make them known; the chattering classes had much to say and diverse forums in which to make themselves heard. Such testimonies are of course not uncomplicated and identifying Courvoisier's own voice is particularly problematic. Chapter 6 pauses the narrative to consider the issue of storytelling, exploring the competing, often contradictory, sometimes heavily mediated, and occasionally suspect narration that complicates the practice of history. The study concludes (Chapter 7) by reflecting on both the causes and immediate consequences of the case and its influence on the evolution of the criminal justice system.

Notes

1 For a recent trade account see Harman, *Murder by the Book*.
2 On the history of policing in London see Radzinowicz, *History of the English Criminal Law*, vol. 4; Critchley, *A History of Police*; Reith, *The Blind Eye of History*; Emsley, *The English Police*, *The Great British Bobbie*, and *Policing in its Context*; Reynolds, *Before the Bobbies*; Beattie, *The First English Detectives*; Cox, *A Certain*

Share of Low Cunning; and Taylor, *The New Police*. On the origins of a detective division within the Met see Emsley and Shpayer-Makov, eds., *Police Detectives in History*; Shpayer-Makov, *The Ascent of the Detective*; and Griffin, 'Detective Policing and the State'.

3 On Bow Street's detective activities in London see Beattie, *The First English Detectives*, 182; for their activities in the provinces, Cox, *A Certain Share of Low Cunning*.
4 The Prosecution of Offences Act, 1879, 42 & 43 Vict., c. 22 created the office of the Director of Public Prosecutions. On the legislative history of this act see Kurland and Waters, 'Public Prosecutions in England'. On police involvement in prosecution during the ostensibly private era see Williams, 'The Power to Prosecute'; Hay and Snyder, 'Using the Criminal Law', and Smith, 'The Emergence of Public Prosecution in London'.
5 6 & 7 William IV, c. 114 (1836), 'An Act for Enabling Persons Indicted of Felony to Make Their Defence by Counsel or Attorney'.
6 See Mellinkoff, *The Conscience of a Lawyer*. On the history of the English criminal trial see Beattie, 'Scales of Justice'; Langbein, *Origins of Adversary Criminal Trial*; Cairns, *Advocacy and the Making of the Adversarial Criminal Trial*; Schramm, *Testimony and Advocacy*; and May, *The Bar and the Old Bailey*.
7 For an overview of the history of public execution see Gatrell, *The Hanging Tree*; Ward, ed., *Global History of Execution*; and Devereaux, *Execution, State and Society in England, 1660–1900*, and https://hcmc.uvic.ca/project/oldbailey/index.php, a database created by Devereaux on capital convictions at the Old Bailey between 1730 and 1837. For works on opposition to capital punishment see Chapter 5, n. 50, below.
8 *English Criminal Law*, 1:30.
9 See Critchley and James, *The Maul and the Pear Tree*.
10 Letter to his sister, quoted in Philips, 'A new engine', 174.
11 Philips, 'A new engine', 174.
12 See *Remarks on the Recent Murders in London* and Griffin, 'Detective Policing and the State', 81–2.
13 See, e.g., the coverage in *The Times* between 8 and 28 April 1842; Good's trial was reported in that paper on 12–16 May and his execution on 24 May 1842. He was also the subject of numerous broadsides, which tended to focus on the dismembering of his victim, and have been described by V.A.C. Gatrell as pornographic. See *The Hanging Tree*, 71. For the police investigation, and press criticism, see Griffin, 'Detective Policing and the State', 74–81. Shpayer-Makov suggests that the attempt on Queen Victoria's life may also have contributed to the recognition of the need for a detective force. *The Ascent of the Detective*, 33.
14 'Detective Policing and the State', 39n146.
15 Borowitz, *The Thurtell-Hunt Murder Case*, 80.
16 *Victorian Studies in Scarlet*, 10, 9, 10.
17 *Victorian Studies in Scarlet*, 67. Judith Flanders's more recent *The Invention of Murder* takes up the same theme of 'the crimson thread that runs through the fabric of Victorian social history' (*Victorian Studies in Scarlet*, 9) but privileges anecdote over analysis.
18 p. 160.
19 *Victorian Studies in Scarlet*, 56. See also Boyle, *Black Swine*, chap. 6; Borowitz, *The Thurtell-Hunt Murder Case*. For a contemporary pamphlet account of this murder see *The Trial of John Thurtell and Joseph Hunt*.
20 See Borowitz, *The Thurtell-Hunt Murder Case*.
21 On the history of this office see Lockwood, *The Conquest of Death*; Forbes, 'Coroners' Inquests in the County of Middlesex' and 'Crowner's Quest'; Burney, *Bodies of Evidence*; Fisher, 'The Politics of Sudden Death', Cawthorn, 'Thomas

18   *Introduction*

Wakley and the Medical Coronership'; Sherrington, 'Thomas Wakely and Reform'; Emmerichs, 'Getting away with Murder?'; Hostettler, 'Thomas Wakley'.
22 Charles Brook, *Battling Surgeon: A Life of Thomas Wakley* (1945), 152, quoted in Emmerichs, 'Getting away with Murder?', 95.
23 On the relationship between the coroner and the new police see Griffin, 'Detective Policing and the State', chap. 2, sec. 2.3.
24 This subject has received little academic attention but see Griffin, 'Detective Policing and the State', chap. 2.
25 On Bow Street and detection, see Beattie, *The First English Detectives*, 182; Cox, *A Certain Share of Low Cunning*, 105–9.
26 On the relationship between murder and detective policing see Shpayer-Makov, *The Ascent of the Detective*; Griffin, 'Detective Policing and the State'.
27 On this subject, see also Schramm, *Testimony and Advocacy*; Cairns, *Advocacy and the Making of the Adversarial Criminal Trial*; and May, *The Bar and the Old Bailey*.
28 HLS MS 4487 (http://nrs.harvard.edu/urn-3:HLS.Libr:12188023).
29 HLS MS 4487, Item 4 (seq. 12).
30 Bentley, *English Criminal Justice*, 84; Williams, 'The Power to Prosecute', 603. See Smith, 'The Emergence of Public Prosecution in London'.
31 HLS MS 4487, Item 4 (seq. 14).
32 Langbein, *The Origins of Adversary Criminal Trial*. See Bentley, *English Criminal Justice*, chap. 12, for nineteenth-century murder trials in which the accused appeared without counsel.
33 This prohibition was intended to spare them from committing perjury in an attempt to save themselves from conviction. See Bentley, chaps. 15–18; Devereaux, 'Swearing and Feeling'.
34 Phillips, as I have discussed elsewhere, a barrister who made his name in the Irish courts in the early nineteenth century, had singularly failed to impress England's civil courts and retreated to the Old Bailey from marked failure in Westminster Hall. In the criminal courts his success in the 1820s and 1830s recalled that of William Garrow in the 1780s. That success owed in no little part to the pre-1836 rules that curbed his tongue in the courtroom. See May, 'Irish Sensibilities and the English Bar'.
35 See Mellinkoff, *The Conscience of a Lawyer*; May, *The Bar and the Old Bailey* and 'Irish Sensibilities and the English Bar'.
36 On the impact of this novel see Buckley, 'Sensations of Celebrity'. The Newgate genre as a whole is briefly discussed below in Chapter 6.
37 *Two Studies in Crime*, 15–16.
38 *Murder by the Book*, 166.
39 'The lamentation of Francis B. Courvoisier, for the murder of Lord Wm. Russell', George Thomas, printer.
40 Steedman, *Labours Lost*, 13.
41 *The Servant's Hand*, 206.
42 Turner's *What the Butler Saw* surveys 'the servant problem' from the eighteenth century through to the twentieth. For servant life in the nineteenth century see Burnett, *Useful Toil*; Davidoff and Hawthorn, *A Day in the Life of a Victorian Domestic Servant*; Horn, *The Rise and Fall of the Victorian Servant*; Huggett, *Life Below Stairs*; May, *The Victorian Domestic Servant*; and Fernandez, *Victorian Servants*. Meldrum's *Domestic Service and Gender* and Steedman's *Master and Servant* and *Labours Lost* are excellent studies of service in earlier periods and I have drawn on them for issues that persisted into the period of my own study. Light's *Mrs Woolf and the Servants* I found equally useful and insightful.
43 Historians have long used legal records as a source of information on the lives of the labouring poor: Dorothy George's *London Life in the Eighteenth Century* (1925) is a notable early example in this regard.

Introduction 19

44 p. 9.
45 *What the Butler Saw*, 20.
46 See Hay, 'England, 1562–1875', 78, 80.
47 On literary representation of the servant class see, e.g., Robbins's admirable *The Servant's Hand*, Fernandez, *Victorian Servants*, and Steedman, *Master and Servant*. Straub's *Domestic Affairs*, while useful in reminding us of the potential for violence inherent in domestic intimacy that included servants, is ultimately more problematic and I would query the existence of a 'leveling energy' (188) in such intimacy. See Sarah Lloyd's review: https://reviews.history.ac.uk/review/814.
(Date accessed: 29 April, 2019).
48 See *The Servant's Hand*, chaps. 3 and 4.
49 'On a Chalk-Mark on the Door', 511.
50 The 1720 Tailors Act (7 Geo. I, st. 1, cl. 13) is the last that allowed forcing an adult servant to work for a master not of his own choosing. I am grateful to Doug Hay for this reference.
51 *The Trial of Laurence Earl Ferrers*, OBP t17670909-1; Brownrigg's trial is reported at t17670909-01. See Seleski, 'A Mistress, a Mother, and a Murderess Too' and Straub, 'The Tortured Apprentice'.
52 Richard Baxter, *Works*, 4 vols. (London, 1707), vol. 1, p. 435, quoted in Meldrum, *Domestic Service and Gender 1660–1750*, 8.
53 OBP t17630223-19.
54 See van Thal, *Ernest Augustus*; Willis, *Ernest Augustus*; and Wardroper, *Wicked Ernest*.
55 OBP t18151045-18. For discussion of this case see, e.g., Gatrell, *The Hanging Tree*, chap. 13, and Seleski, 'Domesticity is in the Streets'.
56 Steedman, *Labours Lost*, 241–54.
57 *The Times*, 19 June 1840.
58 Thompson, 'The Crime of Anonymity', 307 n.1.
59 James, *Devices and Desires*, 271. She had made the same point in *A Taste for Death*: 'the victim was central to his death. He died because of what he was, what he knew, what he did, what he planned to do'. 260.
60 See May, 'Garrow for the Prosecution'.
61 *Ralph Tailor's Summer*, xii.

2   14 Norfolk Street, Park Lane

Upstairs and Down

Introduction

William Russell attracted far greater attention in death than he ever had in life. From the morning of 6 May 1840 people flocked to his London house in droves, 'with the double object of gratifying their curiosity by a sight of the house, and if possible to learn some further news respecting the dreadful affair'.[1] Apart from a host of officials involved in the investigation – police officers of varying ranks, medical professionals, and solicitors – spectators soon thronged the streets, on foot and on horseback, while endless carriages drew up to disgorge aristocrats. According to the *Morning Chronicle*, these included Lord Cowley, Lord Ashburnham, the Marquess of Salisbury, and the Marquess of Aylesbury.[2] Prince Albert, only recently married to the young Queen Victoria, sent messengers to the house to ask for news, as did the Duke of Wellington. 'The excitement produced in high life by the dreadful event', reported *The Times*, 'is almost unprecedented, and the feeling of apprehension for personal safety increases every hour, particularly among those of the nobility and gentry who live in comparative seclusion'.[3]

Why the excitement? Much of it owed to the relationship between the victim and his murderer. Twelve years earlier a servant who killed his master would have been tried not for murder but petty treason, and met with an aggravated form of the death penalty – although not as severe as that accorded to those convicted of high treason.[4] The murder of a master by a servant had for centuries been viewed as a particularly heinous betrayal of trust, and although the law had changed public feeling was unlikely to have altered. More recent political fears, even if not articulated openly, are likely to have contributed to aristocratic alarm as well. Russell's murder took place at the end of a decade which had seen violent unrest in the colonies (the Jamaican uprising of 1831 and riots in 1839, the Canadian rebellions of 1837–38) and on the Continent (the French revolution of 1830 and an anarchist's attempted assassination of Louis-Phillipe in 1835). England itself had experienced parliamentary reform bill riots in 1832 and poor law riots in 1834; the working-class Chartist movement emerged in 1836 and in the year prior to Russell's murder Chartist riots had taken place in Birmingham and a national convention was held in London. Thackeray's unease with Courvoisier's actions evidences a fear of the violent potential of the lower orders that must have been shared, if it went otherwise unvoiced, by the aristocracy.[5]

While an alarmed aristocracy closed ranks following the murder of one of their number, few of the individuals who expressed concern had visited 14 Norfolk Street or shown any interest while 'the aged and respected nobleman', as the *Morning Chronicle* described him, was alive.[6] The widowed, elderly Russell was neither friendless nor a recluse: in the weeks preceding his death he had spent just over two weeks (5–22 April) at a hotel in Richmond and during that time he had paid many visits to his sister-in-law, Lady Sarah Bayley, who lived at Hampton Court Palace. Lady Sarah said that she had seen him 'often'.[7] Russell was also close to his daughter-in-law, the Baroness de Clifford. Generally speaking, however, he led a very quiet life. His company was not sought out by 'society' and he is remembered today not for his life, but for his violent death.

14 Norfolk Street

In the public imagination, an aristocratic household, whether in town or country, is physically large, its inhabitants numerous, and its domestic management stable, an image which has been reinforced by television programs such as *Upstairs Downstairs* and *Downton Abbey*. William Russell's establishment was decidedly at odds with this image. 'With his daughters married and his sons settled in life', wrote Yseult Bridges in her early popular study of the murder, William Russell 'found in 14 Norfolk Street a house large enough to take his books, his collections of fine porcelain and rare prints' yet small enough to suit his quiet life and to be run by a small staff.[8] This description is deceptive, implying a tranquillity Russell was hardly likely to have experienced. The physical premises of 14 Norfolk Street were small and rather mean in proportion. None of the servants employed to look after its sole upstairs inhabitant had been in Russell's employment very long, nor had Russell inhabited the house – or any other, for that matter – for any length of time, taking out a short-term lease in 1839. The master, as well as his servants, had lived a peripatetic life.

Contemporary descriptions of Russell's house and its locale varied. *The Era* described the neighbourhood as both 'fashionable' and 'respectable'.[9] But 'many readers', acknowledged *The Times* in reporting the murder, were 'possibly unacquainted with the locality of the scene of the tragical event'. It continued to enlighten them: 'Norfolk-Street is a small street, containing 31 houses, numbering from South to North, between Park-lane and Park-Street, Grosvenor-square … The whole of the houses in Norfolk-street are inhabited by families connected with the aristocracy'.[10]

Norfolk Street, renamed Dunraven in 1939, dates from the 1750s and by 1761 building had been completed and the houses occupied. The west side, whose houses overlooked the park and had short gardens extending to Park Lane, was the more fashionable. Russell lived on the east side, where the houses were less grand, the frontages narrower and the inhabitants 'more varied', including by the 1790s tradesmen as well as medical professionals such as Sir Lucas Pepys, who had been physician to George III. Two of the original dwellings became public houses and in the 1820s 'a house of ill-fame' had been a cause of concern. The east side also attracted naval or army officers and the street retained this association throughout the nineteenth century. Russell's neighbours included Major Anstruthers at no. 13; when Anstruther and his wife went abroad Sir Howard Elphinstone, commander of the royal engineers in the Peninsular War who had been promoted to major general in 1837, moved in with his wife Frances.[11] Relatively short tenures appear to have been typical on his side of the street and there were only three years remaining on his lease when Russell was killed. *The Times*'s reporter dismissed the house as 'a second-rate one'; the *Southern Star* wrote indignantly, 'The family of the lamented nobleman are blamed for suffering him to live in so dreary a locality'.[12]

Reportage of the trial ensured that the layout of Russell's house was endlessly described and discussed; in the Old Bailey courtroom a model made by Charles Augustus Rivers was placed on a table and would be referred to by various witnesses over the duration of the trial. The word 'small' features prominently in descriptions of the premises. 14 Norfolk Street was three windows wide and three storeys, plus the attic and basement, tall. On the ground floor were a dining room, sometimes referred to as the parlour, cloak-room, and water-closet. There were two rooms on each of the upper floors, the front rooms larger than those at the back: a drawing room and a room used for reading and writing on the first floor, Lord William's bedroom and a dressing room or second, unfurnished bedroom, on the second. The basement comprised a kitchen, scullery, and butler's pantry; the servants slept in two rooms in the attic. The front windows of the house were 'adorned with geraniums, mignionette, &c'.[13] The interior décor remains open to question: the *Southern Star* reported that Russell was 'a great patron of the fine arts' and that his house had contained 'several pictures of rarity and value'.[14] Barrister John Adolphus, retained to prosecute the murder in court, commented similarly that the house was 'beautifully adorned with pictures and china'. 'Unpretentious' yet 'adequate for his lordship's wants' was how he chose to describe the house in his diary.[15] In twentieth-century descriptions of 14 Norfolk Street Yseult Bridges followed the *Southern Star* but David Mellinkoff was dismissive, accepting *The Times*'s report that the house was 'second rate' and saying that its walls had been decorated with portraits of Lord Russell's dog and inexpensive rather than rare prints. We know for certain that these included 'The Vision of Ezekiel', purchased from a Pall-Mall printseller named William Frederick Moltino. Moltino would testify at trial that the brown paper used to wrap it was the same as that found covering stolen items of Russell's plate.[16] Various repairs to Russell's bedroom had been made in April and on the first of May Alfred Hughes had called to fix the bell-pull at the head of Russell's bed, which he would have used to summon his servants.[17] One of Hughes's men, upholsterer John Harris, and Henry Lovick adjusted it again on the 5th of May, the night of Russell's death. Harris also fixed the handle on the door, which had been rehung.[18] Whatever its physical state before the murder, the house would be 'nearly pulled to pieces' during the police investigation so that, both *The Times* and the *Morning Chronicle* reported, a considerable sum of money would be required 'to put it in proper order again'.[19]

Upstairs: Lord William Russell's 'incomplete household'

Contemporary interest in William Russell's murder rested heavily, although not entirely, on the fact that the sole upstairs inhabitant of 14 Norfolk Street was a member of a family which had been important socially and politically since the sixteenth century. 'To be a Russell was to be identified with English history ...'[20] John Russell, advisor to both Henry VIII and Edward VI, was created Earl of Bedford in 1551 (the sixth creation of this title); the fifth earl was made a duke, as well as Marquess of Tavistock, in 1694. All of these names – Russell, Bedford, Tavistock – are physically etched in London's landscape, for the Russells became great property owners in the seventeenth century. In 1669 the son of the fifth Earl of Bedford – a previous William Russell – married a daughter of the fourth Earl of Southampton, who had inherited from her father undeveloped agricultural lands now known as Bloomsbury, the area contained by the present-day Tottenham Court Road, Euston Road, Southampton Row, and New Oxford Street, as well as areas on the other side of Tottenham Court Road and across Euston Road, respectively. When William Russell was executed for treason in 1683 his widow carried on with the property development. The Russell association with Whig politics is equally well known. The seventeenth-century William Russell's commitment to the Protestant succession cost him his life; the posthumous appreciation of William and Mary for that commitment won the family the dukedom and the Tavistock title. In the eighteenth century the fifth and six dukes of Bedford, Francis Russell and John Russell, were Foxites. The latter's third son, another John and a future prime minister, worked all his life with a statue of Fox on his desk.

Among these illustrious Russells the nineteenth-century murder victim was a very minor player, his life and political career undistinguished. The headline for *The Times*'s initial report of the murder identifies his public significance in 1840: 'Horrible murder of Lord William Russell, Uncle to Lord John Russell, Secretary for the Colonies'.[21] William Russell's nephew, whose political career would span 55 years, was born in 1792 and entered the House of Commons in 1813. He had become a member of Cabinet in 1831 and from 1835 led Melbourne's Whig/Liberals in the lower house. John Russell was a great champion of reform, including reform of the criminal law. 'A book could be written', said his biographer in 1972,

> about the impetus he gave to the reform of the criminal law; he drastically reduced the number of offences, including forgery, punishable by

death; he took the chair at the meetings of the select committee on transportation; he pursued a policy of dividing serious offenders, who should be transported for not less than ten years, from less serious offenders who should be sent to prison for not more than five; he established a prison inspectorate, and a prison for juvenile offenders at Parkhurst; and he opened the way to the abolition of the hulks and the construction of a model prison at Pentonville.[22]

John Russell's uncle made no such impact. William Russell was born in August 1767, the son of Francis Russell, Marquis of Tavistock, and grandson, through his mother's line, of the second Earl of Albermarle. His father had predeceased him by five months. 'Strange circumstances attended the commencement as well as the termination of [William Russell's] career', reported the *Era*. 'His father was killed by a fall from his horse, and his mother died of grief soon afterwards, a martyr to her affection for her deceased lord'.[23] This third son – 'Lord' was merely a courtesy title – was educated in the traditional manner for one of his class, at Westminster and Christ Church, Oxford. In July 1789, aged 31, he married 21-year-old Lady Charlotte Anne Villiers, daughter of the fourth Earl of Jersey, whose wife was one of the many mistresses of George IV while he was Prince of Wales.[24] The marriage produced seven children: Gertrude Frances (b. 1791); Francis (b. 1793); George (b. 1795); John (b. 1796); Charlotte Frances (b. 1798); William (b. 1800); and Eliza Laura Henrietta (b. 1803).[25] Virtually empty at the time of his death, Russell's household would once have been a full one. His daughter Charlotte died before her first birthday but six of his children survived to adulthood. The marriage also appears to have been happy: Russell had treasured a locket which contained a lock of his dead wife's hair. This locket was among the items stolen by his murderer.[26]

Whatever personal happiness William Russell's marriage and family had provided him would have been marred by financial worries and, ironically for a member of a family renowned for its London properties, in his old age he could not have afforded more distinguished premises than 14 Norfolk Street, having been plagued by debt all his life. A residence in Streatham, Surrey, on property belonging to his eldest brother, was bequeathed to him in 1802 but sold in 1806. Two years on his financial affairs had become dire indeed and from that date, which coincided with the death of his wife, Russell lived 'a nomadic and anxiety-ridden existence'. In 1809 he was 'skulking in Scotland'; by 1810 he was considering 'perfect seclusion' abroad.[27] At his death William Russell's estate was valued at less than £2,000 – slightly under, that is, the annual income of the middle-class barrister engaged to defend his murderer.[28]

Prior to taking the Norfolk Street lease, Russell had spent some 20 years drifting aimlessly about the Continent. His self-imposed, restless exile coincided for a time with that of his daughter Gertrude. In 1816 Gertrude had married politician Henry Grey Bennet, a man actively involved in various early nineteenth-century campaigns to reform both policing and punishment. Bennet had argued in support of a reduction in the application of capital punishment and in the year of his marriage initiated a special commission to investigate the policing of metropolitan London. His political career, unlike that of his father-in-law, was engaged and successful, but it came to an abrupt end and in 1825 he and Gertrude left England. Publicly, the flight was ascribed to the death of their only son, which had occurred close on the heels of that of one of the couple's three daughters. In fact, it probably owed to scandal. Bennet had been threatened with criminal prosecution for allegedly propositioning a young male servant in August of that year.[29]

William Russell's own life does not appear to have been a happy one in the long years following his wife's death. The chief sources of consolation available to the nineteenth-century widower were thought to be 'work and remarriage'.[30] Work in Russell's case had been the family business of politics: he represented the county of Surrey as a Whig from 1789 until 1807 and briefly held junior ministerial office in the Ministry of All the Talents, as a Lord of the Admiralty. On losing his Surrey seat in the 1807 election he took advantage of the Russell family's pocket borough of Tavistock, serving as MP in that constituency from 1807 to 1819 and then again from 1826 to 1830, when he retired. His political principles were genuinely Whig and progressive. He was against coercion in Ireland[31] and opposed a bill in 1805 to impose an additional duty on salt on the grounds that it would push up the prices of bread and other foodstuffs and 'entirely alter the condition of the lower orders', robbing them of 'the state of independence which was their birthright' and rendering them 'totally dependent on the affluent for support'.[32] He protested against the Seditious Meetings Bill in 1817, arguing that it was inconsistent with the principles of the constitution and that the House 'had already, by suspending the law of Habeas Corpus and trial by jury, given them as much power as the Romans gave to a dictator'.[33] He

> had never before seen so desperate a remedy applied to the wretchedness and distress of the country. The rights of the people, for the protection of which all governments should exist, were trampled under foot and despotism prevailed. It was impossible for the country to part with more liberty ...[34]

The 'tenor of his whole life', Russell claimed in 1827, had been 'the support of liberty in its most extended sense'. He did oppose a motion at that time to repeal one of the Six Acts that eroded free speech, but only because he believed that 'blasphemous publications ought not to be circulated'.[35]

Despite his convictions, Russell rarely spoke in the House and failed to pursue politics in anything but a dilettante fashion. And unlike his more politically active and successful nephew John, who lost his first wife in 1838, William, widowed at 41, failed to remarry. He certainly appeared to have enjoyed female company and to have engaged in a variety of flirtations. His family tended to view them as ridiculous. Perhaps his financial difficulties made him hesitant to acquire another wife; those difficulties may equally have inclined marriageable ladies to look elsewhere for a husband. Regardless of the reasons, in not remarrying he effectively reverted to a bachelor state for the last 30 years of his life, a status that was traditionally regarded as symbolic of 'diminished manhood'.[36] Long before his death 'Old Lord William Russell' had become the object of exasperated pity amongst his extended family. In 1822 a nephew had said, 'He appears such an unhappy wandering spirit' that he had been 'glad' to invite his relative to live with them in Florence while the family was touring the Continent. Russell, however, had been 'too restless to remain in it & wander[ed] about from tavern to tavern without knowing why or wherefore'.[37] In 1829 he had joined them in Switzerland, but he soon left: 'What a strange mode of life, neither respectable nor useful', wrote the younger lord (yet another William) in his diary. 'We could not persuade him to stay'.[38] An exasperated in-law, Elizabeth, Lady Romilly, once commented that the Russells were 'very odd people'.[39] Among his own family, Lord William was considered one of the oddest.

At the time of his murder three of Russell's four sons had predeceased him: 30-year-old bachelor George Russell in 1825; 39-year-old bachelor Lieutenant-Colonel Francis Russell in 1832; and naval Commander John Russell in 1835. John had married Sophia Coussmaker, Baroness de Clifford, in 1822 and they had had four children. Russell's daughter Gertrude, widowed in 1836, had returned to England, ending her ten-year Continental exile as the wife of a 'sexual deviant'. His other surviving daughter, Elizabeth, had married a second cousin, the Reverend Lord Wriothesley Russell, a son of the sixth Duke of Bedford and rector of Chenies, Buckinghamshire, in 1829. But it was the surviving son, Mr William Russell, who like John had provided grandchildren by 1840, who was sent for by the servants on discovery of the murder victim's body. Mr William Russell's address was more prestigious than that of his father: he lived at No. 9, Cheshunt-place, Belgrave-square.[40] William would repeatedly be described by the papers as prostrate with grief.

On the evidence of testimony produced in court and by his servants, in the years immediately preceding his death Russell appears to have relied on his relations, his club, and the dog whose portrait adorned his walls – 'a large animal of the "Swedish sheep-dog breed"' – for company. His predominately solitary life was described by one-time valet James Ellis: 'His Lordship was very punctual and regular in his habits especially in his afternoons and evenings 6 days out of the seven'. 'Going out to dinner of an evening might make a little variation'.[41] Russell's housemaid and cook spoke of a modest dinner party given on 13 April. Four of the seven guests were close relatives.[42] Otherwise, Russell's daily pleasures were small ones, a pipe smoked after breakfast and another between coffee and tea in the evening, a short walk with the dog. On retiring to his bedroom at 11 or 12 o'clock at night he generally read for an hour or so. On the day of his death Russell had breakfasted just before 9 a.m., as usual, and spent the morning at home alone but for his servants and the afternoon at Brooks's, a Whig gentleman's club founded in 1764 and relocated to premises designed by Henry Holland in St James Street in 1778. Like all such clubs, it offered an alternative domesticity, an all-male home away from home.[43]

Aged 72, William Russell's health was somewhat compromised, although the papers reported that on the day prior to his death Russell had cheerfully told the Earl of Erroll, 'I am so well, that I am going to take a fresh lease of my life'.[44] Various of his employees acknowledged that he could be testy. Ellis told the police, 'His Lordship was an irritable man but not ill-tempered the very opposite indeed – liberally disposed and kind to all about him it was impossible any gentleman could have had a better heart than he'.[45] John Harris, who had been involved in furnishing Norfolk Street – hanging the prints, rare or otherwise, and adjusting the book cases – and had known him for three years, expressed the same opinion. Russell, he said,

> was fidgety in his manner, rather feeble on his feet & would walk about talking to himself – he was irritable but not ill tempered, being a very old man he had his little whims & peculiarities which he required to be attended to – he was very precise in having everything placed as he wished to the shadow of a shade – and rather fretful if not done exactly as to suit him. He was difficult to please at times – he was very precise & particular ...

But, Harris concluded, 'I have had many other gentlemen of rank at times more difficult to please than he was – I always thought he was a kind good natured man to those about him'.[46] Harris attributed Russell's mild eccentricities to his advanced age, and the physical infirmity identified in his description was confirmed by Russell's apothecary, John Nussey, who similarly described him as 'feeble', suffering from asthma and a rupture that required him to wear a truss.[47] Russell was also hard of hearing and at trial Thomas Davis testified that his employer had supplied 'auricular devices' or instruments to assist in hearing in June 1836.[48] 'He was very deaf', Ellis reported, 'to a strange voice', although 'by habit' the valet 'could converse with him in an ordinary voice'.[49] Impaired hearing would have contributed to Russell's isolation and loneliness; it also meant that he was unlikely to have woken in the night as his murderer approached. Nussey had speculated as to whether the murder victim had been drugged, but such an action, for which there was no evidence, would not have been necessary.

Downstairs and outside: Russell's 'family'

At 72, William Russell appears to have typified most of the problems identified by Pat Jalland as experienced by older members of the upper-middle and upper classes: 'deteriorating mental and physical health, a declining sense of usefulness, decreasing mobility, loneliness, and increased dependency on family, friends, or servants'.[50] He had no employment and little social life: if he talked to himself, that may have owed to the fact that he had few people to talk to. His wife long dead, his children either dead or married with homes of their own, his household consisted entirely of employees. This household tended, on the whole, to be referred to in the press as his 'establishment', although both the *Era* and barrister John Adolphus chose instead a term fast going out of use, consistently describing those who lived below stairs as Russell's 'family'.[51] The patriarchal conception of the relation between servants and master had been expressed by Dod and Cleaver in the early seventeenth century: 'The householder is called *Pater familias*, that is father of a family, because he should have a fatherly care over his servants as if they were his children'.[52] In his famous mid-eighteenth-century dictionary Samuel Johnson defined 'family' as 'those who live in the same house'. But the 'last *legal* voice' to claim that masters and servants were relatives, Carolyn Steedman tells us, was heard in *Laws Concerning Masters and Servants* (1785):[53] in legal terms, the relationship was subsequently viewed as a contract, and while the Johnsonian linguistic use of 'family' to include all members of a household continued, by 1840 it was decidedly old-fashioned. Regardless of the terminology employed, William Russell was dependent on his servants, who cooked and cleaned for him, waited on him, looked after his possessions, drove him about London, cared for his dog and horses, and, locking the house at night, were ultimately responsible for his personal safety.

As John Burnett points out, despite being 'the largest single employment for English women, and the second largest employment for all English people, male and female', in the nineteenth century, domestic service remains

> a largely unknown occupation. No Royal Commission investigated it or suggested legislative protection of the worker; no outburst of trade union activity called attention to the lot of servants, as it did that of the building workers, the cotton-spinners and the dock labourers; no Joseph Arch or Tom Mann arose as spokesman of their cause to draw forth the pity of the Victorian middle classes. Immured in their basements and attic bedrooms, shut away from private gaze and public conscience, the domestic servants remained mute and forgotten until, in the end, only their growing scarcity aroused interest in 'the servant problem'.[54]

Not until the 1970s did life below stairs begin to attract academic attention; servants, for example, are famously absent from E.P. Thompson's *The Making of the English Working Class* (1963). Interest was one issue, sources another: while prescriptive texts on the master–servant relation abound, the actual experience of life on the other side of the green baize door was rarely recorded.

Despite being a member of a prominent and highly political aristocratic family, William Russell's own life is only faintly documented and his voice is usually heard at second hand. He did not keep a journal or write an autobiography. But he wrote to and received letters from family members and friends; he was also discussed in their correspondence. Parliamentary records testify to his political career. Had he not been murdered, historians would still have been able to piece together the basic contours of his personal and professional life. The same could not be said of his servants. We know of their lives solely by virtue of the fact that they found themselves embroiled in a murder investigation. Thrust temporarily into the spotlight, they spoke involuntarily and to interlocutors.

At 14 Norfolk Street William Russell had three servants who lived in: a cook, Mary Hannell; a housemaid, Sarah Mancer; and, combining the roles of valet, footman, and butler, the male servant who would be charged with, convicted of, and executed for his murder, François Benjamin Courvoisier. Russell also employed a coachman and a groom to drive and tend to his horses; both of these servants lived out. In terms of its complement of staff Russell's household falls somewhere between stools in the hierarchy listed in Thomas Webster's *Encyclopedia of Household Economy*, first published in 1844. Not unnaturally, it didn't meet the standards of a 'first-rate' establishment, which would employ 20–24 servants. Russell's eldest brother, the sixth Duke of Bedford, who died in 1839, employed 300.[55] But such a complement was exceptional: generally speaking, 'five servants made up a large establishment' and these were rare.[56] In Webster's categorization, Russell's household can be located somewhere between the 'fifth-rate', in which a cook, housemaid, underhousemaid, and a single manservant would be found, and the 'sixth rate', comprising a cook, housemaid, and 'footboy'. Aged 23, Russell's in-house male servant was no 'boy' and his formal, combined, role appears higher up the social ladder, in Webster's 'third-rate' category. William Russell's household thus did not fit the contemporary mould in terms of the personnel employed. The short tenures of his indoor servants, however, ranging from the valet's five weeks to the roughly three-year employment of his two female servants, were not unusual. A study based on Ashford, Kent, indicates that by 1851 a mere 7 of the 312 servants recorded in the 1841 census had remained with the same family throughout their lives.[57] Courvoisier, hired at the beginning of April, had not yet been paid at the time of Russell's murder. That none of his staff had long been in his employ is understandable given Russell's Continental wanderings, but 'faithful old retainers' were at any rate largely mythic figures.

The female predominance in Russell's indoor staff was equally typical of the age. In earlier times male servants had dominated indoors and out, particularly in large aristocratic households. In London households, however, the gender balance among Russell's servants had been the norm for centuries: a study of domestic servants in City of London parishes in the 1690s found that some 89% of servant-employing households had between one and three servants, over 84% of whom were women. Tim Meldrum assumed 'a London-wide ratio of four female servants to every one male' at this time. In the period 1660–1750, Meldrum also estimated that 'as many as 43.5 per cent' of male servants worked for knights or the nobility, 63 if the gentry were included. Only the wealthy could afford menservants.[58] Gender also affected 'career' patterns: women tended to be employed as domestic servants in their early to mid-twenties, before they married. For many, it was a life stage rather than a permanent occupation. Menservants tended to stay longer in a single place and also enjoyed greater opportunities for advancement. These trends were not unvaried rules, however, as Russell's household bears witness. Both cook and housemaid were unmarried and in their thirties; the cook also had plans for leaving Russell's household and bettering her employment situation. Before entering Russell's service Courvoisier's previous employment had been for relatively short periods and he too was ambitious.

The female predominance in London domestic service – by the early nineteenth century female servants outnumbered their male counterparts just under eight to one[59] – reflects in large part a change in the status of employers. In the nineteenth century the middle classes increasingly employed servants and their financial means inclined them to hire women. Female domestics were much less expensive, in part because their wages were lower. Apart from the wage differential, female servants were not subject to tax; between 1777 and 1882, male domestics were. This tax, originally set at a guinea per head, had been introduced to help pay for the American war. Prime Minister William Pitt had attempted unsuccessfully to extend the servant tax to females, but the measure proved so unpopular he was forced to abandon it. The tax on male servants however continued and increased, and bachelors had to pay an extra duty. From 1834 boys under the age of 18 were exempted, but Russell's male employees were older than that.

On a variety of fronts, William Russell's household was something of a hybrid. His physical premises and income were more typical of the middle classes, yet as an aristocrat he employed a valet. Middle-class men were much less likely to do so and in the nineteenth century, male servants were seldom found in households with fewer than six servants.[60] Prescriptive texts on the management of servants had also, by this time, begun to assume that a woman would be in charge of running the house, a situation typical of middle-class homes in which the bread winner was absent during the day. Samuel and Sarah Adams's practical manual, *The Complete Servant* (1825), for example, appears directed primarily towards women. This new emphasis on the role of mistresses rather than masters of servants had become evident by the mid-eighteenth century, if not before, and was attributed at least in part to the increasing importance of London houses as employers of servants.[61] Once again, Russell's household was atypical. While they discussed the establishment suitable for a widow, the Adams did not consider that appropriate for the widower. Such a household appears to have been off the prescribed social radar. Yet, as Margaret Ponsonby describes in *Stories from Home*, extraordinary homes are normal. Russell's household is a useful reminder of this fact.

The female servants: cook and housemaid

Neither Russell's cook nor his housemaid had been born in London, but moved to it from the country as young girls, in search of employment. Most domestic staff at this time were country girls; later in the Victorian period, they might equally have come directly from the workhouse. Life below stairs at 14 Norfolk Street however diverged somewhat from the Victorian stereotype. In 1840 female servants were not yet required to wear uniforms – this development dates from the 1850s – so that both cook and housemaid would have worn their own clothes. Leigh Hunt, in an essay both flippant and extraordinarily patronizing, had described these in the 1820s as 'black stockings, a stuff gown, a cap, and a neckhandkerchief' on weekdays while 'a gown of a better texture' and white stockings were donned on Sundays and holidays.[62] The domestic rhythms of cooking and cleaning would naturally have shaped their days, but Russell's servants also enjoyed a degree of personal freedom that is not reflected in prescriptive manuals, nor indeed in the conditions of service recorded in William Cother's 1837 hiring of a cook, which included the following:

> Will obey orders without grumbling ... Ask leave whenever she goes from home. Never leave the House after night. Has no followers ... She is generally to go to Church every other Sunday morning – when she wished to go to see her Friends (say once in three months) she might do so by asking 2 or 3 days previous, at the time she wished, or a day fixed for that purpose.[63]

If Mancer or Hannell had been engaged on similar terms, the rules were not enforced. As discussed below, they visited friends and had visitors in, and on occasion used the front door rather than the area entrance. This freedom no doubt owed in part to the absence of a mistress, possibly to absentmindedness on Russell's part, but also to the fact that their employer was aristocratic rather than middle class: middle-class housewives tended to be much more sensitive about their own social status, and consequently more rigid in the supervision of staff.[64] In 1889 one valet would complain, 'It's only the aristocracy who treat servants properly. I tried one situation out of aristocratic circles, and that was where the man showed me his area gate'.[65] Not all aristocrats, nor indeed all Russells, were so relaxed: the 10th Duke of Bedford (d. 1893) insisted that no housemaid was ever to cross his path after 12 noon, on pain of dismissal from his service. William Russell's cook, however, would remember her employer as a 'kindly gentleman' and good master.

Mary Hannell was a single woman, in 1840, aged 'about' 33 years, who had never been married. She told the police that she had been in Russell's employ for two years and almost nine months, arriving after the housemaid. She had come to his household from that of Lord Southampton's, where she had been a kitchen maid for almost four years, and had been recommended to Russell by Mr Morel of Piccadilly. Previous tenures of service were similarly brief: two and a half years with Sir William Rush at Wimbledon, and a year and a half with Sir Frederick Bakers at Hastings. Her father, a carpenter, was a native of Woburn in Bedfordshire; she had spent her earliest years in London and returned to it from Woburn when she entered service. A younger brother followed the father's trade while her sisters and a cousin were in service with the

Duke of Bedford, employed in the laundry. Her London relatives consisted of her mother's elderly brother and a cousin of her father's. Hannell's history of employment is heavily linked to various branches of the Russell family, or to the locale of their country estates. She was planning to move on again before the murder. 'My only reason for leaving Lord William's service', she said, 'was that he did not keep much company & I wished not to lose my knowledge of cooking – I therefore gave him my notice & he wrote me a recommendation in which he mentions my reason for leaving ...'[66]

Thackeray, for all his acknowledgement of the indignities suffered by the servant class, seems to have found their ambitions amusing:

> Here, dear ladies, is an advertisement which I cut out of The Times a few days since, expressly for you:
> 'A lady is desirous of obtaining a SITUATION for a very respectable young woman as HEAD KITCHEN-MAID under a man-cook. She has lived four years under a very good cook and housekeeper. Can make ice, and is an excellent baker. She will only take a place in a very good family, where she can have the opportunity of improving herself, and, if possible, staying for two years. Apply by letter to,' &c. &c.

Just note, he continued, the conditions specified:

1 This young woman is to be HEAD kitchen-maid, that is to say there is to be a chorus of kitchen-maids, of which Y. W. is to be chief.
2 She will only be situated under a man-cook. (A) Ought he to be a French cook; and (B), if so, would the lady desire him to be a Protestant?
3 She will only take a place in a VERY GOOD FAMILY. How old ought the family to be, and what do you call good? that is the question. How long after the Conquest will do? Would a banker's family do, or is a baronet's good enough? Best say what rank in the peerage would be sufficiently high. But the lady does not say whether she would like a High Church or a Low Church family. Ought there to be unmarried sons, and may they follow a profession? and please say how many daughters; and would the lady like them to be musical? And how many company dinners a week? Not too many, for fear of fatiguing the upper kitchen-maid; but sufficient, so as to keep the upper kitchen-maid's hand in. ...
4 The head kitchen-maid wishes to stay for two years, and improve herself under the man-cook, and having of course sucked the brains (as the phrase is) from under the chefs nightcap, then the head kitchen-maid wishes to go.

    And upon my word ... I will go and fetch the cab for her. The cab? Why not her ladyship's own carriage and pair, and the head coachman to drive away the head kitchen-maid? You see she stipulates for everything – the time to come; the time to stay; the family she will be with; and as soon as she has improved herself enough, of course the upper kitchen-maid will step into the carriage and drive off.[67]

But Mary Hannell's ambitions were more realistic and offer less scope for entertainment. In newspaper reports of the coroner's inquest, pre-trial hearings, and the trial itself she consistently gives the impression of a calm and self-composed woman, neither seeking the limelight nor intimidated by the legal processes to which she was subjected. Hobler commented with satisfaction on the way in which she gave evidence.[68]

The impression left by Sarah Mancer is quite different. Roughly the same age as the cook – 32 or 33, neither woman seemed entirely certain of the year in which they were born – Mancer appears a more fragile individual. A middle-aged woman by the standards of her time, she was referred to consistently by Hobler as 'the girl'. This may simply have reflected linguistic usage of the day; the maid servant 'must be considered as young', wrote Leigh Hunt,[69] and housemaids were called 'girls' just as cooks were given the title of 'Mrs' regardless of their marital status. But it might also indicate vulnerability. Sarah Mancer had been in Russell's employ for almost three years at the time of his murder, and where Hannell found the house too quiet it was just the sort of situation for which the housemaid had been looking. She had come to Russell from Mivart's hotel, where she had stayed three months, followed by two weeks' lodging with a tailor named Don, working for her keep after Don's servant left, in order to save money.[70] This was not unusual. Some servants out of place in 1840 might have enjoyed the good fortune of being lodged in a charitable institution such as the Female Servants Home Society for the Encouragement of Faithful Female Servants, or the Female Aid Mission, both established in 1836. The latter had a variety of aliases reflecting both founder David Nasmith's aims and the precarious lives of the female servant class: the Holborn Female Aid Society/the Friendless Home (Home for Friendless Young Girls)/the Home for Friendless Young Females/the Home for Friendless Young Females of Good Character/Servants' Home (Home and Registry for Female Servants)/ the Home for Penitent Young Women/the Refuge for Indigent Young Females. But servant charities were underfunded and in no position to make a real difference. Contrasting the £332,679 subscribed to Bible and missionary charities in 1861 with the £6,250 received among 21 servant charities in London, Frank Huggett noted that 'the Victorians had an inflexible, and often unfeeling, sense of priorities'. Servants' own efforts to protect themselves, such as the Servants' Institution, founded in 1834 to establish a registry office as well as to provide sickness and retirement benefits, proved no more successful.[71] Working for board and lodging in between placements was thus common.

Mivart's hotel – founded in 1812, it would become Claridge's in 1854 – had been 'a hard place', Mancer said. Prior to that, she had been out of place for four months, following five years' employment with a Mr Lane, No. 1 St Alban's Place near St James's Square, described as 'a sort of lodging house for

Members of Parliament & gentlemen'. The St James's district was the heartland of Victorian gentleman's clubs and notoriously unsafe for young women of her class. Any predations Mancer suffered were unspecified, but this situation too she described as 'a very hard place'; she'd had 'a little difference' with Lane and had left at the same time as another of his housemaids. Apart from a young niece in Holborn she had no relatives living in London: her mother was dead, her father, who was ill and 'quite a poor man', lived five miles from Tunbridge and her four brothers within a mile of him. Three of the four she described as 'labouring men', the fourth ran a small shop. A sister, married to another 'labouring man', lived with their father.[72]

Finding a new position was no easy task for any servant. Footman and (briefly) diarist William Tayler wrote in May 1837,

> It's surpriseing to see the number of servants that are walking about the streets out of place. I have taken an account of the number of servants that have advertised for places in one newspaper during the last week; the number is three hundred and eighty. This was the Times paper. There is considered to be as many advertisements in that as there is in all the rest of the papers put together, therefor I mite sopose there to be 380 advertisements in the rest. I am sertain half the servants in London do not advertise at all. Now, soposing seven hundred and sixty to of advertised and the same number not to of advertised, there must be at least one thousand, five hundred and twenty servants out of place at one time in London, and if I had reckoned servants of all work – that is, tradespeoples' servants – it would have amounted to many hundreds more. I am sertain I have underrated this number.[73]

Mancer did not advertise, enquiring instead of other servants, who in turn enquired of tradesmen – what would now be called 'networking'. This too had been typical for centuries: 'once servants had found their first job they were thrust into a network of information and gossip'.[74] Relations, friends, and acquaintances typically played an important role in a servant's search for work and relatives in service were obvious sources of connection.[75] Family connections among employers were also highly useful. Courvoisier's predecessor as valet, James Ellis, had worked for Lord William's son Mr William Russell and simply traded places with a man named Gilbert, who left the father for employment by his son.[76] Mancer gained her new position by virtue of the fact that Russell, who had stayed at Mivart's hotel, remembered her. An Italian head waiter had recommended her. When Russell returned to England from abroad she said, he had sent for her 'by one of the men out of the stable'.[77] It is also clear that the housemaid had been looking for 'a light place', and at Norfolk Street, for almost three years, she found one. What frustrated Hannell suited Mancer perfectly. A housemaid was essentially a cleaner, responsible for emptying and cleaning grates upstairs and down, lighting the fires, dusting and polishing the furniture and ornaments, sweeping the floors and carpets, cleaning windows, emptying and cleaning chamber pots, airing and making beds, and so forth. It was hard physical labour, but the work required to care for a single elderly gentleman in a small house, and a fastidious man at that, with a bidet in his bedroom and a water closet on the main floor, would not have been arduous. Guests were infrequent. Mancer had been happy in her position.

On the 6th of May, however, this quiet world was shattered, and with it Sarah Mancer's peace of mind. It was the housemaid who discovered Russell's body and she would briefly be a suspect. Privately and publicly examined time and time again, her character was assassinated in the press – Russell's remembrance of her from the hotel was cast in a sinister light and some believed her to have been his mistress – and in court.[78] Press coverage of the murder also reveals the value ascribed to servants' lives in contemporary estimation: both cook and housemaid suffered the indignity of having their names repeatedly misspelt. Courvoisier, as we shall see, declined to speak from the time he first appeared at Bow Street. He did, however, take the stand at the coroner's inquest and 'upon being asked his name, ... he dictated with great precision to the coroner's clerk the exact mode of spelling it'.[79] His fellow servants would have done well to follow suit. Mary Hannell appears in the newspapers as 'Mary Hounell',[80] 'Mary Houston',[81] and Mary Hemmell[82]; at the coroner's inquest Inspector Tedman said he believed he had been let into the house by a cook named 'Arnold'.[83] In the Old Bailey Proceedings Mancer became 'Manser'. The papers did get other names wrong as well, referring, for example, to family solicitor Thomas Wing as 'Wynne' and Inspector Pearce as 'Pearse' or 'Peirse'.[84] Constable Rose is initially reported as 'Coal'.[85] Lady Sarah Bayley's surname was frequently misspelt.[86] Emanuel Young, butler at no. 23 Norfolk Street, was misnamed 'Daniel' in one report, and coachman James Leach appears as 'Leich'.[87] Richard Altick, in his otherwise admirable *Victorian Studies in Scarlet*, gives Courvoisier's middle name as 'Bernard' rather than 'Benjamin'. But where most of these errors are subsequently corrected, the names of the two female servants were constantly misspelt, and in fact frequently conflated, Mancer appearing as 'Sarah Mancel' or 'Sarah Mancell' in many of the newspaper reports.[88] Casual imprecision where members of the lower classes were concerned was not unusual. As P.D. James and T.A. Critchley described in their study of the Ratcliffe Highway murders (1811), the servant victim in the massacre of the Marr household was accorded similar treatment:

> Poor James Gowen was the least regarded of the victims. His short life must have held more toil than pleasure, and he died brutally in an agony of terror. Now, when it came to issuing the reward bill, no one seems to have known his real name. But there was someone who remembered him. A week later an anonymous letter arrived at the Home office from 'a distant Relation of the poor apprentice who was barbarously murdered in Ratcliffe Highway', observing that the lad's name was not James Biggs [as per the original handbill advertisng the reward] but James Gowen. 'Query?' a disbelieving Home Office clerk wrote on the letter...[89]

Like the unfortunate Gowen, Russell's female servants had someone to speak up for them, finding a steadfast champion in solicitor Francis Hobler, who followed and recorded their stories as carefully as he did that of the Russell family. In the maelstrom that engulfed her following William Russell's murder, Sarah Mancer was not friendless.

Menservants: valet, coachman, and groom

While few male servants would be found indoors in the nineteenth century, the number of outdoor male servants – coachmen, grooms, gardeners – grew.[90] Russell had neither garden nor gardener, but he did employ a coachman, 25-year-old William York, and a groom, George Doubleday, aged 22. The two men shared a room at No. 2 Weaver's Court, North Row, Park Lane, and took their meals together. York had been with Russell for four years, Doubleday for one.[91] Neither of the outdoor servants were considered suspects and as such they attracted minimal attention from either the authorities or the press. The third and quickly infamous male servant, Russell's murderer, lived in. Courvoisier was roughly ten years younger than the cook and housemaid, and as indicated above, had been in Russell's employ for a mere five weeks. The new valet was also foreign: the Courvoisier family was Swiss and of farming stock; they lived roughly 15 miles from Lausanne. During the investigation and trial Courvoisier's nationality was endlessly commented on. 'We cannot', said *The Era*,

> [w]ithout entertaining any prejudice against foreigners ... but here give a passing notice of the great increase of foreign servants, a taste for which is now far more in vogue than ever since her Majesty's marriage – cargoes of such gentry coming over from Germany by almost every steamer – opportunities of inquiring into the character, and testing the honesty of these men, exist but to a very limited extent, where there is any such at all; but the ground on which we have noticed it is not one of apprehension of the recurrence on that account of similar tragedies, but on that of the injustice done to our own countrymen, who are thus discarded and left without employment.[92]

The *Southern Star* also commented on 'The Rage for Foreign Servants':

> It is a common saying just now, and no doubt true, that English folks won't go into Switzerland, for fear of the Swiss 'valleys'. But we are quite sure that this is altogether a mistake. The fatal accident which is likely to happen to this interesting foreigner will rather give an *eclat* to foreigners than otherwise. It is already voted a very vulgar prejudice to suppose that foreign valets are more likely to cut throats than English ones, and the foreign servant hiring goes on as briskly as ever. There is not a family of distinction that has not one or more of these foreign creatures about them, and they all look so supple, so polite, so assiduous, that not one of

their masters or mistresses could ever believe, that Francois or Louis, or Bertolph, who is waiting behind their chair, could ever slip a knife gently across their windpipe ... We wonder whether Lord Wm. Russell, when Courvoisier stood behind his chair at dinner, ever thought it possible that so meek-looking a young man had made up his mind a week before to cut his throat. The most affectionate valet in all London did not look more innocent, we will be bound, than Courvoisier did upon these occasions.[93]

If he was foreign, Courvoisier's family connections were respectable. His uncle, Louis Courvoisier, described their background during the course of the police investigation. The family were from the village Mont Caville, 15 miles from Lausanne. Courvoisier's parents and siblings still lived there; Louis and his nephew were the only members to have relocated to England. Courvoisier's father was a farmer owning about 80 acres: in 1840 Switzerland's economy was still heavily agricultural and that holding would have been considered as substantial. The Courvoisiers were not poor. But Russell's valet had chosen to leave the family farm and follow his uncle, employed by Sir George Beaumont for some 17 years, to London to seek employment as a manservant.[94]

Employment histories: 'place' and home

As Bruce Robbins reminds us, servants didn't look for work, but for a 'place', their employment 'less an activity than a dependence'.[95] 'Place' also invokes the physical home in which domestic servants lived, a home which in many senses was not their own, and was usually temporary. Mancer and Hannell's relatively short tenure in Russell's employ appears to have been typical of their immediate neighbourhood: servants interviewed from houses beside and across the street from no. 14 testified to similar ages and in many cases length of employment. Next door at no. 15 George Cutler's household was even smaller than Russell's, consisting of a manservant, Thomas Selway, who served as both groom and valet, and one female servant. Thirty-four-year-old Selway had been with Cutler a total of seven years, three of them at Norfolk Street; before that, he had been 'at various places'.[96] The other servant, 39-year-old Penelope Wilkinson Cook, arrived a month after Cutler had moved into no. 15. She had previously been employed in Lincolnshire.[97] No. 13 changed hands roughly a month before Russell's murder so that Mrs Thomas Blount, who had worked for the Anstruthers three and a half years, was out of a place and living temporarily at no. 7 North Row. Her husband had just joined her there. Questioned by the police Blount provided a more detailed employment history, which is easier to reproduce than to summarize:

> I had been living at my last place Mr Daniels no. 2 Bryanstone Place B. Square I went there on 21st April and left on 1st of May 1 due to illness Capt. Mangin [no. 3 Gloucester Place] had given me a character I had lived with him 6 months I had left him 9 or 10 months before I left

on my own accord ... I married my present wife in London about 18 years ago It may be more than 9 months I was out of place after leaving Capt. Mangin – on leaving Capt M I went back to Major Anstruthers my wife was living there I was not engaged as a servant though I acted as a servant there & he made me a present I continued at Major A's – I had a few words with Major A – he never found fault with me for drinking only for not being home at night I left Major A's in May or June last year and took a lodging & remained there 3 or 4 months – My wife assisted me a little & so my friends in the country did the like – I went out waiting at times ... I then went to a situation at No. 1 Mr Busk's Great Cumberland Street – he had a character from Capt. M – I only stopped a month & left of my own accord on going to Brighton, – I found the family 8 or 9 and they only kept one servant it was too much for me I came back to North Row and lived on what wages I had & what I had before I went out assisting I cannot say how many times I assisted – Young [the butler] opp. no. 23 I went when they had company – assisted him in getting things ready – used to go to Mr W. Prescott's no. 17 Berkeley Square – I am a native of Lenbury [sic] in Worcestershire – I returned to North Row & had a room to myself – Capt. M gave me a character to my place – not slept at No. 13 Norfolk Street for 2 or 3 months – my wife was there in North Row about a fortnight before I joined her – not been to Major A's since I left – since the 1st of May I have been ill I am attended by Mr Dudley North Audley St.[98]

Servants from across the street made briefer statements but 36-year-old housemaid Elizabeth Selzer had been with Jones Loyd in no. 22 for 2 years; his nurse, Harriet Spencer, had been with 'the family' 2 years and ten months.[99]

Servants sometimes left of their own accord, as did Blount, when a situation 'didn't suit'. In other instances the changed circumstances and requirements of those who employed servants, over which servants themselves had no control, were determining factors. Russell's servants lost their jobs following the extraordinary event of his murder. In less unusual circumstances, Mrs Blount lost her place at no. 13 when the upstairs occupants changed: Lady Elphinstone brought her own 'family'. Physical health could also be an issue. At the time of the murder Blount was unable to work due to illness; Sarah Mancer would find herself in the same position after Courvoisier's trial. Spells of unemployment and ways of coping with them are also revealed. A friend of Ellis named Mitchell helped out occasionally in the house, once waiting at table, sometimes helping to clean the plate, assisting in 'setting everything in the pantry to rights' before Ellis left, and then helping him with the move to Kenwood. Hannell's friend Mrs Davies, a 'confidential woman' she had known 'many years' came in to help with the washing up on the rare occasions when William Russell had dinner guests. Mitchell's wife had also come once for two or three hours when Hannell was 'short of time'.[100] The raffling of personal items described in various of the servants' statements – a musical snuffbox, a watch – is not explained, but it was a way of raising cash during periods of unemployment, a more lucrative strategy, certainly, than pawning them or selling them outright to a single buyer. That such exigencies are discernible in the stories of so small a number of servants testifies to the economic vulnerability of this class. Voluntary quittance of employment also reveals dissatisfaction downstairs, as well as a degree of personal agency.

When employed, becoming a member of an employer's 'family' put considerable stresses and strains on the personal families of servants themselves. Thackeray recognized the extent of the travails involved in what amounted to living a double life:

> Henry (who lived out of the house) was the servant of a friend of mine who lived in chambers. There was a dinner one day, and Harry waited all through the dinner. The champagne was properly iced, the dinner was excellently served; every guest was attended to; the dinner disappeared; the dessert was set; the claret was in perfect order, carefully decanted, and more ready. And then Henry said, 'If you please, sir, may I go home?' He had received word that his house was on fire; and, having seen through his dinner, he wished to go and look after his children, and little sticks of furniture. Why, such a man's livery is a uniform of honor. The crest on his button is a badge of bravery. ... Henry is preparing the sauce for his master's wild-ducks while the engines are squirting over his own little nest and brood.[101]

The wife and children of Russell's former valet James Ellis were lodged separately.[102] Blount and his wife of 18 years, who had no children, frequently lived apart. Blount's account of his life – in 1840 he was 40 years old – makes no mention of their ever having been employed in the same household. At the time of William Russell's murder they were together in lodgings only because both were out of a situation.

An out-of-work friend of Courvoisier was also questioned by the police, and his statement like Blount's is rich in detail. On the evening of the murder Courvoisier had entertained Henry Carr to tea at no. 14; the two men had once worked together in MP John Fector's household. The unfortunate Mr Carr must have deeply regretted accepting the invitation, as he became for a short time a suspect in the murder. His statement includes rare information about finances. The 31-year old was single; he had lived for the past year at no. 2 North Terrace, South Street, where he had a room to himself. His meals, he said, he 'took anywhere'. For the lodgings he paid 4*s.* a week (regularly), other expenses he estimated at 3*s.* per day but couldn't say 'how much exactly'. Where gentlemen met at their clubs, servants socialized in pubs, and Carr frequented both the Punchbowl and the Royal Exchange public houses. He had left his employment as coachman to Fector at the end of April 1839, after three years, of his 'own accord with the hope of bettering myself'. These hopes had not been realized. He had been employed as coachman between 22 October 1839 and 4 February 1840, by a widow, Mrs Green, who lived in Piccadilly, again leaving of his own accord, 'the place not suiting me'. Since then he had been 'doing little or nothing' and living on his savings: when he left the Fectors he had had about £80, some of it kept in the Dover Savings Bank; since then he had had no money in any banks, having withdrawn the final £30. He did have £21 in his writing desk, a £10 bank note, and the rest in sovereigns and silver.[103] A little temporary work had come his way. He had returned to Fector for a fortnight, serving as footman until Courvoisier's replacement arrived; he had also done an occasional day's work travelling with horses, once for the Earl of Aylesbury. And he had 'applied to several Hackneys for a situation'. Carr said he owed no money; the previous summer he had loaned Courvoisier £20, which was repaid 2 weeks later. He said he thought 'the Swiss' wanted to send the money home and needed what would now be called a bridging loan.[104] Courvoisier complained to Sarah Mancer that he had had £30 when he first arrived in England, and, with only £8 in a savings bank and still waiting on his wages, was 'not so well off now'.[105]

James Ellis also wished to better himself. William Russell's previous valet had stayed two years and eight months before leaving to become valet to the Earl of Mansfield. Mansfield's household at Kenwood was much larger, and Ellis's pay was higher.[106] The new position was a step up. Another of Russell's former valets, Bernard or Barnard, was less fortunate. There are two conflicting reports on this individual in the Met's archival records: according to one, he was dismissed for making 'improper use' of money entrusted to him to pay bills and Russell refused to give him a reference; Pearce, by contrast, said that Russell had been 'partial' to the servant and gave him a good one. Regardless of which is true, Ellis's predecessor was like Carr out of work at the time of Russell's murder and the police failed to discover an address for him.[107]

Courvoisier had better luck. As the unemployed Carr told him, 'you need not grumble you have not been out of place since you've been in England'.[108] But his employment at no. 14 Norfolk Street is somewhat difficult to categorize: 'Lord' William Russell was an aristocrat, and Courvoisier's salary increased from its previous level, but the household was small. The valet's duties he conceded were 'light' but he also admitted to Carr that 'he found the place rather dull having been used to more servants'.[109] In England, his first employer had been Lady Julia Lockwood; from that place he had gone to John Fector and from thence to Russell's household. At Lady Julia's Courvoisier, as a trainee footman, had not been in livery nor on a wage, although the butler had given him a few pounds from time to time. At Fector's he was paid 25 guineas per annum and served in livery, one of four male servants. Although of lesser social status, Fector's household was much larger than Russell's. The MP lived with his mother and between them, they employed two lady's maids, two housemaids, a cook, and a scullery maid as well as the manservants. Courvoisier's time in that situation had come to an end with his employer's intended marriage: some Englishmen may have had a fancy for foreign staff, but Fector decided that he would prefer an English valet. He also wanted a taller one. It is not unreasonable to suggest that the reasons given for Courvoisier's dismissal must have generated resentment, one which could not be vocalized. While Fector's preferences would raise eyebrows today, physique had traditionally been a factor in the hiring of servants. Footmen were often matched in pairs, like horses, and height was prized. At the end of the nineteenth century a footman of 5'6" could expect wages of £20–22, whereas at 6 foot the range would be £32–40.[110]

While Fector's mother would have been happy to take Courvoisier on, she was reducing her household and moving to the country, which didn't suit him. He wanted a better place, to make his way in the world. He also wanted to get out of livery, the wearing of which constituted deliberate public display and reflected a master's social status, physically marking the social distance between servant and employer. It also effaced the individuality of those who wore it. Liveried servants, having been chosen like horses for their looks, were then imprinted by means of dress with their master's 'brand'. Some servants may have relished the association with a socially prestigious house. Others did not. 'There is some evidence', Tim Meldrum writes, 'that many lower servants wearing the badge of livery felt it emphasized their servile status'.[111]

Lady Julia Lockwood mentioned her former servant to Russell; Fector gave him a good character; and Courvoisier was hired by Russell. At 14 Norfolk Street he was to combine the roles of valet, butler, and footman, and not required to wear livery. The position of valet, or 'gentleman's gentleman', was the closest male equivalent to a lady's maid and in this role he would assist his master with dress and grooming and take care of his clothes, boots, and shoes.[112] As de facto butler and footman he would have been responsible for the wine and for the care of silver, and he would have waited at table. Primarily identified in the press as Russell's 'valet', Courvoisier was in fact a 'man of all work'.

Courvoisier's uncle had visited the young man at the Fectors and was aware that he wanted to get out of livery. On hearing that his nephew was going to William Russell, Louis Courvoisier paid him a brief visit at Norfolk Street. The valet, who was laying the table when Louis arrived, said that he was comfortable and liked his master. On a second visit, Louis again asked his nephew if he were comfortable and received the same answer: 'he seemed', the uncle reported, 'perfectly satisfied with his place'.

Life below stairs

Given that Courvoisier's brief time in William Russell's service ended in a deadly assault on his new master, the valet clearly had not been at all satisfied. In the earliest days of Courvoisier's new employment all had however seemed well, and by contrast with upstairs, life below stairs at 14 Norfolk Street had been convivial. While William Russell dined alone, spent a few hours with his dog and read before bedtime, his servants ate together and the cook and housemaid shared a bedroom. Mary Hannell said that they had lived 'very comfortably together' and used to joke with one another. She had not been planning to leave Russell's service, she insisted, because of any quarrel.[113]

On the night of the murder Hannell had called on a friend and returned around 10 o'clock, and generally speaking the examinations of Russell's servants and those of neighbouring premises bears out Tim Meldrum's assertion that domestic servants engaged in extensive social interactions. They do not appear to have socialized with others in their immediate neighbourhood: when questioned by the police the servants at nos. 15, 22, and 23 all said that they had known Russell's servants only by sight. Thomas Blount's acquaintance with the women was only slightly greater but he had known Ellis and the female servants a little, the stable servants by sight.[114]

If their acquaintance with neighbours was minimal, servants clearly retained connections from previous employment.[115] Apart from taking tea on the eve of the murder, Carr had been at no. 14 a week earlier, together with another servant, William Jones, who had known Courvoisier at the Fectors. The extent of socializing among their own class is not surprising, given William Tayler's assertion that London was 'overrun with servants'. Tayler kept, for a year only, a journal of his daily life, a rare voluntary description of life below stairs. Embarked upon to improve his writing skills – his spelling remained idiosyncratic – Tayler's journal provides a portrait of a mid-nineteenth-century household not far removed in either geographical space or time from that of William Russell. Tayler, like Courvoisier, came from an agricultural family, although his was English (Oxfordshire). He was the first in that family to enter service, employed originally by a local squire but by 1837 – the year in which both Hannell and Mancer began their tenure with Russell – he was in London, working for a wealthy widow at 6 Great Cumberland Street, Marylebone (site of the present-day Cumberland Hotel), near Oxford Street and Park Lane. Aged 29, Tayler was 6 years older than the Swiss valet and like James Ellis he was married, his wife and children respectably, but also secretly, lodged elsewhere, their existence ignored by his employer.

Tayler opens his journal by describing the establishment in which he was employed. He, like Courvoisier, was the only manservant to live in; he does not name a cook but speaks of three housemaids, 'very good quiet sort of bodys', and reported, 'we live very comfortably together'. The coachman lived out and was 'only a sort of jobber'.[116] Tayler's wages were very slightly less than the terms agreed upon for Courvoisier: £42 rather than £45 per annum, despite a slightly larger household. Upstairs was a widow, Mrs Prinsep, rather than a widower, and she had a 40-ish daughter to keep her company. A female employer meant that Tayler did not attend to her personal needs, but many of his other duties overlapped with those of Courvoisier. In his initial entry Tayler described tasks performed on a daily basis: cleaning knives and lamps, getting the parlour breakfast, lighting the pantry fire, clearing breakfast and washing up afterwards in the mornings, in the afternoons taking lamps and candles to the drawing room, laying the table in the dining room, taking up dinner and waiting upon table, taking up tea, washing up after each meal, taking down the lamps and candles at half past ten, and going to bed at 11.[117] Prinsep had a more active social life than William Russell, paying visits on a regular basis, accompanied by her footman, and entertaining both family and friends at home. Two of her sons were dead but their widows and children visited frequently and stayed during holidays. She also held card parties. Days involving the presence of guests were recorded by Tayler as 'very buisy' and occasioned a degree of irritation.[118] When only Mrs Prinsep and her daughter were in residence he was left with ample leisure time: contemporary social commentators indeed grumbled that male domestic servants had far too little to do, and questioned whether their limited responsibilities actually merited the description of 'work'. 'Some of the loudest commentators thought that domestic service (and particularly male service) was hardly work at all but licensed idleness, usually going hand-in-hand with arrogance and insubordination'.[119] 'What a pleasant farce is that of "High Life Below Stairs!"', wrote William Hazlitt.

> What a careless life do the domestics of the Great lead For, not to speak of the reflected self-importance of their masters and mistresses, and the contempt with which they look down on the herd of mankind, they have only to eat and drink their fill, talk the scandal of the neighbourhood, laugh at the follies, or assist the intrigues of their betters, till they them selves fall in love, marry, set up a public-house (the only thing they are fit for), and without habits of industry, resources in themselves, or self-respect, and drawing fruitless comparisons with the past, are, of all people, the most miserable![120]

Tayler's duties certainly afforded him opportunity for personal amusement. He rose between 7 and 8 a.m. and his morning's work was normally accomplished by 11. He then walked and saw friends – or his tailor, or his wife – often taking a glass or two of wine with them. He visited the British Museum, the National Gallery, and Regent's Park zoo. In the afternoons he drew; in the evenings, he wrote, played cards, and read, with *The History of England* (possibly Rapin's, according to his twentieth-century editor) cited frequently. He also read the newspapers and compiled a scrapbook. On some evenings he had friends in and gave them tea. His mistress treated him to a play at Drury Lane one evening.

Like Courvoisier Tayler had ambitions and hoped to rise in his profession. On 15 November he recorded with envy the advancement of George Castle, who was promoted to butler and given the opportunity to be out of livery:

> George is the luckeyest servant I ever heared of or know. No fellow can have tried to get on more than I have, but I cannot get on so fast as he does. He is very steady and well deserves all he has got. People say, when a puple turn out well, there is some credit for the teacher. Therefore I shall claim credit in this case, as I sertainly was his teacher and no one elce, and many people tell me he aught to be thankfull for what I did for him, all the days of his life.

I believe he is very gratefull and is very sencible of the obligation he is under to me for it. If it had not been for me, he sertainly would been following the plough at this time instead of being where he is ...

He and I started in service under very diferent advantages, he under the very best, and I under the very worst. I was four or five years in finding out the way of service, haveing no one to show me, and I taught him the whole art of service in one year or less, as I took an interest and pleasure in showing him everything I could.[121]

Courvoisier had his uncle to thank for the fact that he no longer followed the plough, and unlike Tayler received instruction in the art of being a footman at both Lady Julia Lockwood's and Mr Fector's. But he too may have wished to 'get on fast', just as Mary Hannell relished her elevation from kitchen maid to cook and worried that Russell's lack of entertaining would set her back professionally.

In 1959 Yseult Bridges registered indignation that William Russell's servants did not comport themselves in the manner prescribed in contemporary advice manuals. Sarah Mancer, she assumed, offering no evidence whatsoever, had been 'brought up in the best traditions of domestic service' but Bridges could not fathom why Hannell, the cook, had on the evening of the murder, 'conferred upon herself the privilege' of entering Russell's house via the front door rather than the area entrance.[122] There was a very simple explanation for this: on returning home from visiting a friend Hannell found the area gate locked, so rang the bell of the street door.[123] Courvoisier, who let her in, received the severest of treatment from Bridges. His duties in Russell's household had been 'light, too light', she complained, and he had had no proper supervision, consequently spending far too much time in his pantry reading.[124] On the evidence of Tayler's diary, however, Courvoisier's duties, lack of supervision, and time for reading and socializing do not seem exceptional. They were perhaps instead perfectly normal in a smallish household.

Master and servant relations: unhappy friends?

As Thackeray recognized, there was a profound gulf between master and servants even in the happiest of households:

Between me and those fellow-creatures of mine who are sitting in the room below, how strange and wonderful is the partition! We meet at every hour of the daylight, and are indebted to each other for a hundred offices of duty and comfort of life; and we live together for years, and don't know each other. John's voice to me is quite different from John's voice when it addresses his mates below. If I met Hannah in the street with a bonnet on, I doubt whether I should know her. And all these good people with whom I may live for years and years, have cares, interests, dear friends and relatives, mayhap schemes, passions, longing hopes, tragedies of their own, from which a carpet and a few planks and beams utterly separate me.[125]

How should these 'fellow-creatures' conduct themselves as servants? The famous nineteenth-century writer on cookery and household management, Isabella Beeton, contemplated the situation in 1861 and considered what might reasonably be expected of them:

> 'No man is a hero to his valet,' saith the proverb ... The infirmities of humanity are, perhaps, too numerous and too equally distributed to stand the severe microscopic tests which attendants on the person have opportunities of applying. The valet and waiting-maid are placed near the persons of the master and mistress ... dressing them, accompanying them in all their journeys, the confidants and agents of their most unguarded moments, of their most secret habits, and of course subject to their commands, – even to their caprices; they themselves being subject to erring judgment, aggravated by an imperfect education. All that can be expected from such servants is polite manners, modest demeanour, and a respectful reserve ... Their duty leads them to wait on those who are, from sheer wealth, station, and education, more polished, and consequently more susceptible to annoyance ... Quiet unobtrusive manners, therefore, and a delicate reserve in speaking of their employers, either in praise or blame, is as essential in their absence, as good manners and respectful conduct in their presence.[126]

That Russell's 'family' or 'establishment' was not entirely a happy one is patently obvious. In her study of late-eighteenth-century domestic service Carolyn Steedman writes both of 'the endless longing of the underprivileged' found below stairs and 'the shrill laughter of social disdain' emanating from those who lived above them, the amused condescension to which servants were subjected by employers such as Hester Thrale/Piozzi, who found in her domestic staff a source of anecdotes and the butt of jokes which allowed her 'to celebrate her own perceptiveness, social and psychological'.[127] Leigh Hunt's essay on 'The Maid Servant' (1825) is evidence of similar attitudes. He downplays the work the maid performs ('exercise keeps her healthy and cheerful') while laughing at her meagre possessions (a few coins, a brass thimble and scissors, an enamel box from a fair), her taste in reading material and entertainment, her attempts at 'sophistications' in dress and manners, and her correspondence: 'various letters, square and ragged, and directed in all sorts of spellings, chiefly with little letters for capitals'.[128] Sarah Mancer would have been unlikely to recognize herself in Hunt's portrait. Mary Hannell's thimble was at least a silver one.

Footmen too were a source of mirth, although the pretensions of their employers provided fodder as well. In an essay first published in the *New Monthly Magazine* in 1830, William Hazlitt wrote,

> Footmen are in general looked upon as a sort of supernumeraries in society – they have no place assigned them in any Encyclopaedia – they do not come under any of the heads in Mr Mill's 'Elements,' or Mr Macculloch's

'Principles of Political Economy;' and they nowhere have had impartial justice done them, except in Lady Booby's love for one of that order. But if not 'the Corinthian capitals of polished society,' they are 'a graceful ornament to the civil order.' Lords and ladies could not do without them. Nothing exists in this world but by contrast. A foil is necessary to make the plainest truths self-evident. It is the very insignificance, the nonentity as it were of the gentlemen of the cloth, that constitutes their importance, and makes them an indispensable feature in the social system, by setting off the pretensions of their superiors to the best advantage. What would be the good of having a will of our own, if we had not others about us who are deprived of all will of their own, and who wear a badge to say, 'I serve?' How can we show that we are the lords of the creation but by reducing others to the condition of machines, who never move but at the beck of our caprices? Is not the plain suit of the master wonderfully relieved by the borrowed trappings and mock-finery of his servant?[129]

Condescension aside, domestic servants had long been a source of worry to those who employed them and Beeton's polite intimations of some of the potential difficulties inherent in master and servant relations had been amplified in earlier texts. Fear of theft by servants – potential enemies within doors – had a considerable history by 1840. Legislation specifically targeting 'the preventing and punishing robberies that shall be committed in houses' was passed in 1713.[130] The lengthy title of a work published at the turn of the nineteenth century indicates continued concerns and raises once more the particular anxieties attendant on hiring foreign staff. *Reflections on the relative situations of master and servant, historically and politically considered; the irregularities of servants; the employment of foreigners; and the general inconveniences resulting from the want of proper regulations* was occasioned by a 'bill of regulation' about to be presented to Parliament, the author's intent to enquire into the grievances alleged, the causes of those grievances, and the appropriate remedy, 'to fix the relative boundaries of authority, and obedience'.[131] Schemes to offer financial rewards for merit or long service were dismissed as ineffectual. Concern about foreign servants, it suggested, came not from employers but from British servants who were worried about competition.[132] This fear it also dismissed, arguing that other than in the case of tutors or governesses no such preference existed. But the author was willing to indulge such fears via a tax on every foreign servant employed – 'it is no way unjust that an Englishman should pay for the gratification of having his dinner dressed by a Frenchman, or his ears tickled with the amusing sounds of mutilated English in a personal servant, if such happens to be his particular fancy' – or even an outright ban on them.[133] The author was highly suspicious of servants as a collective body, a fear in accordance with broader post-French revolution concerns about the lower classes as dangerous; he or she also believed this body to be highly indulged, suffering 'fewer hardships than almost any class of men in the kingdom'. He – or she – bemoaned 'the absurd extension of lettered education',[134] an extension subsequently reflected in the fact that all of Russell's servants were literate and which enabled Tayler's journal. Servants' reading, as we shall see in Chapter 6 below, occasioned criticism and alarm.

The growth of London and other towns was also regarded with dismay as a source of depravity where the morality of servants was concerned. The metropolis abounded with 'lazy, faithless, and timeserving' servants.[135] The lower orders, the author feared, were encroaching on their betters. Servants' advertisements were described with scorn:

> every jackanapes, at eighteen, proposes to be a gentleman's valet; or, perhaps, he condescends to be a footman, *where a boy is kept*, that he may thrash the boy, and set him to clean knives, whilst he is diverting himself in gentle dalliance with the maids, and *talking over* the master and mistress.[136]

The author hoped that 'the vast improvements in mechanics' which had been applied to manufacturing would 'soon be able to produce automata, capable of performing all the domestic functions of servants', for the 'capriciousness, discontent, exorbitancy, drunkenness, negligence ... insubordination ... and fraudulent disposition' of servants had become 'more and more the painful theme of remark and lamentation' amongst every class of employer, from noblemen to 'antiquated spinsters'.[137] The author would not go so far as to argue that servants were animated by a spirit of positive sedition but was alarmed by the fact that 'every one of them would wish to *better himself*', perhaps even beyond servitude.[138] Good masters did not make good servants but were instead 'perpetually plagued with bad ones'.[139] Servants were the most 'headstrong' class of men, and prone to leaving places in abrupt fashion, 'from arrant malice, pique, or caprice' – or, tellingly, because they could find better wages elsewhere – 'to the utter distress and inconvenience' of their employers.[140] Wages the author believed to be too high; they had 'risen extravagantly' and domestic servitude was easy labour compared to agriculture or industry.[141]

These complaints were not new: similar concerns had been voiced in the eighteenth century, as had the author's proposed remedy of a register. A public register of men servants in particular, containing physical descriptions, was recommended, with certificates paid for by the servants themselves and all clubs of servants legally banned. An (unflattering) example of the type of description required was provided: 'A.B. a thin man, about five feet eight inches high, in his shoes, native of London, with dark hair, hazel eyes, low forehead, long nose, and small chin'.[142] The certificate would then be endorsed by the employer he was leaving, including the length of service. Such a register would have done nothing to save William Russell's life, as Courvoisier's previous employers had had no cause for complaint. At the valet's trial Lady Julia Lockwood was among those who 'deposed to his good character for kindheartedness, humanity, and inoffensiveness of disposition'.[143]

Other writers, from the eighteenth century through the early twentieth, when traditional domestic service was in its final death throes, acknowledged that the master–servant relationship was in its very nature corrupting. Radical William Godwin's 1797 essay on servants is nothing short of hair-raising:

> A rich man has in his house various apartments. The lower tier of apartments is inhabited by a species of beings in whom we apprehend the most sordid defects. If they are not in an emphatical degree criminal, at least their ignorance makes them dangerous, and their subjection renders them narrow. The only safety to persons of a generous station, is to avoid their society ...
>
> This house is inhabited by two classes of beings, or, more accurately speaking, by two sets of men drawn from two distant stages of barbarism and refinement. The rich man himself, we will suppose, with the members of his family, are persons accomplished with elegance, taste and a variety of useful and agreeable information. The servants below stairs, can some of them perhaps read without spelling, and some even write a legible hand ... [But] their ignorance is thick and gross.[144]

He then elaborated on the consequences of a 'monstrous association and union of wealth and poverty together'[145] under a single roof, contrasting the spacious and luxurious quarters of the master of the house with the dark, cramped and neglected servants' quarters, the physical representation of 'the depression and humiliated state of mind' of their inhabitants.[146] Little wonder, he said, that the servant class was depraved:

> Servants have only the choice of an alternative. They must either cherish a burning envy in their bosoms, an inextinguishable abhorence against the injustice of society; or, guided by the hopelessness of their condition, they must blunt every finer feeling of the mind, and sit down in their obscure retreat, having for the constant habits of their reflections, slavery and contentment. They can scarcely expect to emerge from their depression. They must look to spend the best years of their existence in a miserable dependence.[147]

The root of this incurable evil, Godwin argued, lay in the existence of servitude:

> Treat a servant as you will, he will be a servant still ... He has nothing to do, but to obey; you have nothing to do, but to command ... His great standing rule is to conform himself to the will of his master ...He is destitute of the best characteristics of a rational being.[148]

Alison Light's study of Virginia Woolf's notoriously fraught relations with her live-in servants reveals that such sentiments continued through Courvoisier's lifetime into the opening decades of the twentieth century. Light also provides a perceptive summary of master and servant relations:

14 Norfolk Street, Park Lane 49

> Over the centuries servants learned to be amphibious. None more so than the live-in servant, moving between the classes, making a home within a home, a halfway house between kin and strangers. ... Servants frequently encountered a different world from the one into which they had been born: they observed new codes of dress, manners and behaviour; they saw how the other half lived. If they had their wits about them, they managed to live a double life, adopting their employers' standards, but remaining outsiders, enjoying only a portion of the domestic comfort they made possible. The live-in servant had divided loyalties ... Servants were expected to pin their colours to their employers' masts but they usually kept a foot in both camps.
>
> ...
>
> Service ... has always been an emotional as well as an economic territory ... Service could be brutalizing and estranging; it could also be affectionate and devoted, but, however unequal the parties, it was always something more, or less, than a purely financial arrangement ... Ruled by the cash-nexus, service was a relationship of trust which involved a mutual dependence. The servant, however vulnerable, wielded a precarious power. For what is entrusted to the servant, be it only the crockery, is something of one's self, and being taken care of by a person who is seen as a subordinate, an outsider or an inferior, is never without its anxieties and fears. Servants may leave only vestigial traces in the official histories of the past but they have always loomed large in the imagination of their employers. Inside every servant, or so it seems, is a sorcerer's apprentice whose rough magic is enough to send the rhythms of domestic order and of social life spiralling out of control ... The figure of the servant casts a long shadow, disturbing the hearts and minds of all who like to think themselves in charge.[149]

The servant's shadow is long indeed, and there are remarkable continuities of emotional experience over the centuries. In a fascinating study of the servant in Western literature Bruce Robbins wrote of his frustration with the 'annoying sameness' in their representations that thwarted his desire to 'salvage the servant from [Northrop] Frye's fetishizing of recurrence'. The literary differences proved 'not particularly illuminating' and he found himself instead faced with 'the disturbing fact of continuity'.[150] Robbins is careful throughout *The Servant's Hand* to distance himself from 'the hypothesis of a direct correspondence between the servants of art and those of life'; his own topic is 'analysis of representations'.[151] 'Historical information about actual servants', in his view 'could not offer an organizing principle'.[152] And yet such a principle might be found. Woolf's early twentieth-century diaries evince the same combination of personal revulsion for her own servants with recognition of a flawed social order found in Godwin's eighteenth-century essay. The origin of tensions between master or mistress and servants, she concluded in 1918, despite the venom with which she would continue to describe her own long-suffering housemaid and cook, lay not with individuals but with a domestic system that confined some people to the kitchen and others in a drawing room.[153]

What of the view from below stairs? Tayler's journal is again instructive. Where the anonymous author of the 1800 tract laid the blame for unquiet households squarely on servants' shoulders and their shoulders alone, servants themselves, as Tayler recorded, naturally had a different perspective. Visitors to the Prinseps' kitchen who had left service to run a public house lamented that 'they allways heard servants very much run down and dispised'. Yet servants, especially gentlemen's servants, were 'very much more respectable in every point' than tradesmen. The very fact of their service elevated them:

> everyone must think and must know that servants form one of the most respectable classes of persons that is in existance. In the first place they must be healthy, clean, respectable, honest, sober set of people to be servants; their character must be unexceptionable in every respect. They are in the habit of being in the first of company and are constantly hearing the first of conversation. Being so much in the company of the gentry, from the private gentleman to the highest Duke in the land always traveling about with their masters, learning and seeing hundreds of things which mecanics or tradespeople never knew there was in the country ... I think servants are the most respectable in consequence of their characters and actions being so investigated by their superiors.[154]

If William Tayler did not look upon his employer and her friends with a hostile eye, his was certainly a critical one. And the criticism was not always suppressed: his employer's daughter having kept him out longer with the carriage than he thought right, he 'gave her a little row for it'. 'I hope', he wrote, 'it will do her good. I served the old lady the same way the other day and it did her a deal of good ...'[155] Courvoisier too was not above teaching his master a lesson, even when the fault was his. When Russell's coachman reproached him concerning the carriage not being sent to Brooks's on the day of Russell's death, the valet said that he had forgotten to order it, but would tell his master that it had been ordered for 5:30 rather than 5 p.m. Sarah Mancer protested that 'he had better tell his lordship the truth, and his lordship would forgive him' but he refused: 'his lordship was very forgetful, and must pay for his forgetfulness'.[156]

Tayler's diary records a steady stream of adverse commentary on the manners and mores of those above stairs. At tea parties, he noted with disapproval, they 'talked about every bodeys buisness but their own';[157] the chief topics of conversation were illness and doctors, fashion and 'back biteing their neighbours'; they also discussed 'the cheapest tradespeople' and 'scandalized' each others' servants.[158] In fact, they engaged in precisely the same behaviours that Hazlitt had condemned in describing life in the servants' hall. On Sundays,

Tayler observed, his mistress read novels but 'with the Bible laying by her, ready to take up if any body came in'[159] – just as Richard Brinsley Sheridan's Lydia Languish instructs her maid to 'fling *Peregrine Pickle* under the toilet', '*Roderick Random* into the closet', 'to thrust *Lord Ainsworth* under the sofa', and to secret *The Innocent Adultery* within *The Whole Duty of Man*, which, together with *Fordyce's Sermons*, was to be left on display for guests.[160] While Tayler acknowledged that Mrs Prinsep was 'not a bad one in the end', deference is conspicuous by its absence in his journal entries and there is considerable evidence of both censure and contempt in his commentary. On the day on which he had been treated to the theatre Tayler 'imagined' and drew a picture of 'servants helping themselves in the dining room'.[161] One is taking a swig from a wine bottle behind the screen that separates him from the table. In the penultimate entry of his journal, Tayler concluded:

> The life of a gentleman's servant is something like that of a bird shut up in a cage. The bird is well housed and well fed but is deprived of liberty, and liberty is the dearest and sweetes object of all Englishmen. Therefore I would rather be like the sparrow or lark, have less houseing and feeding and rather more liberty.[162]

At 14 Norfolk Street Mary Hannell and Sarah Mancer appear to have been content with their lot. While female servants employed in the household of a widower might have been at risk of sexual abuse or harassment, given Russell's age and physical weakness this risk would have been slight and no mention of it was made in their interviews with Hobler or testimony in court. Courvoisier, however, does appear to have cherished the 'burning envy' Godwin cited, and a resentment of his master. In *A Present for a Servant Maid* (1737) Eliza Haywood had acknowledged that servants shared 'the same appetites' as their employers: she was referring specifically to appetites for food and warning kitchen maids not to covet leftovers.[163] But shared appetites extended beyond food to material positions. Female servants coveted their mistress's fine clothing and longed for cast-offs. Employers' fears of servants mishandling – or appropriating outright – intimate personal possessions would be reflected in late nineteenth-century novels. In Miss Poole's *Without a Character: A Tale of Servant Life* (1870), a housemaid covets her mistress's jewellery and takes one of her rings to the kitchen to show it off; in Helen Briston's *Lottie: Servant and Heroine* (1898), Lottie has her mistress's mantle altered so that she can wear it comfortably herself.[164] Courvoisier was less brazen, and more secretive in his actions. As described in the next chapter, he stole from his employer, but the majority of the items were hidden in his pantry rather than shown off to the female servants. Russell's valet, who was said to have taken great care with his own dress and personal appearance, clearly coveted his master's jewellery and toiletry items, none of which would have come to him in any ordinary course of events.[165] Russell may have been poor by aristocratic standards, but Courvoisier had told the housemaid that 'Old

Billy is a rum old chap. If I had his money I would soon be out of England'. Mancer protested,

> I have said his lordship was not a very rich man & he has shook his head & said aye he has got money – or some words to that effect – he has made this remark more than once – 2 or 3 times I have heard him repeat it.[166]

Mary Hannell had also heard him say it, when the three servants were at tea.[167] At trial, Courvoisier's counsel, Charles Phillips, explained the remark as evidence of homesickness:

> It was not an unnatural wish for a foreigner to express, toiling for his daily sustenance yet longing to visit his fatherland, rugged though it be – 'I wish I had the wealth of such a one, I would not be long away from my own country!' Ambition's vision, glory's bauble, wealth's reality, were all nothing as compared to his native land. Not all the enchantments of creation, not all the splendours of scenery, not all that gratification of any kind, could make the Swiss forget his native land …

But Mancer's testimony suggests that the valet had a keen interest in baubles as well as money.

Mancer told the police that she had noticed Courvoisier 'looking into all his lordship's property, and every thing that he could': 'I had often seen him in his Lordship's bedroom busy turning over things and looking at them', and examining the contents of the bedroom closet. Sometimes, on being asked what he was doing, he 'made excuses' and left the room; other times Mancer left first. The housemaid had 'observed this conduct in prying about as much as he possibly could, with a few days after he first came', and commented on it to Hannell. Ellis, she said, had never behaved in that way. On one occasion she had 'noticed that he had his lordship's dressing-case down in his pantry' for two or three days, for 'cleaning', and the valet had shown her a ring, asking whether it was gold.[168]

Courvoisier also resented Russell's manner towards him. Mancer told the police that on supping together on the evening of the murder they had discussed changes to 'the family' and the potential of a new cook arriving; Mancer had recommended a friend for the position but another person was also applying and she would not care to wait on that person. Courvoisier said, 'I wish I had not come into the family, as I do not like it so well as I thought I should'.[169] William Russell appears, to use Mrs Beeton's gentle phrasing, to have been 'susceptible to annoyance' and precise in his instructions. Ellis, questioned about Russell's general health, commented on his wearing spectacles for reading but said his sight was fine for 'ordinary purposes': 'He could see very accurately if a picture were hung correctly or not'.[170] Courvoisier complained that his lordship was 'fidgety, and he thought not pleased with him, and that he was cross and peevish'.[171] The valet had, Mancer said, spoken in a similar fashion on various occasions. He had complained of Russell's treatment of him during a visit to

Richmond a week before the murder, again accusing him of 'cross and peevish' behaviour, and fretted that he would not be able to stay in Russell's employ: 'he said he did not know how the late valet could have stopped so long with his lordship; he did not think his temper would allow him to stop so long'.[172]

Any relationship between master or mistress and servants was an unequal one, and sensitive employers acknowledged both potential abuses of power and the feelings of those on the receiving end of the authority of even good and caring persons. In 1737 the Marchioness de Lambert had urged mistresses to be kind and compassionate in dealing with servants; she also, somewhat surprisingly for her time, attributed the difference in their social situation as 'owing merely to chance'. Servants ought, she advised, to be viewed as 'unhappy friends'.[173] Even in undemocratic ages, dependency was often felt as a burden and engendered resentment. Nor did subjection of the will to that of another always come easily. William Russell may have been a kindly master, but he was a master nonetheless. In *Great Expectations* Charles Dickens would describe the sense of burning injustice created by a societal imposition of inferiority as 'the smart without a name'. Pip is not a servant but Estelle has made him aware of their social distance, of 'his coarse hands and common boots'; humiliated, he cries, kicks the wall, and pulls his hair in a bitter rage.[174]

Conclusion

William Russell's household at 14 Norfolk Street defies the categorizations offered by texts on early Victorian homes. An aristocrat by birth, 'Lord' William Russell's physical household space resembled that of the middle classes. As a widower with grown-up children, his home was incomplete. His servants were also few in number, yet he employed a footman/valet, which few middle-class men would have done. Russell spent his final years living a betwixt and between life. His housemaid, desiring a quiet life herself, was content but his cook was restless, and his manservant's attitude might best be described as contemptuous. I would surmise that the explanation given for Courvoisier's dismissal from Fector's service – he was foreign and too short – rankled, and that he is likely to have arrived at his new situation with something of a chip on his shoulder that made him unwilling to tolerate Russell's irritability. And Russell's household and lifestyle allowed the newly employed valet to take advantage. His new situation had a single, elderly male upstairs; below stairs, his only fellow servants were two middle-aged females. Courvoisier was unlikely to have been so cavalier in handling his employers' personal possessions in his previous places. The stolen property discovered after Russell's murder included a locket with his wife's hair in it. This theft seems particularly spiteful and its disappearance caused Russell considerable distress, which his valet would have witnessed. And of course Courvoisier went further still, taking his master's life in the most violent way possible. Resentment of his 'place', in every sense of the word, must have been common amongst servants. The explosion of rage it occasioned, discussed in the following chapters, was not.

Notes

1. *The Times*, 11 May 1840.
2. 9 May 1840.
3. 9 May 1840.
4. The change was made in the Offences against the Person Act, 1828 (9 Geo. 4, c. 31, s. 2).
5. I thank Simon Devereaux and Doug Hay for raising these issues.
6. *Morning Chronicle*, 7 May 1840.
7. HLS MS 4487, Items 13 (seq. 75–6), deposition, n.d.; 77 (seq. 356–57), copy of deposition, n.d.; OBP t18400615-1629.
8. *Two Studies in Crime*, 13.
9. 10 May 1840.
10. *The Times*, 8 May 1840.
11. Item 42 (seq. 168), statement of Thomas Blount, 15 May 1840; Sheppard, ed., *Survey of London*, vol. 40, 194–95.
12. 11 May 1840; 17 May 1840.
13. *The Times*, 11 May 1840.
14. 10 May 1840.
15. Henderson, *Recollections*, 204–5.
16. *The Era*, 21 June 1840; OBP t18400615-1629.
17. Items 29 (seq. 126), 30 (seq. 127), statements of Thomas Prest, Joseph Burr, and Alfred Lund Hughes, 20 May.
18. Item 6 (seq. 37–40), statements of Henry Lovick and John Harris, 6 May 1840.
19. 'The Murder of Lord William Russell', *Morning Chronicle*, 14 May 1840.
20. Prest, *Lord John Russell*, 73.
21. *The Times*, 7 May 1840.
22. Prest, *Lord John Russell*, 150. For the basis of this précis, see Radzinowicz, *History of English Criminal Law*, vol. 4.
23. *The Era*, 10 May 1840.
24. A portrait of Lady Charlotte Russell was painted in 1790 by John Hoppner.
25. Russell's children were identified in both the *Era* and the *Southern Star*, 10 May 1840.
26. See Chapter 3 below.
27. Fisher, *The House of Commons, 1820–32*; Thorne, *The House of Commons, 1790–1820*.
28. PROB 6/217/221; UCL: Brougham papers, 36,815; *Law Times* 33 (1859): 19.
29. *ODNB*.
30. Jalland, *Death in the Victorian Family*, 264. See generally ch. 12.
31. *Hansard. Parliamentary Debates*, 1st series, vol. 9, House of Commons 13 Aug 1807.
32. *Hansard. Parliamentary Debates*, 1st series, vol. 3, House of Commons 4 Mar 1805, col. 696.
33. *Hansard. Parliamentary Debates*, 1st series, vol. 35, House of Commons 3 Mar 1817, cols. 850–59.
34. *Hansard. Parliamentary Debates*, 1st series, vol. 35, House of Commons 14 Mar 1817, cols. 1083–132.
35. *Hansard. Parliamentary Debates*, 2nd series, vol. 17, House of Commons 31 May 1827, col. 1083. A brief sketch of Russell's political career appeared in the *Morning Chronicle*, 9 May 1840.
36. Tosh, *A Man's Place*, 173.
37. Blakiston, *Lord William Russell*, 65.
38. Blakiston, *Lord William Russell*, 195, 197.
39. Quoted in Prest, *Lord John Russell*, p. xvi.
40. OBP t18400615-1629.

14 Norfolk Street, Park Lane 55

41 Item 19 (seq. 90), statement of James Ellis, 12 May 1840.
42 Item 27 (seq. 123), statement of Mary Hannell, 15 May 1840. These included Russell's daughter-in-law, the Baroness de Clifford, Mr and Mrs William Russell, and (Elizabeth Anne) Lady William Russell, the wife of Lord William's nephew George.
43 See Milne-Smith, *London Clubland*.
44 *Morning Chronicle*, 14 May 1840; repr. in *The Era*, 17 May.
45 Item 18 (seq. 89), statement of James Ellis, 9 May 1840.
46 Item 37 (seq. 137), statement of John Harris, 12 May 1840.
47 Item 71 (seq. 315), undated copy of Nussey's deposition.
48 OBP t18400615-1629; the *Examiner*, 21 June 1840.
49 Item 19 (seq. 90).
50 Jalland, *Death in the Victorian Family*, 144.
51 14 June 1840; Hobler scrapbook.
52 *A Godly Forme of Household Government: for the Ordering of Private Families, According to the Direction of God's Word*, quoted in *Domestic Service and Gender 1660–1750*, 37.
53 *Labours Lost*, 18.
54 *Useful Toil*, 135.
55 May, *Victorian Domestic Servant*, 4.
56 Steedman, *Labours Lost*, 39. See generally ch. 2.
57 May, *Victorian Domestic Servant*, 8.
58 *Domestic Service and Gender 1660–1750*, 15–6, 22, 170, 174.
59 Horn, *The Rise of Fall of the Victorian Servant*, 8–9, 28–9; http://www.londonelectoralhistory.com/PDF's/LEH-THE-LED/LEH-4.2SHOP-&-SERVANT-TAXES.pdf.
60 Burnett, *Useful Toil*, 144.
61 *Domestic Service and Gender 1660–1750*, 43.
62 http://essays.quotidiana.org/hunt/maid-servant/.
63 'Conditions of service of a cook employed by William Cother, landowner, of Longford, Gloucestershire, 14 January 1837', reproduced in Horn, *Rise and Fall of the Victorian Servant*, Appendix B, p. 216.
64 See 'Conditions of service of a cook employed by William Cother, landowner, of Longford, Gloucestershire, 14 January 1837', reproduced in Horn, *Rise and Fall of the Victorian Servant*, Appendix B, p. 216.
65 British Weekly Commissioners, *Toilers in London*, 120, quoted in Huggett, *Life Below Stairs*, 35.
66 Items 21 (seq. seq. 97), 27 (seq. 121–22), statements of Mary Hannell, 9 and 15 May.
67 'On a Chalk-Mark on the Door', 511–12.
68 Item 21 (seq. 101).
69 http://essays.quotidiana.org/hunt/maid-servant/.
70 Items 6 (seq. 24), 6 May; 12 (seq. 62), 8 May; 15 (seq. 79), 13 May.
71 *Life Below Stairs*, 115, 160.
72 Items 12 (seq. 62) and 15 (seq. 79), statements of Sarah Mancer, 8 and 13 May 1840.
73 *Diary of William Tayler*, 33.
74 Meldrum, *Domestic Service and Gender 1660–1750*, 20.
75 Meldrum, *Domestic Service and Gender 1660–1750*, 20, 30, 33.
76 Item 15 (seq. 80), statement of Sarah Mancer, 13 May 1840. It was erroneously stated in various of the papers that Ellis had been in Russell's service 'upwards of ten years', and Courvoisier was very jealous of him. See, e.g., *Morning Chronicle*, 7 May 1840.
77 Item 12 (seq. 62); *Southern Star*, 21 June 1840; OBP t18400615-1629.
78 See Chapter 3 below, 35.
79 *Morning Chronicle*, 7 May 1840, repr. *The Era*, 10 May 1840.

56   14 Norfolk Street, Park Lane

80   *The Times*, 11 May 1840.
81   *Morning Chronicle*, 8 June 1840.
82   *Examiner*, 24 May 1840.
83   *The Times*, 7 May 1840.
84   *The Times*, 11 May 1840.
85   *The Times*, 7 May 1840.
86   She appears as 'Baillie' in the *Era*. 31 May 1840.
87   *Examiner*, 24 May 1840. Similar errors appear in reputable historical studies, unfortunately including mine: to my eternal mortification, in proofreading *The Bar and the Old Bailey* I did not notice a typo whereby Courvoisier's solicitor Thomas Flower became 'Flowers'.
88   *The Times*, 11 May 1840; *The Era*, 10 May 1840.
89   *The Maul and the Pear Tree*, 2134.
90   Horn, *The Rise and Fall of the Victorian Servant*, 84.
91   Items 21 (seq. 105 and 110), statements taken 9 May. Foreign servants had caused resentment in the mid-eighteenth century as well, with Bow Street magistrate Thomas De Veil urged in 1744 to prevent a meeting of footmen protesting the employment of foreigners. The English footmen marched upon De Veil's house and he arrested three of them, but the others stormed in to secure their release. De Veil, *Memoirs*, 60–1.
92   *The Era*, 10 May 1840. In a subsequent issue the paper grumbled that it was 'not only in private families that we have to deplore this predilection for the employment of strangers, the evil is still more extensively felt in what are called the houses of businesses of our great dress-makers ...' 31 May 1840.
93   10 May 1840.
94   Item 37 (seq. 141–44), statement, 12 May 1840.
95   *The Servant's Hand*, 53.
96   Item 43 (seq. 167).
97   Item 42 (seq. 161).
98   Item 42 (seq. 168–69), statement of Thomas Blount, 15 May 1840.
99   Item 39 (seq. 152, 153).
100 Items 15 (seq. 80), statement of Sarah Mancer, 13 May 1840; 27 (seq. 123), statement of Mary Hannell, 15 May 1840.
101 'On a Chalk-Mark on the Door', 510.
102 Item 20 (seq. 93), statement, 18 May 1840.
103 The police were particularly interested in the note, as one for that sum had been found hidden in the butler's pantry.
104 Item 21 (seq. 101–4), statement of Henry Carr, 9 May 1840.
105 Item 14 (seq. 77), statement of Sarah Mancer, 12 May 1840.
106 Item 18 (seq. 85), statement, 9 May 1840; Item 19 (seq. 90), statement, 12 May 1840.
107 MEPO 3/44 (DSC 01730, n.d.); (DSC 01741, 24 May 1840).
108 Item 14 (seq. 77), statement of Sarah Mancer, 12 May 1840.
109 Item 21 (seq. 104), statement of Henry Carr, 9 May 1840.
110 May, *The Victorian Domestic Servant*, 9; Huggett, *Life Below Stairs*, 27–8; Horn, *Rise and Fall of the Victorian Servant*, 200. More unusual was the 11th Duke of Bedford's insistence on 5'10" as a minimum height for his housemaids at Woburn Abbey. In their own time, women of such a height would practically be giantesses, especially among the working class. Booth and Argyll, 'Domestic Household Service', 227–28.
111 *Domestic Service and Gender 1660–1750*, 200.
112 James Ellis gave a very detailed account of his daily routine and duties as valet to Lord William Russell in a statement made to the police on 12 May 1840. Item 19 (seq. 89–92).
113 *The Era*, 21 June 1840.

14 Norfolk Street, Park Lane 57

114 Item 42 (seq. 169–70), statement of Thomas Blount, 15 May 1840.
115 *Domestic Service and Gender 1660–1750*, 124.
116 Tayler, *Diary*, 9.
117 Tayler, *Diary*, 9–10.
118 Tayler, *Diary*, 10.
119 *Domestic Service and Gender 1660–1750*, 164.
120 'Footmen', 341–42.
121 *Diary*, 57.
122 *Two Studies in Crime*, 21.
123 Item 21 (seq. 99), statement of Mary Hannell, 9 May 1840.
124 *Two Studies in Crime*, 17.
125 Thackeray, 'On a Chalk-Mark on the Door', 510.
126 *Book of Household Management*, 416.
127 *Labours Lost*, 7–8.
128 http://essays.quotidiana.org/hunt/maid-servant/.
129 'Footmen', 341–42.
130 12 Anne c. 7.
131 *Reflections*, 2.
132 *Reflections*, 4.
133 *Reflections*, 5.
134 *Reflections*, 7.
135 *Reflections*, 8.
136 *Reflections*, 9.
137 *Reflections*, 10–11.
138 *Reflections*, 13.
139 *Reflections*, 20.
140 *Reflections*, 31.
141 *Reflections*, 36, 39.
142 *Reflections*, 43.
143 OBP t18400615-1629.
144 'Of Servants', 204, 205.
145 'Of Servants', 207.
146 'Of Servants', 208.
147 'Of Servants', 209.
148 'Of Servants', 210.
149 Light, *Mrs Woolf and the Servants*, 2, 3–4.
150 *The Servant's Hand*, x.
151 *The Servant's Hand*, 15.
152 *The Servant's Hand*, xi.
153 Woolf, *Diary*, 1:314. Woolf later acknowledged that changes had occurred, and within her own lifetime, so that the boundary lines between kitchen and drawing room were no longer impermeable: 'The Victorian cook lived like a leviathan in the lower depths, formidable, silent, obscure, inscrutable; the Georgian cook is a creature of sunshine and fresh air, in and out of the drawing room, now to borrow the *Daily Herald*, now to ask advice about a hat. Do you ask for more solemn instances of the power of the human race to change than that?' *Mr Bennett and Mrs Brown*, 5. The green baize door had vanished and Woolf's servants lived in greater physical proximity with their employer – one had even the temerity to order Woolf from her bedroom, a shock from which the author of *A Room of One's Own* ironically took days to recover. Ultimately, however, that change had not affected a basic inequality in social relations; in fact, on Woolf's account, it merely exacerbated traditional frictions.
154 Tayler, *Diary*, 34–5.
155 Tayler, *Diary* 36.

156 Item 12 (seq. 66–7), statement of Sarah Mancer, 8 May 1840; OBP t18400615-1629.
157 Tayler, *Diary*, 18.
158 Tayler, *Diary*, 25.
159 Tayler, *Diary*, 19.
160 *The Rivals, a Comedy*, 25.
161 Tayler, *Diary*, Plate II; the diary entry for 27 Jan. is on p. 14.
162 Tayler, *Diary*, 62.
163 Quoted in *Domestic Service and Gender 1660–1750*, 47.
164 Cited in *Domestic Service and Gender 1660–1750*, 47.
165 This was the first point made by 'R.J.' in a letter speculating on the crimes. Item 65 (seq. 242) (n.d.).
166 Item 17 (seq. 81), statement of Sarah Mancer, 18 May 1840.
167 Item 16 (seq. 81), statement of Mary Hannell, 18 May 1840.
168 Item 17 (seq. 82), statement of Sarah Mancer, 18 May 1840.
169 Item 12 (seq. 68–9), statement of Sarah Mancer, 8 May 1840.
170 Item 19 (seq. 90), statement, 12 May 1840.
171 OBP t18400615-1629.
172 *Morning Chronicle*, 15 May 1840; OBP t18400615-1629. The quotations are a slight variation of the wording recorded in Mancer's second police interview, 8 May: Item 12 (seq. 69).
173 *Advice of a Mother to her Son and Daughter*, 65–6, quoted in *Domestic Service and Gender 1660–1750*, 44–5.
174 Dickens, *Great Expectations*, 92.

3 Inspectors Call

The Investigation

The murder discovered

Although a member of one of England's most prominent political families, Russell's life had been quiet and unremarkable, and his last day was no different. He left his home at around 1 o'clock, with instructions that he should be fetched by carriage from his club at 5 p.m. There was a mix-up with this request, Courvoisier neglecting to pass it on to the coachman, so that Russell had to return by hackney cab, arriving just before 6 p.m. He rang for his manservant from the dining room and gave him a letter to deliver; Courvoisier also brought in Russell's dog, which Russell walked for about half an hour before dinner. At 7 p.m. Russell dined alone waited on by his valet; after dinner, he went to his back drawing room to read or write. The coachman collected the dog around 9 p.m. and returned him to the stables; housemaid Sarah Mancer lit a fire in Russell's bedroom just after 10 p.m., before retiring for the night herself. Russell went up to bed at half-past 12.

On the morning of 6 May 1840, Mancer rose at 6:30: late-ish for a female domestic but Russell's household was a small one and the housemaid would describe her start as 'rather earlier than usual'. At about quarter to 7, she made her way downstairs from the attic bedroom she shared with Mary Hannell and found the house in disarray. A warming-pan used to warm Russell's bed before he retired, which would normally have been returned to the kitchen, lay on the landing outside his bedroom on the second floor. The Davenport writing desk in her master's back drawing room on the first floor was open, and letters and papers were scattered across the carpet and hearthrug, where she also saw Russell's keys. She noticed a screwdriver on a chair. Opening the shutters in the front drawing room all seemed in order, but in the hall on the ground floor, Mancer found a thimble belonging to the cook and by the front door, wrapped up in a neat cloth parcel, Russell's large cloak, opera glasses, and various other small items: a gold pencil case and a toothpick case, a silver caddy spoon, the top of a saltcellar, a silver dredger, and a cayenne spoon. The cloak she remembered as normally being kept in the dining room, the opera glasses in her master's bedroom. Moving to the dining room, she found silver candlesticks and other items of plate on the floor. Mancer turned and ran back to the attic to tell Hannell what she had discovered. The cook told her to call Russell's valet, who slept in a bedroom next door to the two women. Mancer found the manservant up and dressed but for his coat. What, she asked him, had he been doing with the silver? Nothing, the valet replied, and after running downstairs himself, declared that the house had been robbed. In the basement pantry and kitchen, drawers had been opened and the cook's workbox ransacked. At this point the agitated housemaid requested that Courvoisier go and see where Russell was. She followed him back up the stairs and together they entered the bedroom. The door was never locked. The valet crossed it to open the shutters while Mancer approached the foot of the bed, calling, 'My Lord, my Lord'. Then she saw blood. On the bed lay their master, a towel across his face and covering his slashed throat. Mancer screamed and began to run upstairs again to the cook but changed her mind and instead fled into the street to seek help, ringing the bells of both no. 22 and no. 23 opposite. Emanuel Young, the butler from no. 23, went first to Russell's house and then to the Marylebone Station House to fetch the police. Henry Lake, footman at no. 22, went directly to the station. When she returned to the house Mancer found Courvoisier sitting on a chair in the dining room with a pen in his hand and a small piece of paper on the desk. 'What the devil do you sit there for?' demanded the housemaid. 'Why don't you go out and send for someone, or a doctor?' The valet replied he was writing a letter to Russell's son but Mancer insisted someone must go to him in person. The two servants went back out into the street and Courvoisier beckoned to 'some sort of labouring man going past', but Mancer 'told him not to call a man such as that'. Russell's coachman then appeared, and with Young went up to Russell's bedroom to view the body. A servant from the house next door also entered the house, having heard Mancer and Hannell screaming. Various police officers began to arrive just after 7 a.m. Doctors were sent for. William Russell's once quiet house was in an uproar, teeming with officials: a murder investigation had begun.[1]

Investigating officers

While Police Commissioner Richard Mayne personally oversaw the investigation into Russell's death, officers drawn from the full array of police ranks were involved and would testify at trial. The investigation would also cross official geographic boundaries. The Metropolitan Police Act, 1829 defined the force's original district as an area of roughly 7 mile radius from Charing Cross, and within the next year 17 police divisions were established. Marylebone police station, in D Division, was physically closer to Russell's house, and it was to that station that Young and Lake ran to report the murder.[2] Technically, however, no. 14 lay within C Division, whose headquarters were on Vine Street, Piccadilly. Two constables from Vine Street, Alfred Slade and George Glew, had patrolled the street on the night of the murder, from 9 p.m. to 6 a.m. and 5:30 a.m., respectively. Slade's beat was on the side opposite to Russell's house and he had passed through the street every 12 or 13 minutes. Glew's beat was on Russell's side of the street; he had passed the house every 12 minutes and tried the front door and side gate 'several times' during the night. All had seemed in order when the two men went off duty in the morning.[3] At just after 7 a.m. Constable John Baldwin (C Division), on duty in Green Street, 'saw a number of persons' including Constable William Rose (D Division), running up North Street towards Norfolk Street. Rose had been told of a robbery at number 14, but not the murder, by a groom exercising horses. The two officers arrived at the door at roughly the same time. They were let in by the housemaid. Courvoisier was sitting behind the parlour door. Baldwin told Hobler that he had asked the valet,

> What in the world are you sitting there for, to see a house in this state as it is here? As soon as I spoke he put both his hands up before his face so that I did not see his face and he never gave me any answer.

Baldwin and Rose then began to collect the items scattered about the passage. Courvoisier remained seated, which Baldwin told him was 'very strange' and subsequently said, 'There must be something very strange about him he must know something about it, – I then spoke to Rose said there is something wrong about this'. Courvoisier by this time had retreated downstairs to the pantry, where he was later found sitting in the same position, his head in his hands. 'I strongly suspected him in a moment', Baldwin continued, '& I said you've made a devilish pretty mess of this'. The two constables searched the yard at the back to see if anyone was concealed there and found marks on the door and post. Searching the walls and upper yard and peering into the adjoining property they could detect no signs of an intruder from outside.[4] When Inspector John Tedman arrived the three officers together with the household servants went up to Russell's bedroom, where Courvoisier again sat down, still hiding his face, this time with a handkerchief. Tedman lifted the small towel covering Russell's head, revealing the wound. The inspector then sent for a medical man; surgeon Henry Elsgood came, as well as John Nussey, an apothecary who had attended Russell. The two men examined the body. The fact that the victim's eyes were closed raised questions[5] and Hobler would later write to both doctors:

> does a person in death close the eyes – or is it an invariable fact that in articulo mortis the eyes become prominent & staring wide open – if that be the case some person must have gently closed Lord Williams eyes to give them the appearance of sleep.[6]

When Baldwin saw that Russell was dead he contacted Superintendent Baker and told him to 'come directly' as he suspected a murder had been committed. He then went to fetch Inspector Henry Beresford and returned to the house with him. Baldwin spent the rest of the day outside the front door, leaving only for the inquest held in the evening.[7] Mayne arrived shortly afterwards; Inspector Nicholas Pearce of A Division entered the house at 5 in the afternoon. Pearce, who had begun his policing career in 1825 as a member of the Bow Street Patrol, was a very active officer who rose quickly through the ranks of the Metropolitan Police, becoming a cosergeant in 1831. As an inspector he had initially served in D Division but at the time of Russell's murder he was working within Division A (Westminster): his involvement in the investigation was at the invitation of Commissioner Mayne.[8] A coroner's inquest was convened for 6 o'clock in the evening.

The coroner's inquest

The coroner and the new police

In 1840, involvement of the Metropolitan Police in the investigation of murder was still something of a novelty: in the previous decade, John Beattie reports, they had participated in 'only about 18 murder cases at the Old Bailey'.[9] Cases of homicide had traditionally reached the criminal courts via the long-established system of coroners' inquests into suspicious deaths: murder had never been Bow Street's priority and on the occasions in which its force was involved, detective activities had been somewhat ad hoc and members of other forces also played a role. Investigation into the notorious Ratcliffe highway murders in 1811, in which two East End families had, like Russell, been murdered in their sleep in their own homes, provides an example. Former police officer T.A. Critchley and crime writer P.D. James listed the policing 'officials' operating in London's east end at that time:

> one Night Beadle, one High Constable, one Constable, thirty-five old night watchmen and twenty-four night patrols employed by the vestry of St George's-in-the-East; three magistrates at their Public Office in Shadwell, with their eight police officers; and an inquisitive old adventurer, [John] Harriott, with a force of River Police and five land constables.[10]

The River Police were relatively new at the time, created in 1798 by magistrate Patrick Colquhoun and Master Mariner Harriott. Based in Wapping High Street, this force's mandate was to combat theft from ships anchored in the Pool of London as well as the docks and lower reaches of the Thames. The location of the first victims' home, on the south side of the highway, between Cannon Street Road and Artichoke Hill, meant that the first official to arrive on the scene was Constable Charles Horton, like Harriott, a member of the River Police. Harriott himself searched ships on the river for the murderer.[11] Bow Street magistrate Aaron Graham subsequently assumed leadership of the investigation just as, six years earlier, Graham had spearheaded the enquiry into Richard Patch's 1805 murder of his business partner Isaac Blight.[12] This particular magistrate clearly viewed himself as an active investigating officer and is described by Critchley and James as 'a true detective'.[13] Officially, however, investigating murder was not his role.

When committees of the House of Commons sat in 1833–34 and 1837–38 to consider the police of the metropolis which had been created by the Metropolitan Police Act 1829, the Bow Street model of detective policing was again ignored. Detection might occasionally be required of London's new force, but the general consensus remained that a special detective division was not necessary. The force's constables were 'fully competent', perfectly able, Commissioner Mayne and his colleague Colonel Charles Rowan testified, to conduct any such investigations.[14] Mayne has been characterized as 'the more articulate and imaginative' of the two men, but he shared with Rowan a suspicion of creating a force of 'spies'.[15] When questioned they had also been thinking primarily in terms of property crime, and during a period of 'historically low levels of violence'.[16] The Russell investigation would be one of a cluster of murder cases that sorely tested the authorities' – and the public's – belief in the competence of preventive officers to act in a detective capacity.

Police participation in murder enquiries did not come about as the result of any deliberate decision made by the commissioners. Instead,

> the establishment of police stations in each division and the regular presence of the Met constables on the streets, day and night, meant that from time to time unexplained deaths would be reported to them, opening the possibility that divisional sergeants and inspectors might be drawn into their own investigations, even as the coroner was conducting his.[17]

The relationship between the new police and the coroner's office remained to be determined. In 1835, the commissioners of police had ordered that

> in all cases of violent or sudden death, or casualties, where a coroner's inquest should be held upon the body, the police, wherever a case comes under their cognizance, will, in addition to giving information to the parochial authorities of the district, give information to the coroner also ...[18]

In 1839, the commissioners considered whether officers of the Metropolitan police should 'undertake the duty of summoning the coroner's jury within the police district, in all cases where an inquest is to be held'. 'It has been decided', wrote Richard Mayne in October of that year,

> that for the present it would not be expedient that the metropolitan police should undertake the performance of this duty, but they shall continue, as heretofore, to give notice to the coroner in all cases where it shall be thought desirable that an inquest should be held.[19]

It was not merely relations between the new police and the ancient office of the coroner that had to be resolved: like policing, trial, and punishment, at the time of Russell's murder the coroner's office itself was in the throes of profound change.[20] Thomas Wakley, a medical journalist – founder in 1823 of *The Lancet* – and member of Parliament, had been elected coroner of West Middlesex in 1839, having offered himself as a candidate since 1830.[21] This election broke new ground, Wakley's predecessors for centuries having been lawyers rather than medical men.[22] The battle lines had been drawn in his original, unsuccessful attempt, remembered in George Eliot's *Middlemarch*, published in 1871 but set 40 years earlier: 'I hope', says the town's coroner Mr Chichely,

> you are not one of the *Lancet*'s men, Mr Lydgate – wanting to take the coronership out of the hands of the legal profession ... I should like to know how a coroner is to judge of evidence if he has not had a legal training.

Lydgate of course *was* a *Lancet* man, retorting that 'A lawyer is no better than an old woman at a post-mortem examination'.[23] In the 1839 Middlesex election that followed from the death of solicitor Thomas Stirling, who had held the office of coroner for 23 years, both candidates were keen to emphasize that the contest did not turn on party-political grounds but lay instead between the choice of a medical or a legal coroner. Several solicitors had put themselves forward for election but successively withdrew, leaving only a Mr Adey to face his medical opponent. *The Times* reported in detail the nominations for the election held on hustings erected before Hick's Hall on Clerkenwell Green, on 14 February. On this account, the majority of those who attended favoured Wakley's candidacy: he was repeatedly cheered while Adey met with 'mingled cheers and disapprobation'. Adey's candidacy was proposed by Mr Oliver and seconded by Mr Gude. Both candidates then addressed the audience at some length, Adey asserting that the legal profession supported the continuance of a lawyer-coroner, Wakley keen to point out the folly of such a course. Such men could not distinguish between male and female skeletons, nor indeed between that of a human or a rhinoceros or a dead man from a living one. At the close of the poll, Wakley had bested his solicitor opponent by 808 votes.[24] By the second poll held on 20 February Wakley's majority had increased to 1,419 and Adey at this point withdrew his candidacy, admitting with good humour that as 'he was by his own confession dead as far as regarded the struggle for the present situation, his opponent, Mr Wakley, would no doubt stand up and dissect him'.[25] Wakley could not be declared the victor until ten days following the initial poll, but on 25 February the final poll was officially announced as Wakley, 2,015, Adey, 582.[26] The medical profession had won. Wakley's first inquest was held the following day.[27]

Wakley had various reforms in mind when he took office. At the time of his election, and until 1860, justices of the peace controlled payments to coroners; as inquests were expensive JPs were selective in authorizing such payments. With justice for the dead discretionary, the poor tended to be marginalized in death, as they had been in life. Wakley found this abhorrent – there was a strong connection between reform of the coroner's office and radical politics – and was among those insistent that deaths in custody, whether prison or workhouse, merited investigation.[28] He was determined to extend the powers of the coroner's office and insisted that the investigation of *any* sudden or suspicious death was a medical matter, that every such death within his jurisdiction would be investigated, criminal activity exposed, and that the medical witnesses who facilitated such enquiries would be paid. Adey had claimed that Wakley supported the new poor law of 1834, but in fact, the new coroner had opposed it with all his heart and was determined there should not be one law for the rich and another for the poor. The poorest of England's subjects were as deserving of inquest as the rich.

William Russell was neither a pauper nor a convict, the circumstances of his death could not have been more suspicious, and there was no question but that an inquest would be held on his body. As it happened, Wakley himself would not preside over the inquest into Russell's death: he was ill and a deputy, Thomas Higgs, was called in to preside.[29] This substitution too was an instance of recent innovation. The use of deputy coroners was controversial and disputed by Middlesex's magistrates, who at this time were, like solicitors, engaged in something of a turf war with the medical profession, as documented in the report of a parliamentary enquiry in July 1840. The committee deemed the use lawful under 6 & 7 William IV, c. 105 when illness prevented the coroner's attendance.[30]

While by 1839 the medical profession had triumphed over the lawyers with respect to who was properly qualified to fulfil the position of coroner, uncertainty with regard to the precise responsibilities accorded to that office and to the new police in investigating a suspicious death is reflected in early press coverage of Russell's murder. The inquest into William Russell's death took place at the City of Norwich on the corner of Norfolk Street and North Row, the public house frequented by Russell's former valet, Ellis. Deputy Coroner Higgs's jury comprised the right honourable Mr Dawson, who served as foreman, and 13 other men. They spent 20 minutes in Russell's house, examining his body, then returned to the inquest room. The first witness to be called was surgeon Henry Elsgood. Elsgood testified that he had found Russell, in bed and wearing a night dress, lying partially inclined on his right side. The victim had, he said, been dead not more than three or four hours. The coroner's jury was adamant that they had seen that the ball of Russell's right thumb had been nearly cut off; Elsgood claimed he had seen no such wound. John Nussey was then examined; he confirmed Elsgood's testimony except that he had seen the injury to Russell's thumb and considered it consistent with an attempt to ward off an attack. Both practitioners were convinced that the evidence did not support suicide. The victim was unlikely to have been able to inflict the wound, four or five inches deep and seven inches long, and certainly could not have placed the napkin or towel covering his face and head. The three servants who lived in, as well as police inspectors Tedman and Beresford, also gave evidence. The jury returned a verdict of wilful murder 'by some person or persons unknown.'[31]

66 *Inspectors Call*

The police investigation

On the morning the murder was discovered William Russell's servants, indoor and outdoor, were examined by Inspector Jarvis of C Division – his first and last involvement in the investigation, Jarvis's place subsequently assumed by Commissioner Mayne. Jarvis also examined James Ellis and the two workmen, ironmonger Henry Lovick and upholsterer John Harris, who had been in the house the day before, both engaged in repairing the bell pull in Russell's bedroom.[32] Mayne took over on the 8th of May, and from that date solicitor Francis Hobler recorded all of the statements taken at the house. Sarah Mancer's cross-examination at the Old Bailey revealed that she had originally been unaware of Hobler's identity. All of the servants' rooms were examined; nothing incriminating was found. Courvoisier, Mancer, and Hannell were detained at the house in separate rooms and forbidden to speak to one another. The cook was quickly determined not to have been involved in the murder and both Hobler and the police also eliminated the housemaid from their list of suspects. Others were less charitable about Sarah Mancer, as discussed below. But among those officially responsible for the investigation, suspicion focused from the start, and unanimously, on Russell's valet. Constable Baldwin's conviction that the behaviour of Courvoisier was 'strange' was shared by every officer who entered the house.

One thing that immediately strikes the modern reader of Hobler's scrapbook is what would now be considered serious contamination of the crime scene during the police investigation. The various statements and depositions of the police, servants, workmen, and Russell's neighbours reveal a high degree of casual public access to 14 Norfolk Street on the day the murder was discovered, including the room in which the murder victim lay dead. Inspector Tedman, who had arrived at 7:30 a.m., reported that when he entered the kitchen to question the cook, 'there were several other persons standing by at this moment they seemed to be strangers who had come into the house in consequence of the alarm'.[33] He does not appear to have asked anyone to leave. The 'strangers' would have included Young, the butler from across the street whom Sarah had asked to fetch the police, and a man named Franklin he had brought with him, described as someone 'who had lived with some of his Lordship's family'. Young had also sent for York, Russell's coachman, who accompanied him upstairs to see if 'His Lordship is dead or alive'. The two men were in the room when Tedman entered and remained while the body was examined by Elsgood. They subsequently went downstairs to the basement and watched the back door being inspected. Superintendent Baker arriving, however, ordered that 'all strangers must leave the house'; Young then left 'immediately'.[34] In the days following, a great many aristocratic spectators – many of them women – appear to have been let in.[35] Aristocratic access to 'the chamber in which the dreadful occurrence took place' was finally curtailed on 20 May, a full two weeks after the murder had been discovered, 'when positive orders [were] issued by the authorities that no person should be admitted at the house, unless provided with an order to that effect, signed by Mr. Wing'.[36] Wing was the Russell family's solicitor. The *Morning Chronicle* reported that 'numbers of the nobility' continued to request access to Russell's bedroom, and to the places where stolen items had been hidden, but they were now refused.[37]

William Russell's neighbour at no. 15, George Henry Cutler, had also wandered about the house.[38] Having been roused by his man servant sometime between 7 and 8 a.m. and told of the murder, he promptly went next door and was admitted by Russell's groom. He spoke to the female servants and looked at the disordered items in the dining room before going downstairs. Seeing the officers in the kitchen Cutler suggested that they accompany him to the corner house, which was unoccupied. They did so. He then took them to his own house and the stables which adjoined Russell's. Returning to no. 14, he talked with both the police and the servants about the murder, peered into Russell's bedroom but did not approach the bed, then returned to the ground floor and spoke briefly to Courvoisier before leaving the house. During the time spent in Russell's kitchen, he said, 'there was a great deal of conversation respecting the murder ... between the police Elsgood, the apothecary the maids – the groom & myself'.[39] Cutler, like the police, suspected Courvoisier, and told his manservant so on returning to no. 15. Selway later heard his employer tell Superintendent Baker 'it was evident someone in the house had committed the murder'.[40]

Thomas Selway was potentially of greater use to the investigation. Selway occupied the back attic of no. 15 and the staircase of no. 14 was against the inner wall of his room. He could hear the stairs next door, and people's voices, but had not done so on the night of the murder. He had gone to bed at midnight and his sleep was not disturbed. He did however hear screaming within the house between 7 and 8 in the morning; he had put his ear against the wall to 'hear more distinctly', but to no avail. Leaving the house he went next door, where he found Russell's female servants wringing their hands. Having had a brief look around the ground floor, observing the scattered items and seeing Courvoisier seated behind the dining room door, he left as Constables Rose and Baldwin were arriving. The valet had asked him to fetch the butler of no. 100, Park Street, but Selway did not know the butler in question and did not go. Nor did he know Courvoisier. In statements taken on 15 May both Selway and Cook said they had been slightly acquainted with Russell's female servants, but hadn't been in the house, nor had Hannell or Mancer visited them. Selway hadn't realized James Ellis had left, nor had he seen Courvoisier before the murder was discovered.[41] Back in no. 15, he watched from the drawing room window the constables' search of the rear of Russell's premises. The police, he noticed left prints in the dust. Selway would testify at both Bow Street and the Old Bailey.[42]

The police also took statements, on 13 May, from the three servants of Mr Jones Loyd at no. 22: housemaid Elizabeth Selzer, nurse Harriet Spencer, and Lake, the footman. Like Selway and Cook, they knew Russell's servants only by sight. Lake did not enter no. 14 on his return from Marylebone Station House.[43] Spencer claimed to have seen lights on in the attic rooms on the night of the 5th, including in a room where she'd never seen a light and which she presumed was Courvoisier's.[44]

Sergeant Pullen was put in charge of the house from the day the murder was discovered. While Commissioner Mayne took initial statements from its inhabitants other officers began at once to dismantle the premises, looking for both stolen items and the murder weapon. According to Belton Cobb, Mayne had a list 'compiled of policemen who were particularly skilled in specific branches of work'.[45] Two on that list were deemed especially adept at searching out missing items; thus, despite belonging technically to E Division, Constables Frederick Shaw, who had been with the force for ten years, and George Collier were sent for. With Inspector Pearce, Shaw searched the house for potential hiding places. A number of workmen were called in to assist them. These included carpenters and builders Henry Battin, George Simmons, and John Crake, and plumber William Winter. Another carpenter, John Christie, would be employed as an expert witness and testify at trial with respect to the 'bruises' on the damaged back door.[46] On the 6th Battin was involved in the search of Russell's water closet on the ground floor and another located in the basement. Neither search yielded any results. On Friday 8 May, at Pearce's direction, Battin removed the skirting boards and plate rack and took up the hearth stone in the butler's pantry. He assisted in taking up the floor of the pantry that evening and helped to empty the scullery cesspit (the soil was put through a sieve).[47] The heavy work having been done, Pearce discovered, behind the skirting board:

1 gold Napoleon
1 40 franc Napoleon
2 double Maria Louisa
1 thick plain gold ['wedding' has been struck through] ring
1 wedding ring
1 gold seal ring boy & dog
1 gold ring ruby
1 gold seal ring onyx black – with a white streak – 2 hands joined

These items were contained within a gold net purse. In the same spot were found a £10 bank note, number 41447 (January 4) and a Waterloo medal and ribbon which had belonged to the victim's son, Captain Francis Russell.[48] Much effort would be extended to determining that the note in question had been in Russell's possession.[49]

Pearce and Constable Collier immediately confronted Courvoisier, who was sitting in the parlour with another constable, with the items discovered and informed him of where they had been found. Courvoisier responded, 'I know nothing about them, I am innocent, my conscience is clear, I never saw the medal before'. Taken down to the pantry and shown the site behind the skirting board, he repeated that he was innocent.[50] In his master's bedroom, questioned by Tedman, the valet had already indicated that some of his employer's rings were missing, as well as his watch.[51] Now, identifying them, he told Collier 'I am innocent of it, but it would not look so bad against me, if the property had not been found in my Pantry'. When Collier agreed it looked 'very suspicious', the valet replied, 'he should say nothing till the last until he heard if the whole truth was told'.[52] This cryptic statement would subsequently be puzzled over, but theft by servants was by no means uncommon; in fact, in 1837 such thefts accounted for the largest total loss of property in the Metropolitan Police area.[53] The location of the stolen items obviously suggested that Courvoisier was a thief if it did not prove him a murderer.

Pearce, together with Shaw, then proceeded to Courvoisier's bedroom at the top of the house for a second search of his belongings and the clothes he was wearing:

> I searched the Prisoner's Boxes in his Bed Room on Friday the 8th of May instant in the Afternoon, there was a Box, a Portmanteau and three or four drawers, I turned all the Clothes out I therein found, I saw nothing that attracted my attention, I also searched a Carpet Bag but found nothing that attracted my notice, I saw one or two Shirts but I am not quite sure whether I examined them very minutely, I saw some dirty Linen which I examined but found no particular marks, soon after the Prisoner came into that room and I left him there replacing the articles in the presence of a Constable, I had not made any search of the Box, Portmanteau and Drawers before this time though I had been in the Room and looked about generally.[54]

Whether he was aware of the loss of other personal possessions is uncertain, but William Russell had been distressed by the disappearance of a silver locket containing a twist of hair tied with a silk ribbon. During his Easter visit Lady Sarah Bayley noticed that it had fallen onto a table from a pocket book and that when it was returned to him, Russell hadn't put it back in the book. Russell subsequently missed it and wrote asking if he'd left it at the palace. He had not.[55] James Ellis told the police that Russell kept the locket in either a small Russian leather box or a silk note case and 'never went anywhere even for a night without the little box'.[56] A locket was discovered on Courvoisier's person, but it was not the one lost by his employer.

On the same day, under Pearce's direction and within his presence, George Simmons took up the paving stone in the yard and searched the drains and pipes of the back area. He also took up the floor and trap of the servants' water closet and cut away the wall where the pipe came down from Russell's closet above it. He removed beer tubs and their stands. None of these searches yielded results.[57] On Saturday the 9th Shaw and Collier, again with the assistance of Battin, continued to take apart the butler's pantry. Battin removed a plate rack from above the sink, behind which, seven feet up, were three pipes. Candle in one hand and Collier by his side, he felt behind the pipes with his other hand and saw secreted a seal with the stone facing outward. Collier removed it. Roughly a quarter of an hour later Winter, the plumber, called the constable to again feel behind the pipes as he could see something shining there. Collier extracted a split gold seal ring, bent from its hiding place. Searching the floor from which Battin had prised the hearth stone the previous day, and sifting the dirt, Shaw – Charles Dickens's 'little wiry Sergeant of meek demeanour and strong sense'[58] – found the missing locket.[59]

Constable Paul Cronin, C Division, who had witnessed Pearce's discovery of the purse and £10 note on the 8th, found another stolen item on the 12th. The sink from the pantry had been removed to a wash house leading out of the scullery at the rear of the house; feeling along the brick ground of it he drew out a gold chased watch key. The next day he examined the sink itself and found hidden between the lead and its wooden cover Russell's missing watch. It too had been damaged, the glass broken.[60] The watch, Ellis told the police on identifying it, Russell had worn with his seals on a black ribbon and placed in a fob. At night it was laid on a stand on the convenience beside his bed.[61] Charles Ignatz Klaftenberger, of Regent St clock and watchmakers Aubert & Klaftenberger, would be called at trial to confirm it the watch found was Russell's.[62]

Missing silverware was not discovered, nor had the murder weapon been identified, and Courvoisier persisted in denying responsibility. He was told on the 8th, after the discovery of the stolen items in the pantry, to consider himself in custody at the house, and Sergeant Humphries watched over him from that time. But enquiry was also made by the police into the possibility that the valet's unemployed friend, Henry Carr, who had taken tea with Courvoisier on the 5th, was involved. Mayne sent Inspector Beresford to fetch him and Carr was examined at the house on 9 May. *The Times* reported that a 'loose' woman claimed she had met a servant named Carr in a pub, and that he had told her he was about to leave for Australia; it also reported false rumours to the effect that some of the missing items had been found in his bedroom chimney.[63] But the inspector found Carr's character 'good',[64] and he had an alibi. After he left Norfolk Street on the evening of the murder Carr paid a couple of brief calls relating to his employment search and visited a cousin at 8 Hanover Square around 9 p.m., staying for half an hour, and then attended a raffle held at the Royal Exchange Public house, leaving just after 11 p.m. On returning home he found another lodger at the door of his house and let him in. In bed by 11:30, he had heard the clocks strike 12. Hobler dismissed the possibility that Carr was the murderer, just as he eliminated Russell's cook from suspicion:

> Hannell gave her evidence in a very clear & satisfactory manner, and so did Carr – there was not to my mind any ground whatever for supposing that they or either of them had any knowledge of or participation in the murder.[65]

Carr was released, and after testifying at Courvoisier's trial, he disappeared from the historical record. There is nothing suspicious or unusual about this disappearance; he was only briefly visible by virtue of being accidentally caught up in a murder investigation. In ordinary circumstances, an unemployed man-servant in a city teeming with such men was unlikely to attract attention.[66]

The physical evidence gathered by the police in the days following Russell's murder indicated that the house had not been broken into; stolen items of Russell's property had been found secreted in the butler's pantry; and everyone thought the valet's behaviour on the day the murder was discovered was odd. Courvoisier was consequently charged and removed to Bow Street Station House on Sunday 10 May. The pre-trial examinations, discussed in the next chapter, began on Monday the 11th.

A succinct summary of the police investigation up to 17 May was filed by C Division's unnamed 'responding officer' – presumably Jarvis. He wrote that he had been told of the murder at 9 a.m. on the morning of the 6th and that when he arrived at 14 Norfolk Street, he found Inspectors Beresford and Tedman already there. He confirmed that Russell's throat had been cut and his writing table broken into, but could not ascertain precisely what had been stolen as Courvoisier, with only five weeks' service, was not 'in possession of what Property there was in the House'. Neither the silver furniture on the desk or dressing table nor a silver night candlestick had been removed. In the dining room, a silver dish and other silver articles had been taken out of the side table and left on the floor. The drawers of the side table were all pulled out but no locks had been broken. In the passage behind the front door were found Russell's cloak, a silver dish cover, a pair of spectacles, a silver thimble, a tea shell hidden in a cloth, also a gold opera glass, a silver sugar dredger, an ivory toothpick, and a gold pencil case, laid on the cloak, 'no doubt for deception'. In the back kitchen some drawers and a cupboard had been forced open and the silver routinely used by Russell, including dinner forks, table spoons, dessert spoons, and tea spoons, all marked with the Bedford family crest, was missing. Personal items including rings and a gold watch were also missing. The servant's rooms had been searched and a chisel found among the clothes of the valet that corresponded exactly with the marks made on the drawers and cupboard in the back kitchen. Marks had also been found on the back kitchen door leading into the area which appeared to have been made with a dull instrument, and

> from the appearance of the Poker in the pantry being bent and half broken completely corresponds with the size of the marks which causes great suspicion that this was the instrument used and that the door was never broken from the outside.

An examination of the walls and roofs leading to the back of Russell's premises failed to discover the slightest marks that would indicate that someone had entered that way.

Courvoisier, the report continued, stated that he fastened the front door in the early part of the night and it had been found the next morning by the housemaid, on the latch. The police constable on the beat [Glew] had been 'particularly questioned' and stated that he had seen nobody about the house during the night and that he had found the door locked fast just before 6 o'clock on leaving his duty. The two workmen who had been in the house on the afternoon of the 5th had been questioned and properly accounted for their time during the night. The coachmen and groom had likewise 'very satisfactorily accounted for themselves during the night'. Their lodgings had been searched. The inspector also reported that the seats of the water closets had been taken up, the dust holds, cisterns, and 'every other part of the house strictly examined'. Nothing had as yet 'been discovered to give the least clue to the horrid deed'. Inspectors Beresford and Pearce were pursuing enquiries; Inspector Tedman together with a sergeant and a police constable remained in charge of the premises and property. Nothing had emerged in evidence at the inquest other than what the police were already in possession of. 'Every exertion', the report concluded, would 'be made to endeavour to bring to justice the perpetrators of the deed'.[67] At the time of this report the murder weapon remained elusive: no. 14 Norfolk Street was full of razors and knives but Tedman told the coroner's inquest, 'I have searched very carefully all over the house, but did not find any Cutting Instrument with which the wound might have been given.'[68] Physical evidence connecting the valet with his master's violent death was similarly lacking. And when such evidence was discovered, it was highly suspect.

Tainted evidence?

Inspector Pearce was not the first officer to have searched Courvoisier's belongings. On the 6th of May, after Baker had left and before Mayne had arrived, Tedman and Beresford searched all of the servants' attic rooms. In the valet's, Tedman reported,

> we found a box – for clothes, on searching this over I found a £5 Bk note & 6 sovereigns – they were in a bead purse & placed among the clothes, so as easily to get at if wanted – I immediately showed it to him & asked him where he got the note & money from – C said he gave Lord William change for the note a few days ago & the other money is my own I have had it bye me some time – I found nothing else in his box – [struck through: there were shirts clean & dirty in this box] only cloth garments in this box. I then examined a portmanteau which he had near him I found a number of shirts both clean & dirty – only one good one clean for use – the other clean shirts were apparently washed but not ironer – I opened all the shirts, clean & dirty – saw no marks of blood or anything else on them & they were replaced – the portmanteau was turned completely out & nothing left in it – besides the shirts there were stockings & drawers & cravats, stocks & such like articles all of which were closely examined – there were several pairs of leather gloves which I also examined every one & found nothing. I did not see a pair of white cotton

Inspectors Call 73

gloves had they been there they could not have escaped my search. I then examined a chest of drawers in his room & a carpet bag – very minutely found they contained linen every piece of which I examined & turned over, but found no marks of blood or otherwise in any of them.

Courvoisier also opened the waistcoat and shirt he was wearing and turned out all his pockets, revealing nothing but a few shillings, the locket belonging to him, and a small bunch of keys.[69]

Further searches were made after Courvoisier had been removed from the house. Sergeant Shaw and Constables Humphreys and Collier went through the valet's belongings on the day of the first pre-trial hearing, 11 May. On this third search, as on the first two, the officers found nothing. The fourth search took place on 14 May, following a request from Louis Courvoisier for some items of clean clothing, including a clean shirt, for his nephew. In fulfilling this request, Inspector Tedman, this time accompanied by Sergeant Lovett (D Division), went through Courvoisier's belongings yet again. On this occasion when Tedman unfolded one of the shirts, a pair of white cotton gloves fell from it, the left-hand glove very slightly stained with two marks of blood. He believed it was the same shirt he had examined previously, and asked Constable Collier to make further search 'in case I had overlooked anything'.[70] On the fifth search Constables Collier and Cronin recovered, 'nearly at the top' of Courvoisier's portmanteau, two handkerchiefs, likewise faintly stained, and a shirt front minus both shirtsleeves and body.[71] 'Neither', as David Mellinkoff points out caustically,

> the handkerchiefs nor the shirt front had been noted in the four previous searches of Courvoisier's clothing, which had now been inspected by nine different policemen, including a Police Commissioner and three Inspectors, three of the police having been in on the search in the attic twice each.[72]

The Metropolitan Police archives contain both a copy of Courvoisier's first confession and notes breaking it down into separate, numbered paragraphs. Courvoisier had said,

> The gloves were never placed in the shirt by me [?] to my knowledge, when I left Mr Fector's I gave all my white gloves to the coachman – the handkerchiefs that were found in my portmanteau were never put there by me, they were in my drawer where I used to keep my dirty linen, or in my bag with my dirty linen in the pantry, if there is blood upon them, it must be from my nose, as it sometimes bled.[73]

Fector's coachman, James Leach, who had overlapped with Courvoisier's service for two years, said that the valet had always worn white cotton gloves when he went out with the carriage,[74] but Sarah Mancer told the police on 18 May that she had never seen Courvoisier wearing white gloves while in Russell's service, 'at any time'. When serving Russell at table, he used a napkin. Mancer did admit – presumably on being asked – that she never saw any of Courvoisier's things except those in 'immediate use'. She was in his room daily to make the bed, but he kept his clothing locked in his box.[75]

A police memo acknowledged that of the assertions relating to the conduct of the police, 'some seem to impute conspiracy and fabrication of evidence, the rest would show great incapacity, want of tact and vigilance in the principal officers employed':

> The assertions [numbered 13, 14, and 15 in the memo] are those which impute to the police conspiracy or fabrication of evidence. In addition to what was stated before the magistrates and at the trial on those points it may be observed with regard to the gloves when produced at Bow Street both Mr Wing and Mr Hobler saw Courvoisier look at them while in the hands of his Solicitor Mr Flower and point out a wound or cut on his hands from which they inferred that the prisoner was accounting for the stain of blood and admitting the gloves to be his; it is also worthy of observation that if it can be [conceived?] any of the police were capable of preparing gloves and placing them where found the stains would not have been such as they were, it would have been much easier as well as more conclusive to have made the marks of blood more like what would appear to have been caused had they been worn when the murder took place.

The memo argued that the marks of blood found on the handkerchief 'appeared to be such as were made in the way the Prisoner himself states, and whether found in his drawers or portmanteau is not material'. With respect to the shirt front, 'the same sort of observation' could be made as with respect to the gloves: 'it affects the prisoner too remotely to suppose it placed there by any one designing to fabricate evidence of party to a conspiracy to convict him'.[76]

These protestations notwithstanding, it is inconceivable that the police officers involved in the searches – including two renowned for their skill in finding lost objects – could have been so incompetent as to have missed potentially damning evidence in their first explorations of Courvoisier's belongings. The suspect gloves, handkerchiefs, and shirt front must have been planted. Mellinkoff suggests financial motivation, 'attempts by those whose duty is to enforce the law to serve themselves an extra helping of public reward'.[77] The *London Gazette* had announced on 8 May that the Treasury was offering £200 and Russell's relatives the same sum for the apprehension and conviction of the murderer. Another £50 was subsequently offered for the discovery of silverware missing from the house: four forks, four tablespoons, four dessert spoons, and two teaspoons, all bearing the Russell family crest (a standing or walking goat).[78] At trial defence counsel certainly accused the police of corruption for monetary gain, as discussed in the next chapter. Here I disagree. Various officers did share in the reward, but the individual sums received were small.[79] The actions of the police, discreditable as they are, were far more likely to have been rooted in desperation. They were convinced they had arrested the right man, as indeed they had. But they had no positive proof of Courvoisier's guilt. This late discovery, however, created only suspicion. As one press report commented,

> The gloves, spotted with blood, would certainly have formed a very strong circumstance, if the gloves had been proved to have been the valet's, or if they had been discovered in the first instance. But the policeman positively says, that there were no gloves in the portmanteau when he first searched it; and it was not until a subsequent search, eight days afterwards, that the discovery is made; yet this seems to have strengthened the suspicion of the valet's guilt more than any other circumstance. We confess, in our minds, it removes a great portion of the previous opinion which we had formed, that he was the man.[80]

The chief suspect

Twentieth-century crime novelist Patricia Wentworth nicely sums up the predicament of a murderer once an investigation has begun:

> The murderer does not walk an easy path. He must keep the dust from his shoes, the stains of crime from his garments. He must not touch, he must not handle. But he must not only glove the bare skin lest it leave the mark of his guilty sweat – he must hood his thoughts and heed his tongue, he must mask his eyes from being the mirror of his mind, and walk the naked edge of danger easily. What to others are little things, sifted out afterwards by patient question and answer, are to him all the time an ever-present menace – the teeth of the trap which may at any moment spring to catch him. He must watch everything and everyone. He must not appear to watch at all. With thought at its most abnormal, all that he looks, or says, or does must be so normal as to merge into an accustomed background and provide nothing that will catch even the most scrutinizing eye.[81]

In 1840, the grain of dust, the smear of a fingerprint, or the speck of blood, as the events of Courvoisier's trial would prove, did not so easily combine to convict a man. But Russell's valet was quickly suspected of being involved in the robbery and murder: his behaviour from the time Baldwin and Rose entered the house on 6 May had appeared abnormal; he offered no assistance and Baldwin reported that during the course of the entire day he had never seen the valet's face.[82] On Baldwin's first mention of Courvoisier hiding his face in his hands, Francis Hobler wrote on the facing page to his statement, 'Witness should have pulled aside his hands & shook him from his chair & made him stir himself'.[83] Sarah Mancer reported that the valet 'appeared very much concerned'. Inspector Tedman used the same phrase and also said that he 'frequently drank water during the day'.[84] Taking Courvoisier to the back door, Inspector Tedman had informed him, 'this deed has been done by someone amongst you in the house'. When Courvoisier replied, 'if so I hope they will be found out', Tedman said, 'there is not much doubt but what they will'.[85] If he raised suspicions, the valet nonetheless managed to maintain a degree of composure into the second day of his trial, saying little and repeatedly denying both theft and murder. His thoughts were hooded, and he carefully heeded his tongue.

'The persecution of Sarah Mancer'

On 11 May *The Times* reported that Henry Carr had been released from custody and that while the two female servants were still in the house their movements were no longer restricted and 'their entire innocence' was established: 'we believe we may with perfect confidence state, that [the police] have, to a considerable extent, succeeded in fixing the guilt of the murder upon the party to whom suspicion pointed from the first'. On the 14th, the paper reported, 'The opinion which from the first moment obtained general concurrence, that there was a strong case of suspicion against the valet Courvoisier, daily becomes stronger'.

But not everyone was convinced of Courvoisier's guilt. Russell family solicitor Thomas Wing received a letter dated 9 June which suggested that female servants sometimes had 'sweethearts & acquaintances that are not always of the best character'.[86] The housemaid did tell the police she had a 'male friend', a shopkeeper from High Holborn, who used to visit her at Norfolk Street, but she hadn't seen him for a year. She also mentioned James Don but said prior to the inquest she hadn't spoken to him in three months.[87] There is no evidence of either Sarah Mancer or Mary Hannell secreting gentleman callers in the house to commit theft and murder, but various members of the public were not convinced of the innocence of Mancer in particular. Hannell was never subject to public suspicion, but having suffered the trauma of discovering Russell's body Sarah Mancer's troubles would only increase. Following the inquest rumours about the housemaid's character and past conduct began almost immediately to be circulated and a number of persons accused her of dishonesty in previous employment. Someone wrote on behalf of Mr Geldent in Westminster that a person by the name of Sarah 'Mansell' had been dismissed for dishonesty from a previous position.[88] As a consequence of such reports, Hobler noted,

> Inspector Beresford took Sarah Mancer to two or three persons who it was said she had robbed, & they all declared they had never seen her before in their lives – the Girl was cruelly used – for even 2 or 3 <u>Ladies</u> of Title who came to see the House of Lord Wm R while she was in it – before they quitted spoke to her and told her they thought she must know something about it.[89]

As Courvoisier's trial approached, *The Times* reported the police enquiries as essential not merely to clearing the housemaid of guilt, but to establishing her as a reliable witness:

> Several insinuations prejudicial to the character of Sarah Manser, the housemaid of the deceased nobleman, having from time to time appeared in some of the public prints, the police authorities felt it their duty to institute every inquiry in order to arrive at the truth of those statements, that the credit of so important a witness might not be left doubtful at the trial. Amongst other charges against Manser, it was alleged that before she entered the service of Lord William Russell she lived in the establishment of Dr. Thompson, of Kingston, Surrey, and was discharged by that gentleman in consequence of her having committed a theft. To ascertain the truth or falsehood of this statement, it was arranged that Inspector Beresford should accompany Manser to Kingston, which he did a few days ago, and the result was, that Dr. Thompson's lady declared that the young woman had never lived in her service, that she never saw her to her knowledge before, and consequently that the alleged imputation upon her honesty had no foundation whatever in fact. The witness, it is stated, courts the fullest inquiry into her conduct and character.[90]

Mancer was also suspected of having been an accomplice in the murder if not the murderer herself. 'Mr Trail the magistrate at Union Hall', Hobler wrote, 'expressed to me a very strong conviction in his mind that she & not Courvoisier was the guilty party'.[91] In a letter to Mayne dated 18 May 'G.W.' said he found it odd that neither Courvoisier nor Mancer had knocked on the door or spoken outside it before entering Russell's bedroom. Once in the room the maid had remained silent and still, waiting for Courvoisier to open the shutters. The fact that the two servants had never announced their presence or sought permission to enter suggested they knew Russell would be unable to respond and 'were prepared for the spectacle which afterwards presented itself'.[92] The author of another, undated and unsigned, letter wrote in distress of attempts by 'Courvoisier's friends' to implicate the two female servants in the murder. He had overheard a conversation in Kensington Gardens in which the speakers, one a servant out of livery, 'were rejoicing that <u>no</u> circumstantial evidence could hang a man, and that it was as easily proved that either of the women did it'. They were 'gloating over the pleasurable certainty' that Courvoisier could not be convicted.[93]

Most vocal in the imputations made against Mancer was M.M.G. Dowling, a police inspector from out of town. 'There was', reported an incensed Francis Hobler,

> an attack ... openly made upon [Mancer] by Mr Dowling the Police Inspector of Liverpool who wrote a letter against her which appeared in the Morning Chronicle under the signature of '*Blue Rock*' – & this busy

meddling Ass – carried his indecent impertinence so far as to come to London to attend one or two Examinations & afterwards had interviews with the Home Office & Police Commissioners & he declared his opinion that the case was mismanaged – that we were pursuing the wrong person & that I was quite incompetent to the conducting of the case & in fact he should have said that he & he alone was able to unfold the mystery –[94]

Dowling had written privately to Mayne of his suspicions on 12 May:

Will you excuse me for suggesting to you one or two possibilities respecting the probable murderers of Lord Wm Russell. Suspicion does not seem to have been pointed at the Housemaid, whom I believe to be implicated with the valet.

Newspaper reports of the crime led him to believe that the cook's beer had been drugged, causing her to sleep heavily. He found Mancer apparently 'eager' to point out the broken back door to the police suspicious and questioned how she could have known Russell's throat had been cut when a towel lay upon it. He concluded his letter,

I have been so much in the habit of making these sort of investigations of late years that the necessity of leading you to them lest they should have escaped notice was strongly urged upon me by my anxiety for the success of your enquiries after the murderers.[95]

The letter attributed to Dowling, dated 27 May, was published on the 28th. The coroner's inquest, he believed, had firmly established that 'some inmate of the house was concerned in the murder'. Press and public alike appeared convinced that the inmate in question was the valet, and Dowling acknowledged that the evidence against Courvoisier was strong. But, he warned, 'let us not be so far blinded by prejudice as to overlook the, to my comprehension, improbable evidence of the housemaid'.[96]

Dowling's efforts were not welcomed by the Metropolitan police or Hobler. On 7 June the very angry inspector, having returned to Liverpool, wrote to the chief clerk of the Commissioners of the Police:

Dear Sir,
   I have just received your letter of yesterday date in which you state you have been directed by the Commissioners of Police to write to me upon the subject of the imputation which has gone forth against the Character of Sarah Mancer. Housemaid to the late Lord William Russell.
   With respect to the statement of her having lived with Dr A.J. Thompson [illeg.] that was made to me the evening before the day on which I quitted London – I thought it my duty to acquaint some person in authority of what I had heard in order that enquiry might be made into its truth or

falsehood. I consequently communicated with Captain Hay stating at the same time that I could not vouch for its truth but that it had been told to me, and I thought it desirable that enquiry should be made. If it be slander I am prepared when necessary to name the person from whom I obtained the information.

Now with respect to any Newspaper Reports – I declare that I have never written nor caused to be written one word upon the subject, but if it be a crime to express an opinion deduced from the circumstances and evidence on the case – as every person naturally will do – why then I am in common with thousands of others guilty of feeling anxious that the perpetrators of this atrocious murder should be brought to justice.

I am very much astonished that the Commissioners should have directed you to insinuate a wish that I should cause what you are pleased to call a 'Contradiction or Explanation' to be inserted in the Newspapers. Contradiction of what? I have neither directly nor indirectly caused the insertion in the newspapers of an observation relative to the affair, and cannot therefore comprehend what I can have to contradict. In short why such a letter was written to me I cannot understand.

The threat of an action against him for expressing an opinion, Dowling continued, 'was lost' on him. 'Hundreds and thousands' of persons were expressing the same opinion. He repeated his denial of being responsible for any 'insertions' in newspapers. He hadn't even seen such reports, other than one in the *Morning Chronicle*. He concluded by asking the commissioners to provide the name of their informant.[97]

A week later the *Southern Star* reported on Dowling's attempt to 'fix the murder' on the housemaid; the paper believed his letter to the *Morning Chronicle* to be a 'tissue of falsehoods' and that its author would come to regret having sent it. It also reported with some indignation that

a person, holding the rank of gentleman, has been circulating a report, which is now in almost every person's mouth, that Sarah Mancer, the housemaid, has been taken up and tried; also, that she has been discharged from many places for dishonesty and immorality. Now, the girl evidently suffers greatly under this infamous report; and she has given a full and perfectly satisfactory account of her life, and where she has lived from a child. She has entreated the police to make every possible inquiry into her character, and to confront her with her accusers. She implored them to do so; and we are certain that the inquiry has been made, and the result is every way satisfactory. Then, why do not the Commissioners of the Police contradict such reports publicly? Does the individual who circulated the report, think that he has done the case any good? Does he think that he will get off comfortable and easy? If so, he is sadly mistaken. Why did he come to London to interfere with the case? Can his employers spare him, to blast the poor girl's character?

The paper dissociated Flower, Courvoisier's solicitor, from these attempts to implicate Mancer in the murder: 'He is too honourable a man to countenance such dirty work'.[98]

Hobler's scrapbook also contains a copy of a snippet published in another newspaper, *John Bull*, on Sunday 24 May, pasted in under the handwritten heading: 'The villainous & unjust attack on the Housemaid Sarah Mancer which appeared in the John Bull newspaper':

> The examination of Mr. Courvoisier, the gentleman from Switzerland, who we perceive was accommodated with a seat during his examination at Bow-street on Friday, and of which the most ample details will be found in our paper, elsewhere, have excited the greatest and most painful interest. We *have* a view of that case peculiarly our own; we certainly do not feel justified in promulgating that view, inasmuch as public suspicion has never to our knowledge fallen upon the person whom we believe to have been, if not A principal – perhaps actually THE principal actor, in that horrid scene, as least an accessory before, in, and after the act.[99]

The exasperated solicitor took swift action:

> In consequence of this Paragraph Mr Wing & myself went to the John Bull office & not finding the Editor we went to the Solicitor Mr Hopkinson Red Lion Square my old schoolfellow and guardian when at Apsley – He was vexed at the paragraph when he read it and expressed himself that in his opinion it was one of Mr Theodore Hooks brags – but that he would have it set right.[100]

Theodore Hook was a highly irreverent and now largely forgotten early nineteenth-century journalist, biographer, dramatist, and novelist; his publications include a tongue-in-cheek account of Old Bailey trials in the semi-autobiographical *Gilbert Gurney* (1836), but Hook is most famous as a hoaxter or prankster.[101]

In response to his reproof Hobler received an unrepentant confidential communication from Hook – yet another commentator who conflated the female servants' surnames:

> I can have no difficulty in stating the reasons I have for making the remarks to which you call my attention – nor any object in making them but a desire that justice should be done to the murderess of a nobleman so universally esteemed and to whom in my earlier days I had the pleasure of being personally known.
>
> The object of my suspicions is the house-maid Mancele [sic] – I have no facts to adduce – but take the following circumstances –
>
> During the day of the murder Mancele and Curvoisier [sic] were much together alone – it is in evidence that Courvoisier & Mancele agreed that

Curvoisier should tell Lord William a falsehood about the carriage – it is in evidence that a bell-hanger came to do something to the door of Lord William's bed-room which bell-hanger Mancele kept in conversation during the time he was doing the work whatever that was to <u>the exclusion of the cook</u> – Where is the bell-hanger? – Who is he – who is his master if he was a journeyman?

At night Courvoisier goes for beer – Mancele declines it. So does he – the Cook drinks it – was it drugged? –

It seems scarcely possible that in a small bed-roomed house a man sleeping in one garret should be able to get up, go down stairs commit a murder and get rid of all evidence of it & return to bed without being heard more especially as (I believe) it is in evidence that groans were heard[102] about the time according to the measurement of the rush-light the murder must have been committed by someone in the adjoining house. When Mancele discovers the robbery – ie <u>the packing up of the things</u> at ½ past 6 & when she wakes Curvoisier & he comes down & sees the confusion – What does she say? Does she say run up and tell my Lord that the house has been robbed? – not she – she says or at least she says she said – 'go & see how Lord William is' or 'What has become of Lord William' – Why should she say this? She was safe – Curvoisier was safe & the Cook was safe – Why should she apprehend that anything had happened to her Lord. Then when Curvoisier goes up to my Lord's room she goes too – and she does not stay at the door she follows him in – no remark is made according to her own account and instead of going to his Lordship's bedside to tell him what had happened Curvoisier opens one of the windows and <u>then</u> they find his Lordship murdered

And then when they come downstairs Curvoisier is greatly confounded & confused & begins to write a letter, whereupon the house-maid recalls him to a sense of the position of affairs & says, '<u>What the devil</u> do you do sitting here, go & call on somebody' & when he acts upon her advice & proceeds to call on some poor labouring man who is passing, she says, 'Don't call on such a person as <u>that</u> call somebody more respectable as a witness'.

Then see how strongly her evidence goes <u>against</u> Curvoisier – then look at the extraordinary fact that the bloody gloves were <u>not</u> (according to the police account) in Curvoisier's box when first searched & to which <u>she had access</u> and that they <u>were</u> found there when <u>he</u> [double underscore] (Curvoisier) <u>sent a policeman to the trunk</u>, in which if he had put them there, he must have known they were, in order to get a change of linen.

Then is it likely – is it possible that Curvoisier having committed this murder should have put all the stolen property behind the skirting-board of <u>his own pantry</u> or is it creditable that the murder was committed with a view of robbery at all – I think not – a much deeper character seems to attach itself to the whole affair.

Under any other circumstances I should not venture to allude to <u>that</u> which under existing ones, & in <u>perfect confidence & sincerity</u> seems essentially necessary to the elucidation of this barbarity. I mean the consideration of the terms upon which the late lamented nobleman was with the woman – I know that when his Lordship lived at Mivarts this woman was peculiarly employed about him in attendance. And during this period her style of dress generally improved, and that although Mr Mivart as I hear is ready to afford testimony to the badness of her character, Lord William selected <u>her</u> to be his house-maid when he took the house in Norfolk street.

If <u>this</u> sort of connexion can be established the mystery seems much lessened – we find Curvoisier stating on the day of the murder that if a particular servant does <u>not</u> come he shall go & Mancele stating that if a particular servant <u>comes</u> she will not stay – in the way this is given in the reports it does not sound important but coupled with anything which involves a <u>personal</u> interest on the part of the woman and Lord William it seems to be everything.

<u>One</u> person could not have done the deed – but who the second one was, is the question –? I repeat my conviction that the murder was not a murder in which robbery was the object – all I urge upon those who are either personally or professionally engaged in the detection of the crime is to look after Mancele. – and above all to conceal nothing of the real state of the case – Curvoisier says 'I am innocent but I shall not speak <u>till I see whether the whole truth is told</u>'

Perhaps while I write this much more is known at Bow Street but I write <u>unreservedly</u> because it is a duty to do so.[103]

The accusations made by Dowling and Hook were dismissed by those officially engaged in the investigation into Russell's death. Hobler wrote,

A full Inquiry about Sarah Mancer was made of Mr and Mrs Mivart who both gave her an excellent character & their readiness to speak on her behalf & at my request they remained at home during all the Trial ready to be sent for should it be required for them to attend – this they would never have done had not the girl borne a good character different to the opinions of Mr Hook and Mr Dowling.

Almost incandescent with rage, the prosecuting solicitor said of Dowling that he

should have liked to make the dirty rip[?] eat a copy of the Morning Chronicle with his Blue Rock letter in it & a copy of each of Courvoisier's confessions by way of satisfying him upon his extreme sagacity & as a cure for his discreditable conduct – I suppose his volubility of speech and pomposity of manner ignorant presumption I may fairly add gain upon some persons in authority.[104]

Public 'assistance'

Hobler's scrapbook contains a great deal of less vitriolic correspondence related to the case. Some of this is professional, consisting of communication between Hobler and the police commissioners and inspectors, the coroner, and the solicitor for the defence. But he also collected letters received from members of the public. Aristocratic interest in Russell's murder may have reflected personal unease about their physical safety, but the general public was equally mesmerized by the investigation as the story unfolded in the press. A few people wrote in search of potential business advantage. George Smith made a macabre offer to the police commissioners on the 7th of May.

> I take the liberty of acquainting you, that I have completed my arrangements for introducing into this country the Process for arresting the progress of Decomposition, discovered by M. Gannal of Paris, and adopted by the Government of France, in similar cases.[105]

French chemist Jean-Nicolas Gannal preserved cadavers for anatomical purposes by injecting a solution of acetate of alumina, sometimes supplemented by small amounts of arsenic and carmine, into the carotid artery without draining any blood from the body. His *Histoire des embaumements* had been published in Paris in 1838; an English translation appeared in the year of Russell's murder. Samuel Lovegrove's offer was more mundane: witnesses, he suggested, might like to make use of his home during Courvoisier's trial. Lovegrove had 'private doors' at nos. 3 and 8 Old Bailey.[106] Shorthand writer Henry Buckler wrote to Hobler on 11 June asking, 'In the event of a Report in the case of the Queen agst Courvoisier I shall esteem it a particular favour if you will kindly use your favour on my behalf'.[107] Buckler was at the time the Old Bailey Proceedings' official shorthand writer; presumably, he wanted to publish a separate pamphlet account of the trial.

Other correspondents were simply seized with curiosity. 'The extraordinary murder of Lord William Russell', wrote Charles Greville in his journal on 15 May, 'has excited a prodigious interest, and frightened all London out of its wits. Visionary servants and air-drawn razors or carving knives dance before every body's imaginations'. And though 'every day produces some fresh cause for suspecting the man Courvoisier, both the facts and the motives are still enveloped in great mystery'. Greville himself was so intrigued that two days before this entry he had gone to Tothill Fields Prison to see the suspect, reporting, 'He is rather ill-looking, a baddish countenance but his manner was calm'.[108]

In 1840, just as it does now, murder attracted cranks of all sorts and myriad persons wrote to the newspapers, various of the police officers, Bow Street magistrate Thomas Hall, Mr William Russell, Lord John Russell, and Hobler, hoping to assist in resolving the mystery and offering advice during the course of the investigation. *The Times* commented on the volume of this correspondence as early as 14 May, and reproduced some of it within its own pages; on the

18th the *Morning Chronicle* similarly noted letters offering suggestions to Inspector Tedman. On the eve of Courvoisier's Old Bailey trial the letters continued: 'It is a great pity that persons take so much trouble, and make such fools of themselves, in such a serious matter', reported the *Southern Star*.[109]

One letter arrived from someone with a personal connection to the Russell family: T.I. Manning wrote to solicitor Thomas Wing offering his thoughts because he had served on the same ship as William Russell's sons George and John and dined at high table with 'these fine young lads' for almost three years. Having read the newspaper reports carefully, Manning speculated at some length as to whether Russell had been smothered before his throat was slashed, and whether a razor or carving knife had been used to inflict the wound. Like Hobler, he criticized the constable (Baldwin) who had not made Courvoisier hold up his face, instead allowing him to cover it throughout the day on which the murder was discovered.[110]

While Manning was acquainted with the family of the victim, most correspondents opened their communications with a variation on 'you don't know me, but', and apologized for intruding at a difficult time. Some, especially in the early days of the investigation and prior to Courvoisier's arrest, offered general advice. Almost all of the letters assumed or presumed Courvoisier to be the murderer, although a brief note to Hobler, written in a very shaky hand, claimed that the valet was 'as innocent of the murder as the queen of England, *in act thought or Deed*.[111] After reading of the murder in the *Salisbury Standard* Daniel Tabor wrote to Russell's son offering his service as a self-styled 'Inspir'd Man': his suggestion that Courvoisier be detained while a suspect does not seem particularly inspired.[112] Edward Mordet Pereira thought Courvoisier should be asked whether he could put one hand on his heart and take his dead master's hand in the other, and swear on oath that he had not committed the murder. If he were guilty, placed in this situation he could not but confess.[113] James Pearson recommended to Lord John Russell that he ascertain whether Courvoisier was a Roman Catholic; if he were, 'take a cross and confess him up on it and mark his countenance and you will have the truth out of him'.[114] A correspondent identifying himself as belonging to the Asmonean Jewish Ministry wrote, again to Lord John Russell, 'I would have summoned the suspected murderer to touch the wounded part of the body or else to look the deceased in the face pointing to it in the presence of a jury'. He also said, 'the man against whom the dog might evince an evil disposition I would consider guilty, and instantly have him tried and punished'. [115] A rare female correspondent (almost all of the letters were from men) had written to Tedman on the 12th to enquire similarly why no one appeared to be investigating the habits of Russell's dog. Was it watchful? Was it 'attached or otherwise' to the valet? Anticipating Sherlock Holmes's remarks regarding the curious incident of the dog in the night-time (*The Adventure of Silver Blaze*), she also asked if it had been heard barking.[116] As the dog in question had been returned to the stable where it slept hours before the murder, these queries were irrelevant.

A few correspondents concerned themselves with missing stolen items. Superintendent Baker was told of a man offering for sale a seal that may have had the Bedford crest on it; a public house address was given and Baker informed that the man in question may have had a wooden leg ...[117] Another gentleman wrote to the commissioners of the police telling them of a suspicious character who, taking an arm out of a sling to eat an orange on a street step, he had witnessed wearing 'brilliant rings'.[118] But many of the writers were preoccupied with the potential locations of the missing murder weapon. A letter to Inspector Tedman signed 'a Magistrate' and dated 10 May read,

> Sir, I am not known to you, but take the liberty to suggest that if the weapon, with which the murder was perpetrated has not been found, may it not have been thrust through the aperature in the throat into the body of the victim. —[119]

Someone suggested the weapon might have been thrown out of Courvoisier's window, at the back of the house.[120] John Ritter wrote to Mayne to suggest that the entrance to the street sewer should be examined; a 'country clergyman' likewise recommended that the drains in the street should be inspected.[121] On the 17th a brief letter to Hobler urged him to search the beds, particularly Courvoisier's. Hobler annotated this item, 'done'.[122] 'Justitia' from Lincoln's Inn similarly wrote Tedman to ask – acknowledging that the suggestion had probably already been made – whether the bedding and mattresses of both Courvoisier and Russell had been searched.[123] On the 25th, 'a Friend' wrote to the murder victim's son that he understood proof was 'not yet sufficient to condemn that coldblooded ungrateful wretch the valet'; in a murder case in his own neighbourhood evidence had been found in an outdoor water tank. Was there such a thing on Russell's premises?[124] Another wrote, from Birmingham, to Hobler suggesting that Courvoisier may have had a friend who 'carried off' the murder weapon. Henry Carr could not have been the only acquaintance of the valet who had been in the house, and the family servants should be examined as to who else had visited.[125] Boot and shoemaker William Edwards informed the 'Honored Gentlemen' investigating the case of 'a remarkable dream' his daughter had had concerning the whereabouts of the weapon. In this dream, a knife had been discovered in a flower pot on the drawing room windowsill. If the weapon still remained unfound such a hiding place was not, Edwards believed, improbable and worth checking. Edwards concluded by saying he took an interest in such cases as he had formerly been in the force himself, as a sergeant in F Division.[126] 'P.Q.' also suggested that 'the flower pots which ornament the windows of the drawing room of his late lordship's mansion' be searched for the murder weapon.[127] The windowsill flowers noted in newspaper descriptions of 14 Norfolk Street had clearly imprinted on the public.

Unsurprisingly, most of this correspondence was inserted into Hobler's scrapbook without comment. But in one lengthy annotation the solicitor wrote of correspondent F.W. Buchanan's previous involvement in a murder case with a missing knife, and the means by which the weapon had been discovered:

> I will make a note of a curious circumstance which was related to me by Mr Wing, as connected with the writer of these letters – Soon after the receipt of these letters Mr Wing had occasion to be at or near Nuneaton & on enquiring for Mr Buchanan he found him & called on him & learned that he was an old solicitor retired from practise & he had indeed been induced to write from the following circumstances which had occurred to him many years ago whilst in his profession – a murder had been committed as was supposed with a knife but which could not be found the belief was it was thrown into a particular field – Mr Buchanan being professionally concerned to conduct the prosecution against the supposed murderer who was in custody committed – he made search for the knife in the field which was of some acres extent, by employing about 300 little boys to search the field over – to each of whom he gave a shilling & to the one who should find the knife half a crown – the result was the knife was found[.][128]

Buchanan's child recruits bring to mind the 'Baker Street Irregulars', street urchins – far fewer in number – employed by Sherlock Holmes in the course of various investigations.[129]

Unsurprisingly, none of these suggestions yielded results and the murder weapon's lodging place turned out to be the most obvious: the knife used to cut Russell's throat was one of the household knives, and modern forensics would quickly have identified it as such. A rare sensible letter from a member of the public had urged the authorities to consider precisely this possibility and examine the table knives, 'particularly the carvers'.[130] Opposite the fourth page of James Ellis's statement on 9 May, Hobler noted that three dozen silver knives, with corresponding dinner forks (four of them were among the missing items), were kept in a sideboard in Russell's front parlour. Ellis, Beresford, and Pearce had examined them and found the knives included four poultry carvers; one had a small mark of yellow water rust under the balance of the handle and the blade was duller than the others.[131] The draft of the letter sent to Nussey and Elsgood in which Hobler had queried whether someone had closed Russell's eyes ended with another enquiry: 'Did you see the poultry knives which were at Lord William's house if so should you think the wound one likely to be caused by such an Instrument?'[132] Nussey responded on 1 June. He had not seen the knife, but could 'readily conceive' that such an instrument could have caused the wound.[133] Elsgood said he had not seen a description of any knife other than a clasp knife, as he had explained to Hobler in his examination.[134]

Hobler himself was certain one of the poultry carvers had been used. 'I had no doubt', he wrote,

> this was the knife of murder the blade was not so long so as to be in the way. It was so very compact & handy that Inspector Pearce brandishing it in his hand declared he thought he could cut off a man's head at a blow.

Again he repeated, 'I have no doubt it is the knife –'[135] In one of the first pages of his scrapbook Hobler also annotated a newspaper account that identified four Damascus table knives with ivory handles – a 'little mistake' had been made, he said, in that the blades were not Damascus blades but had 'the rough sharp edge of Damascus steel which would cut through anything'. He also corrected the report that one of the four knives had been separated from the rest and sent to Russell's bank. 'Not so' was underlined in his marginal notation. All of the knives had been sent.[136] Following Courvoisier's conviction, Hobler recorded,

> I got Mr Cope to ask Courvoisier if he should know the knife he did it with & he said no, but it was true he took it from the side board drawer & when it was over he cleaned it & threw it back again – & it was one of the carvers. – Now in Lord Williams bedroom there was a Bidet with some water in it which was slightly tinged with blood but in the absence of proof it is a conjecture to say he washed the knife & his hand there – the blades were so bright it is not probable that much blood would remain on one of them – for being so polished it would run off & so would water.[137]

The puzzling absence of seriously stained items of clothing was another topic of interest. 'G.F.' wrote to *The Times* on 13 May that he had recommended the police examine Courvoisier's shirt and offered potential explanations as to why no marks of blood had been discovered on it.[138] Bow Street magistrate Thomas Hall received a letter suggesting Courvoisier's washerwoman be applied to, as she could account for the number of the valet's shirts.[139] An annotation from Hobler on a later page indicated that he intended to follow up with washerwomen in both London and Richmond.[140] An 11-year-old girl recommended a search of the valet's pillow and bolster for bloody clothing.[141] Other correspondents suggested an alternative explanation. On 11 May, George Pryme wrote to the 'Chief Officer of the Police at Lord William Russell's':

> Sir,
> I yesterday heard from a prominent Physician that blood must have spouted from the wound of Lord William Russell – & that if an inhabitant of the House had committed the act, he might have taken the precaution to be naked at the time – & that therefore the person suspected should be examined without his clothes on & the insides of his shirts also examined.
> Late as it is, I think it right to trouble you with this suggestion, tho it may perhaps have already occurred.[142]

Pryme was not the only person to raise the possibility that Courvoisier had been naked when he slit Russell's throat. 'Amicus' on the 22nd and two further individuals on the 28th made the same suggestion.[143] Buchanan, who wrote first to Lord John Russell and subsequently to Hobler, amplified it, claiming to have heard gossip at a dinner party to the effect that 'two females' in a neighbouring house had seen the valet naked on the morning Russell's body was discovered.[144] The women in question were likely to have been the female servants at no. 23 across the street: yet another correspondent had claimed two women had seen a naked man washing himself at 3 a.m.[145] Among Hobler's 'scraps' is a business card for Charles Dix, Messr. Thos. McLeod & Co, Scotch Brewery, Cold Harbour Lane, Camberwell, on the back of which is written in pencil, in Hobler's hand, 'evidence to prove that a man was seen to undress himself in Ld W Russells house quite naked & afterwards to wash & then dress – on the night of the murder'.[146] But Dix was not called at trial, and the owner of no. 23, Frances Latham, wrote on 10 June to say that he had questioned his servants and been informed they had seen nothing out of the ordinary on that night.[147]

The idea that Courvoisier had committed his crime in the nude would take firm hold in the popular imagination. It would explain the absence of significant blood stains on any of his clothing. The valet himself however never gave any such indication, saying instead that he had turned his right coat and sleeve up,[148] nor does Pryme's suggestion that Courvoisier be examined naked appear to have been taken up by the police. 'R.J. or Reader of The Times's supposition that Courvoisier burnt or otherwise destroyed any bloodied garments seems more likely.[149] 'A Friend of Justice's recommendation that the dust hole be examined for 'any quantity of tinder' tends towards this view;[150] 'J.N.' similarly wrote to Hobler urging that the ashes in the fireplace be examined for evidence that Courvoisier had destroyed any 'traces of his guilt'.[151] No such evidence appears to have been found.

Consideration was taken of a letter which said that if Russell's throat had been slashed from left to right, the perpetrator must have been left-handed. At the bottom of this letter, Hobler scribbled, 'Does C use his left hand at his meals'.[152] Another correspondent wrote that he hoped Hobler would 'not fail to produce evidence that the prisoner was accustomed to shave with his left hand'.[153] Opposite a statement made by William York, the coachman, on 9 May Hobler commented: 'knows Courvoisier to be able to use his right hand & his left hand in shaving himself – has seen him shave several times & use both hands'.[154]

Less helpful were letters from Henry Jones and William Green. Jones enquired of the governor of Lancaster Castle, on 13 May, if Courvoisier and the prison's former assistant turnkey in 1835, a man named Kemper, were one and the same person. Jones was 'haunted' by coverage of the murder and couldn't get the possibility out of his mind.[155] Green's letter of 16 June, written in response to newspaper coverage of the Bow Street hearings in the *Daily Sun*, was even more peculiar. He understood from the paper's reports that Beresford had claimed not to have seen Mr Russell in the house when Lord William Russell's watch was discovered. Green had travelled by coach from Newark to Lancaster with a Mr Russell on 7 May, and as far as he was aware, Russell was still in Doncaster as of 13 June. He found him 'a very curious person'. This is hardly surprising, as the evidence for Russell's presence consisted of an enclosed poster advertising a Mr J. Russell's 'Vocal Entertainment ... known as Russell's Recollections of Things that May or May Not Have Happened'. The Russell in question was described as, 'of the Theatres Royal Drury Lane, Covent Garden, and Haymarket, and English Opera House, and formerly of the Theatres Royal York, Hull, and Doncaster'.[156]

There were, inevitably, false confessions. The *Era* published one:

> It was I who killed Lord Russell. Yes, me. Who would have thought it was me who has stained my hand in blood, and that of an old man 74 [sic] years old. It is no good weapon; it can't be helped. I have done the deed. Tomorrow I am on the Continent, and to leave this country for ever.
>
> W.B.[157]

Hobler's scrapbook contains another, undated and unsigned, written in a beautiful hand:

> My mouth is tied – but my conscience nevertheless upbraids me with the part I have taken in quieting the man whose image I constantly see pointing at me – If I were sure no harm would come to me – but I dare not – yet if I might speak by correspondence – I could alter the present feature – But I daily read the Morning Chronicle and a communication consistent with my safety might be attended to.
>
> x x x x[158]

More dramatic was the letter received on 13 May, which read:

> Sir,
> What will you think when i tell you the wrighter of this letter was and is yeat in existence
> the very Murder of Lord Wm Russell may the lord God have marcey on my soul i was bribed i was bribed it is ever on my mind may God have marcey up on me i have stained my hands in Eoniscent. Eonocent **blood x** [written in red ink] his blood was bought by a price had i never taken it i would bean happy i maid my eccape in a ship i took som property and hid it a bout the primises and soon in a sertin place whare i thought it if found would condem the buttler and they would never look after a nother but i can not rest my mid is in confusion his lordship maid a little struggle you will find the instrument wich i in flicted the death blow a bout the primises i was in the house conciled best part of the day if you up on your oath will advertise what fate i will get fi i give up the name of the parson that bribed me and I can put confidence in it i will send you word ho it was if not i will never wright again.
> i am very much timbed to put end to my self and if i do i will leave a last(?) document of the awful affair i was bribed bribed bribed
>
> > Lord have mercy on my sol
> > Christ have macy on my sol
> > [small drawing of a gallows with noose]
> > Amen[159]

90   *Inspectors Call*

Of all these letters one stands out, that of Robert Blake Overton, a surgeon who wrote to Lord John Russell on 16 May to suggest that fingerprint evidence be used in detection:

> I find upon reading the evidence taken from the Coroners Inquest the marks of <u>bloody fingers</u> were found upon the sheets and pillows and now perhaps it is not generally known that every individual has a peculiar arrangement of the grain of the skin the impression of which may be distinctly seen by the aid of a high magnifying glass and every line counted from about the centre [illeg.] which varies, from the bend of the joint in every person. Therefore the impression made from the fingers of different persons will produce different shapes.

Overton's letter was illustrated with two sets of prints taken from the middle fingers of two separate persons and he suggested that impressions be taken 'from the fingers of the suspected individual' to assist in bringing the 'diabolical wretch' to justice.[160]

Blood had indeed been found on Russell's sheets: 'I have no doubt', the apothecary Nussey wrote to Hobler, 'the murderer after the deed wiped his hands & perhaps the Instrument on the sheet which covered the body, as a large portion of this was smeared with blood just in the way such an act alone would explain'.[161] Impressions of Courvoisier's fingertips may very well have been discernible from the sheets, and if he had been fingerprinted, a match might have been made. That the suggestion was not taken up by the police, however, is not surprising, despite the fact that recognition of the utility of fingerprints as a means of identification has a very long history.[162] Fingerprint impressions had been used as a way of signing government or business documents in fourteenth-century Persia, and in China possibly as long as 5,000 years ago; archaeological discovery was made on a cliff face in Nova Scotia, Canada, of prehistoric Mi'kmaq handprints exaggerating the unique ridges and whorls found on fingertips. But it wasn't until the nineteenth century that attempts were made to classify fingerprints. Professor Johannes Evangelista Purkinje of the University of Breslau published an essay in 1823 which described, illustrated, and named nine different pattern types; Purkinje also argued that every individual's prints were unique. Overton may have been aware of the essay, or he may simply have been thinking along parallel lines. But official, government use of prints by the English originated much later in the century, in India. William Herschel, while a civil servant in Bengal, used full (right) handprints to identify workers on the back of their contracts, thereby preventing fraudulent claims to payment or pensions. A Scot, Dr Henry Faulds, suggested that criminals might be identified from prints left at crime scenes: the two men subsequently engaged in an undignified squabble about which of them was the true pioneer in the field. But when Faulds approached the Metropolitan Police with his idea in 1886 – almost 50 years after Russell's murder – the force, which by this date had a Criminal Investigation Department, was still not interested. Only in the 1890s did the Met become receptive to the detective possibilities offered by fingerprint evidence.[163] A Home Office committee appointed to enquire into it recommended, in 1894, that fingerprinting be employed by the police.[164] By that date, American novelist Mark Twain had made dramatic use of fingerprint evidence in a courtroom scene to convict a murderer in *Puddn'head Wilson* (1893). But in the English courtroom, such evidence would not be employed until the early twentieth century, after another Indian Civil Service officer, Sir Edward Henry, devised an acceptable system of fingerprint classification. First recognized by the Indian Evidence Act of 1899, Henry's system was adopted by the British police in the same year and when Henry became assistant commissioner in the Met (1901), he established a central fingerprint bureau. Fingerprint evidence was used to convict a burglar in 1902 and in 1905, it was successfully employed in a murder trial.[165] In 1840, Overton's suggestion was considerably ahead of its time.

The investigation and the press

In commenting on the volume of correspondence streaming in from the public early in the investigation, *The Times* indicated that the suggestions made were redundant:

> Numerous letters have been received at the house by Inspector Tedman, from persons in all parts of the country, offering suggestions, which, in the opinions of the writers, would lead to the elucidation of the deep mystery in which the dreadful transaction is enveloped; but, singularly enough, the whole of them had been anticipated by the police authorities.

It offered as an example the letter that recommended searching the wound for the murder weapon, as it might have been thrust into Russell's throat. The body, the paper noted, had already been opened.[166]

If they failed – Overton's letter is an obvious exception – to raise any lines of enquiry the police were not already following, the letters from the public tucked into Hobler's scrapbook reveal close perusal of the press reports of the investigation into William Russell's murder. Many of them directly reference specific newspaper coverage. That coverage was extensive; within days of the report of the murder, it was also critical. Russell's murder had followed on the heels of a clutch of previous lethal assaults, the majority of which remained unsolved. Two women, Hannah Brown and Eliza Davis, had been murdered in 1837, Eliza Grimwood in 1838, Robert Westwood in 1839, and John Templeman just two months earlier than Russell, in March 1840. Only Brown's murderer, James Greenacre, had been caught and brought to justice.[167]

Both the new police and the older institution of the coroner's inquest came under fire:

> In the short space of three or at most four years, no fewer than six such murders have been committed; and the perpetrators remain to this day

undetected. Are the murderers of Mr Richardson, who was shot near Epsom, detected? The murderer of Eliza Grimwood, in Waterloo-road, where is he? Of Eliza Davis, the bar-maid, near Regent's Park, where? What have the police done towards the detection of the brutal murderers of Mr. Westwood, in Princess-street? The recent case of Mr. Templeman affords no reason to praise the acuteness or dexterity of the favourite force of the Whig Government; and now we have the murder of Lord William Russell, a crime involved in as much mystery as any of the preceding, committed to their sole investigation, because the coroner's jury has chosen to abdicate its functions. The last case, if the mystery which hangs around it be not removed, will give the average of two undetected murders per annum.[168]

The *Morning Chronicle* also criticized the inquest:

In defence of the conduct of the inquest, we see it argued in the *Globe* that the business of the inquests is confined to the question how the deceased was destroyed, whether by his own hand or that of another. Does the *Globe* thus mean to say, that inquests, in finding verdicts of wilful murder against individuals, have exceeded their functions? And further, how are verdicts of manslaughter and justifiable homicide arrived at but by as searching an investigation of all the circumstances as a criminal court could effect! Moreover, in the cause of death, the agency is generally so involved that it is impossible, were it desirable, to separate the one from the other. What other opportunity than that of a coroner's inquest is there for obtaining evidence, and clues to guilt, in cases in which suspicion is not strong enough to justify a charge against anyone, and an examination of him by the magistracy?

Coroners are not the functionaries they ought to be, but their juries, with occasional exceptions, bring to the investigation intellects sharpened by the intense interest they feel in the detection of a great crime. With all the faults of coroners' inquests – and the faults lie for the most part with the president, as apathetic as the juries are earnest (the business being the trade of the coroner, and generally a new and exciting duty to the juror) – many murders would have been undiscovered but for the active and searching inquiries of coroners' inquests.[169]

The *Examiner* too was scathing about the conduct of the coroner's inquest:

if its object had been to avoid the discovery of the assassin, its proceedings would have been most skillfully conducted for the purpose. Questions the most necessary were unasked, and no attempt was made to clear up discrepancies in the evidence; indeed, though glaring enough, they seemed to escape notice.

'Mancel' had said there was no cloth over Russell's face; Courvoisier and Inspector Tedman said there was and Mancer was not cross-examined on this point. Mancer had not been asked if she and Courvoisier had rapped at the door before entering Russell's bedroom; Courvoisier had not been asked why he went straight to the window and not his master's bed. Worse still, when questioned about a chisel in his possession the deputy coroner had intervened to tell Courvoisier any answer he provided would be taken down. 'Was this inquest – was this inquiry? A witness, not a prisoner accused, was before the Coroner, and the business of the Court was to obtain from him the fullest disclosure, and not to close his lips …' No inquiry had been made as to where in the house the murderer might have washed his bloody hands, or the state of the towels. Carr had not been detained:

> It might be quite right not to detain the man on suspicion, but the search of his lodgings was a step due both to his character and to public justice, and this was *not* done. One of the medical witnesses had been so careless in his examination of Russell's body that he missed the wound on the thumb. This inadvertence was 'curious in connection with such a tissue of imperfect investigation.[170]

The Russell murder would continue to be invoked in criticism of the way in which inquests were conducted in subsequent years. Thomas Wakley argued in 1843 that the coroner's court should not always be open, nor its proceedings always publicized. Russell's inquest had been open and Courvoisier not yet apprehended. The murderer thus 'had the means of ascertaining all that transpired and of taking his measures accordingly'. The murderer of Westwood, Wakley claimed, had similarly benefitted from hearing the evidence presented at the inquest, which 'taught him how he might escape'. Only when an accused was in custody should open proceedings take place and 'respectable and real reporters' be allowed to attend.[171]

Between the inquest's verdict of wilful murder and Courvoisier's trial attention naturally focused on the activities of the police. The press at first applauded police efforts: 'Mr Beresford is most unremitting in his exertions, and several policemen were in readiness to proceed against any supposed party', reported *The Times* the day after the murder had been announced.[172] But praise soon turned to anxiety, impatience, and censure. The following day *The Times* commented,

> Of the activity, zeal, and intelligence of the new police as a body there can be no doubt; and as far those qualities can be exerted, we are sure they will be in the present instance. It would be frightful, indeed, to suppose that from any defect in the system of police as at present constituted, however admirable it works in other respects, they should be found unequal to the duty of bringing offenders to justice stained with the most atrocious crime that can disgrace a civilized community. We hope and trust that constables the most experienced in the whole force may be selected on the present occasion, so that the cold-blooded murderer of a kind-hearted and unoffending nobleman may be brought to sure and speedy justice.[173]

94   *Inspectors Call*

By the 9th, the paper was exasperated by the search of the house:

> The workmen have not as yet finished their search, but it appears very surprising that both the pantry and watercloset should not have undergone a minute and strict examination before yesterday, and we cannot but feel that such a delay on the part of the police implies a want of tact and foresight of which experienced constables would never have been guilty in prosecuting an inquiry of this important description.[174]

The *Morning Chronicle* had also become fretful:

> Throughout the proceedings in this horrible case the search for clues has been wanting, and clues will never be found unless they are sought for with the minutest attention. Many circumstances, slight and insignificant in themselves, must be investigated in order to get on the traces of crime. Indeed, much that does not bear upon the crime must, in many cases, be inquired into to get at what does bear on the crime. Many crimes enveloped in the deepest mystery have been brought to light by investigations: proceeding on the principle of attaching importance to every fact and circumstance, including the most minute and apparently insignificant, but widely different from such inquiries has been the conduct of recent investigations. It seems to us that the fear of raising suspicions against persons who may be innocent is carried to an extreme incompatible with that vigorous pursuit of the truth.[175]

The Metropolitan Police, like the coroner and his jury, would thus work under increasingly critical public scrutiny. The public interest owed in part to the fact that the murder victim was a member of the Russell family, but timing was also an issue. The press and the public wanted and expected quick results; when an arrest was not immediately forthcoming, they were quick themselves with criticism of the new police. The *Southern Star*, a Chartist newspaper, drew attention to two of the previous unsolved murder cases in the same vicinity and commented,

> Here are three diabolical crimes, the perpetrators of which are undetected, while the public pay enormous sums for the support of a police for their protection. There must be something wrong in the system of police, or surely murderers could not thus evade justice. We know that in France, the case would be different; and the opinion is gaining ground, that under the old system of police, the perpetrators of such horrible crimes would not have remained so long undiscovered. The confidence of the public in the police is shaken ... [T]he police must display more activity than they have yet done; and the government must see that a more intelligent and searching spirit pervades the force. ... It is impossible to remove the

impression that had the police been possessed of proper intelligence, and proper spirit, the murderers of Westwood and Templeman would, long ago, have been taken. The government must look to this. The public pays heavily for the protection of the police, and ought to be protected.[176]

'To the disgrace of those who have the control of the executive in our criminal laws', wrote *The Town* a week later,

> *this* murder makes the *fifth*, within a short period of time, which the *sagacity* of the police has failed to discover the authors of. That it were otherwise would be the wonder of all men acquainted with the characters, the habits, and the superlative stupidity and ignorance of the new force, who, in the *main*, are raw Irishmen or yokels, who hardly know the statistic difference between Aldgate pump and Hyde-park corner. When a murder happens, these blundering fellows swarm about the spot like an army of locusts, and, by their misplaced alacrity, prompted by interest, and uncontrolled by one scintillation of judgment or discretion, defeat the very object they seek to accomplish, viz., the discovery of the murderer! Any man of common intelligence, however ignorant he might be of police matters, WOULD HAVE HAD NOT THE SLIGHTEST DIFFICULTY in fixing the murder upon the assassins of Eliza Grimwood, Westwood, Templeman, and Lord William Russell, provided his energies had not been encumbered or clogged by the stupid interference of a set of meddlers, calling themselves inspectors, sergeants, or whatever other title designates this new force of ignoramuses. Could it, we ask, have been possible that, in the days of Ruthven, Ballard, Keys, Jem Smith, Goddard, Ledbitter, Shackell, Plank, and other members of the *old force*, such assassinations as those to which we have referred would have remained in the disgraceful state of mystery which now characterize them? The members of the old police made their avocation as much a *study* as professional men do in other walks of life; they mixed with the world in all its varied forms, features and aspects; their experience taught them to trace the springs of motive and of purpose up to the developments in the *overt* act ...[177]

Bow Street's study of and mixing with London's underworld had by the time of the Runners' demise been the subject of considerable government and public unease: now, it was missed. Of the individual Runners named by the paper Ballard, Goddard, Keys, and Shackell had been employed from the mid-1830s, in the last of that force's final years. Ruthven had served from 1818 to 1839, James John ('Jem') Smith from 1821 to 1839. Some of the men cited retired when Bow Street was disbanded. Ballard, Goddard and Keys accepted pensions of £100 each; Ruthven's long service and reputation won him the larger sum of £230.[178] But during their coexistence Bow Street and the Metropolitan

Police had not merely run in parallel lines: a not unsurprising overlap is easily discernible. Shackell had actually begun his policing career as a sergeant with the Met, one of three of its officers transferred to Bow Street in the 1830s. He returned to the Metropolitan Police as an inspector when Bow Street was disbanded, an indication, as John Beattie has argued, of the esteem in which his abilities were held.[179]

A pamphlet titled *Remarks on the Recent Murders in London* raised similar concerns with the performance of the new police, albeit much more politely, and like the *Town* article lamented the passing of Bow Street. The author noted that only one of the perpetrators, James Greenacre, the murderer of Hannah Brown, had been brought to justice and bemoaned the fact that credit for the discovery of Greenacre's identity lay with the victim's brother and friends and the offer of a reward rather than the police investigation. It was far from the author's

> intention to seek to cast any slur on the new Police. We are unwilling to do so for two reasons: in the first place, because we think very highly of their services in general; and in the second place, because we should think it very unjust and very unwise to sap that opinion of safety through their protection universally entertained by the public. The services which they have rendered both to person and to property since their full establishment, are incalculable and above all praise …

Yet he or she concluded regretfully 'that the languor on the part of the Police in this case looks very bad for the public safety, and must have been encouraging to the class of murderers'. The efficiency of the Met's officers in patrolling the streets, the author suggested in a rather novel interpretation of the effects of the new police, had driven criminals into its houses, 'in the same manner as a disease which, at first rested on the skin, may have been driven into the blood'. It recommended locking internal doors at night as a precautionary measure – and this might in fact have saved Russell from the deadly attack.

Press grumbling continued.

> The investigation of the murder of Lord William Russell has proceeded as it commenced … it appears a miracle that anything has been found out. With the means at disposal, the whole house might have been picked to pieces in twenty-four hours; but instead of any such hasty doings, after some days the money and trinkets were found, and after some more days, the watch.

The discovery of the watch, said *The Examiner*, exemplified 'the whole tenor of the search'. It had been found in the sink removed from the pantry and thrown into the yard; there it eventually attracted the attention of a sergeant from the C Division who prised the watch from where it had been wedged between lead and wooden frame. Until that point, the police had been using the four-legged sink as a stool. 'The sergeant of the C Division', wrote *The Examiner* with considerable exasperation,

> had found the watch because he did what no one else had thought of doing – searched, and searched thoroughly ... The sink should hereafter be the judgement seat of the Magistrate, whose parts are so aptly represented by its wood and its lead. As a sink for facts it typifies the genius of the procedure in this remarkable case ... No one discovery has resulted from the directions of the Magistrates, or the Chief of Police. For all that has been discovered hitherto we have to thank the acuteness of the inferior officers and the chapter of accidents.[180]

An editorial published in *The Times*, by contrast, criticized not the lack of progress in discovering Russell's murderer, but the resources devoted and attention paid to that crime compared to the earlier murders. 'One of the most glorious characteristics of our British jurisprudence, whether civil or criminal', it asserted solemnly,

> is its perfect impartiality ... the rich and the poor, without distinction, are equally amenable to its authority, and equally entitled to its protection ... the entire administrative *corps* of the country, comprising magistrates, judges, and the responsible advisors of the Royal prerogative, are solemnly sworn ... to measure out equal justice to all ranks of men; to show no favouritism for one class more than for another; and to maintain just as sacred a regard for the life and property of the poor as for those of the opulent and the great.

This impartiality, the (Tory) paper claimed, had been disregarded by the 'Whig Ministry'. It charged Melbourne's government with

> having shown a *most shameful respect of persons* in regard to the comparative value of the lives of HER MAJESTY's subjects, and to the absolute indifference wherewith the Government contemplate the murder of a man in humble life, as contrasted with that of a noble partisan of their own. A marked distinction in favour of birth or rank in such a sacred matter as this is offensive and revolting in the extreme. The blood of one assassinated Englishman, in the eyes of the state, is just as precious, and just as much to be avenged, as the blood of another; but the Whigs, ever the most fawning parasites in existence, have given evidence to the whole country that, in their opinion, the lives of all classes of her Majesty's subjects are by no means equally valuable, nor entitled to equal protection; nay, that if murderers will only content themselves with cutting the throats of common people, there need be no great fuss about the matter.
> Upwards of six weeks ago, an obscure individual named TEMPLEMAN was barbarously butchered ... In the case of *poor*

TEMPLEMAN, however, the non-discovery of whose assassins must impart proportionable insecurity to all persons of his comparatively defenceless class, HER MAJESTY'S Government did not think it worth while to offer a single penny of reward for the conviction or apprehension of the principal murderer.

The 'tardy' reward in the Templeman case subsequently posted in the *Gazette*, the paper argued, 'would never have been heard of, unless the melancholy fate of a Liberal nobleman had absolutely shamed the Government into a tardy notice of it ...'[181]

Conclusion

The Russell murder investigation was in many ways exceptional, and the resources devoted to it bear out *The Times*'s indignant assertion that greater value was accorded to Russell's life than to the lives of more ordinary victims. One of the two Metropolitan police commissioners assumed command of the investigation, replacing the divisional head; an undersecretary from the Home Office visited the house on a regular basis and, as described in the next chapter, involved himself in the preparation of the brief for the prosecution. But this case also reveals issues common across all such investigations in this era. One is new public expectations. As late as 1811, the year of the infamous Ratcliffe Highway murders, the future Earl of Dudley had argued passionately that he would rather such murders took place on a regular basis than submit to a French system of policing. In a matter of decades the public had accepted a uniformed police force, albeit only in London, and expected that force to identify, apprehend, and bring to justice not only robbers but murderers. Throughout the Russell investigation the Met's officers were subjected to a form of 'trial by newspaper', their efforts condemned and disparaged on an almost daily basis. But in their attempts to uncover conclusive evidence incriminating their prime suspect, in this murder case as in any other, these amateur detectives were severely handicapped by the lack of forensic procedures and techniques we now take for granted. That the crime scene was contaminated by extensive, promiscuous, public access was less significant at a time when both fingerprint and DNA evidence lay far in the future. The 'scientific persons', as barrister John Adolphus would term them at trial, brought in to inspect Courvoisier's attempts to simulate a break-in were ordinary workmen, not scene of the crime officers. It is difficult, in fact, to see how Belton Cobb could describe the Courvoisier investigation as revealing 'an immense advance in methods of detection'.[182] There was no such advance; the police, for example, literally took Russell's house apart in failed efforts to find a murder weapon that had been hidden in plain sight.

Convictions in high-profile murder trials had in the past occasionally been secured on the basis of circumstantial evidence: this was true in *Aram* (1759,) *Patch* (1806), and *Thurtell* (1824). But reliance on such evidence was risky, and in the Russell investigation the police were clearly desperate to avoid it. Their denials notwithstanding, the only physical evidence seemingly linking Courvoisier with Russell's murder appears to have been planted, and at the 11th hour. This possibility is not referenced or discussed in Hobler's scrapbook. His lack of commentary on the highly suspect bloodied items found on the final (fourth and fifth) searches of Courvoisier's possessions is diplomatic and hardly surprising: Hobler was the police prosecutor and unlikely to bite the hand that fed him. At trial, the defence would suggest that the officers involved had been motivated by the prospect of financial reward. This is possible but unlikely: the reward was divided among many. The planted items are better read as an attempt to incriminate a suspect who the police, working under intense public scrutiny and pressure, believed to be guilty. The late discovery of items of bloodied clothing, however, almost backfired. As we will see in the next chapter, the prosecution team virtually – and wisely – ignored this 'evidence' in arguing their case, which still gave Courvoisier's counsel the opportunity to accuse the police of corruption.

Planting evidence was a serious error in judgment. But in terms of investigative techniques, the police might legitimately be criticized for carelessness in intelligence gathering. Here, in my view, lies their true failure. Courvoisier, like Mancer, spent some time at a hotel when between places, in his instance the Hotel de Dieppe, in the Leicester Square area, and while employed by Russell he deposited there a brown paper parcel containing readily identifiable stolen silverware. Had the police been more diligent in their enquiries, the valet could conclusively have been tied to theft and confronted with the evidence that would prompt a confession of guilt before the trial opened. Hobler noted, somewhat defensively, beside *The Times*'s report of the second day of the trial,

> In the course of the Inquiries that were made during the time I was occupied at the house of Lord William taking Examinations Inspector Beresford & I frequently conversed on the subject of foreign Hotels or Hotels frequented by foreigners and the necessity of Inquiry being made among them & Inspector Beresford visited 3 or 4 houses in Leicester place & Square but it so happens he did not visit Madame Piolaines & thus it was unknown – but even if he had as the name of Courvoisier was not known to her, but only that of Jean it is not all improbable that she might not have recollected and thus even then it might escape his Search [.][183]

Public criticism of this failure was minimal, but at least one paper commented, 'It is a matter of surprise to those well acquainted with matters of police, that no inquiries were instituted at the several foreign hotels and coffee-houses in London with respect to Courvoisier'.[184] Given the lack of such enquiry, when the case, resting precariously on circumstantial and suspect evidence, came to trial at the Old Bailey there was every possibility that Courvoisier would be acquitted. The police had failed.

Notes

1. These details were first reported in Mancer's initial examination at the house and would be repeated at the pre-trial hearings and trial itself. See Item 12 (seq. 61–74); *The Times*, 7 and 12 May, 19 June 1840; OBP t18400615-1629.
2. HLS MS 4487, Items 71 (seq. 288), statement of Emanuel Young, 9 May 1840; 39 (seq. 154), statement of Henry Lake, 13 May 1840.
3. Item 60 (seq. 232–34), statements of Slade and Glew, 20 May 1840. Baker had sent them to Hobler for examination. Item 60 (seq. 232), memo, n.d.
4. Item 60 (seq. 211–17), statements of Baldwin and Rose, 18 May 1840.
5. Item 60 (seq. 219), statement of Tedman, 20 May 1840.
6. Item 167 (seq. 580). Draft, n.d.
7. Item 60 (seq. 214), statement of Baldwin, 18 May 1840.
8. MEPO 3/42 1839;7/1; 21/3 1855.
9. *The First English Detectives*, 261.
10. Critchley and James, *The Maul and the Pear Tree*, 33–4.
11. In the twenty-first century, Constable Horton would become the hero of Lloyd Shepherd's series of historical thrillers: *The English Monster* (2012), *Poisoned Island* (2013), *Savage Magic* (2015), and *The Detective and the Devil* (2016). The first of these gives Horton a primary role in the Ratcliffe murders investigation.
12. *The Trial of Richard Patch for the wilful murder of Isaac Blight*; Graham's examination of Patch is reproduced at 132–43.
13. Critchley and James, *The Maul and the Pear Tree*, 86, 92.
14. *Committee on the Police of the Metropolis* (1834), 21–2.
15. *ODNB*. Called to the bar in 1822, Mayne had practised on the Northern circuit for seven years prior to applying to Home Secretary Peel for the position of one of two commissioners for the new Metropolitan Police. He accepted without an interview. On Mayne and the new police see Cobb, *The First Detectives*, Smith, *Policing Victorian London*, and Palmer, *Police and protest in England and Ireland*.
16. Beattie, *The First English Detectives*, 260.
17. Beattie, *The First English Detectives*, 261.
18. *Report from the Select Committee on the Office of Coroner for Middlesex*, Appendix 1, 10.
19. *Report from the Select Committee on the Office of Coroner for Middlesex*, Appendix 1, 10.
20. See Burney, *Bodies of Evidence*, and Fisher, 'The Politics of Sudden Death'.
21. For Wakley (1795–1862), see Sprigge, *Life and Times of Thomas Wakley*, Brook, *Thomas Wakley*, Sherrington, 'Thomas Wakley and Reform', Burney, *Bodies of Evidence*, and Fisher, 'The Politics of Sudden Death'.
22. See also Fisher, 'The Politics of Sudden Death', chap. 4. Burney, in *Bodies of Evidence*, casts this struggle in different terms, highlighting an alignment between political radicalism and the medicalization of the inquest, and viewing its nineteenth-century development as 'forged out of a powerful, persistent, and often unstable confluence of the ostensibly divergent historical narratives of participatory democratic politics and medical expertise' (20). The issue of legal expertise is not addressed, and the relationship between the coroner's inquest and the new police falls outside the scope of Burney's book.
23. Eliot, *Middlemarch*, 186.
24. *The Times*, 15 Feb. 1839.
25. *The Times*, 21 Feb. 1839.
26. *The Times*, 26 Feb. 1839.
27. *The Times*, 27 Feb. 1839.
28. See Sim and Ward, 'The Magistrate of the Poor?'.
29. For Higgs, who committed suicide in 1857, see the *Annual Register* vol. 99 (1858), 7.

30 *Report from the Select Committee on the Office of Coroner for Middlesex*, 27 July 1840.
31 Hobler included copies of the evidence sworn under oath during the inquest. Item 10 (seq. 46) Henry Elsgood; (seq. 47) John Nussey; (seq. 47–9) Sarah Mancer; (seq. 49–51) John Tedman; (seq. 51–2) Henry Beresford; (seq. 52–3) Mary Hannell; (seq. 53–4) François Benjamin Courvoisier. At the end of this record, after noting the verdict, he wrote, 'The above is a true copy'. See also *The Times*'s coverage, 7 May 1840.
32 Item 6 (seq. 36–40), the first statements taken at 14 Norfolk Street, 6 May 1840.
33 Item 60 (seq. 217), statement of John Tedman, 20 May 1840.
34 Item 21 (seq. 107–9), statement of Emanuel Young, 9 May 1840.
35 The *Morning Chronicle* commented on female interest in the house on 11 May.
36 *Morning Chronicle*, 21 May 1841.
37 *Morning Chronicle*, 15 May 1840.
38 Cutler's occupation was identified in the *Southern Star* (5 July 1840) as 'country magistrate'; presumably he is the Devon magistrate of that name. His manservant Selway said his master was 'a good deal out of town'. Item 42 (seq. 161), 15 May 1840.
39 Item 59 (seq. 209–11 at 211), deposition, n.d.
40 Item 42 (seq. 167), statement of Thomas Selway, 15 May 1840.
41 Item 42 (seq. 168), Selway; Item 43 (seq. 167), statement of Penelope Wilkinson Cook, 15 May 1840.
42 Item 42 (seq. 161–63), statement 15 May; Item 71 (seq. 281–84), deposition. Cutler was anxious about his servant being called, and wrote to Hobler asking if the police request had been made and if so when Selway should arrive at Bow Street. He hoped Selway would be called early and swiftly released. Item 44 (seq. 164–66). On 9 June he wrote solicitor Thomas Wing to outline his servant's previous employment history and establish his good character, 'understanding the respectability of the Witnesses summoned for the impending trial, is likely to be questioned'. Item 170 (seq. 587–89). In another letter (13 June), with the Old Bailey trial approaching, he appeared equally anxious: 'I shall be much obliged if you direct that no unnecessary attendance or waste of time shall take place'. He was however 'aware of the importance of a witness being prepared, and I will guarantee his presence when it may be necessary for the ends of justice'. Item 179 (seq. 611–13).
43 Item 39 (seq. 154).
44 Item 39 (seq. 152–53).
45 Cobb, *The First Detectives*, 166. Cobb's text is unfortunately unreferenced and I have been unable to locate the list itself.
46 Item 68 (seq. 253–55). Undated witness statements.
47 Item 68 (seq. 253–54), witness statement, n.d.
48 Item 12 (seq. 74), Hobler's itemized list.
49 Item 13 (seq. 75–6), deposition of Lady Sarah Bayley, n.d.; Item 61, examinations taken at Hoare's in Fleet Street, 21 May: Thomas Wing and Richard Harrison.
50 Item 74 (seq. 327–28), copy of deposition for the prosecution, Nicholas Pearce, n.d.
51 Item 60 (seq. 220), statement of John Tedman, 20 May 1840.
52 Item 74 (seq. 329), copy of deposition for the prosecution, George Collier, n.d.
53 Select Committee on Metropolis Police Office, *PP* 1837–38, vol. 15, 304.
54 Item 74 (seq. 325–28), copy of Pearce's deposition for the prosecution, n.d.
55 Item 13 (seq. 75), statement of Lady Sarah Bayley, n.d.
56 Item18 (seq. 85), statement of James Ellis, 9 May 1840.
57 Item 68 (seq. 254).
58 *Household Words*, 13 July 1850.

102 *Inspectors Call*

59 Item 74, copies of depositions for the prosecution (Pearce, Collier, Shaw) (seq. 327–30); Battin's witness statement, Item 68 (seq. 253–54).
60 Item 77 (seq. 336–38), copy of Cronin's deposition for the prosecution.
61 Item 18 (seq. 88), statement, 9 May 1840.
62 Item 33 (seq. 129), business card with Hobler's note, n.d.
63 9 May 1840.
64 Item 67 (seq. 249–50), Beresford's statement, 21 May 1840.
65 Item 21 (seq. 101).
66 Claire Harman's study of the Russell murder ends, very oddly to my mind, with a paragraph devoted to Carr, saying he 'seemed to have got away, or disappeared'. Repeating *The Times*'s report of a woman who had met him in a pub, the final sentence of the book reads, 'He was expecting his fortunes to turn very shortly, he told her, and was about to leave this country for Australia'. *Murder by the Book*, 170.
67 MEPO 3/44, 17 May 1840 – C Division Inspector's Report (DSC01688).
68 Item 10 (seq. 51).
69 Item 60 (seq. 228–29), statement of John Tedman, 20 May 1840.
70 Item 60 (seq. 230).
71 Item 74 (seq. 329), copy of Collier's deposition for the prosecution, n.d. He makes no mention of his participation in the 11 May search which had not discovered the items in question.
72 *The Conscience of a Lawyer*, 35.
73 MEPO 3/44 (DSC 01763).
74 Item 71 (seq. 287), copy of deposition for the prosecution, n.d.
75 Item 17 (seq. 81), statement, 18 May 1840.
76 MEPO 3/44 (DSC 01766).
77 *The Conscience of a Lawyer*, 209.
78 MEPO 3/44 (DSC01728).
79 See Chapter 7 below, 215.
80 *The Era*, 31 May 1840.
81 Wentworth, *Pilgrim's Rest*, 142.
82 Item 60 (seq. 214).
83 Item 60 (seq. 212).
84 Item 10 (seq. 48, 51), copies of informations taken at the inquest.
85 Item 60 (seq. 227).
86 Item 169 (seq. 584–86).
87 Item 13 (seq. 79), statement of Sarah Mancer, 13 May 1840.
88 Item 171 (seq. 590–92).
89 Item 79 (seq. 352).
90 *The Times*, 15 June 1840.
91 Item 79 (seq. 352).
92 Item 146 (seq. 517–19).
93 Item 168 (seq. 581–83).
94 Item 52 (seq. 191–92).
95 Item 149 (seq. 526–28).
96 *Morning Chronicle*, 28 May 1840.
97 Item 134 (seq. 482–84). For Matthew Maurice George Dowling's career – which began in the navy under Nelson and included a brief stint in London's Metropolitan Police before he was appointed to Liverpool in 1833 – see his obituary, *Liverpool Mercury*, 22 Nov. 1853.
98 14 June 1840.
99 Item 52 (seq. 190).
100 Item 52 (seq. 191–92).

101 See Barham, *The Life and Remains of Theodore Edward Hook*, Dunn, *The Man who was John Bull*, and the *ODNB*.
102 Hobler wrote of this claim, 'As to the groans supposed to be heard in the next house, Mr Traill of Union Hall got hold of the same story & to be able to decide on the point Inspector Pearce went into the bedroom of Lady Elphinstone [at no. 13] who was said to have heard the groans and Inspector Beresford and myself remained in Lord William's room wch is only separated by the party wall & we found it impossible a voice could be heard unless either by a loud scream or a loud calling – no truth in this report – '[.] Item 53 (seq. 192), n.d.
103 Item 53 (seq. 192–96).
104 Item 53 (seq. 192).
105 Item 145 (seq. 514–16).
106 Item 165 (seq. 576).
107 Item 178 (seq. 608).
108 Greville, *Memoirs*, 4:293. For Tothill Fields see below at 138n39.
109 14 June 1840.
110 Item 154 (seq. 541–45).
111 Item 157 (seq. 554), 29 May 1840.
112 Item 125 (seq. 453–55), 10 May 1840.
113 Item 126 (seq. 456), 11 May 1840.
114 Item 135 (seq. 485), 19 May 1840.
115 Russell forwarded this letter to Beresford. Item 176 (seq. 603–5), n.d.
116 Item 147 (seq. 520), 12 May 1840.
117 Item 63 (seq. 240), n.d.
118 Items 138 (seq. 494–95), 1 June 1840; 139 (seq. 498), n.d.
119 Item 22 (seq. 112–13). The body had already been opened.
120 *Morning Chronicle*, 1 June 1840.
121 Item 127 (seq. 459); Item 155 (seq. 548).
122 Item 46 (seq. 177).
123 Item 55 (seq. 197–98) (n.d.). The same suggestion is found in an undated letter to Mayne (Item 140 (seq. 500)), in a letter from John Wilks dated 25 May (Item 150 (seq. 529)), in letters to Hobler from 'G.D.', 26 May (Item 151 (seq. 532–34) and 'P.G.', 30 May (Item 159 (seq. 559)), and in an unsigned letter of 30 May (Item 164 (seq. 574)).
124 Item 54 (seq. 196).
125 Item 68 (seq. 238–39), n.d.
126 Item 128 (seq. 462–66), 14 May 1840. Edwards wrote again on 17 June after the Bow Street examinations to raise issues about the messages Courvoisier had been charged with on the day of the murder. See Item 185 (seq. 631–33).
127 Item 142 (seq. 505), 16 May 1840.
128 Item 161 (seq. 564).
129 For Holmes's Baker Street Irregulars see *A Study in Scarlet* (1887), *The Sign of the Four* (1890), and 'The Adventure of the Crooked Man' (1893).
130 Item 152 (seq. 536), 26 May 1840.
131 The discovery of the rust spot was reported in *The Times*, 22 June 1840.
132 Item 167 (seq. 580).
133 Item 72 (seq. 318).
134 Item 72 (seq. 321).
135 Item 18 (seq. 88). The date of Hobler's note is not recorded.
136 Item 3, n.d. (seq. 12).
137 Item 99 (seq. 397), n.d.; written below pasted-in newspaper coverage of Courvoisier's confessions.
138 *The Times*, 14 May 1840.

104 *Inspectors Call*

139 Item 66 (seq. 246–47), 21 May 1840.
140 Item 75 (seq. 331) (n.d.). A washerwoman named Lettice Banks gave evidence about Courvoisier's socks at trial. OBP t18400615-1629.
141 Item 38 (seq. 147–49), 15 May. She also suggested searching the fireplace, water closet, and stableyard for the murder weapon. Once the trial had opened, Mr Powell wrote to prosecuting barrister John Adolphus to suggest that the missing weapon might be found up the chimney in either Russell or Courvoisier's room or in a bend in the pipe of a water closet. Item 187 (seq. 637–39).
142 Item 23 (seq. 113–14, 119).
143 Item 132 (seq. 476); Item 161 (seq. 563).
144 Item 60 (seq. 562, 565–66); Item 162 (seq. 567–69).
145 Item 175 (seq. 600).
146 Item 177 (seq. 606).
147 Item 173 (seq. 596–98).
148 MEPO 3/44, Courvoisier's confession, 22 June 1840 (DSC 01753).
149 Item 65 (seq. 243), n.d.
150 Item 130 (seq. 471).
151 Item 153 (seq. 538–39), n.d.
152 Item 43 (seq. 163), 13 May 1840.
153 Item 174 (seq. 598–99), n.d. and unsigned. The author also suggested that Courvoisier be told to try the blood-spotted gloves on it court to see that they fit.
154 Item 21 (seq. 105–7), 9 May 1840.
155 Item 131 (seq. 473–75).
156 Item 182 (seq. 619–24).
157 *The Era*, 10 May 1840.
158 Item 40 (seq. 156).
159 Item 40 (seq. 155–56).
160 Item 133 (seq. 479–81).
161 Item 72 (seq. 318). Letter to Hobler, 1 June 1840.
162 For an introduction to this history, see http://www.academia.edu/5908317/A_History_of_Fingerprints.
163 An Argentine police officer, Juan Vucetich, used fingerprint identification in 1892 to catch a woman who had murdered her two sons via a bloody print left on a doorpost. In England in the same year anthropologist, geneticist, and eugenicist Sir Francis Galton published a study of the science of fingerprinting.
164 At this point, the technique was to be complementary to a system of identification via body measurements devised by French policeman Alphonse Bertillon, known as anthropometry.
165 *R. v. Harry Jackson*, OBP t19020909-686; *R. v. Alfred and Albert Stratton*, OBP t19050502-417.
166 *The Times*, 14 May 1840.
167 *Awful confession of Greenacre to the murder of Hannah Brown*.
168 *The Courier*, 8 May 1840, reprinted in *The Era*, 10 May 1840.
169 *Morning Chronicle*, 11 May 1840.
170 10 May 1840.
171 *The Times*, 8 Nov. 1843.
172 7 May 1840.
173 8 May 1840.
174 *The Times*, 9 May 1840.
175 11 May 1840.
176 17 May 1840.
177 23 May 1840.

178 On these men see Beattie, *The First English Detectives*, 179, 218, 222, 254, 257, and 258. See also Cox, *A Certain Share of Low Cunning*.
179 Beattie, *The First English Detectives*, 258.
180 *Examiner*, 17 May 1840.
181 12 May 1840.
182 Cobb, *The First Detectives*, 169.
183 Item 91 (seq. 381).
184 *Southern Star*, 28 June 1840.

4 The Case for the Prosecution Rests … with Francis Hobler

Introduction

William Russell's murder became a cause célèbre from the time it was discovered, and as described in the previous chapter a critical, highly opinionated public had closely followed and commented on events from the initial report of the murder through the inquest, police investigation, and the pre-trial hearings. When Courvoisier's Old Bailey trial came on, new concerns would arise. That the post-trial revelation of the valet's mid-trial confession of guilt, and barrister Charles Phillips's decision to continue in his client's defence, caused as much public uproar as the crime itself is entirely understandable. Those responsible for passing the Prisoner's Counsel Act four years earlier had been motivated by a desire to protect innocence by allowing defence counsel to speak in place of the accused. The implications of the new legislation for the conduct of the defence of guilty persons had not been considered. When academics turned their attention to Courvoisier's trial, the focus was similarly on the case made for the defence and the role played by this trial in the professional elaboration of standards of conduct. The valet's prosecution, by contrast, occasioned little public comment. And until recently, apart from the fact that Francis Hobler's appearances in the pre-trial hearings at Bow Street were covered by the press, the mechanics involved in assembling the case for the prosecution have largely been hidden from sight. Details regarding how John Adolphus was briefed, or how the case he presented was constructed, have only come to light in Hobler's scrapbook. The statements the solicitor took down as the police questioned witnesses, and the depositions he later copied, are marked, usually in red ink, in preparation for the brief he wrote, with the first person changed to 'the witness', information not deemed relevant struck through with a diagonal line, and so forth. Queries and notes regarding leads to be followed up are scribbled in pencil in the margins; passages of interest sometimes have a long X beside them; sentences are underlined. On the basis of police interviews and evidence sworn to on oath at the coroner's inquest and at Bow Street Hobler drew up and edited lists of witnesses to be called at Courvoisier's Old Bailey trial. He worked on a daily basis with Police Commissioner Mayne, and under the supervision of the Home Office. The

DOI: 10.4324/9781003481638-4

notes Adolphus made for his opening speech, and the lines of questioning he pursued in the courtroom, reflect the solicitor's weeks of labour.

'Publick prosecutions'

How did Francis Hobler come to be employed in the prosecution of Courvoisier? At the time of William Russell's murder criminal prosecutions technically remained in private hands: there was as yet no official public prosecutor. The attorney general, appointed from the practising bar, served as legal adviser to the government of the day and while the bulk of his work concerned civil matters he also led for the Crown in state trials. The Treasury Solicitor played a role as well, with responsibility for preparing prosecutions and briefing counsel in trials of treason and sedition.[1] Their participation, however, was the exception rather than the rule. In 1824 Thomas Denman, then Common Serjeant in the City of London and a future attorney general and lord chief justice of the Court of King's Bench, had puzzled over the lack of a public prosecutor; a decade later Lord Chancellor Henry Brougham had suggested that Treasury counsel might usefully be employed in preparing and overseeing *all* prosecutions at the Old Bailey. Charles Phillips, whose fame – or infamy – rests largely on his activities as a defence counsel, and ultimately on his defence of Courvoisier, was convinced that in London at least there was a very real need for a public prosecutor. He lobbied Brougham both for a provision to create the position in the Central Criminal Court Act of 1834 and for his personal appointment to such a new role.[2] Entrenched public suspicion of state involvement in prosecution, however, precluded the creation of any formal office. It did become common practice for the Treasury Solicitor to nominate counsel in serious cases. But state prosecution retained its association with the political tyranny experienced under the Stuarts and the Commonwealth in the seventeenth century. A Director of Public Prosecutions was only appointed in 1879 and that office was ineffective.[3] What we would now recognize as formal public prosecution was a twentieth-century development.

In certain cases involving the public interest, however, various government agents had over the centuries quietly become involved in criminal prosecutions. Prior to the Restoration central government intervention was accomplished via the Privy Council and it was usually restricted to cases of treason. After 1660 secretaries of state, in particular, the secretary for the Northern Department, served as a link with local officials including justices of the peace; in the early eighteenth century, two undersecretaries were themselves sworn as magistrates. Again, the cases of interest tended to be political, specifically concerned with threats to the newly established Hanoverian regime. A solicitor to the Treasury had been appointed in 1696 to assist in organizing the prosecution of perceived enemies of the state and government involvement deepened after 1715 in response to fears over attempts to restore the Stuart monarchy. Rioters and those overheard uttering treasonable words, printers and publishers of seditious political pamphlets and the booksellers who sold them, and editors of suspect newspapers were all targeted. There were also prosecutions of smugglers who evaded customs, and protesters such as the Waltham Blacks in 1723, who objected to the loss of customary forest rights. The solicitor for the Treasury paid the costs of conducting these 'Publick Prosecutions'; the attorney-general reviewed the evidence and in some cases conducted the prosecution. 'Entry Books' containing material related to the undersecretaries' prosecution work, which first appeared in the reign of Queen Anne, were retitled 'Criminal Entry Books' when George I came to the throne and recorded an increase in such work. There was admittedly a slight retreat in involvement from 1724, with the attorney general's role eliminated and the government choosing instead to finance such private prosecutors who could be found to inform on their neighbours and fellow subjects. This change in policy, as John Beattie indicates, was significant in that it reaffirmed executive belief in private prosecution. But it also coincided with a broadening of the type of case in which the government would intervene. Beattie cites two cases of violent crime – attempted rape and attempted murder – in 1721, as attracting the attention of the secretary of state in the first instance and George I in the second. The would-be rapist, Arthur Gray, was like Courvoisier a violent servant, one who had broken, armed with a sword and pistol, into the bedroom of his master's daughter. The following year the secretary wrote to the attorney general indicating the king's personal interest in the prosecution of four watermen who had raped and murdered a woman, and murder would again result in prosecution at the government's expense in 1723 and 1726.[4]

Violent crimes as well as treason or sedition had thus begun to attract official concern over a century before the Russell murder. Outside London the Crown became involved in prosecuting violent offences at the request of local magistrates, although such interventions were extremely rare.[5] A similar development can be seen within the narrow confines of the City of London, with the corporation's City Solicitor effectively acting as a public prosecutor in certain cases from the late 1730s. In the first three decades of the nineteenth century he prosecuted an established mix of individuals who had assaulted the City's constables or stolen City property, or kept bawdy houses, but the City Solicitor's remit, like that of the central government, also seems to have expanded. By the late 1840s it included prosecution of habitual offenders, sexual offences, and domestic violence.[6] A case has also been made for a form of public prosecution for minor property crimes: it has recently been argued that from the Middlesex Justices Act of 1792 public officials in London played 'considerable (and considerably underappreciated) roles in prosecuting cases of misdemeanor' and that

> persons suspected of petty theft were, in fact, *routinely* arrested, prosecuted, tried, convicted, and sentenced in ways that dispensed with the involvement of private victims altogether. In many such cases, public officials rather than private victims carried out the essential investigative and forensic tasks of criminal prosecution.[7]

Despite historic reluctance to establish or commit to a formal system of public prosecution, government agencies clearly felt it necessary to act in certain instances. It is equally clear that they did so in a discreet fashion, and originally in the lower courts. As Bruce Smith comments, 'Given the political sensitivity associated with "public" prosecution', it is not surprising that English criminal justice administrators vested prosecutorial power in public officials who toiled in tribunals removed from the glare of the Old Bailey, and in a manner that permitted contemporaries (and later historians) to cling to the illusion of "private" prosecution'.[8] Yet he also points out that in the opening decades of the nineteenth century officers were occasionally found, in the absence of identifiable victims, prosecuting cases of theft involving persons discovered in possession of suspicious goods. Where theft was concerned, successful police prosecutions in the lower courts, Smith suggests, may have encouraged the application of this prosecutorial model to the higher courts.[9]

As John Beattie described, the private initiative of Bow Street magistrates in the eighteenth century played a significant role in enabling the development of this form of public prosecution. The origins of the Bow Street office are well known. Appointed to the commissions of the peace for Middlesex and Westminster in 1729, Thomas De Veil opened his first office in what is now Leicester Square, subsequently moving to Thrift Street, Soho, before settling at Bow Street in Covent Garden in 1739 or 1740. His keen interest in promoting public order soon attracted government attention and the government rewarded De Veil's service financially in a variety of ways, including Treasury grants and a 1738 appointment as inspector-general of exports and imports that provided him with a salary of £500 per annum. Government funding also paid for his clerk. De Veil was knighted in 1744 and by the time of his death two years later he had become metropolitan London's leading magistrate, consulted by and relied upon by secretaries and undersecretaries of state.[10] His successors at Bow Street, Henry and John Fielding, proved equally active prosecutors and the government links were maintained and strengthened, with the brothers receiving more direct support as anxiety grew about violent property crimes in the capital. Henry Fielding was paid a stipend of £400 a year from Secret Service funds when he assumed the office in 1746. Preoccupied with a seeming rising tide of crime and perceived weaknesses in policing Fielding collected a group of officers and persuaded the government to finance their activities. By the early 1750s an equally alarmed central government was looking for solutions to the perceived crime wave; the Duke of Newcastle, as secretary of state, turned to Bow Street and Fielding for advice. When Henry died in 1754 his half-brother John was granted the same personal stipend and funds for policing and prosecution, and the original grant of £200 had been increased to £600 by the 1760s. In 1782 the Northern and Southern departments were replaced by the Foreign and Home Offices; from that time the secretary and undersecretary for the Home Office would work with Bow Street in pursuing criminal prosecutions. These would include murder: Critchley and James suggest that Bow Street magistrate Aaron Graham's involvement in the Ratcliffe Highway investigation of 1811 was probably 'at the request of the Home Secretary', and various police officers reported to the Home Office during that investigation. But there is no evidence that their reports were collated, or of attempts to coordinate their activities.[11] The Home Office would play a much more active role in investigating Russell's murder.

Hobler and Whitehall

We know little of the details of the history of police prosecution before 1850, noted Douglas Hay and Francis Snyder in 1989,[12] and that situation has unfortunately not changed. The opacity is a matter of sources: no records survive of the Bow Street Magistrates Court, nor, with very few exceptions, have those of metropolitan London's police offices in the first half of the nineteenth century.[13] Yet there clearly was a system. In 1840 Hobler had been the 'police solicitor' for some three years. This position predated the Met, originating with Bow Street, but liaison work with the Home Office had always been part of its remit. The precise mechanics of the relationship between that office and Whitehall remain obscure, but by the early nineteenth century the chief clerk of the court was a pivotal figure within it. For almost four decades (1800–37) the incumbent was John Stafford, a barrister of the Inner Temple who began his career as a Crown draughtsman and also served as clerk of the indictments for Middlesex. Stafford's tenure at Bow Street was not without criticism: in 1816 he was examined by the Committee on the State of the Police of the Metropolis – more specifically, by William Russell's son-in-law Henry Grey Bennet – which took issue with the way in which the office was staffed. Stung by what he considered allegations of 'negligence and irregularity' in carrying out his duties, an indignant Stafford defended himself at some length in *The Times*.[14] The 1816 report aside, Stafford's service was valued, and for reasons which echo government concerns from earlier centuries. A biographical notice printed after his death stated that he had been

> frequently consulted by the authorities at the Home-office and during the Spa-fields riots and other occasions of difficulty and danger to the Government which occurred during his long service, he was in constant attendance at Whitehall and Lord Sidmouth attached great value to his advice in all matters connected with criminal justice. Mr. Stafford was also the medium of communication with Whitehall when Sir Robert Peel filled the office of Home Secretary...[15]

Francis Hobler was Stafford's successor, courtesy of William Russell's nephew John. In his scrapbook Hobler explained that

> The Lord John Russell Secretary of State for the Colonies & Nephew of the deceased Nobleman ... kindly when Home Secretary of State directed Police business to be sent to me after the decease of Mr John Stafford of Bow Street now about 3 years back.[16]

Employing a particular solicitor to conduct police prosecutions appears to have become an established practice not just in London but in major provincial towns such as Leeds, Birmingham, and Manchester, among others, although there was considerable local variation in practice.[17] Having successfully applied to Russell for police work on Stafford's death, in 1840 Hobler again put himself forward, volunteering to conduct the prosecution of Courvoisier:

> The murder of this aged and much respected nobleman in the secret and methodic manner in which it was effected created a very extraordinary feeling and sensation of horror throughout the whole Country, most especially in the Metropolis and amongst the nobility & gentry dwelling at the Court end of the Town ...
>
> I felt it my duty immediately that I knew of the murder, to tender my services for its discovery, and I accordingly went & wrote to the Commissioners of Police on the 7th of May & on the 8th they sent for me...[18]

The relationship between the Metropolitan Police and prosecution was comparatively recent, dating to the establishment of that force in 1829, and again the detailed mechanics remain to be uncovered. But it is clear, as Hay and Snyder argue, that while they did not immediately monopolize it, once the new police had been established they 'increasingly took a leading role in prosecuting', especially in serious cases.[19] Precedents for such prosecutions are found in the eighteenth century, when parish constables occasionally prosecuted murderers. They did so in law, however, as private citizens, as would the new police. Although some nineteenth-century reformers recognized that a police force could formally assume the role of public prosecutor, Robert Peel did not even mention the possibility in devising and presenting his plans for the Metropolitan Police in the 1820s: such an innovation would have been deemed constitutionally unacceptable. If 'by 1879 the private prosecutor often wore blue', 'a policeman was, in the eyes of the law, merely another private prosecutor who happened to wear a uniform'.[20]

Like Bow Street magistrates, the new police worked in conjunction with the Home Office where prosecution was concerned. From the time his offer to act in the Courvoisier prosecution was accepted Hobler, 'the solicitor for the police', worked with the assistance of Russell family solicitor Thomas Wing, in close collaboration with Metropolitan Police Commissioner Richard Mayne, and under the supervision of undersecretaries of state. He wrote of his initial involvement,

> I went with Mr Commissioner Mayne to the House of Lord William [on 8 May] and began taking [?] Examinations & remained so engaged till past 12 – that night – this day brought me the honour of the company of Mr Wing the Solicitor of the Duke of Bedford – Lord William, Baroness de Clifford & other members of the Bedford family, I dined with him that day after 7 o'clock at the Gloster Coffee House close by & returned to

my work – I reached home soon after 1 o'clock in the night – this was my first day – I continued at work at the House from day to day beginning usually at 10 in the morning & ending at 11 to 12 at night & sometimes at 10 – & on Sundays I usually either met Mr Wing there or had to make some arrangement for what was to take place in the course of the ensuing week or would be useful or likely to happen – for time was wearing on & the case getting very voluminous could only be brought to a proper conclusion in good time by hard fagging & incessant application[.] So that I never went near my office for the first 3 weeks above one day or afternoon in the week – all my other business neglected & left to do itself.[21]

The Home Office had, like Commissioner Mayne, been physically present from the earliest days of the investigation: Lord Normanby (Constantine Henry Phipps), the home secretary, and Fox Maule, one of the undersecretaries, were among the officials who attended at 14 Norfolk Street.[22] Normanby was shown over the house for an hour on 13 May by Mayne and 'expressed his approbation of the conduct and exertions of the police'.[23]

The Marquess of Normanby's tenure as home secretary was short-lived: he had been transferred from the colonial office in 1839 and would lose the position when the ministry fell in 1841. He was also little thought of: Wellington considered his appointment 'very bad and very foolish'.[24] The undersecretaries would at any rate play a more substantive role in the prosecution of Russell's murderer. A former army officer, Maule had been named after Charles James Fox, a political as well as personal friend of his father, and belonged to the Liberal political establishment of which William Russell had been a member. He acquired the post of undersecretary of state in Melbourne's government in 1835.[25] In preparing the case for the prosecution, however, Hobler's primary contact would be another permanent undersecretary, Samuel March Phillipps. Phillipps, who had been called to the bar of the Inner Temple in 1806 but never practised law, served in the position from 1827 to his retirement in 1848. His testimony before a Select Committee in 1833 revealed unease with the new police. Commenting on the activities of Sergeant William Popay, who in that year had infiltrated the National Political Union and incited its members to violent action, he complained that the Metropolitan Police were employed as spies to monitor political meetings.[26] Phillipps and Commissioner Mayne had also developed personal differences in the 1830s and their working relationship would have been strained.[27]

As described in the previous chapter, Hobler's first task at 14 Norfolk Street was to record Commissioner Mayne's interviews with William Russell's servants and other witnesses. In building a legal case against the valet, he would work from personal conviction:

On my first going to the house I had a full and satisfactory opportunity of observing the valet Courvoisier agst whom my mind had been excited from what I read in the newspaper, and from what I then observed in him & his manner of behaviour & from the places where the property had been secreted & also by a careful consideration of the appearances in Lord William's bedroom of the bed clothes, and of the servants sleeping rooms and also by a minute examination of the female servants Mancer & Hannell & their manner & behaviour I felt satisfactorily confirmed in my own mind & never quitted the conclusion I thus formed that not only was Courvoisier the murderer but that he was the only murderer notwithstanding the unjust aspersions cast publicly on Sarah Mancer.[28]

The pre-trial hearings: Bow Street

Once Courvoisier had been arrested, Hobler's task was to shape the evidence he had recorded in witness statements taken at the house, and that given at the coroner's inquest, into a case for the prosecution sufficient to convince a magistrate that Russell's valet should be sent forward to trial. Six pre-trial hearings would be held at Bow Street, which had survived the policing reforms of the previous decade. With the creation of the Metropolitan Police, Bow Street's continued existence had appeared threatened, and there had been rumours on the death of chief magistrate Sir Richard Birnie in 1832 that the office would be abolished and its functions assumed by the two police commissioners. This did not happen. A new police station opened in that year across the street at numbers 25 and 27, but the old court remained the principal magistrate's office within London. With the passage of the Metropolitan Police Courts Act, 1839 (introduced by William Russell's nephew John), the Bow Street runners were legislated out of existence but the court was not. Under the 1839 Act 'Public Offices' became 'Magistrate's Courts' and Bow Street acquired official status for the first time in its history, formally incorporated into the stipendiary system established in 1792 and given a specific jurisdiction.[29] Thus when, at 12 o'clock on Sunday 10 May Courvoisier, attended by Inspector Pearce and Superintendent Baker, had been removed from Norfolk Street, he was taken to the Bow Street Station House of F Division.

At 2 p.m. the following day Courvoisier, accompanied by Pearce and three constables, was transferred to the court and placed in the dock. Hobler had arrived some 15 minutes earlier; Thomas Flower, a Hatton Garden solicitor who worked in partnership with James Harmer, attended on behalf of the prisoner.[30] Although in the eighteenth century it appears common for barristers to conduct these examinations, by 1840 such work had become the purview of the lower branch of the legal profession.[31] During the pre-trial proceedings, the two solicitors worked very much in the public eye. Hobler made careful record of the dates of the hearings, 11, 14, 22, 23, 27, and 29 May, and *The Times*'s coverage was pasted neatly into his book.[32] By the eighteenth century, magistrates' courts had assumed responsibility for sifting evidence and ensuring there was sufficient to warrant and enable trial rather than simply committing a suspect to jail to await it. The emphasis in pre-trial hearings remained, however, on the case for the prosecution, hence Hobler, not Flower, dominated the hearings that preceded Courvoisier's committal for trial at the Old Bailey. Flower rarely cross-examined the witnesses called by the prosecuting solicitor, although a slight skirmish did take place between the two men at the end of the sixth and final hearing.[33]

Seated on the bench was Bow Street's chief magistrate, Thomas James Hall, who had transferred from Hatton Garden in 1839.[34] Hall 'enjoyed the reputation of being a sound lawyer and an able and impartial administrator of justice'[35]; he was also firmly of the belief that proceedings in the police courts should be open to public scrutiny – but via publication of quarterly abstracts.[36] The public, however, was present in person and in full force during these particular examinations. Courvoisier's midnight transport, conducted with as much secrecy as possible, had been designed to evade crowds, and once at the station, the valet was formally charged in a private room rather than the public charge room. But his removal quickly became public knowledge and by early Monday morning spectators had abandoned the scene of the murder for Bow Street. Police constables struggled to keep the crowds outside in order while inside Hall shared the bench with the Duke of Brunswick and his equerry, Baron Audlan, the earls of Clarendon, Mansfield, and Essex, Sir George Beaumont, and the private secretary to the archbishop of Canterbury, among others.

When the hearing opened Flower told the chief magistrate he had been denied the opportunity to speak with his client and requested permission to retire with him for a short time. Flower 'had been called upon to [appear for the prisoner] on Sunday, and as he was out of town yesterday he had not an opportunity of consulting with him privately'.[37] Permission granted, Courvoisier and his solicitor withdrew briefly.[38] On their return Inspector Pearce took the stand: he was the only witness to testify on that first day. Hobler subsequently informed the magistrate of the reason he had confined himself to the evidence of Inspector Pearce: he had wanted to establish a case of suspicion against Courvoisier sufficient to warrant the valet's detention. Thursday the 14th was established as the date of the next hearing and Courvoisier was handcuffed and, 'strongly guarded', taken to the 'Westminster Bridewell, in Tothill-street', also referred to in the press as 'Tothill-fields prison'.[39] Back at Norfolk Street, the investigation continued. Undersecretary Phillipps had been seen entering the premises at 10 a.m., family solicitor Wing at 11. Phillipps stayed for about an hour and then proceeded directly to the Home Office. Wing was joined by Hobler and Commissioner Mayne once the hearing had been concluded; shortly thereafter Superintendent Baker and Inspector Pearce arrived. Mayne and Wing left the house around 7 p.m.; Baker and Pearce stayed much later.[40]

When the second hearing opened Hobler informed the court that he would begin at the beginning and call the two female servants. Sarah Mancer took the stand first and her examination and cross-examination lasted three and a half hours. Hall clearly found the detail excessive and stopped Hobler at one point to ask whether his course of examination with respect to the minutiae of the day preceding Russell's death 'was intended to lead to some result', for he could not see the relevance of the solicitor's line of questioning. Hobler replied that his 'object was to form a connected chain of facts from first to last' – he was clearly anticipating a case that would rely on circumstantial evidence. Flower declined to cross-examine and Mary Hannell was only briefly examined; she corroborated Mancer's testimony and was likewise released without cross-examination. When Mancer told the court of seeing her master's bloodied face and pillow, she had 'shed tears and appeared much affected' and *The Times* reported that she appeared 'depressed in spirits' as she left the court.[41] Mancer and Hannell returned to Norfolk Street, which remained the operating base for the prosecution. There they would find little peace: wet weather did not prevent crowds from continuing to gather outside the house and 'a great number of the nobility', including Lord Normanby and, less explicably, Lord Jersey and Russell's next-door neighbour Lord Elphinstone were permitted inside to inspect the premises. The press reported the comings and goings of Wing, Hobler, and Commissioner Mayne.[42]

At 10 a.m. on 22 May the court reconvened for a third time. Aristocratic presence continued in full force, with the Earl of Errol, Lord Lowther, Lord Blaney, Lord George and Lord William Lennox, Lord Robert Grosvenor, and Lord George Ponsonby cited in addition to those whose attendance had been noted in previous hearings. Mancer ('Mansell' in *The Times*'s report of the examination) was resworn as a witness and questioned by Hall rather than Hobler. The magistrate was particularly interested in whether she had had any suspicions with regard to Courvoisier's behaviour. Hannell ('Hanwell') was likewise resworn and re-examined by Hall. Thomas Selway, the manservant from no. 15, recounted his involvement and impressions after the discovery of Russell's body. He was cross-examined by Flower, who complained that he would have liked to have pursued his cross-examination at greater length but, having been denied access to the Norfolk Street house, he could not do so. The solicitor was assured by Hobler that he would be given the opportunity 'in sufficient time for his purpose'.[43] He was not. When the Old Bailey trial opened on 15 June Flower had still not been granted access. His clerk, Edward Wolff, sent an aggrieved letter:

> As you must be aware that at this late period any advantage that the prisoner's counsel might have derived from an inspection of the house of the late Lord William Russell will now, from the very short time allowed, be unable to make use of any information which might have been so acquired (permission having been refused of Mr Flower to do so on his application) I have to inform you that Mr Flower declines naming any appointment for inspection of the house in question.[44]

At this third hearing, in contrast to the previous two, a host of witnesses were questioned by both Hobler and Hall. Russell's coachman, William York, and

James Leach, the coachman to Courvoisier's previous employer, Fector, were called, as were Latham's butler Emanuel Young, police constables Baldwin and Rose, Inspector Tedman, and surgeons Elsgood and Nussey. At this third exam, the 'discovery' of bloodied gloves in Courvoisier's box was made public. Flower cross-examined Inspector Tedman to establish that the discovery had been made eight days after the first search of the box, and four days after Courvoisier had been removed from the house. Inspector Beresford was the last witness to take the stand and at the conclusion of his testimony Hobler informed the court that another examination was required: he anticipated that Inspector Pearce's testimony would be lengthy, and he had a further nine witnesses to call.[45]

On Saturday 23 May police constables George Collier and Frederick Shaw testified with respect to their successful search of Russell's premises for various of the stolen items. Pearce was recalled and questioned by Hall; Constable Paul Cronin testified to having found Russell's watch. Superintendent Baker, present in court, suffered his own personal tragedy on this day. He passed to Hobler a note which read,

> Dear Sir,
> Do you think I can go, having just recd. Information of the <u>Death</u> of <u>Mrs. Baker</u>. I shall order Mr. Beresford to be in attendance.[46]

Hobler tried twice to call the two constables who had been patrolling Norfolk Street, but Hall could not see the relevance of their testimony. James Ellis identified various of Russell's possessions; Harrison, chief clerk of Hoare's bank, testified with respect to the bank note; Wing was sworn to confirm this evidence.

At the conclusion of these examinations, Hobler considered that he had made a sufficient case for Courvoisier to stand trial for the wilful murder of William Russell. Yet he had not finished. The depositions of the witnesses called at Bow Street, he told Hall, were so 'voluminous' – a description he would record in his book – that he requested Courvoisier be remanded until the following Wednesday. This would allow Hobler time to read over the whole of the evidence offered, 'in case he might have omitted anything material, which could be supplied when all the witnesses were in attendance to have their depositions read and be bound over'. Flower, he suggested, might likewise wish to put further questions to the witnesses. Both solicitors were granted copies of the depositions.[47]

No one could fault Hobler for lack of diligence. The solicitor was all too aware that the 'case of strong suspicion' even Flower acknowledged against Courvoisier relied solely on circumstantial evidence. He must have had private doubts about the late police discovery of incriminating evidence in Courvoisier's portmanteau; at the very least, he was sufficiently experienced to have anticipated how such evidence would be treated by defence counsel in court, hence the painstaking pursuit of 'minutiae' that occasionally exasperated Hall. Establishing both that a break-in had been staged, and the honesty and credibility of his witnesses, was important.

The Case for the Prosecution Rests ... with Francis Hobler 117

When the Bow Street court reconvened for its fifth hearing – *The Times* at this point gave up naming 'the persons of distinction' who crowded the bench individually – Hall's clerk was ready to read over all of the depositions taken so far. But Hobler wished to call one further witness, Lady Sarah Bayley, who testified as to Russell's locket, signed her deposition, and was bound over as a witness for trial. Hall read the evidence of the two medical witnesses and asked a few additional questions before binding Elsgood and Nussey over as well. Sarah Mancer (still referred to as 'Mansell' by *The Times*) took the stand for the third time and was questioned at greater length by the magistrate. New evidence was introduced in the course of this questioning: Mancer had remembered that on the night of the murder Courvoisier had offered her both a glass of ale as well as something poured out of a pint bottle into a wine glass and that she had felt 'sleepy, very sleepy' after drinking the ale. Hannell's deposition was read, a few questions asked, and she signed it. When Tedman took the stand, Flower asked to see the bloodied gloves discovered so late in the police investigation. Pearce was questioned about a silver teaspoon which had been given to him by Mancer: it looked as though an attempt had been made to remove the crest. Sergeant Collier's deposition was read, and he added that he had searched in the drains and everywhere possible for the body of the shirt front which was found with the bloodied gloves. James Ellis, apart from confirming his deposition, testified that a penknife found by Pearce in a pantry drawer had belonged to Russell and was usually kept in the bottom of his dressing case. He could not identify the teaspoon.

All told, the reading of the evidence taken from witnesses in previous hearings occupied three and a half hours. But Hobler informed the magistrate that he had another witness to call: Charles Ellis, the landlord at the Castle Hotel at Richmond, where Russell had stayed over Easter. Russell had written to the landlord as he had to Sarah Bayley, asking if he had left a locket behind. Hobler also persisted in being allowed to call the two Norfolk Street beat constables, Alfred Slade and George Glew, to testify as to the state of the street and no. 14 on the night of the murder. The two men gave their evidence and were bound over for the trial. Still the pre-trial hearings were not concluded: Hall now had a question to resolve before signing the committal of the prisoner and Courvoisier was remanded until Friday.[48]

At quarter past two on 29 May the valet made his final appearance at Bow Street. *The Times* reported that Courvoisier 'entered the dock with a light step and a cheerful countenance', and that 'his appearance indicated increased confidence' as the proceedings wound to a close. Hall told him there was no longer reason to delay signing his commitment and that he would now be conveyed to Newgate Prison to await trial. Further evidence might still be brought against him, and he would likewise have the opportunity to produce evidence in his defence. Courvoisier was invited to make any statement or observation that he wished and cautioned, 'whatever you do say will be taken down in writing, and may be produced in evidence either for or against you'. Just as at the conclusion of the first hearing, he declined the invitation. Flower told the court, 'He has nothing to say, Sir, at present, but that he is entirely innocent of the murder'. Hall replied that the prisoner then stood committed to Newgate. A portion of the crowd outside Bow Street pursued the police van that transported him 'for a short distance'.[49]

Briefing the prosecution

With Courvoisier committed for trial, Hobler's next task was to shape the information he had amassed into a brief for counsel. In 1840, in the absence of an official public prosecutor and legal aid, counsel were not always employed for either the prosecution or the defence, and even when they were, professional etiquette requiring barristers to be 'briefed' by a solicitor was not always adhered to.[50] Collaborations between the upper and lower branches of the legal profession remained the ideal, however, and such etiquette was naturally followed in a high-profile case like the Russell murder. After his Bow Street appearances Hobler would disappear from the public stage, his efforts unacknowledged in the drama subsequently played out in the Old Bailey courtroom.

Hobler was briefing a prosecution team that he had envisioned as being led by long-term Old Bailey counsel William Clarkson: 'intended but not used', he recorded on the first page of his book. Clarkson 'then became one of the counsel for the prisoner'.[51] In 1840 there was as yet no distinction in practice between prosecution and defence; criminal barristers appeared for either side, as they were hired, and that this barrister had been the prosecution's first choice is unsurprising. Called to the bar in 1823, Clarkson had become the closest thing that Charles Phillips, who led the defence, had to a rival in the Central Criminal Court, although he appeared in no more than half the number of cases. The two men had otherwise little in common in terms of character. Clarkson is perhaps the single example of an Old Bailey barrister who epitomized the criticisms so often levied against the bar found at that court. An aggressive, greedy practitioner with a corrosive manner of speech, no one appears to have had a good word to say of either his private or public life.[52] Why Clarkson was 'not used' is not explained, but counsel for the prosecution were instead led by John Adolphus and included William Bodkin and Montagu Chambers.[53] The police might have had a regular solicitor, but Crown counsel did not yet exist: the barristers employed were all in private practice.

John Adolphus was a good second choice; damned with faint praise as 'nearly a great man', he had more experience of Old Bailey practice than most. He had been called to the bar in 1807, at almost 40 years old, after an earlier career as an attorney. Roughly the same age as the murder victim, Adolphus was in reasonable health, although suffering from cataracts: his clerk read his briefs for him.[54] He was not a flashy advocate; in terms of professional oratory, in fact, this phlegmatic, unimaginative Englishman was the polar opposite of the voluble, emotionally charged Irishman who defended Courvoisier: Phillips's rhetoric, easily parodied, was memorably characterized by Samuel Taylor Coleridge as a 'vertiginous *Waltz* of stultification and Derangement'.[55] Adolphus's idiom, by contrast, was described as 'purely and unaffectedly English ... never chargeable with a false or vicious taste'.[56] The difference in rhetorical style of the two would be neatly skewered by *Punch* in 1841.[57]

An affectionate testimonial published by Adolphus's daughter, Emily Henderson, after his death reproduced entries from the barrister's professional notebooks, the manuscript originals of which have vanished. Henderson's *Recollections* reveal that in this particular prosecution Adolphus, like Hobler, worked from personal conviction of Courvoisier's guilt: 'I saw the bed on which [Russell] was murdered', he had written, 'just as it was, the pillow saturated with blood, and the furniture in disorder. I viewed the pantry, and all the places where property had been found. I have not the slightest doubt of the wretch's guilt'.[58] Adolphus was understandably concerned, however, that all of the evidence against the accused was circumstantial. And he was decidedly unhappy with Hobler's brief.

'I had been at great pains and trouble preparing my Brief', wrote the aggrieved solicitor. But Undersecretary Samuel March Phillipps wasn't satisfied and demanded alterations:

> when I had got it complete Mr S.M. Phillips undersecretary for the Home Departmt. requested to see it. I had submitted it to Mr Wing – & had spent 4 hours over it with him – Mr Phillips had it & kept it 3 or 4 days & when I saw him again he spoke of it in disdain & as carrying no convincing feeling with it & he for near half an hour dictated what he said should be the Brief – I listened attentively & being very solicitous to obtain his good opinion I felt almost as a boy under a pedagogue. Knowing full well that to please or displease a man situated as Mr Phillips, is making or marring without any regard to merit or feeling – I listened & went home in the state of dismay natural to such a trial – Jane [Hobler's wife] & I after tea went to work & in about 3 hours produced a Brief in the style required by Mr Phillips but which was barely more than a Summary – I had it fair copied & took it to him he perused every word & made a few alterations with his pencil & he suggested also some matters – I went to work again & altered & recopied & again showed it him & he expressed himself satisfied saying such a brief as that must convince & convict the Prisoner – the Briefs were fair copied & handed to Counsel.[59]

Phillipps, the author of a textbook on evidence of which an 8th edition, revised with the assistance of Andrew Amos, had been published two years earlier, had no practical experience in the courts and his revision found no favour. Hobler had scribbled in the left-hand margin to his note, beside Phillipps's opinion that the brief he virtually dictated would 'convince and convict': 'I did not think so'. Adolphus agreed with the solicitor:

> when I next saw Mr Adolphus preparatory to consultations he asked how I came to make him such a Brief for it had obliged him to make his own Brief – I told him the circumstances & he expressed himself that he would have been much better satisfied to have had my Brief in its original state

The barrister consequently spent the day before the trial opened studying the depositions made before the coroner's court and Bow Street and making notes for his opening speech, which he later donated for Hobler's book:

> The following Manuscript notes were written by Mr Adolphus who led the Case for the Prosecution & although it is usual with Counsel to make notes preparatory for their addressing the jury yet on the present case they were made by Mr Adolphus at much length and fullness ... These notes are what Mr Adolphus calls his Brief and instead of destroying them he very kindly gave them to me when I made it known to him that I wished them for this book
>
> They are all in his own writing & are anylizations of my proofs.[60]

These circumstances were highly unusual. But even lacking the brief Hobler had originally drafted, in falling back on the Bow Street depositions Adolphus drew on the solicitor's work, or as Hobler described them, his 'proofs'. Briefs for the prosecution typically ended with a list of witnesses, beside each name an explanation of what they would be called upon to prove. Hobler's initial list of witnesses had included a great many people who were gradually weeded out as he put together the case for the prosecution.

Adolphus's notes, written in a column on the left-hand side of each page, begin with the heading General Observations. The first page reads:

> Public Prints
> >   Rumours &c
> Family &c of the deceased
> >   His father & Brother
> His own State
> >   age about 73
> Had the infirmities incident to his years –
> >   spare habit of body
> >   walked feebly
> >   heard imperfectly
> He was a widower
> >   family married away – &
> >   provided for
> He lived alone
> >   14 Norfolk Street Park Lane
> >   Size & description of the house   Plans – Model.[61]

'An attempt', he later noted, 'may be made to set up a Phantom – that some other Person has committed this'.

I have much reason to think a furious attack will be made on Mancer –/
If mere genl abuse – the Jury will/know how to treat it –/ ... Is she

unchaste? – I cod. afford to give away the Point – But the accusation is false. – Was she – as has been intimd. – the paramour of her Master – If it were true ... while she has neither settlement nor legacy be the least likely to assent to his murder. But it is false/Mr and Mrs Mivart.

He also anticipated a 'Run at the Police – But reward never offered till the lost material discovd'. These notes, 12 pages in all, constitute a rough but very recognizable outline of the opening speech Adolphus would make in court.[62] *The Times*'s report of that speech was also pasted into Hobler's book.[63]

The Old Bailey trial

Courvoisier was one of 237 persons tried at the Old Bailey sessions which opened on Monday, June 15. They included Edward Oxford, accused of high treason for his attempt to assassinate the young Queen Victoria – the first attempt made on her life – firing at her open carriage with pistols. Adolphus was involved in this prosecution as well. To the annoyance of both the queen and Home Secretary Lord Normanby, on conviction Oxford was not hanged but confined in a lunatic asylum; 27 years later he expressed contrition and was permitted to emigrate.[64] The sessions also included the second trial of Richard Gould: acquitted of the murder of John Templeman which, like that of Russell, had attracted great public interest, Gould now stood charged with burglary. Hobler had been solicitor for the prosecution in this case as well. Courvoisier was the only prisoner to be tried for murder in this session; the remaining cases included a mix of cutting and wounding with intent, burglary, assault with intent to rob, housebreaking, robbery, sacrilege, forgery and counterfeiting, receiving stolen goods, stealing letters from the Post Office, and embezzlement. The vast majority (183) were trials of larceny.

On the first day of the sessions Common Serjeant William St Julien Arabin, deputizing for the recorder, who was ill, delivered the charge to the grand jury. Commenting first on the wide range of offences, he then concentrated on the three he wished particularly to call to their attention: the trials of Oxford, Courvoisier, and Gould. The common sergeant's description of the case against Courvoisier reveals the difficulty under which Hobler and Adolphus worked:

> The evidence would prove beyond a doubt, from the nature of the wound inflicted, and the situation of the body, that the deceased nobleman met his death by the hands of another; but the case throughout depended upon circumstantial evidence only, which, however, was a species of evidence peculiarly fitted for a jury to consider. In weighing the evidence in the case, it would be well to examine the witnesses upon the point as to whether the marks of violence upon the back area door would lead to the conclusion that the house had been entered from without on the night of the murder, or whether those marks had not been made by some person on the inside, and this inquiry would lead the grand jury to consider whether the murder

was committed by any person residing in the house at the time. The next point of inquiry would be as to whether any property was missing, and if so, in what part of the premises it had been secreted. Generally speaking, when thieves effected a burglarious breaking, their first object was to secure and carry away whatever property they found; but in this case, according to the evidence of the police, the missing property was found concealed on the premises ... the question was by whose contrivance were they so secreted, if not by some person in the house at the time? Again, it appeared that two pocket-handkerchiefs spotted with blood, and also a pair of white gloves with marks of blood upon them, were found in the prisoner's portmanteau by some of the police, but in common justice to the accused it was right to mention that his person, as well as his box and this same portmanteau, had been previously searched on three different occasions – namely, on the 6th, 10th, and 13th of May, and those articles had not been found. It was right these dates should be borne in mind in considering the evidence against the prisoner. However, there were circumstances connected with the concealment of the property which undoubtedly cast a strong degree of suspicion up him, coupled with the marks on the inside of the door. He repeated, however, that the circumstances of the case were purely circumstantial from beginning to end...[65]

Grand jury deliberations are wholly secret and not recorded, but the *Examiner* reported,

On Tuesday the grand jury found a true bill against Courvoisier. We understand that there was some difference of opinion and considerable discussion in the grand-jury room before the bill was found. Some of the jurors, we believe, were for ignoring the bill, on the ground that the evidence adduced on the part of the prosecution was not sufficiently conclusive against the prisoner to warrant his being sent for trial.[66]

Courvoisier's trial began on Thursday, 18 June, some two weeks after the conclusion of pre-trial proceedings. From this point, Hobler, Flower, and Wing recede from public view, although Wing would be called as a witness. The trial proceedings were reported in all the main papers but it was *The Times*'s account which the ever-watchful Hobler chose to paste into his scrapbook. The trial also, of course, made its way into the *Old Bailey Proceedings*, pamphlet accounts published from the late seventeenth century. By this date the OBP no longer reproduced opening or closing speeches but in this particular trial it recorded the examinations and cross-examinations in greater detail than that found in *The Times*. Both sources were occasionally inaccurate with names but *The Times* was the worst offender in this regard: Inspector Tedman appears as Tidman, Sergeant Pullen as Pulling, Constable Cronin as Cronan. Latham's butler Emanuel Young becomes footman Daniel Young, Madame Piolaine, Madame Piolaire.[67]

Public interest continued to be intense. The spectators who had flocked first to the scene of the murder and then to Bow Street now vied for attendance in court: some 73 applications, reported *The Times*, had been made by members of the aristocracy.[68] By 1840 the Old Bailey had three separate courtrooms. Courvoisier was tried in what had become known as the Old Court, and to accommodate the unprecedented number of spectators the principal door was blocked, with benches covered in green baize laid against it and other seats erected elsewhere. One of the courtroom's boxes was set aside for the aristocracy, and chairs were also provided. What would Courvoisier have thought as he reached the top of the stairs leading to the court and stepped into the dock? Charles Dickens had imagined the feelings of such a man, on trial for his life, in the penultimate chapter of *Oliver Twist*, published a little over a year before the murder of William Russell: 'The court was paved, from floor to roof, with human faces. ... Before him and behind: above, below, on the right and on the left: he seemed to stand surrounded by a firmament, all bright with gleaming eyes'.[69] Many of the 'gleaming eyes' in this particular courtroom were patrician. *The Times* named the Duke of Sussex, the Countess of Charleville, Lady Burghersh, Lady Sonder, Lady G. Lennox, Lady Julia Lockwood, Lady Bentinck, the Earls of Sheffield, Mansfield, Clarendon, Lucan, and Louth, Lords Rivers, Gardiner, and A. Lennox, the Dutch ambassador, the Portuguese ambassador extraordinary, Sir Gilbert Heathcote, Sir Stratford Canning, Colonel Fox, and Lord Frederick Gordon as being present, along with 'many others whose names we could not learn'.[70] Also present were the customary City of London officials: the common serjeant who had addressed the grand jury, the lord mayor, and several aldermen.

Clark, the clerk of arraigns, read out the indictment, which charged Courvoisier with having murdered William Russell

> by having with malice aforethought struck, cut, and wounded the said Lord William Russell with a knife or some sharp instrument, whereby a deadly and mortal wound was inflicted on his throat, of the length of five inches and four inches in depth, of which deadly and mortal wound the said Lord William Russell did then and there die.

To this charge Courvoisier answered in a 'firm voice': not guilty. As a foreigner, he was entitled to be tried by a jury composed equally of foreigners and Englishmen, but he waived this right and asked to be tried by an English jury. Neither the accused nor his counsel made any objection to the trial jury sworn in. Courvoisier's judges then entered the courtroom: Lord Chief Justice Nicholas Conyngham Tindal (two of his sons were spotted among the spectators) and Baron James Parke, who had been Tindal's pupil.[71]

Making the case for the prosecution

When John Adolphus rose to make his opening speech he began by cautioning the jury to dismiss anything they may have read about the case in the past five weeks and attend solely to the evidence presented in court and to the judge's summing up.[72] He described William Russell's household and the events of the day and evening preceding the murder and the discovery of the murder itself, drawing attention to the fact that on entering Russell's bedroom Courvoisier had gone straight to the window while Mancer – 'the girl' – 'more naturally' went to her master's bedside: 'Would he who attended an aged man, – would he, if innocent, have gone to the window to open the shutters, trusting to the clamour of a female servant to waken his master?' The back door, he indicated, would become a 'very material subject of inquiry' for the jury, and he would produce 'scientific persons ... who had inspected it through a magnifying glass'. He regretted that on discovery of the 'simulated burglary' the police had not immediately taken into custody the person of whom they were almost instantly suspicious. He was very careful to distance himself from the stained items of clothing found in Courvoisier's portmanteau: he

> did not rely on anything found in the box on any occasion ...something might have transpired with respect to linen found in the prisoner's box, marked in a particular way; but he (Mr Adolphus) attributed no weight to it, and he repeated that nothing arose in the present case from anything discovered in the prisoner's box.

This evidence was not merely unhelpful, but potentially dangerous. He acknowledged, as the common serjeant had advised the grand jury, that the prosecution of Courvoisier relied on circumstantial evidence, and quoted at length from a famous murder trial heard 35 years earlier, that of Richard Patch for the murder of Isaac Blight, which had similarly depended on circumstantial evidence. Patch's counsel had not been allowed to make a speech but the defendant had read out in court a defence which had clearly been drafted or reviewed by a lawyer:

> When you consider that circumstantial evidence consists of a chain of proofs, connecting by the interposition of various facts two things which have no connection with each other, you will readily perceive how dangerous it is to rely on a case proved by such evidence. If any one link be defective, the strength of the whole chain fails; and although the broken members may be sufficient to create suspicion, they can in no rational minds induce conviction. All hope of that moral certainty which alone can authorize you to say on your oaths that a man is guilty is gone the moment the least disagreement in the connecting points is discovered...

Adolphus was an experienced counsel and no fool. The almost certainly tainted evidence of the items found in Courvoisier's box was useless in constructing a case for the prosecution. In the absence of a confession from the valet with respect to either the theft or the murder, circumstantial evidence was what Hobler and subsequently Adolphus had to work with. Each link had indeed to be secure. Phillips immediately objected that the opinion quoted was not judicial authority and was limited to one specific case, but Tindal 'intimated that the general observations might be quoted with reference to the nature of evidence as the expression of the learned counsel's own opinion'.

Adolphus then addressed a variety of problems that might arise in the course of the prosecution, as identified in the rough notes he gave to Hobler. Due to the newspaper coverage of suspicions cast on Sarah Mancer's character, her testimony might be deemed 'unworthy of credit'. It was not within his power to call witnesses to correct this impression, 'but in answer to the general declamation which might be addressed' to the jury, 'he would say this, that her character was unblemished in every particular'. Phillips immediately objected to this anticipation of an attack which had not yet been made, but Tindal again allowed it, saying that it was 'quite competent to the counsel for the prosecution to put the case hypothetically of the character of one of his witnesses being attacked'. Adolphus said that he was 'quite content' to put his concerns 'in that general way', and further 'he challenged, he dared, he defied his learned friends, to impeach [Mancer's] testimony of the grounds of character'. He continued with the further prediction that an attack would be made on police testimony, given the substantial reward on offer for a conviction. This he dismissed by reminding the jury of the number of officers among whom the award would have to be shared, and the unlikelihood of the conspiracy which would have been required on their part. He concluded his speech by advising the jury that the Russell family, in offering the reward, had not been motivated by 'the desire to hunt a hapless foreigner into the jaws of death' or by any 'feelings of personal revenge'. They were instead 'petitioners for public justice':

> He could feel, as every other man must, for the case of a foreigner, distant from his own country, and charged under the most solemn circumstances with the commission of a capital crime. But there was a circumstance of even paramount consideration – the safety of the vast family of the British community, for on their unbiased verdict in such a case must depend whether the old man, retiring to rest, and the defenceless female and the helpless child, having addressed their prayers to Almighty God, should be subjected with impunity to the assassin's knife.

The case required 'firm and upright hearts' and 'cool and intelligent heads', both of which he was certain the jury possessed. Adolphus spoke for roughly an hour; when he sat down, one of his juniors, William Bodkin, rose to call the first witness for the prosecution.[73]

Counsel for the defence

Charles Phillips's professional reputation was mixed even before his controversial defence of Russell's murderer. Like all Old Bailey counsel, he was an advocate rather than a lawyer and Lord John Campbell dismissed Phillips with contempt: 'Nothing could have prevented him from attaining to great eminence, except a head which not only was not "a head for law", but into which no law could be crammed, and which repelled all legal definitions and distinctions'.[74] 'Counsellor O'Garnish's' flowery rhetoric, as described above, was also deemed too Irish for English courtrooms: on leaving Ireland Phillips had failed spectacularly, and immediately, in Westminster Hall. But in the criminal courts he enjoyed extraordinary success before his fall from grace: between 1825 and 1834, Adolphus was named in the Old Bailey Proceedings as appearing in just under 600 cases, Phillips in well over 2,000. In 1840 he might be said to have been at the height of his fame, not merely the leader 'but really everything', as Henry Brougham described him, at the Old Bailey.[75] Courvoisier had the best defence counsel in England.

Just as Adolphus was not a Crown counsel, Phillips should not be thought of as wedded to defence work, nor should it be assumed that he worked from political convictions about the rights of the accused. The Old Bailey's premier defence counsel had, in the discussion preceding the Central Criminal Court Act 1834, argued that trial at that court was skewed in favour of the accused. London magistrates, he said, seldom granted legal costs for prosecution, and thus few private prosecutors employed counsel. On his account, '19/20' trials at the Old Bailey went forward without prosecuting counsel, which goes some way towards explaining the predominance of defence work in his own caseload in that court. Phillips had also argued vehemently against full advocacy for 'prisoners', believing that allowing counsel to make speeches for the defence, which they had been forbidden to do before 1836, would disguise rather than promote revelation of the truth. An element of self-interest can be discerned in both positions: a salaried appointment, as Phillips admitted, would have eased his anxieties about providing for his family; adding speeches to the cross-examinations carried out by counsel would increase their workload without the likelihood of any increase in pay. Their clients tended to be poor. But there was also principle at work and Phillips's views were founded on years of practical experience.[76]

New evidence

When Phillips was engaged to defend him, Courvoisier was still protesting his innocence with respect to both theft and murder. On the evening of the day on which the trial had commenced, however, new evidence emerged which shook the valet's confidence and resulted in a private confession. Hobler described the finding of evidence that definitely tied Courvoisier to theft from Russell, and prompted the valet's confession to the murder, as follows. 'The first days trial concluded just before six o'clock – about which time a note underneath was brought to me in Court'. The brief note, from solicitor Richard Cumming, read: 'Dear Sir, I believe I now have in my possession some of the missing property belonging to the late Lord William Russell'. Madame Piolaine, wife of the proprietor of the Hotel de Dieppe, a London hotel popular with foreigners, had read of the trial while abroad, recognized Courvoisier, though she knew him by another name, and remembered that he had deposited a parcel at the hotel. She contacted her husband, and Piolaine's business partner Joseph Vincent, together with a watchmaker, Louis Gardie, had gone to Cumming.[77] 'Knowing Mr Cumming', Hobler continued,

> I desired the officer to let him come in and he sat behind me until the Trial ended for the day – he had brought Vincent and Gardie with him & we all adjourned to Newgate, where we examined the parcel & Mr Cope took Vincent and Gardie to see Courvoisier who was with other prisoners – they did not recognize him but he knew them & he then knew their errand & the next morning Friday the 19th before going into Court he sent for his attorney Mr Flower & told him it was all over he did the Deed – he afterwards saw his two Counsel Messrs Phillips & Clarkson & told them the particulars & when I came into Court a few minutes before 10 on the Friday morning I saw them both leaving the Dock before the prisoner was put to the Bar –
>
> The parcel when opened was found to contain all the missing articles – I had the two female servants and the men servants and Ellis brought into Newgate & they examined the articles and identified such as were Lord William Russell's
>
> The other articles which were considered to be the prisoners were given to Inspectors Pearce & Beresford to see & get proved by the next morning the brown paper I found came from Moltino's & I sent there also – & other articles to other places & by the next morning I had got up all the additional proofs as the appear at the latter part of the Evidence given on the 19th beginning with Madame Piolaine – I had between 10 & 11 o'clock of the 19th handed a letter across in Court to Mr Flower to tell him the plate was discovered & he might see it – copy of the letter is ante.

That letter read,

> Sir, I beg to inform you that the missing plate & some other articles have been found at the Hotel de Dieppe, No. 4 Leicester Place Leicester Square kept by Piolaine & Vincent & that evidence will be adduced to show that it was deposited there by the Prisoner previously to the murder. – You may inspect the Plate & if you wish it also some articles of dress which were found with them & which are believed to belong to the Prisoner.

Piolaine, as Hobler's notes indicate, would be called to prove Courvoisier's deposit of the parcel on 3 May, that the watchmaker Gardie and Piolaine's partner Vincent had been present at the time of that deposit but neither remembered Courvoisier himself, that Gardie and Vincent had called on solicitor

Cummings, who had then gone to Piolaine. 'Having occupied myself till near 12 o'clock at night over this additional Evidence', Hobler continued,

> I went next morning Friday 19th June to Newgate before 9 o'clock and there met Mr Cummings Mad^e Piolaine Gardie and Vincent. Mr Cope had taken Mad^e Piolaine to see Courvoisier & although there were many other prisoners in the place she recognized him directly & he also knew her – I then sat down & took fuller notes in pencil as on the other side [they have been traced over in ink] and afterwards left them all in Mr Cope's parlour – when I had quitted and Mad^e Piolaine began to think on the inevitable result of the new discovery she fainted and ultimately was put to bed where she received every possible attention from Mrs Cope and a medical man & at last she was sufficiently recovered as to come into Court about 4 o'clock where she gave her evidence exceedingly well although exposed to a cross-examination from Mr Phillips conducted not in the politest manner or with the strict attention to facts which I could have wished to have seen...[78]

From the time in which he was made aware of the new evidence Phillips laboured under a heavy burden. Despite the confession of guilt made to his two barristers as well as Flower, Courvoisier had no intention of changing his plea, instead expecting Phillips and Clarkson to continue to defend him to the best of their ability. Having protested against the introduction of legislation that allowed barristers to assume the role of mouthpiece for their clients, Charles Phillips now found himself in a deeply unenviable position, not merely having to make a speech, but required to speak on behalf of someone who had privately confessed to murder. This decision resulted in public scandal but the bar, which spent the subsequent decade mulling over whether Phillips deserved the public opprobrium that followed once Courvoisier's mid-trial confession came to light, eventually agreed with the advice provided privately by Baron Parke during the trial itself. Phillips could not have abandoned his client mid-trial but, given the personal knowledge of Courvoisier's guilt he now possessed, he should have confined himself to testing the evidence presented in court. On no account could a barrister in his situation imply that any other person had been responsible for the murder. Many contemporary critics felt Phillips did just that, in both his cross-examination of Sarah Mancer and in his closing speech, when he knew she had been in no way involved in either the theft or Russell's murder.

Were these criticisms fair? Phillips certainly attempted to prove that Mancer had perjured herself. When the trial opened the housemaid was the first witness to be called – she too would have faced the 'inquisitive and eager eyes' of the spectators who filled the court – and as Bodkin began to examine her Phillips interrupted to request that depositions taken before the coroner be placed before the court. The reason became obvious during his initial cross-examination. Had Mancer not, Phillips pressed, in the coroner's court deposed that when she first entered Russell's bedroom she had seen her master murdered in his bed, rather than referring only to blood on his pillow?[79] In discussing this line of questioning *The Examiner* blamed not Mancer but the conduct of the coroner's inquest:

> If the coroner's inquest ... had done its duty, the discrepancy between Sarah Mancell's [sic] evidence and that of the other persons who saw the napkin over the face of the murdered nobleman would have been cleared up. The discrepancy was evidently nothing more than an inaccuracy of expression; but the effect of leaving it unexplained was, as we have seen, to expose the principal witness to a charge of falsehood.[80]

Phillips returned to the alleged perjury in his closing speech: 'The depositions taken by the coroner were now before the learned judges, and perhaps they would consider it their bounden duty to tell the jury whether that woman swore before the coroner as she did before the court'.[81] He also questioned other of Mancer's actions and speech.

> The prisoner had seen his master retire to his peaceful bed, and was alarmed in the morning by the housemaid, who was up before him, with a cry of robbery, and some dark, mysterious suggestion of murder. 'Let us go', said she, 'and see where my Lord is'. He did confess that that expression struck him as extraordinary. If she had said, 'Let us go and tell my Lord that the house is plundered, that would have been natural, but why should she suspect that any thing had happened to his Lordship? She saw her fellow servant safe, no taint of blood about the house, and where did she expect to find her master? Why, in his bedroom, to be sure. What was there to lead to a suspicion that he was hurt?...[82]

Although Phillips expressly denied imputing any guilt to either of the female servants, this passage suggests that Mancer was already aware that Russell had been wounded. Her expression of exasperation on finding Courvoisier seated, writing a letter to Russell's son – 'what the Devil are you doing there?' – Phillips described censoriously: 'feminine exclamation!' And why, he asked, if she wanted Mr William Russell fetched personally rather than written to, had she stopped Courvoisier from sending the first person he saw on the street?

Phillips also, as Adolphus expected, made a considered 'run at the police'. Here, as Adolphus recognized, he had a great deal of ammunition. Tedman, after the initial examination of Courvoisier's trunk, should have had it locked. Invoking – in typically inflammatory language – the once-maligned Bow Street runners Phillips asked, 'What would a practised policeman of the old school have done – one of those who, after years of experience and drudgery, dismissed to poverty in the street to make way for the regiment?' After sealing it he would have 'sent it to a place of safety, where no miscreant, speculating on his share of 450*l.* reward, could have tampered with it to insure the conviction of the unfortunate man at the bar'. Instead, someone inserted items at a later date: 'some villains must have been at work here to provide proofs of guilt against the prisoner'. In this accusation Phillips was almost certainly correct, just as he was correct in saying that Pearce – 'he who would intimidate a poor wretch in the fangs of the police' – had not, on his first examination, admitted to having asked Courvoisier, 'Dare you look me in the face?'. This query Phillips interpreted as an attempt to elicit a confession. Mayne and Hobler were condemned for allowing the interview in question to take place: 'Such treatment was worthy of the Inquisition'. Commissioner Mayne was an 'iniquitous ruffian' and Courvoisier had been 'tortured by every interrogatory' that police 'ingenuity could suggest'. In his closing speech Phillips referred to the police as 'myrmidons' and a 'gang'. Various reference was made to the police sharing blood money over Courvoisier's coffin and of a police 'conspiracy to share the wages of blood'. Constable Baldwin, described as a 'miscreant bloodhound', he singled out for having 'equivocated and shuffled, and lied on his oath' before admitting to knowledge of the reward offered. But Phillips's claim that 'over every portion of the case doubt and darkness rested' was not true. The discovery of the missing silverware, proved in court, removed any doubt that Courvoisier was a thief. He also insinuated that the Piolaines' hotel was not respectable, when, as an indignant Hobler recorded, 'he must or ought to have been informed by the attorney Flower that her house was not a gaming house or complained of as he attempted to make out'.[83]

Strong – and ultimately controversial – as Phillips's closing speech was, there were rumours to the effect that it had been considerably toned down. 'We presume', reported *The Times* on 22 June, that Courvoisier's communication

> entirely changed the line of defence intended to be taken by his counsel; for it was generally rumoured that a severe attack would be made on the fellow-servants of the prisoner, and also on the police who were engaged in the investigation. We must, however, do Mr Phillips the justice to state, that with the honourable zeal which always distinguishes him for his clients, he made the best of a very bad case; and, although surrounded by difficulties, his speech for the prisoner was most energetic and impressive.

Other papers went further:

> While the preliminaries for the approaching execution were in progress, and a large number of gentlemen were assembled in a room adjoining the prison, waiting for admission, it was stated by one of the city authorities, as an admitted fact, that the line of defence which Mr. Phillips, the criminal's counsel on his trial, intended to have taken was, that the female servants had been engaged in criminal intrigue with some of the police, and had admitted them into the house for the purpose; that the robbery and murder had been perpetrated by them. The secretion of the jewellery and other articles in the butler's pantry was to have been

thus accounted for; and the subsequent discovery of the blood-stained gloves, &c., so strangely rolled up in Courvoisier's line, after the real perpetrator of the deed was in custody, and had left the house, was to have been adduced as further presumptive proof of the police being the guilty parties, for the purpose of incriminating the prisoner. The effect of such a defence, especially if it had been followed by an acquittal of the prisoner, must have been most injurious, as tending to create a prejudice against, and weakening public confidence in the integrity of the metropolitan police.[84]

The most serious of the accusations made against Charles Phillips's defence of Courvoisier was the suggestion that he had gone so far as to express a personal belief in the innocence of a client he knew to be guilty of murder. It is also the most difficult to prove. Over the years Phillips protested vehemently that far from having made any such claim, he had gone out of his way to avoid doing so. Reports of the exact phrasing varies, with perhaps the most damning – and unlikely – coming from the *Southern Star*, which recorded Phillips as saying, 'From my soul I believe Courvoisier is innocent'.[85] *The Times* reported instead that he had said 'the Omniscient God alone knew who committed this crime' – a statement which by this point was not strictly true. On this particular charge, I am inclined to acquit the beleaguered counsel. In 1833 Phillips had been employed at the Old Bailey to defend one Henry Berthold, a 'native of Saxony' who had been living in England since 1824 and was a well-known political radical, accused of stealing a boa from the warehouse of Leaf & Co. 'According to the instructions of his brief' the barrister had called two character witnesses, but one, Julian Hibbert, refused to be sworn on the Bible, asserting that he was an atheist: 'the hisses with which Hibbert's avowal was received by the whole court were loud and unanimous' and Phillips then 'repelled all communication with such a being'. The response of both the public gallery and Berthold's counsel was described as useful in instructing 'foreigners as to the ingrain [sic] religious feeling of the English nation'.[86] This case, seven years prior to Phillips's subsequent disgrace, was widely publicized and won him considerable positive notoriety; it might also be taken as an indication of the barrister's own religious feelings. Alderman Brown, addressing Phillips, said, 'the public owe you much for the course you have pursued'.[87]

I would also argue that Phillips's attack on the conduct of the Metropolitan Police seems not without foundation. Following Courvoisier's private confession, Phillips's task in the Old Bailey courtroom was to ensure that his client was not convicted other than on legal evidence submitted there which proved Courvoisier's guilt beyond reasonable doubt. As discussed in the previous chapter, and even if the police had not been motivated by financial reward, as Phillips suggested, the late discovery of incriminatory evidence in Courvoisier's portmanteau remains highly suspicious. Phillips had every right to challenge it at trial, and any damage to the integrity of the police had arguably been caused by their own actions.

For both his cross-examination of Sarah Mancer on the second day of the trial and remarks made during his concluding speech, however, Phillips might legitimately be thought to have earned the public's – and posterity's – disapprobation. He did cast Mancer's actions on the morning the murder was discovered in a suspicious light. The perjured evidence he sought to prove was merely a matter of an understandable confusion of speech. Phillips exercised a degree of restraint, however: he may have found her speech unladylike, but he did not go so far as to imply she was unchaste, with her master or anyone else, or a thief. Mancer had not conspired with the police, just as she had not conspired with Courvoisier, whom she had known for little over a month. Any such possibilities – and they were only rumoured – were not raised in Phillips's speech to the jury.

The trial concludes

When Phillips sat down, Clarkson called a number of witnesses to speak to Courvoisier's character rather than material evidence: Peter Cherry, proprietor of the British Hotel, Jermyn-street; James Noble, head waiter at the above hotel; servants of Lady Julia Lockwood and Lady Julia herself, as a former employer of the accused. Tindal then summed up for the jury. Sarah Mancer must have been relieved by the portions of his summation that related to her testimony:

> With regard to the observations which had been made upon the expressions used by the housemaid, 'Let us go and see where his Lordship is' he thought it was merely a natural expression of anxiety for his Lordship's safety under the circumstances. With regard to her preventing the prisoner sending to Mr Russell by a labourer passing by, her idea might have been that a man of that description sent to such a distance as Belgrave Square might have loitered by the way, or perhaps not gone at all; however, they had heard the observations of the Counsel upon it and it was a question entirely for them to determine. ... With regard to what had been said by the counsel about the seeming contradiction in the evidence given by the housemaid in the Court and before the Coroner, he ought to have had the evidence given before the Coroner read, and to have given her the opportunity of explaining it; as it was, her evidence was uncontradicted; and even admitting all that the Learned Counsel had said, he really did not think it was a discrepancy of any importance whatever.

In fairness to the accused, Tindal also instructed the jury,

> With regard to the expression used by the prisoner, 'Old Billy was a rum old chap, and had money,' he thought the jury must not lay too much stress upon expressions used by persons in the prisoner's class of life when discoursing with their fellow-servants; all the inference that could be drawn from the expression was that the prisoner thought Lord William Russell was a rich man.[88]

The jury then retired. Dickens had imagined at some length the feelings of a man in the dock as his case was brought to a close, just as he had speculated on what they must have been when it opened:

> He stood there, in all this glare of living light, with one hand resting on the wooden slab before him, the other held to his ear, and his head thrust forward to enable him to catch with greater distinctness every word that fell from the presiding judge, who was delivering his charge to the jury. At times, he turned his eyes sharply upon them to observe the effect of the slightest featherweight in his favour; and when the points against him were stated with terrible distinctness, looked towards his counsel, in mute appeal that he would, even then, urge something in his behalf.
>
> ... Looking round, he saw that the juryman had turned together, to consider their verdict. As his eyes wandered to the gallery, he could see the people rising above each other to see his face: some hastily applying their glasses to their eyes: and others whispering their neighbours with looks expressive of abhorrence. A few there were, who seemed unmindful of him, and looked only to the jury, in impatient wonder how they could delay. But in no one face – not even among the women, of whom there were many there – could he read the faintest sympathy with himself, or any feeling but one of all-absorbing interest that he should be condemned.
>
> ...
>
> He looked up into the gallery again. Some of the people were eating, and some fanning themselves with handkerchiefs; for the crowded place was very hot. There was one young man sketching his face in a little notebook. He wondered whether it was like, and looked on when the artist broke his pencil-point, and made another with his knife, as any idle spectator might have done.[89]

Courvoisier too had been sketched in court, by C.A. Rivers, the same man who had made the model of 14 Norfolk Street and drawn the plan of its basement. Two of Rivers's portraits were pasted into Hobler's scrapbook, the first sketched on the 18th, the opening day of the trial, and the second on the third day, during the course of Phillips's address to the jury. Hobler noted of the second portrait: 'Rivers has made him a little crosseyed which is an inaccuracy & the only one –'[90] Courvoisier had not long to wait for the verdict: the jury having retired at 5 p.m. came back at 6:30. Russell's valet was found guilty and sentenced to death.

Conclusion

The prosecution of François Benjamin Courvoisier for the murder of William Russell can only be described as a public prosecution, involving as it did Police Commissioner Richard Mayne and police solicitor Francis Hobler working under the supervision of the Home Office. That collaboration was not without friction, nor was it particularly successful: public prosecution is not automatically efficient. Undersecretary of State Samuel March Phillipps may have been the author of a standard textbook on evidence, but he had no practical experience of the criminal courts and his interference with Hobler's brief hindered rather than assisted counsel. The police investigation into the crime produced little in the way of useful evidence and what they did offer damaged the case to be made. As prosecuting counsel John Adolphus was only too aware, the late discovery of bloodied items of clothing in Courvoisier's portmanteau was a positive liability at trial. Adolphus was careful to distance himself from this evidence, explicitly telling the jury that he attached no weight to it and rightly anticipating the ammunition it provided to defence counsel. In constructing the case for the prosecution he had instead to rely on the physical evidence that ruled out the likelihood of a break-in, and circumstantial evidence connecting Courvoisier with theft. He had also to contend with the negative publicity attached to Sarah Mancer. When Courvoisier's trial opened some doubts might still have been entertained about her involvement in the crime, or of her reliability as a witness. But for the surprise evidence of Madame Piolaine introduced on the second day, Adolphus may very well have failed to convince the jury that Courvoisier's guilt lay beyond reasonable doubt. The *Examiner* was quick to point out that '[b]ut for the lucky accident which produced the decisive evidence as to the stolen plate of Lord William Russell ... it is highly probable that Courvoisier would have been acquitted'; *The Times* attributed the conviction to 'the singular intervention of Providence'.[91] It certainly owed nothing to the police investigation into the murder.

At the conclusion of the trial, Hobler was nonetheless a happy man. In an undated letter to Mayne informing the commissioner that Courvoisier had been found guilty and sentenced to death, the police solicitor described the circumstances and content of the valet's in-court confession to Phillips and Clarkson. In this version – as described in the next chapter, there would be others – Courvoisier claimed to have been found by Russell in the act of secreting some of the stolen goods, that Russell threatened to discharge him in the morning, and that he had been 'so frenzied' by the threat he determined to kill his master before it could be carried out. The knife used he had afterwards cleaned and Hobler asked Mayne if he 'would be so kind as to recollect that on one of the poultry knives there is a minute spot of new rust'. The solicitor ended his letter by saying he was 'extremely satisfied that so very important a trial has been so successfully terminated'.[92]

'Laus Deo', Hobler later wrote with some satisfaction, 'that I was at all instrumental in however small a way' in securing Courvoisier's conviction. In the letter to Mayne he had also referred to Madame Piolane as 'my female witness'. But she was not, strictly speaking, 'his', having come forward long after Hobler had researched and drafted his two briefs. In terms of the conviction, like that of the police, his role was small indeed. Ultimately, the guilty verdict depended on neither the police investigation nor Hobler's efforts to construct a convincing brief: it rested instead on evidence provided by a member of the public at the 11th hour. Press coverage of proceedings played an important role in this regard, as police magistrate Thomas Hall would be reminded three years later. On being examined by the Select Committee of the House of Lords regarding libel and defamation about the utility of press reporting of hearings, one of the questions asked of Hall was whether 'the System attended with any Advantage in the discovering of Crimes?' Persons had appeared with information after having seen a police case reported, he acknowledged, but added that he did not believe such instances numerous. Lord Campbell reminded him of the Courvoisier prosecution: 'Are you not aware that in the late Case of Courvoisier it was by the Circumstance of a Newspaper having gone over to France that he was convicted, who must needs have been acquitted otherwise?' 'That was one Case', Hall agreed, 'and a remarkable Instance'.[93]

Having ordered and commented on the various material he collected for the prosecution Hobler might have consoled himself by a belief that his efforts had not been in vain. That consolation was subsequently tainted by personal resentment. His work, he felt, had not been recognized or appreciated. On 22 December 1840 Hobler had written in distress to the police commissioners as Undersecretary Phillipps had not approved his bill of costs. On 16 December the Home Office had approved a payment of £375.14.2, but £58.4 had been deducted on taxation that included charges for copies of papers supplied to Wing, the Russell family's private solicitor; charges for the personal attendance of Mr Hobler at 3 guineas per day during the whole of the proceedings had also been deemed excessive. In the Home Office's view the charges for paper copies could not be paid out of police funds, and Hobler's submission was

> not made in the usual and ordinary form of an attorney's Bill of Costs; it affords no due means of check, and Lord Normanby feels much difficulty respecting it…Lord Normanby is quite of opinion, that two guineas per day will afford Mr Hobler a full and fair remuneration for the time he employed in the case.[94]

The Russell family to whom he had happily offered his services appeared indifferent to them and Hobler's reflections on their professional relationship are bitter by the end of his 'book'. Albeit to a lesser degree, just as the relationship between Russell and his murderer had been soured by class differences, Hobler records personal resentment of his treatment. After describing the various post-trial fates of William Russell's servants, he added,

> As regards myself I have not much to say – On the discovery of the murder I acted as stated in my preliminary remarks of offering my <u>gratuitous</u> services to the Commissioners because when Lord John Russell, nephew of the deceased Nobleman was Secretary of State for the Home Department he very civilly sent me/on applying to him/the business of the Home Office after Mr Stafford's death – However I was directed to make

out a Bill of Charge which I did & also an account of all my expenditure – copies here inserted & all the letters I had from the Commissioners & the Home Office on the subject –

After much cavilling the expenditure was allowed and repaid. But it was a very long time before I got any final settlement which was concluded in February this year/1841/ & their magnificence just allowed me £105 for my Labour, 'though when I shewed the Bill to Mr Jones at the Crown Office he said he should have allowed it all –

So much for <u>nobility</u> – and never did any of the family personally or by their Solicitor Mr Wing write me one line to say they were satisfied with my exertions – there was a small sum deducted from my Bill by the Home Office for copies of papers supplied by Mr Wing £11.3.4 although it ought to have been more at proper charges – I was a year and a half getting this money from the Russell family which I did at last on 9 Sept 1843 – the murder was committed in May 1840 the trial took place in June 40 – thus 3 years & 3 months getting £11.3/4 from these very wealthy personages[.][95]

Notes

1 For the history of this office see Sainty, ed., *Office-Holders in Modern Britain*.
2 See May, *The Bar and the Old Bailey*, 194–97.
3 Bentley, *English Criminal Justice*, pp. 83–7. See also Edwards, *Law Officers of the Crown*.
4 See Beattie, 'Sir John Fielding and Public Justice', esp. 65.
5 See Hay and Snyder, 'Using the Criminal Law', 23.
6 Beattie, *Policing and Punishment in London, 1660–1750*, 392; May, *Bar and the Old Bailey*, 238.
7 Smith, 'The Emergence of Public Prosecution in London', 32.
8 Smith, 'The Emergence of Public Prosecution in London', 61.
9 Smith, 'The Emergence of Public Prosecution in London', 61.
10 Beattie, 'Sir John Fielding and Public Justice', 68 and n26.
11 *The Maul and the Pear Tree*, 84, 18, 79.
12 See 'Using the Criminal Law'.
13 There are letter books from the Thames Police Office plus related correspondence in the Home Office papers. Smith, 'The Emergence of Public Prosecution in London', 56.
14 'Police Report', 4 Sept. 1818.
15 'The Late Mr. John Stafford', *The Times*, 11 Sept. 1837.
16 Item 4 (seq. 13).
17 See Hay and Snyder, 'Using the Criminal Law', 39, and *Report on Public Prosecution* (1856).
18 Item 4 (seq. 13).
19 'Using the Criminal Law', 38.
20 Hay and Snyder, 'Using the Criminal Law', 47, 37, 39.
21 Item 4 (seq. 13–14).
22 *The Times*, 8 May 1840.
23 *Morning Chronicle*, 14 May 1840.

24 *Wellington and his Friends*, 122.
25 *ODNB*.
26 Popay had acted on his own initiative and was dismissed from the police. For contemporary views see *Report from the Select Committee on the Petition of Frederick Young and Others* (1833); see also Emsley and Shpayer-Makov, *Police Detectives in History*, 7.
27 Browne, *The Rise of Scotland Yard*, 101.
28 Item 4 (seq. 14).
29 Babington, *A House in Bow Street*, 232–37; Browne, *The Rise of Scotland Yard*, 111.
30 Harmer, who dominated defence work in the opening decades of the nineteenth century, was the more famous of the two. See May, *The Bar and the Old Bailey*, 80. A third partner, John Sandell, had formally left on 1 February 1836. *London Gazette*.
31 May, *The Bar and the Old Bailey*, 89–90. In a perfect world, Flower would also have left a record of his involvement in the case. If he did, it has either not survived or remains to be discovered. It might prove difficult to decipher: the handwriting in the few examples of his correspondence with Hobler is atrocious.
32 Item 71 (seq. 263); Items 47 (seq. 182–85) and 49 (seq. 186–88).
33 Flower raised the issue of an item of lost property; a missing seal, his client informed him, had, on application to Mr William Russell been handed over and promptly supplied by Courvoisier to the investigating police officers. Hobler objected that amending the evidence with respect to the seal required not merely Courvoisier's new assertion but the production of Mr Russell at trial to prove it. 'I know your objection perfectly well', Flower countered, 'I was not born yesterday'. Hall commented that it was not his place to tell either gentleman how to conduct their cases, but it was 'quite a new thing' to ask him, once the evidence had been closed, to allow questions to be put on behalf of the prisoner 'with a view to alter the testimony given by the witnesses for the prosecution'. Flower then asked Hobler if he would undertake to produce Russell at trial; Hobler refused to commit himself but said that Flower was free to call him. Hall weighed in on Hobler's side: how could the evidence for the prosecution be altered by a mere assertion of the accused? Flower insisted it was capable of proof and called on Hobler to produce Russell or pledge to produce him at trial. Hobler would pledge nothing. Flower complained his client was being ill-treated; Hobler denied any unfairness. *The Times*, 30 May 1840.
34 Jamaican-born, Hall was educated at Harrow and Trinity College, Cambridge and called to the bar of the Middle Temple in 1815. He practised briefly on the Northern Circuit, a typical choice for a barrister without local connections to draw upon for work, and then returned to Jamaica to serve as Judge Advocate General and King's Justice. Subsequently declining both the office of attorney general in Canada and a judgeship in Penang, back in England, he became sole stipendiary magistrate in Liverpool – in this port town which had grown rich on the slave trade Hall may have had some family connections. At Hatton Garden, his tenure probably overlapped with that of Allan Stewart Laing, the police magistrate who had the misfortune to be made a guy of, as 'Fang', by Charles Dickens in *Oliver Twist*. Roughly half a year after chap. 11 of *Oliver Twist* was published Laing was removed from office by Home Secretary Lord John Russell. While Dickens's portrait had been exaggerated, Laing had attracted censure. Hall, it appears, did not. See May, 'Fiction or "Faction"?', 171–72.
35 *The Solicitors' Journal and Reporter* 20 (1 Apr. 1876): 439–40.
36 HO 45/4492 A letter from Thomas James Hall concerning the bill for improving the police and his suggestion that quarterly abstracts of the proceedings of the Magistrates should be made public, 11 June 1851.
37 *The Era*, 17 May 1840.

38 *ODNB*. Who paid for Flower's services is unclear: Courvoisier himself, with his meagre £8 in a savings bank, was in no position to do so. It was rumoured that Sir George Beaumont had stepped forward – not the famous art collector, who had died in 1827, but his 'rather lacklustre heir', a second cousin of the same name whose butler was Courvoisier's uncle, Louis. Beaumont denied this in the papers.
39 *The Times*, 12 May 1840. From 1850 onwards, it would be restricted to female convicts and boys younger than 17 and in 1869, it was given yet another name: the Westminster House of Correction. Cardinal Manning's solicitor purchased the site in 1884, selling part of it onto a property developer but retaining the western half for Manning. Westminster Cathedral, Clergy House, and the Choir School currently stand on that site, rubble from the demolition possibly contributing to the cathedral's foundations. The stone doorway from the original prison alone survived and was relocated to Little George Street in 1969. Mayhew and Binny, *The Criminal Prisons of London*, 364–65; *Old and New London*, 4:1–13; http://www.westminstercathedral.org.uk/history_before.php.
40 *The Times*, 12 May 1840.
41 *The Times*, 15 May 1840.
42 *The Times*, 16 May 1840.
43 *The Times*, 23 May 1840.
44 Item 34 (seq. 130).
45 *The Times*, 23 May 1840.
46 Item 47 (seq. 186). Hobler has mistakenly said he received the note on Monday 25 – the hearing was on Saturday 23, and the newspaper report of it was dated Monday.
47 *The Times*, 28 May 1840.
48 *The Times*, 28 May 1840.
49 *The Times*, 30 May 1840.
50 May, *The Bar and the Old Bailey*, 81–4.
51 Item 1 (seq. 4).
52 For Clarkson's reputation, see May, *The Bar and the Old Bailey*, 51, 52–3.
53 For the Old Bailey experience and reputation of these men, see May, *The Bar and the Old Bailey*: 47–8, 51–2, 85, 123–24, 133, 138, 142 (Adolphus); 51–2, 123, 212, 248 (Bodkin); 212, 249 (Chambers).
54 Ballantine, *Some Experiences*, 69–70.
55 Coleridge, *Notebooks*, 5: 5872. On Phillips's rhetoric, see May, 'Irish Sensibilities and the English Bar'.
56 *Evening Chronicle*, 23 July 1845.
57 *Bonbon v. Punch*, vol. 1 (4 Dec. 1841). See also Schramm, 'Anatomy of a Barrister's Tongue', 294–95.
58 Henderson, *Recollections*, 204.
59 Item 90 (seq. 370).
60 Item 90 (seq. 370).
61 The plan of the basement of 14 Norfolk Street drawn by C.A. Rivers is included in Hobler's book. Item 177 (seq. 435–46).
62 Item 90 (seq. 370–77).
63 20 June 1840; Item 87 (seq. 364–68).
64 Hibbert, *Queen Victoria*, 421–22.
65 *The Times*, 16 June 1840.
66 *Examiner*, 21 June 1840.
67 *The Times*'s coverage of the three-day trial can be found on 19, 20, and 22 June 1840, pasted into Hobler's scrapbook as Items 87 (seq. 364–68), 91 (seq. 378–81), and 93 (seq. 382–85). The OBP reference is t18400614-1629.
68 17 June 1840.
69 Dickens, *Oliver Twist*, 466.

70 19 June 1840.
71 *The Times*, 19 June 1840.
72 The *Morning Chronicle* named the trial jurors as Edward Mellor, William Payne, George Coates, Philip Bring, Henry E. Newington, Stewart Helmstone, John Molton Maxwell, John Parke, Henry Marshall, William Elstone, Robert Feldon, and William Monk.
73 *The Times*, 19 June 1840; Item 87 (seq. 364–65).
74 *Life of John, Lord Campbell*, 2: 75.
75 PRO 30/22/2C, Russell papers, ff. 31–7.
76 See May, *The Bar and the Old Bailey*, 189–97.
77 In 1837 Cumming's address was listed as 5, King-square, Goswell-road. *Central Criminal Court Minutes of Evidence, taken in Short-hand by Henry Buckler* (London, 1837), 7: 192.
78 Item 98 (seq. 368–69).
79 OBP t18400615-1629; Mancer's cross-examination is reported at 223–28 in the original pages; quotation at 224–25.
80 28 June 1840.
81 *The Times*, 22 June 1840; Item 93 (seq. 380).
82 *The Times*, 22 June 1840; Item 93 (seq. 382).
83 *The Times*, 22 June 1840; Item 93 (seq. 383). Respectable as their hotel may have been, and despite reward money received for discovering the stolen plate, the Piolaines did not prosper. In 1841 Louis Jacque appeared before the bench of the Insolvent Debtors' Court. A Mr Woodroffe, acting for a butcher named Westlake, and a baker named Closse, opposed Louis Jacques's application to be discharged:

> The opposition was to inquire into the disposition of the Dieppe Hotel ... which had been kept by the insolvent and a person named Vincent, to whom he had given a warrant of attorney, under which property had been and which had cost 800*l.* at a great loss. Vincent had put the insolvent in prison, and he declared it was not a friendly proceeding.
>
> The complaint was, that meat was obtained from the opposing creditor up to the time of the execution, which had swept way all the property.
>
> The insolvent said, his wife had received the sums above mentioned in reference to the trial of Courvoisier (together 70*l.*), and the opposition was because he had not given up a part of it. He paid his rent and other matters as soon as he received the money.
>
> The Court eventually adjourned the case to complete the service, and told the insolvent he would not be immediately discharged. It was clear no tradesman in his senses would have supplied the goods if it had been known that an execution was in the house.

Piolaine was remanded to prison. *The Times*, 26 June 1841.
84 *Morning Chronicle*, 8 July 1840, repr. from the *Globe*. A briefer report appears in *The Era*, 28 June.
85 28 June 1840.
86 'Extraordinary Scene', the *Standard*, 28 November 1833, reproduced in the *Londonderry Sentinel*, 7 December 1833. See also 'Extraordinary Scene', *Lancaster Gazette*, 7 December 1833, which reported Phillips as responding to the witness with 'great energy ... Begone sir; I will not insult this Christian jury and assembly by putting another question to you'; 'Extraordinary Scene at the Old Bailey', *Morning Chronicle*, 29 November 1833; *Examiner*, 1 December 1833; *Morning Post*, 3 December 1833; *Morning Chronicle*, 6 December 1833; 'Atheistical Witnesses', *Essex Standard*, 7 December 1833; 'Curious Scenes at the Old Bailey', *Leicester Chronicle*, 7 December 1833; 'Pair of infidels', *Royal Cornwall Gazette*, 7 December

1833; 'Extraordinary Scene', *Sheffield Independent*, 7 December 1833. The exchange, which clearly made headline news across the national press, is not reported in the OBP's report at t18331128-23.
87 *Lancaster Gazette*, 7 December 1833.
88 *Examiner*, 21 June 1840.
89 Dickens, *Oliver Twist*, 466–67.
90 Item 94 (seq. 386).
91 28 June, 22 June 1840.
92 MEPO 3/44 (DSC01751). I have not found a copy of this letter in Hobler's own scrapbook.
93 *Report from the Select Committee of the House of Lords Appointed to Consider the Law of Defamation and Libel* (1843), 132.
94 MEPO 3/44 (DSC01844, 01849).
95 Item 110 (seq. 413).

The Case for the Prosecution Rests ... with Francis Hobler   141

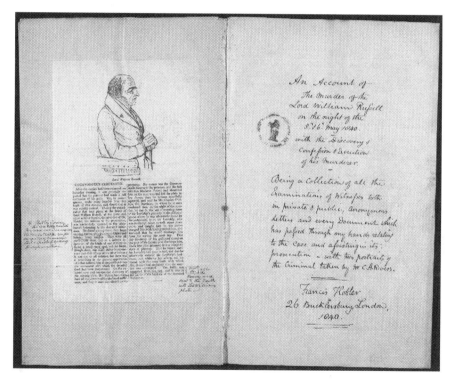

Figure 1 The title page of Francis Hobler's scrapbook demonstrates that he clearly envisioned his collection of materials as constituting a 'book'. The text is reproduced on page 7. Hobler, Francis. Scrapbook of documents relating to the investigation of the murder of Lord William Russell and the subsequent trial of François Benjamin Courvoisier, compiled by attorney at law Francis Hobler, 1840. HLS MS 4487. Harvard Law School Library, Historical & Special Collections.

Figure 2 A newspaper sketch of the exterior of 14 Norfolk Street, Park Lane. The murder victim's modest house was endlessly described in the newspaper press and subsequently in the Old Bailey courtroom. The sketch establishes that these premises were indeed small, more akin to a middle-class dwelling than one inhabited by an aristocrat. Hobler, Francis. Scrapbook of documents relating to the investigation of the murder of Lord William Russell and the subsequent trial of François Benjamin Courvoisier, compiled by attorney at law Francis Hobler, 1840. HLS MS 4487. Harvard Law School Library, Historical & Special Collections.

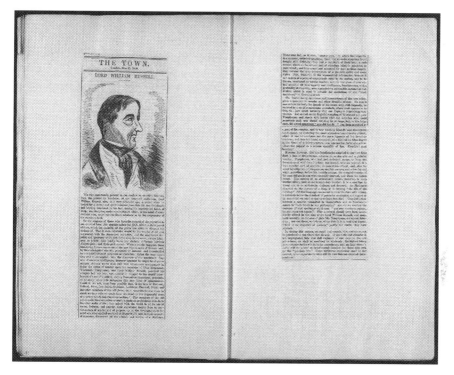

Figure 3 Another portrait of Lord William Russell, from *The Town*. He looks much younger in this portrait and has all his hair. The two newspaper sketches could easily represent two entirely different men. Hobler, Francis. Scrapbook of documents relating to the investigation of the murder of Lord William Russell and the subsequent trial of François Benjamin Courvoisier, compiled by attorney at law Francis Hobler, 1840. HLS MS 4487. Harvard Law School Library, Historical & Special Collections.

144 *The Case for the Prosecution Rests ... with Francis Hobler*

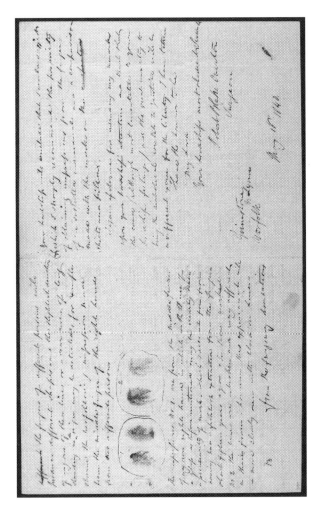

Figure 4 Surgeon Robert Blake Overton's explanation of fingerprint evidence. Overton wrote to Lord John Russell on 16 May 1840 saying that fingerprint evidence might be useful in identifying Lord William Russell's murderer. Hobler, Francis. Scrapbook of documents relating to the investigation of the murder of Lord William Russell and the subsequent trial of François Benjamin Courvoisier, compiled by attorney at law Francis Hobler, 1840. HLS MS 4487. Harvard Law School Library, Historical & Special Collections.

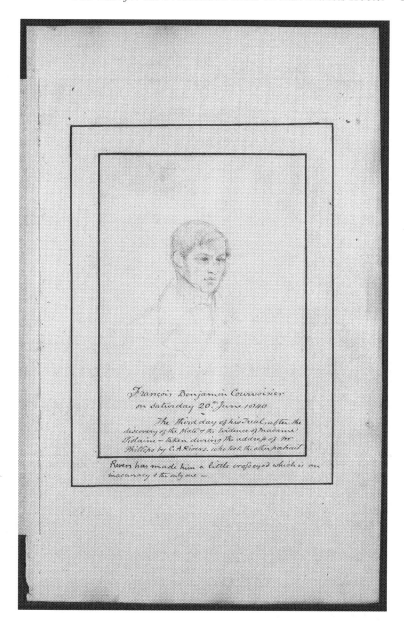

Figure 5 One of two pencil courtroom sketches of François Benjamin Courvoisier by C.A. Rivers. This sketch was made on the third day of the trial (Saturday 20 June 1840). Solicitor Francis Hobler thought Rivers had made Courvoisier look slightly cross-eyed but was satisfied that it was otherwise an accurate portrayal of the murderer. Hobler, Francis. Scrapbook of documents relating to the investigation of the murder of Lord William Russell and the subsequent trial of François Benjamin Courvoisier, compiled by attorney at law Francis Hobler, 1840. HLS MS 4487. Harvard Law School Library, Historical & Special Collections.

Figure 6 A newspaper representation of Courvoisier at the scaffold, 6 July 1840. Such illustrations were a routine feature of execution coverage and tended to be generic. Hobler, Francis. Scrapbook of documents relating to the investigation of the murder of Lord William Russell and the subsequent trial of François Benjamin Courvoisier, compiled by attorney at law Francis Hobler, 1840. HLS MS 4487. Harvard Law School Library, Historical & Special Collections.

5 'Going to See a Man Hanged'

Introduction

Two men died a violent death as a result of the Russell murder: William Russell himself, at the hands of his murderer, and François Benjamin Courvoisier, executed by the state as punishment for that murder. Russell, who had endured a private lethal attack in the dead of night, was accorded a public, formal, and ceremonial funeral procession and a burial attended by members of his family. Courvoisier, by contrast, met with the most public – and legally sanctioned – of deaths, his execution witnessed by perhaps 10,000, even 40,000 people (estimates vary considerably),[1] while the burial of his remains was both ignominious and private. The contrast is described below. This chapter also considers a remarkable shift in discussion of the case once Courvoisier had been hanged. After his death, in unsurprising accordance with the practice of the time, waxwork effigies and plaster casts of the valet were made to satisfy public fascination with the murder and murderer.[2] But Courvoisier also became the subject of a more curious response and a new one. From the time Russell's body had been discovered the Swiss valet had attracted no sympathy, and the public became positively enraged once details of his mid-trial confession were released. It is interesting, then, that one of the reasons this case continues to attract historical interest is public reaction to the execution itself, as expressed by a young William Makepeace Thackeray. Thackeray, as discussed in the next chapter, was a vociferous opponent of the Newgate novels, which he believed glamourized criminals – yet in his essay 'On Going to See a Man Hanged', published in *Fraser's Magazine* shortly after the execution had taken place, the murderer himself assumes the role of victim.[3] This essay has been viewed as evidence of a significant change in public sensibilities where capital punishment was concerned, both in terms of a new squeamishness and a new capacity to feel empathy across the class divide that typically separated respectable society from those hanged. Subsequent publications, however, suggest that within the space of a few years, Thackeray adopted a more nuanced and ambivalent position on state executions. Taken as a whole, Thackeray's writings also reveal considerable ambiguity where his views of the servant class were concerned. As Brian McCuskey has pointed out, Thackeray's novels and journalism

DOI: 10.4324/9781003481638-5

positively teem with 'objectified servants': Fritz in *The Luck of Barry Lyndon* (1844)/*The Memoirs of Barry Lyndon* (1856), the 'gigantic footmen' in *Vanity Fair* (1847–48), John and Jeames in *Pendennis* (1848–50), and the 'huge', 'big', 'fat', 'splendid and enormous' footmen referenced throughout *The Book of Snobs* (1856).[4] Thackeray's eye, McCuskey argues, 'singles out' male servants rather than female ones and he describes Thackeray's footmen as eroticized, 'fetishized objects of flamboyantly homosexual desire'.[5] This may be true (I'm not entirely convinced), but they clearly inspired fear as well as desire, and not merely on sexual grounds. Thackeray empathized with the servant class of his day in a way in which previous generations had not, but the empathy expressed in essays such as 'On a Chalk-Mark on the Door' (1861) co-existed with a deep unease rooted in apprehension of the physical power of servants. This fear arguably tempered the evolution of the novelist's opinions on capital punishment, and it had its origins in Courvoisier's murder of Russell.

'The old honest way of cutting throats'?: William Russell's private execution

William Russell died as the result of a savage physical attack that left him nearly decapitated. Given this circumstance, the manner of his death might, in 1840, have been considered somewhat old-fashioned. In his study of Victorian poisoners Ian Burney discusses Thomas De Quincey's 1827 essay, 'On Murder, considered as one of the fine arts', and Leslie Stephen's lesser known revisitation of that essay in 'The decay of murder' (1869). Where De Quincey's adopted persona had lamented an apparent increase in poison over violent physical assault, this view was challenged in the mid-Victorian press, which instead lauded the mystery and 'poetry' of poisoning cases. Stephen, signing himself 'a cynic', offered yet another take. Commenting 'on those who professed to mourn the passing of an era of "heroic" murder', his cynic claimed that the decline of violence reflected the emergence of a dull, increasingly respectable, and increasingly homogenous modern world. 'Taken together', Burney writes, re-readings of de Quincey 'delineate a modern aesthetics of criminal violence, in which bold physicality had been displaced by a more insidious form of subterranean (or sub-cutaneous) violation'.[6] On this view, Courvoisier could be perceived as a throwback, a virile and colourful murderer of the old school. The degree of violence involved in the slashing of William Russell's throat is, as I have suggested, a clear indication of the extent of Courvoisier's anger. Taking a more pragmatic view, the method chosen might also have reflected the valet's agricultural upbringing, which would at the very least have exposed him to the slaughter of animals, even if he had not personally participated in their slaughter. And given the presence of a cook and housemaid in Russell's tiny household, poisoning would have posed greater logistical challenges as well as requiring a premeditation that cannot be substantiated by the valet's post-trial confessions.[7] Russell was arguably butchered. But the attack was made by an assailant almost 50 years younger, and while the victim slept: 'old school' the murder might have been in its method, but there was nothing bold or heroic about it. If raising a hand in defence, as the wound on Russell's thumb suggests he may have done, can render the assault a contest, it was grotesquely uneven. Not merely the social status but the age and physical frailty of Courvoisier's victim undoubtedly contributed to public horror at this crime. There is little 'bold physicality' to be found in a midnight attack on a deaf septuagenarian asleep in his own bed. That the assailant was a resident employee, trusted with the safety of Russell's home and person, added to the public's terror.

The victim laid to rest

William Russell's life had been highly privileged but unremarkable. Apart from producing children he had accomplished very little and appears to have been regarded with exasperated, if affectionate, pity by his near relations. The notoriety attendant on his death, the publicity and intrusive public attention that ensued in its wake, would have been extremely unwelcome, and in arranging Russell's burial the family, with the help of the police, made every effort to regain a degree of control and restore appropriate dignity and decorum, which had been conspicuous by their absence in the manner of his death.

The body of William Russell had been removed from 14 Norfolk Street on 12 May, six days after the murder. Every attempt was made to keep the time of the removal a secret but Superintendent Baker, with a few serjeants and constables from C Division, attended before 4 o'clock in the morning, rightly anticipating that crowds would assemble. According to *The Times*, when the hearse and mourning coaches drew up to the house at 6 a.m. some 200 spectators were waiting. The coffin, the paper reported, 'was covered in dark purple (not black, as previously stated) cloth, richly studded with gilt nails'.[8] The *Morning Chronicle* had reported a black covering on a 'remarkably plain coffin'. The coffin had been brought to the house at 10 p.m. the night before from a Holborn undertaker named Richards, whose premises had been 'thronged throughout the day by persons anxious to see it'.[9] Both papers agreed that the hearse, drawn by four horses, was 'decorated with velvets and [ostrich] plumes'. The *Chronicle* reported that the Norfolk Street house had

> been besieged by messengers from members of the royal family, the cabinet ministers, members of the nobility and gentry ... requesting that they might do honour to [Russell's] obsequies by their carriages at the funeral following in the mournful *cortège*.

The young queen and Prince Albert – who had been married three months earlier – were said to have made a similar request. All of these offers had been 'respectfully declined', Russell's family desiring as quiet an internment as possible.[10] The carriages would at any rate have been empty: 'Among the aristocracy when a person dies, unless he is some great general or other public character, no one attends the funeral except the immediate family of the deceased. Friends of the family send only their empty carriages'.[11] In this particular instance empty carriages would have been singularly fitting, as few of their absent passengers would have graced William Russell with their presence during his lifetime. But in accordance with the family's wishes, Russell's funeral cortège consisted of the hearse and three mourning coaches containing various of his relatives. The press detailed the arrangement as follows:

<blockquote>
Inspector Tedman and Sergeant Smith, in deep mourning, with silk hatbands.

The undertaker, with silk hatband and scarf,

Messrs. Wing and Bennett, the town and country agents of his Grace the Duke of Bedford, with silk hatbands and scarfs.

Two mutes on horseback.

A page   A lid of feathers   A page

Six of the principal tenantry of the Duke of Bedford, residing in the neighbourhood, in deep mourning, with silk hatbands.

Porters with Silk Hatbands and Staves.	THE HEARSE Containing the Body of the Deceased.	Porters with Silk Hatbands and Staves.
A Page with Wand	The first Mourning Coach, containing – Mr. William Russell (the only surviving son of the deceased Lord), the Rev. Lord Wriothesley Russell, and Lord John Russell.	A Page with Wand
A Page with Wand	The second Mourning Coach, containing – Lord Edward Russell, Lord Charles Russell, and Lord Cosmo Russell.	A Page with Wand
A Page with Wand	The third Mourning Coach, containing – Lord Alexander Russell, Marquis of Abercorn, and Fitzstephen French, Esq., M.P.[12]	A Page with Wand
</blockquote>

Bound for the parish church of Chenies, Buckinghamshire, 22 miles from London, Russell's final journey would last seven and a half hours. The cavalcade rested 15 minutes at Edgeware at half past eight and broke its journey again at Watford in Hertfordshire at 10 a.m. When it moved off at 11:30, the road was lined 'by respectable persons'. From Rickmansworth, four miles from their destination, 'a similar tribute of respect was shown by the inhabitants', and spectators again lined the road from thence to the village of Chenies, which was reached at roughly half past one.

The church, reported *The Times*,

> is of the Anglo-Norman style of architecture, and ha[d] been recently repaired and beautified. Attached to it is the chapel of the Russell family, which was erected in the year 1556 by Elizabeth, Countess of Bedford, wife of John, first Earl of Bedford ... It contains magnificent monuments erected to the remains of numerous members of the illustrious house; whole-length figures, in polished marble, of the first and second Earls and Countesses, in the armour and dresses of the time of Henry VIII, and Queen Elizabeth, surmounting their tombs. The vault which is underneath contains the remains of 61 members of the Russell family, amongst which are those of some of its earliest ancestors, as well as those of the lady of Lord William Russell, who died in the year 1807, and of his gallant son, Captain George Russell, R.N., who died September 15, 1825, &c. The windows of the chapel have the family arms emblazoned on them, whilst from its vaulted roof hung pendant the banners of the Dukes of Bedford, with their escocheons, &c.

At three o'clock the family assembled at the rectory; 20 minutes later the funeral cortège proceeded to the church. Inspector Tedman and Serjeant Smith, who led the procession, had been brought in to supervise the local constabulary's crowd control at the church. The Duke of Bedford's tenants served as pallbearers and the burial service was conducted by the Reverend Mr Bower, rector of St Paul's, Covent Garden. In the chapel, the pulpit, reading desk, communion table, and family pews were all draped in black. Lord John Russell did not follow the coffin to the vault but remained in his pew, his own recent losses preying on his mind.[13] The family left the chapel by a private door leading to the rectory rather than face more crowds: the *Era*, a Sunday paper, estimated the size of the congregation as between 500 and 800 persons.[14] All of the newspaper accounts reported that the Reverend Mr Bowers struck his head on a protruding stone during the descent to the vault, suffering a 'severe contusion' on his forehead, but continued in his duties.[15]

Courvoisier's final days

As the *Era* commented in verse, Courvoisier's end was predictable:

> What Courvoisier felt when the jury were trying,
> And Phillips, his counsel, the truth was belying:
> 'Tis finished—again with his death to begin—
> The reward of his murder—the wages of sin.[16]

Unlike William Russell, Courvoisier would have been very aware of both the timing and manner of his end. Convicted on 21 June, he would spend the next two weeks in the condemned cell at Newgate awaiting execution. The ceremony attendant on his death, like that accorded to Russell posthumously, included a significant degree of public pomp and circumstance, but in Courvoisier's case it preceded and encompassed the execution itself.

Public hangings, once common, had by 1840 become relatively rare events and from 1836 only murderers were executed outside Newgate prison. Sentenced to hang at 8 a.m. on Monday 6 July, Courvoisier would make one more public appearance before his execution. At 10:30 a.m. on Sunday the 5th the Ordinary of Newgate, the Reverend James Carver, preached the condemned sermon in the prison's chapel. The public was there in full force; cards had been issued by the sheriffs and a gallery closed since the execution of the forger Henry Fauntleroy in 1824 was opened to accommodate the spectators. Courvoisier – described as a 'wretched man' and 'wretched culprit' – entered the chapel just before the sermon began, flanked by two turnkeys, and was seated on a bench beneath the pulpit. 'He never once', the *Times* and the *Morning Chronicle* reported,

> raised his eyes during the service. In fact, his looks denoted extreme sorrow and contrition, and he seemed to suffer great inward agitation when the ordinary particularly alluded to his crime. He was as attentive as possible to the service, and held the Prayer book with a steady hand'. Oxford sat behind him, and apart from a single observed 'foolish grin' likewise behaved with a 'decent seriousness'.[17]

Carver took as his text Job 14:21: 'For his eyes are upon the ways of sin, and he seeith all his goings. There is not darkness nor shadow of death where the workers of iniquity may hide themselves'.[18] *The Times* reproduced passages from Carver's sermon that 'referred to the wretched criminal more especially', such as

> that special deed of darkness which has subjected you, the midnight assassin of an aged, amiable, and unoffending master, to prison and death, has yet, and in a few hours too, to be judged of by Him 'whose eye is upon your heart (as well as upon your ways), and who sees all your thoughts as He saw all your goings'.

Acknowledging that Courvoisier had eventually, albeit 'tardily', confessed to his sin, Carver did not refrain from commenting on the 'evasions, subterfuges, and inconsistencies which have occurred in your recorded verbal statements on minor details', which 'very naturally induced the fear that "your heart is not right in the sight of God"'. Interestingly, he also referenced legal issues relating to the trial: 'God, in the wonderful workings of His providence, by a marvellous chain of circumstantial evidence, fixed upon you the guilt of [murder]'.

Courvoisier might still have escaped the noose. He had 'almost reached the very verge' of triumph; 'so strong was the impression of your innocence, from your long-established character for mildness and probity, that a mortal stab was about to be inflicted upon the reputation of your fellow-domestics and other innocent persons'. Here, presumably, Carver was referring to the anticipated attack by Charles Phillips on housemaid Sarah Mancer in his closing speech to the jury, an attack largely, if not entirely, abandoned in the wake of Madame Piolaine's evidence.

On returning to his cell after the sermon concluded, Courvoisier was visited by the Swiss consul, who delivered to him a letter written by his mother. He was said to have replied in a few conventional lines resembling letters written by schoolboys in much less serious circumstances: 'the answer was an attempt to console the unhappy parent for the misery and disgrace which his crime had brought upon his family'.[19] Following his attendance at the condemned sermon the convict retired from public view until he reappeared at the scaffold the following morning.

In these days of less frequent executions contemporaries, including Charles Dickens, had developed a morbid fascination with a capital convict's final night. Just as he would imagine the feelings of a defendant watching the jury withdraw to consider his fate, Dickens contemplated the condemned man's experience in *Sketches by Boz*:

> Conceive the situation of a man, spending his last night on earth in this cell. Buoyed up with some vague and undefined hope of reprieve, he knew not why – indulging in some wild and visionary idea of escaping, he knew not how – hour after hour of the three preceding days allowed him for preparation, has fled with a speed which no man living would deem possible, for none but this dying man can know. He has wearied his friends with entreaties, exhausted the attendants with importunities, neglected in his feverish restlessness the timely warnings of his spiritual consoler; and, now that the illusion is at last dispelled, now that eternity is before him and guilt behind, now that his fears of death amount almost to madness, and an overwhelming sense of his helpless, hopeless state rushes upon him, he is lost and stupefied, and has neither thoughts to turn to, nor power to call upon, the Almighty Being, from whom alone he can seek mercy and forgiveness, and before whom his repentance can alone avail.
>
> Hours have glided by, and still he sits upon the same stone bench with folded arms, heedless alike of the fast decreasing time before him, and the urgent entreaties of the good man at his side. The feeble light is wasting gradually, and the deathlike stillness of the street without, broken only by the rumbling of some passing vehicle which echoes mournfully through the empty yards, warns him that the night is waning fast away. The deep bell of St. Paul's strikes – one! He heard it; it has roused him. Seven hours left! He paces the narrow limits of his cell with rapid strides,

154 *'Going to See a Man Hanged'*

cold drops of terror starting on his forehead, and every muscle of his frame quivering with agony. Seven hours! He suffers himself to be led to his seat, mechanically takes the bible which is placed in his hand, and tries to read and listen ... The voice of the clergyman recalls him to himself. He is reading from the sacred book its solemn promises of pardon for repentance, and its awful denunciation of obdurate men. He falls upon his knees and clasps his hands to pray. Hush! what sound was that? He starts upon his feet. It cannot be two yet. Hark! Two quarters have struck; - the third - the fourth. It is! Six hours left. Tell him not of repentance! Six hours' repentance for eight times six years of guilt and sin! He buries his face in his hands, and throws himself on the bench.

...

A period of unconsciousness succeeds. He wakes, cold and wretched. The dull, gray light of morning is stealing into the cell, and falls upon the form of the attendant turnkey. Confused by his dreams, he starts from his uneasy bed in momentary uncertainty. It is but momentary. Every object in the narrow cell is too frightfully real to admit of doubt or mistake. He is the condemned felon again, guilty and despairing; and in two hours more will be dead.

Three years later Dickens returned to the theme of a capital convict's last night, in chapter 52 of *Oliver Twist*, first published in April 1839. Fagin is less contrite and does not turn to God; he raves and blasphemes and drives away 'with curses' the Jews brought to pray with him. But he nonetheless suffers 'the tortures of his evil conscience' in the few days between conviction and execution: the 'paroxysm of fear and wrath' demonstrated by their prisoner made even his guards recoil in horror so that a single man would not sit alone with him and 'two kept watch together'. The terror and despair with which Fagin contemplates his fate are not drawn entirely unsympathetically: he is afraid of the dark, bloodies his hands beating on the cell door for a candle, and is stricken by the hourly striking of church clocks.[20]

Courvoisier's own last night was much reported and rumour appears to have run riot, aided in part by the convict himself. The convict's turnkeys had been 'most active and vigilant' following his conviction, the *Morning Chronicle* reported, as prison governor William Cope was convinced that Courvoisier might attempt to anticipate 'the hangman's business' and end his criminal career in self-murder, as the alleged Ratcliffe highway murderer John Williams had done – in Williams's case before the trial could be held. Various reports were made to this effect. On the night prior to the execution, Cope was said to have discovered among Courvoisier's clothes a strip of cloth that might have been used in an act of private strangulation. He also replaced the convict's mattress, and Courvoisier reputedly told Cope that secreted within the original was a piece of sharpened wood with which, in the absence of a pin, he could have 'opened his arm'. No such piece of wood was found within the mattress in question: 'In the hurry and confusion of removal it might have been lost; or the prisoner might have indulged himself with another lie before his exit'.[21] The latter explanation seems the most likely; Courvoisier pretended to have led the police in a merry chase for secreted stolen goods before he was removed from Russell's house. *The Times* similarly reported that the valet had 'a short time before his execution' 'contemplated self-destruction, but the vigilant superintendence under which he was kept ever since he was placed within Newgate rendered it impracticable ...'[22] Courvoisier retired at 11 p.m. and slept until 4:30 a.m.

Courvoisier at the scaffold

On the day of execution Carver, the ordinary of Newgate, as well as a Swiss cleric, Charles Baup, together with Sheriff Wheelton, attended Courvoisier just after 7 a.m. and prayed with him until the convict received the sacrament at 7:30. By a quarter to 8 there were also well-dressed spectators in attendance. 'Hundreds of applications', reported the *Morning Chronicle*, 'had been made to the sheriffs for orders of admission', but few had been issued.[23] 'In some instances', the anxiety of those who succeeded in gaining entry

> to witness the preparations for the execution of the last sentence of the law on the criminal, led them to crowd and press noisily into the cell, utterly regardless of that decorum which all ought to observe in the chamber of death.[24]

There was also an unseemly scuffle between the sheriffs and one of the prison inspectors, the inspector demanding entry to observe the final preparations and Sheriff Evans maintaining the prisoner was in his custody and the inspector had no right to be present. At one of the undersheriff's urging the inspector was eventually allowed in, on the condition that he did not interfere with proceedings. Courvoisier was said to have ignored these various distractions. The executioner, William Calcraft, entered the cell after the convict had received the sacrament, and bound his arms. Some degree of solemnity was attempted in the procession to the scaffold. Prison governor Cope led the way, followed by the sheriffs and undersheriffs and the two clergymen. Carver read the burial service as he preceded Courvoisier to the gallows.[25] Yet in his scrapbook, Hobler commented censoriously,

> The day or day after the Execution of Courvoisier I spoke to two of the newspaper reporters Mr Archbold/since dead/ and Mr McFarlane both of whom attended the last scene, and they named to me several noblemen & men of rank who were present, and that when the moment arrived for the Criminal to walk to the spot for Execution the procession was formed in the usual way and in passing along through the narrow passages of Newgate leading to the door at the opening whereof the scaffold is placed – these titled men made such a rush to get a good place that in

156 *'Going to See a Man Hanged'*

> their zeal they pushed over the chaplain and the Criminal & nearly threw them down – so much for the taste of this sort of man[.][26]

Hobler also pasted into his book a cutting from the *Hampshire Independent* which excoriated the behaviour of the upper classes. That paper reported,

> Can anyone have read the account of the execution of the wretch Courvoisier without being satisfied of the folly of taking human life – without being disgusted at the circumstances which attended it? It was not merely the lowly, the poor, the ignorant, and the depraved that glorified this villain in his death, – but the rich and the noble were there to do honour to his exit. Yes, – the educated and puissant of the land gloated their beastly appetites over the throbs of a murderer. They came to see *how* he died. They wished to know (in cant phrase) if he was '*game to the last*'. Why, is this not the way to encourage murder – is it not giving *ton* to blood and crime? We say distinctly that it is. Every high-born personage present at this execution merits and ought to receive the censure of society.

The paper then 'named and shamed' the aristocrats in question, as they were identified in the London press: Lord Glentworth, Lord Lowth, Lord Alfred Paget, Lord Fitzharris, Lord Lichfield, and Count D'Orsay. Several of these men, the *Independent* noted, were known to frequent the prize ring. The implication is that their attendance owed more to a penchant for physically violent spectator sports than to sympathy for the murder victim. The presence of 'elegantly-dressed females' who watched the proceedings from neighbouring houses with 'opera glasses in their hands!!!' was also censured. No sympathy was expressed for the hanged man himself: Courvoisier was described as both a 'cowardly villain' and a 'mucilaginous murderer'. The 'whole affair', the paper concluded, 'from first to last, has been a libel on the Law, the Justice, and the Police of the country. He was within an ace of getting off scot-free …'[27] As indeed he was.

Outside the prison, the execution attracted an enormous crowd. Among the spectators was 28-year-old Charles Dickens. So incensed had he been by the conduct of Courvoisier's defence, Dickens is unlikely to have felt any sympathy for this confessed murderer or to have lost sleep contemplating the last hours of this particular convict on earth. Not Dickens but another novelist would write sympathetically about Courvoisier's execution. Thackeray, in 1840, like Dickens, a young man in the early stages of his career and reliant on occasional journalism for an income, happily accepted a commission to write about the event and on the morning of the hanging met up with men, including his friend Monckton Milnes, MP, who had spent the preceding evening carousing and telling gallows jokes rather than sympathizing with the plight of the condemned man. The execution proved an unexpected shock to Thackeray's sensibilities.

Thackeray, it has been claimed, had brooded on public execution long before the Russell murder. The subject is first referenced in letters written to his mother in 1829, during his time at Cambridge, when he noted the arrival of the Assize judges, who stayed at Trinity College. Whether any of the trials held resulted in conviction he does not say, but he refers to the fact that some men organized breakfast parties to see convicts hang. When studying art in Paris in 1836 Thackeray himself attempted to witness the execution of Giuseppe Fieschi, guillotined for his part in the unsuccessful conspiracy to assassinate Louis Phillipe, but the authorities did not publish the date of the execution and it was carried out in a remote location. He subsequently tried to attend the guillotining of poet and murderer Pierre François Lacenaire but arrived after the fact. In 1839, Thackeray became preoccupied with the case of Sebastien-Benoît Peytel, convicted, despite the efforts of Balzac on his behalf, of murdering his wife and their servant. The young journalist thought the trial too theatrical and the evidence on which Peytel was convicted too slight. He did not attend Peytel's execution in Bourg but read about it in the press. Collectively, these three cases led him to reflect on the efficacy of public execution as a deterrent. Thackeray was horrified by crowd behaviour at such events, by the evident pleasure, even joy, taken in the suffering of others. He could detect no 'moral profit' in such exhibitions and found no 'moral basis' for criminal sanctions.[28]

By the time of Courvoisier's execution – the first he witnessed in person – Thackeray had thus already become an opponent of capital punishment. What he saw on 6 July 1840 only confirmed him in his opinions. He wrote to his mother,

> I have been to see Courvoisier hanged & am miserable ever since. I can't do my work ... It is most curious the effect his death has had on me, and I am trying to work it off in a paper on the subject. Meanwhile it weighs upon the mind, like cold plum pudding weighs on the stomach, & as soon as I begin to write I get melancholy.[29]

Thackeray, like Dickens, had contemplated the feelings of a man who goes to bed in full knowledge that in the morning he will meet with death, but in his instance, a particular man: Russell's valet.

> I could not help thinking, as each clock sounded, what is he doing now – has he heard it in his little room in Newgate yonder – Eleven o'clock. He has been writing until now, can hold out no longer, and is very weary. 'Wake me at four,' says he, 'for I have still much to put down.' From eleven to twelve the gaoler hears how he is grinding his teeth in his sleep. At twelve he is up in his bed and asks, 'Is it the time – 'He has plenty more time yet for sleep; and he sleeps, and the bell goes on tolling. Seven hours more – five hours more. Many a carriage is clattering through the streets, bringing ladies away from evening parties; many bachelors are reeling home after a jolly night; Covent Garden is alive; and the light coming

through the cell-window turns the gaoler's candle pale. Four hours more! 'Courvoisier,' says the gaoler, shaking him, 'it's four o'clock now, and I've woke you as you told me; but there's no call for you to get up yet.' The poor wretch leaves his bed, however, and makes his last toilet; and then falls to writing, to tell the world how he did the crime for which he has suffered. This time he will tell the truth and the whole truth.[30]

At 4 a.m., as Courvoisier was wakened, Thackeray and his friends made their way to Newgate, where they would wait four hours for the execution to take place. Others had been gathering from Sunday evening. 'Sixty constables', the *Globe* reported, 'marched to the Old Bailey for the purposes of preserving order' when the carpenters arrived to erect the scaffolding at roughly two in the morning, and another 60 were sent in an hour later. 'As we enter Holborn', Thackeray wrote,

> the town grows more animated; and there are already twice as many people in the streets as you see at mid-day in a German Residenz or an English provincial town. The ginshop keepers have many of them taken their shutters down, and many persons are issuing from them pipe in hand. Down they go along the broad bright street, their blue shadows marching after them; for they are all bound the same way, and are bent like us upon seeing the hanging.
>
> It is twenty minutes past four as we pass St. Sepulchre's: by this time many hundred people are in the street, and many more are coming up Snow Hill. Before us lies Newgate Prison; but something a great deal more awful to look at, which seizes the eye at once, and makes the heart beat ... There it stands black and ready, jutting out from a little door in the prison. As you see it, you feel a kind of dumb electric shock, which causes one to start a little, and give a sort of gasp for breath. The shock is over in a second; and presently you examine the object before you with a certain feeling of complacent curiosity. At least, such was the effect that the gallows produced upon the writer, who is trying to set down all his feelings as they occurred, and not to exaggerate them at all.

'Scarcely a word', Thackeray reported,

> had been said about Courvoisier all this time. We were all, as far as I could judge, in just such a frame of mind as men are in when they are squeezing at the pit-door of a play, or pushing for a review or a Lord Mayor's show.[31]

But as the hours wore on, the atmosphere changed:

> It was past seven now; the quarters rang and passed away; the crowd began to grow very eager and more quiet, and we turned back every now

and then and looked at St. Sepulchre's clock. Half-an-hour, twenty-five minutes. What is he doing now? He has his irons off by this time. A quarter: he's in the press-room now, no doubt. Now at last we had come to think about the man we were going to see hanged.

... at last – ding, dong, dong, dong! – the bell is tolling the chimes of eight.[32]

Courvoisier, Thackeray wrote,

bore his punishment like a man, and walked very firmly. He was dressed in a new black suit, as it seemed: his shirt was open. His arms were tied in front of him. He opened his hands in a helpless kind of way, and clasped them once or twice together. He turned his head here and there, and looked about him for an instant with a wild imploring look. His mouth was contracted into a sort of pitiful smile. He went and placed himself at once under the beam, with his face towards St. Sepulchre's. The tall grave man in black twisted him round swiftly in the other direction, and, drawing from his pocket a night-cap, pulled it tight over the patient's head and face. I am not ashamed to say that I could look no more, but shut my eyes as the last dreadful act was going on which sent this wretched guilty soul into the presence of God.[33]

Newspaper reports of the execution largely confirm Thackeray's description of Courvoisier's scaffold behaviour. *The Times*, for example, wrote:

The prisoner's manner was marked by an extraordinary appearance of firmness. His step was steady and collected, and his movements free from the slightest agitation or indecision. His countenance indeed was pale, and bore the trace of much dejection, but it was at the same time calm and unmoved. While the executioner was placing him on the drop, he slightly moved his hands (which were tied in front of him, and strongly clasped one within the other) up and down two or three times; and this was the only visible symptom of any emotion or mental anguish which the wretched man endured.[34]

Courvoisier's personal control, the solemnity of the convict being 'turned off', and Thackeray's horror at what he was witnessing were not matched by the behaviour of some of the spectators. A 'gang of thieves' reportedly caused chaos by shouting 'mad bull!', leading to a panicked stampede of spectators trying to escape in Giltspur street; 'many hundreds' were thrown to the ground and carts were overturned.[35]

The hanged man's body was cut down at roughly 9 a.m., crowds remaining in place until that time, and removed to the 'dead room' within Newgate, where the Earl of Lichfield and various other noblemen were said to have viewed it. Casts were also taken of his head. In contrast to the dignified burial arrangements made for William Russell, his murderer's corpse was interred without fanfare, or the presence of family, in an unmarked grave within the prison walls at 8 p.m. that night.[36]

On a purely physical level, the spectacle had come to an end. Public interest and discussion, however, continued. A troubled Thackeray mused at some length on the meaning and effects of what he had witnessed:

> If a public execution is beneficial – and beneficial it is, no doubt, or else the wise laws would not encourage forty thousand people to witness it – the next useful thing must be a full description of such a ceremony, and all its entourages, and to this end the above pages are offered to the reader. How does an individual man feel under it – In what way does he observe it, – how does he view all the phenomena connected with it, – what induces him, in the first instance, to go and see it, – and how is he moved by it afterwards? The writer has discarded the magazine 'We' altogether, and spoken face to face with the reader, recording every one of the impressions felt by him as honestly as he could.
>
> I must confess, then (for 'I' is the shortest word, and the best in this case), that the sight has left on my mind an extraordinary feeling of terror and shame. It seems to me that I have been abetting an act of frightful wickedness and violence, performed by a set of men against one of their fellows; and I pray God that it may soon be out of the power of any man in England to witness such a hideous and degrading sight. Forty thousand persons (say the Sheriffs), of all ranks and degrees, – mechanics, gentlemen, pickpockets, members of both Houses of Parliament, street-walkers, newspaper-writers, gather together before Newgate at a very early hour; the most part of them give up their natural quiet night's rest, in order to partake of this hideous debauchery, which is more exciting than sleep, or than wine, or the last new ballet, or any other amusement they can have. Pickpocket and Peer each is tickled by the sight alike, and has that hidden lust after blood which influences our race.[37]

For all the condemnation Courvoisier had met with, now the state seemed equally a murderer:

> I fully confess that I came away down Snow Hill that morning with a disgust for murder, but it was for the murder I saw done. ... This is the 20th of July, and I may be permitted for my part to declare that, for the last fourteen days, so salutary has the impression of the butchery been upon me, I have had the man's face continually before my eyes; that I can see Mr. Ketch at this moment, with an easy air, taking the rope from his pocket; that I feel myself ashamed and degraded at the brutal curiosity which took me to that brutal sight; and that I pray to Almighty God to cause this disgraceful sin to pass from among us, and to cleanse our land of blood.[38]

'Constraints on sympathy': class and execution[39]

Thackeray's immediate response to witnessing the execution of Courvoisier attracted significant attention in his own time and continues to absorb the attention of both criminal justice historians and literary scholars. The issue of class tends to be a constant in such discussions. Thus in chapter 10 of *The Hanging Tree* V.A.C Gatrell contrasts the attitudes of James Boswell in the eighteenth century and Thackeray in 1840, arguing that in Boswell's time 'emotional distances between the propertied classes and most victims of the law' effectively prevented true sympathy, and that 'an economy of the emotions' was 'organized along lines of class'. On his view, what distinguishes Thackeray's response to public execution was that 'Here, at last and extraordinarily we do encounter a man who transcended class boundaries by associating himself' with Courvoisier's 'scaffold terror'.[40] Boswell had shared Thackeray's morbid fascination with execution, enjoying hangings and attending 'as many as he could'. Unlike Thackeray, he also believed public execution was an effective deterrent if properly conducted. In 1783 he had advocated that capital convicts be dispatched as if they were oxen: rendered unconscious by a blow to the head, throats slit, and corpses dismembered with an axe. Such an execution would reduce the suffering of its victim while properly inducing terror in spectators. Hanging, by contrast, allowed for a transference of sympathy, and inclined spectators to view the law as cruel. Pity, Boswell believed, 'should be allowed no place' at the scaffold.[41] But, as Gatrell argues, the pity Boswell had felt was limited to convicts of his own class. He cites two examples in this regard: Boswell's attendance at hangings in 1763 and 1774. In 1763, his sympathy was reserved for highwayman Paul Lewis, whose execution shook him as Courvoisier's would Thackeray, inducing shock, melancholy, and 'gloomy terrors'.[42] Boswell neglected to mention the other two convicts hanged on the same occasion, and Gatrell finds the omission of Hannah Dagoe, convicted of burglary, particularly significant. Dagoe, an Irish woman, had not left the world meekly or calmly, instead struggling with her executioner and removing and throwing her clothing to the spectators before flinging herself from the cart so that she broke her own neck. The vulgarity of this 'big unconcerned being', Gatrell argues, precluded any sort of 'sympathetic connection' on the part of a gentleman like Boswell. 'With Lewis, conversely, identification depended on a projection mediated through a fantasy of social likeness'. Boswell felt a similar empathy in 1774 with sheep-stealer John Reid, who had been a former client, and on whose behalf he spent seven weeks petitioning for a pardon while simultaneously urging Reid to confess if he were truly guilty. Boswell was unsuccessful in both efforts and claimed that he 'suffered much more' from the conviction and execution than Reid had done himself. Once again, Boswell had 'projected his personality into that of another being', but in a narcissistic way. Lewis had attracted his sympathy by virtue of a similar social status, Reid on the basis of a former personal relationship.[43] Empathy thus depended on some form of social connection and, as Gatrell argues, 'in an era when most of the condemned were

Dagoe-like rather than Lewis-like, those conditions were rarely achieved'. The majority of capital convicts 'remained remote'.[44] Gatrell also challenges Sir Leon Radzinowicz's assertion that the execution of the reverend and forger Dr Dodd in 1777 marked a turning point in public opinion where public execution was concerned. Dodd, he claims, attracted sympathy by virtue of his class. Unlike Dagoe he had died 'politely' and his execution engendered horror because 'executing a clergyman turned the world upside down'.[45] Gatrell contrasts public reaction to Dodd's execution with that of 15-year-old Joseph Harris, hanged on the same occasion: where Dodd had 'tried to get away with £4,300' Harris had been convicted for robbing a stage coach of a couple of half guineas plus a few shillings. He also points to the execution of 25 Gordon rioters in 1780: their fates, like that of Harris, failed to attract sympathy in part for political reasons but also because the terror of such people 'could not easily' be replicated within the 'feeling selves' of polite society.[46]

To find true change and the erosion of eighteenth-century social constraints on empathy, Gatrell argues, we must 'leap forward' 60 years to the execution of Courvoisier:

> Either we meet in Thackeray just another young man going to a hanging thoughtlessly and being shocked by it; or we meet a new or different kind of sensibility – a modern one, we might call it, by which we might mean one intelligible to use: inheriting the precepts of eighteenth-century sympathy certainly, but responding to a hanging *democratically* at last, through identification with a humble victim regardless of his social status. Either that, or another way of interpreting the episode entirely. Might it be merely that in 1840 we enter a different material and political world, which offered peculiarly appropriate (though unstable) conditions for the release of empathy across class boundaries?

Gatrell favours the latter explanation, but regardless, class boundaries had been breached to allow empathy even for a convict who had himself violently transgressed them in murdering his employer. Thackeray's identification with Courvoisier's terror was not dependent on any presumption of a shared social standing. A 'great divide had been crossed': 'pity for a common murderer and disgust at those who took his life had never been so nakedly discussed in print before'.[47]

While Thackeray's article clearly struck a chord – the *Era* saw fit to quote at length from the author's 'truly graphic description' of Courvoisier's execution[48] – this passionate protest was not sustained. Monckton Milnes, who had persuaded Thackeray to attend the hanging, proposed in Parliament in 1845 that public hangings should be banned and executions take place instead within prison walls. They would retain a degree of publicity, in that both the authorities and journalists would be on hand to witness events. Milnes, that is, was by 1845 no longer an opponent of capital punishment per se, rejecting only the continued public spectacle, which he described as 'gladiatorial exhibition'.

Dickens would make the same transition: at the time of Courvoisier's execution he was an abolitionist; by 1849, he argued instead for private hanging.[49] In the 1840s, this suggestion was not entirely novel – Henry Fielding had urged it in 1751 – but it remained unsuccessful. Public executions would continue until 1868, and in 1856, the hanging of Martha Brown for the murder of her husband would be witnessed by another famous Victorian novelist, Thomas Hardy.[50] Hardy was only 16 years old when Brown was executed, but the memory of her body turning in the wind stayed with him and is commonly acknowledged as inspiring *Tess of the D'Urbervilles* (1891).

Although, at the time of Brown's execution, abolitionists were thin on the ground, there were still some to be found, and they included the barrister who had unsuccessfully defended Courvoisier 16 years earlier. In the manner of its expression Charles Phillips's *Vacation Thoughts on Capital Punishment* is a prime example of the rhetorical, bordering on hysterical, excesses for which he had long been known. But beneath the melodrama was a clearly argued rationale that combined Christian morality with the practical concerns of criminal justice administration. Phillips, like the young Thackeray, did not believe capital punishment served as an effective deterrent; public executions failed to instil terror into spectators but brutalized them instead. Convicted murderers, he argued, rather than being hanged, should be incarcerated in institutions built in isolated locations and specifically reserved for them.[51]

The lack of legislative response to calls for abolition or private execution testifies to the fact that public opinion remained divided. When, on 12 July, *Bell's Weekly Messenger* contrasted the respective fates of Gould and Courvoisier, tried at the same Old Bailey Sessions, it considered Courvoisier's execution an exemplary moral lesson and a clear indication that 'the retention of capital punishment is necessary' to secure confession. 'A public good' had been effected and 'public benefit' achieved. Gould, by contrast, acquitted of Templeman's murder but convicted of theft, had 'cheated the hangman'. Transported rather than hanged, he enjoyed 'a kind of triumph over the law'. And for all his reforming instincts where the criminal law was concerned, William Russell's nephew, Lord John Russell, would not have objected to the public execution of his uncle's murderer. Like Robert Peel, he did not believe that 'the publicity should be done away with'. Three years earlier, in 1837, there had been protests in Parliament about 'disgusting exhibitions' at two executions. Lord John had acknowledged the criticisms but blamed 'the low religious and moral standards' of those who had attended them.[52]

Thackeray and execution

Whether Thackeray himself subsequently changed his position on capital punishment is unclear. Deborah A. Thomas reviewed opinions expressed on the issue and concluded that his 'eventual position' remains 'a matter of disagreement'.[53] Were the beliefs expressed in 'On Going to See a Man Hanged' modified over time?

Albert Borowitz is convinced Thackeray didn't change his views at all: 'It is doubtful that Thackeray ever qualified his abolitionist beliefs, based as they were on the repugnance which his flesh had felt on the hanging of Courvoisier'.[54] Others are equally convinced that he came to accept that execution carried out privately, in the presence of only official witnesses rather than large crowds, might be considered just. Gatrell asserted that Thackeray, like Dickens, reluctantly came to accept the utility of private executions, a claim Thomas finds 'plausible' if unsubstantiated. Gatrell merely comments that after 'On Going to See a Man Hanged', Thackeray fell 'silent'.[55] In searching for evidence of Thackeray's ultimate position, Thomas argues that claims that he changed his mind rest on a 'sweeping statement' made by Thackeray scholar and editor George Saintsbury in 1908: 'The anti-capital-punishment fad was one of the special crochets of mid-century Liberalism, and [Thackeray] kept to it for some time, but in his later and wiser days admitted that he was wrong'.[56] Thomas follows Harry Potter in believing that this claim, like Gatrell's, lacks substantiation, resting solely on remarks made by a distant cousin of Thackeray's, Richard Bedingfield.[57] In praising his relative's essay – the date of their conversation was not specified in Bedingfield's reminiscences – the young man met with the following response: 'I think I was wrong. My feelings were overwrought. These murderers are such devils after all'. But Bedingfield adds, 'Nevertheless, he did not like capital punishment'.[58] Thomas herself believes that Thackeray did come to accept private execution and within a few years of witnessing the execution of Courvoisier.[59] As evidence, she cites 'more equivocal' references to capital punishment in stories published in *Fraser's Magazine* in 1843 and 1844: 'The ____'s Wife' and 'The Princess's Tragedy'. In these works, Thomas writes, 'Thackeray seems to have shifted his emphasis' from a 'clear-cut disapproval of capital punishment … to a more complicated and less clearly disapproving sense that executions are horrible events that people with normal, humane feelings would wish to keep at a distance'.[60] Here, she invokes Gatrell's conclusion that 'squeamishness' rather than humanitarianism won the day where public execution was concerned.[61]

Regardless of any subsequent equivocation, Thomas believes that Thackeray's response to the execution of Courvoisier affected the direction of his fiction. *Vanity Fair* (1847–48), she notes, has long been acknowledged as a 'novel of enigmas', and one of its puzzles is why Thackeray fails to reveal whether Becky Sharp actually kills Joseph Sedley. This ambiguity has been commonly considered a matter of deliberate artistry. But Thomas suggests we consider another explanation: that while Thackeray might 'privately conceived of Becky as murdering Jos', he had equally developed a profound revulsion for public execution. Expressly identifying Becky Sharp as a murderer would have required him to describe the legal consequences of her crime. Thackeray 'may not have been fully conscious of the degree to which his experience of Courvoisier's hanging entered into his later treatment of the demise of Jos', but 'connections between fact and fiction' might still be drawn out. *Vanity Fair*'s ambiguity, Thomas argues, places the novel within the context of public debate over capital punishment.[62]

Conclusion: 'The household shiver of razors'

What remains striking, from my point of view, in Thackeray's response to witnessing Courvoisier's execution, is the identity of the convict who occasioned the writer's horror, a convict who had attracted universal condemnation until the hour of his death. That even a servant convicted of murdering his master could become an object of pity is remarkable. He is arguably not the first: 22-year-old Eliza Fenning, hanged in 1815 for the attempted poisoning of the Turner family who employed her as cook, attracted considerable sympathy. Like Courvoisier's her employment had been of short duration, six weeks rather than five, and she was alleged to have been resentful of rebukes on her conduct. But in Fenning's case, public opinion had been divided from the time of her arrest. And where, in Courvoisier's trial, the public was incensed by the conduct of counsel for the defence, in 1815 it was the conduct of the judge, recorder John Silvester, that attracted opprobrium.[63] Some believed Fenning to have been wrongly accused and convicted. As Gatrell puts it, the public 'smelled cover-up, malicious prosecution, wrongful conviction ...'.[64] Courvoisier's case differs in that crucial aspect: he was widely assumed to have been guilty of the crime for which he was hanged. And still Thackeray felt pity.

We should, however, remember the more complicated shadow the Russell murder cast on Thackeray, which has attracted less comment. For all of the distress demonstrated in 'On Going to See a Man Hanged', Thackeray was clearly haunted not merely by Courvoisier's execution, but by his crime. A new sympathy for the servant's experience of life coincided with an enhanced recognition of the physical threat they posed to their employers. Thackeray, as we have seen, became highly sensitive to 'the historical pressure of subalterny'.[65] But his sympathy for servants was also tinged, as Bruce Robbins has explored, with fear of the lethal potential of the servant's hand. Arthur Munby eroticized it, but that hand could also be dangerous.[66] Robbins has commented on both Thackeray's 'fondness for the historical viewpoint of the valet, for whom no man is a hero' and the 'less obvious corollary' in 'an enlarging of the powers' of his valets, 'at his heroic masters' expense'. He points first to the comic essay 'The History of the Next French Revolution', published in *Punch* in 1844: the army of one of the noble aspirants to the French throne includes a unit made up of 'indomitable English footmen'. But 'suggestions of domestic conflict', of 'private, rebellious violence', Robbins argues, are 'unmistakable' in this farce. The '*cold steel*' of the valet's razor – the italics are Thackeray's – becomes bayonets used by 'Jenkins' Foot' to annihilate French regiments. But the battle concludes with Jenkins' hand around a duke's collar, prepared to throttle him. 'As he snickers at military glory', Thackeray replaces it with an order of violence that his readers will feel is closer to home: 'the household shiver of razors at the neck and hands at the collar'. The footmen's violence is rooted in class conflict, the fact that their own material interests 'clash with those of their alliances' and military victory aside, this conflict results in mutiny and rebellion as well.[67] The 'spectre of throat-cutting' is also invoked in *Vanity*

Fair. Jos Sedley, who lives in fear of having his throat cut by Napoleon's armies, is unaware that his valet Isidor is a Bonapartiste and in chapter 12 offers himself, removing his neckcloth and turning down his collar, for a shave. For a brief moment, Isidor believes Sedley has gone mad and is asking his manservant to cut his throat. While only a shave of moustaches ensues, 'it is a shave', as Robbins argues, 'heavy with historical implications'.[68] He also cites a 'mildly comic shave' in chapter 36 of *Pendennis* (1848–50), in which the Major is nicked by his valet Morgan – who later orders Pendennis out of his own house – as he mocks 'pore men'. And Robbins points to a similar 'tonsorial allusion' in Thackeray's Christmas 'fireside pantomime'/fairy tale 'The Rose and the Ring' (1854), 'the shaver and the executioner' conflated in a scene in which a valet shaves a prince before he is guillotined.[69]

'The translation of political revolution into domestic insurrection', Andrew Miller writes, 'understood as the desire of servants to discard the appurtenances of subjection and acquire the material possessions of their masters is one of William Thackeray's obsessive concerns by the late 1840s'.[70] While neither Miller nor Robbins makes the direct connection, domestic insurrection and desire for material possessions, and the invocation of class conflict involving footmen/valets, aristocrats, and throat-cutting/shaving motifs found throughout Thackeray's work arguably have their origins in Courvoisier's murder of William Russell. Three years earlier – in the same year, that is, that footman William Tayler was writing his private diary – Thackeray, tongue firmly in cheek, had produced a fictional memoir of Cockney footman William J. Yellowplush.[71] After 1840, the flippancy would be abandoned. Revulsion for 'the hangman's rope' did not preclude fear of 'a ruffian's knife'.[72] Both were terrifying and the threat of the knife may explain Thackeray's apparent acceptance, however reluctantly, of the noose. In acknowledging the social inequities that defined a servant's experience of life, Thackeray was 'critiqu[ing] a culture in which he knows he remains invested'.[73] That investment rendered him, and other members of his class, vulnerable, and placed continued and significant constraints on sympathy.

Notes

1. The *Morning Chronicle* (7 July 1840) estimated 10,000 spectators; the *Globe* (12 July) 15,000; the *Era* (12 July) 20,000; the *Examiner* 'not less than 30,000' (12 July); Thackeray, in 'On Going to See a Man Hanged', 40,000.
2. See Chapter 6 below.
3. On this article, see Borowitz, 'Why Thackeray Went to see a Man Hanged'; Gatrell, *The Hanging Tree*, chap. 10; and Thomas, 'Thackeray, Capital Punishment, and the Demise of Jos Sedley'. Simpson, 'Thackeray and the Execution of Courvoisier', should be treated with caution as, relying on Yseult Bridge's study of the Courvoisier case, it contains factual errors.
4. 31; 110 and 161; 118; 170.
5. 'Fetishizing the Flunkey', 384–85.
6. *Poison, detection, and the Victorian imagination*, 12.
7. See Chapter 6 below.

8   13 May 1840.
9   12 May 1840.
10 12 May 1840.
11 O'Daniel, *Ins and Outs of London*, 359.
12 *The Times*, 13 May 1840; the *Era*, 17 May 1840; see also the *Morning Chronicle*, 13 May 1840, the *Standard*, 13 May 1840, the *Examiner*, 17 May 1840. 'Mutes' were paid, professional, silent mourners, ostrich feathers a traditional Victorian accompaniment in funeral processions.
13 His first wife, Adelaide Lister, Lady Ribblesdale (1807–38), had died two years earlier. The year after Lady John's death Lord John lost his father, the Duke of Bedford. Both were buried in the crypt at Woburn Abbey. Lord John's marriage, if short-lived and a source of discontent to various family members, appears to have been happy When they met she was a young widow (Ribblesdale died in 1832) with four children. Russell married her on 11 April 1835, the day before he was sent for by Melbourne to help form an administration. Prest, *Lord John Russell*, pp. 85, 135–36 and plate 6, 'A Day after the Wedding'.
14 17 May 1840.
15 Russell's funeral was reported in the *Standard* (13 May 1840) and the *Era* and the *Examiner* (17 May) as well as the *The Times* and the *Morning Chronicle*.
16 The *Era*, 21 March 1841.
17 6 July 1840.
18 The full text of Carver's sermon was pasted into Hobler's scrapbook: Item 104 (seq. 400–6).
19 *The Times*, 6 July 1840.
20 Dickens, *Oliver Twist*, quotations at 469, 470.
21 *Morning Chronicle*, 7 July 1840.
22 7 July 1840.
23 See also the *York Herald*, 11 July 1840.
24 *Bristol Mercury*, 11 July 1840.
25 *Era*, 12 July 1840.
26 Item 110 (seq. 412).
27 11 July 1840.
28 Borowitz, 'Why Thackeray Went to See a Man Hanged', 17–9. Borowitz also links Thackeray's preoccupation to the novelist's personal 'strong anxieties about death and illness'.
29 Thackeray, *Letters* 1:453, quoted in Borowitz, 'Why Thackeray Went to See a Man Hanged', 19.
30 'On Going to See a Man Hanged', 150.
31 'On Going to See a Man Hanged', 151.
32 'On Going to See a Man Hanged', 155.
33 'On Going to See a Man Hanged', 156.
34 7 July 1840. See also the *Morning Chronicle* of the same date; and the *Southern Star* and the *Era*, 12 July.
35 *Freeman's Journal*, 8 July 1840; *Blackburn Standard*, 8 July 1840.
36 *Morning Chronicle*, 7 July 1840; *Blackburn Standard*, 8 July 1840.
37 'On Going to See a Man Hanged', 156.
38 'On Going to See a Man Hanged', 156.
39 Gatrell, *The Hanging Tree*, 280.
40 Gatrell, *The Hanging Tree*, 280–81.
41 Gatrell, *The Hanging Tree*, 287.
42 Gatrell, *The Hanging Tree*, 288.
43 Gatrell, *The Hanging Tree*, 291.
44 Gatrell, *The Hanging Tree*, 292.

168 *'Going to See a Man Hanged'*

45 Gatrell, *The Hanging Tree*, 294. On the emotional response to the Dodd case, see also McGowen, 'Doctor Dodd and the Law'.
46 Gatrell, *The Hanging Tree*, 294.
47 Gatrell, *The Hanging Tree*, 296.
48 9 August 1840.
49 Hansard, col. 1413; *Letters of Charles Dickens* 5:644–45, 651–54, quoted in Thomas, 'Thackeray, Capital Punishment, and the Demise of Jos Sedley', 5. Martin Wiener argues that Thackeray described Courvoisier's execution as a 'pornographic exhibition, a public loss of control over the passions, and an invasion of the integrity of the body, incited by the government itself'. 'Market culture', 153–54, quoted in 'Thackeray, Capital Punishment, and the Demise of Jos Sedley', 15.
50 On the end of public execution, see Cooper, *The Lesson of the Scaffold* and 'Public Executions in Victorian England'; Potter, *Hanging in Judgment*; McGowen, 'Civilizing Punishment'; Gatrell, *The Hanging Tree*, Epilogue; and Devereaux, *Execution, State and Society*, chap. 9. See also McGowen, 'History, Culture, and the Death Penalty', and Gregory, *Victorians against the Gallows*.
51 See May, *The Bar and the Old Bailey*, 60–1.
52 Radzinowicz, *History of English Criminal Law*, 4:345.
53 'Thackeray, Capital Punishment, and the Demise of Jos Sedley', 4.
54 Borowitz, 'Why Thackeray Went to See a Man Hanged', 20.
55 *The Hanging Tree*, 591.
56 *The Oxford Thackeray* 3:xiv–xv, quoted in *The Oxford Thackeray*, 4.
57 *The Oxford Thackeray* 3:xiv–xv, quoted in *The Oxford Thackeray*, 4. For Potter, see *Hanging in Judgment*.
58 Collins, ed., *Thackeray*, 1:124n6.
59 'Thackeray, Capital Punishment, and the Demise of Jos Sedley', 5.
60 'Thackeray, Capital Punishment, and the Demise of Jos Sedley', 7.
61 *The Hanging Tree*, 297.
62 'Thackeray, Capital Punishment, and the Demise of Jos Sedley', 16–7.
63 On the public reaction to the trial and execution of Fenning, convicted of attempting to poison the family for whom she worked, see Gatrell, *The Hanging Tree*, chap. 13; Seleski, 'Domesticity is in the Streets'.
64 *The Hanging Tree*, 355.
65 *The Servant's Hand*, 206.
66 See Atkinson, *Love and Dirt*.
67 See Atkinson, *Love and Dirt*, 133–35.
68 See Atkinson, *Love and Dirt*, 138.
69 See Atkinson, *Love and Dirt*, 139.
70 Miller, '*Vanity Fair* Through Plate Glass', 1042.
71 'The Yellowplush Correspondence' (1837); see White, 'Thackeray's Contributions to *Fraser's Magazine*'.
72 *The Irish Sketch Book of 1842*, 17.
73 McCuskey, 'Fetishizing the Flunkey', 387. Where McCuskey finds the critique cynical, I would describe it rather as sincere but conflicted.

6 Who Speaks?

Voice, Image, Agency – and Truth

Introduction

The legal records generated by a violent death constitute a particular form of storytelling. It has become common practice among historians to remind us that investigations into criminal activity and the ensuing trial records illuminate incidentally, if briefly, the lives of those whose stories otherwise tended to be extinguished at their death. But those stories were told by and filtered through others. The speech involved was mediated and often reluctant. And the testimonies recorded were also driven and shaped by external needs and agendas: the legal need to establish guilt or innocence, to confirm or eliminate suspects, and to prove or cast doubt on the reliability of witnesses. In the event of a conviction, profit had for centuries also been made via publication of 'last dying speeches'. This chapter thus considers the issue of voice: Courvoisier's voice – and his personal silence in court – the voices of those eager to profit from his story, and those who sought to appropriate it as ammunition in a contemporary literary debate. Russell's murder having taken place prior to routine photographic imagery, it also reviews the portraits produced of the murderer. It concludes by considering the voice-over provided by Francis Hobler, whose 'book' constitutes one of the many tellings of this story.

Servants, voice, and history

In the twentieth century, authors of crime fiction – P.D. James is a prime example – frequently remarked on the fact that the temporary spotlight shone on victims, suspects, and witnesses during a murder investigation reveals secrets unrelated to the actual crime.[1] For historians, they also reveal the mundane, not necessarily secret, but matters that wouldn't otherwise attract attention or comment:

> Witnesses, abruptly snatched from the usual obscurity of their lives, must recollect trivial circumstances which, had it not been for the fortuitous intrusion of a murder, would never again have figured in their memories. The actors in a once private play ... in effect repeat the performance in the theater of English justice ...[2]

DOI: 10.4324/9781003481638-6

170 *Who Speaks?*

But the performances in question are of the command variety, prompted rather than volunteered, and all of these revelations occur secondhand. Records of private discourse between master and servant were likewise mediated and controlled. In discussing Victorian barrister Arthur Munby's transcription of servants' speech, Bruce Robbins notes that it is the employer who establishes 'the framework, limits, tone, and center of the reported conversations', and then only when such conversations took place.[3] Munby was by no means a typical employer. In many households, these conversations would have been rare: 'We never speak a word to the servant who waits on us for twenty years', commented Thackeray in *Punch*.[4] As a domestic servant, Courvoisier's speech with his master had always been proscribed. Robbins notes that direct verbal friction between employers and their servants was 'often explicitly disallowed' in novels; most assuredly such friction would not have been tolerated in real life.[5] Servants were expected to hold their tongues. If they did speak, their speech was considered compromised by virtue of their position: 'If your plate and glass are beautifully bright, your bell quickly answered, and Thomas ready, neat, and good-humored, you are not to expect absolute truth from him. ... You get truth habitually from equals only'.[6] Courvoisier would not have been permitted to defend or explain any perceived deficiencies in his service; he could not respond verbally to Russell's criticisms except to complain behind his master's back. Nor would anyone have been interested in the valet's perspective had he not drawn a carving knife across his master's throat. This violent act gave him both an avid audience and competitors for the privilege of recording his words. In the process of that recording, others shaped and framed versions of Courvoisier's story.

We should also remember that Courvoisier's was only one story among the many associated with Russell's murder. If I were a novelist rather than a historian, and permitted a degree of artistic licence, I would have been tempted to write a version of the murder of William Russell and the investigation and trial that followed from the perspective of Sarah Mancer, beginning with her discovery of the body, backtracking to her personal history prior to that event, reporting on the influx of police officers, government officials, and titled women into 14 Norfolk Street as seen through her eyes, recounting her various ordeals – carted about the country to be viewed by alleged former employers as well as appearing as a witness in a variety of tribunals – and summarizing her afterlife. That too would be appropriation and it would inevitably contain countless errors of fact as well as interpretation. Sarah Mancer's story has instead to be pieced together from fragments of second-hand tellings. Mancer was fortunate indeed to have had Francis Hobler to speak on her behalf and in her defence. In his 'book', Hobler told her story sympathetically and with compassion. But Mancer's own voice, like that of Courvoisier, was never fully owned.

Servants as storytellers

In 1847 Charles Dickens, famous for his interest in crime, established, with the financial backing of Angela Burdett-Coutts, a house to 'reclaim' fallen women by training them for domestic service and marriage in the colonies. For 11 years he questioned these 'servants in the making' at Urania Cottage and wrote down 'their' versions of their lives. 'Was this the price they had to pay for their warm beds and the passage out to Australia?' asks Jenny Hartley in her history of the institution. 'Or was there anything in it for them?' In attempting to answer the latter question, Hartley points to a present-day American psychological study of disturbed teenagers confined to locked wards of a residential psychiatric hospital: the psychologists found 'that the act of shaping and telling your autobiography can be a force for good. "When mistakes become stories, people can learn from them"'.[7] But capital convicts, unlike the women Dickens attempted to give a second chance – albeit a chance constrained by the gender and class boundaries of his age – had neither time nor opportunity to learn from their mistakes. The use made of his protégés stories by Dickens is also to be considered; presumably, traces of them contributed to his fiction, which constitutes a different form of appropriation. As Pat Thane's review of Hartley's book concludes, 'We learn more about Dickens than about these other sad lives'.[8]

Examples of servants writing their own accounts, of their own accord, as William Tayler did, are much rarer.[9] But novelists have certainly employed the servant storyteller as a narrative device. As Carolyn Steedman reminds us, there are two famous examples in this regard: Samuel Richardson's Pamela, who ostensibly writes of her travails during employment with Mr B, and Emily Brontë's Nelly Dean, who provides Lockwood and the readers of Brontë's novel with the backstory of the inhabitants of Wuthering Heights and Thrushcross Grange.[10] Neither author, of course, was a servant themself. But Steedman argues that you can let Dean 'speak of the service relationship and of being a servant, because those stories are there, embedded in her as a figure and in the story she tells'.[11] On Steedman's view *Wuthering Heights*, published in 1846 but set in 1801, can be read in part as 'a social history of service and a psychology of servitude'. Incorporating Nelly Dean within her account of the real-life relationship between a Church of England clergyman and the servant he impregnated also enables Steedman 'to recognize properly, and have others recognize, the full implications of the proposition that "history" is a form of writing, a particular genre of literary production'.[12] Steedman's recourse to *Wuthering Heights* has been described as 'a somewhat peculiar experiment' as well as novel and innovative, but response to her 'retool[ing] of literature as a form of historical evidence' has tended to be appreciative if cautious.[13]

Courvoisier and translated speech

Courvoisier had little control over his narrative from the time the murder was discovered. As we have seen, the police were almost immediately suspicious of Russell's valet and confronted him with their doubts at the house. According to their various statements and depositions, he said little on the day the murder was discovered other than to agree that it was 'a very strange thief' who would leave so many valuable items behind. He did not respond to Constable Rose's accusation that he must know something of the events which had taken place.[14] When Inspector Tedman drew back the bedclothes to reveal Russell's corpse Courvoisier 'threw himself into a chair hiding his face with his hands & saying o dear this is a shocking job what shall I do I shall lose my place & character'.[15] He did inform Inspector Tedman, on being asked, that some of Russell's rings were missing; similarly, he confirmed that certain forks and spoons were gone. But from the time the police began to accuse him of involvement in the theft and murder, and prior to his employment of legal counsel, Courvoisier otherwise confined himself to protestations of innocence.[16] The only comment of any interest, and one which was endlessly speculated on, was his remark to Constable Collier that he would say nothing more until he 'heard if the whole truth was told'.[17] This mysterious invocation, never explained, led some to speculate that even if guilty, Courvoisier had not acted alone.

In the valet's first formal statement, taken by Inspector Jarvis, C Division, on the morning of 6 May, Courvoisier related the same account of the events of the previous day as those provided by Mancer and Hannell, including the visit of Carr and the arrival of workmen to mend the bell pull. At the end of his statement, he said that the two female servants had gone to bed between 10 and 11 p.m. and that Lord William Russell went upstairs at around quarter to 12. He had rung for his servant at about ten past; Courvoisier had left his master's room some ten minutes later 'and went directly to bed'.[18] On the evening of the 6th, testifying to the coroner's court, he elaborated slightly on the details of Russell retiring to bed but told essentially the same story. He had heard nothing in the night, nothing until the housemaid knocked on his door in the morning.[19] The area door at the rear of the house had been bolted when he went up to bed. He was always, he told the court, 'the last up'. At this point in the proceedings Courvoisier was cautioned by Deputy Coroner Higgs, a move which, as discussed, incensed some critics who believed the valet to have been effectively silenced when he should have been queried further. Prior to his conviction, this was the last public occasion on which the valet spoke at any length. At Bow Street Thomas Flower, his attorney, cross-examined Hobler's witnesses for the prosecution, and when, on the initial and closing hearings, Courvoisier was asked if he had anything to say he declined other than again to assert his innocence. Once the formal processes of the law had been set in motion, Courvoisier fell silent.

François Benjamin Courvoisier remains something of an enigma and identifying his own voice is difficult. His speech was reported second hand by his fellow servants and various police officers – Baldwin, Rose, Tedman, Collier – as they were questioned by Mayne and Hobler at 14 Norfolk Street, by the coroner and his jury at the inquest, by Bow Street attorneys and magistrate Thomas Hall during the pre-trial examinations, and by counsel at the Old Bailey. The discourses recorded were also shaped by the questioners and we have no record of the questions asked by the police as witnesses made the statements Hobler took down, nor, in fact, do we know who recorded the initial statements taken by Inspector Jarvis, before Hobler had been employed. English, moreover, was not the valet's mother tongue. Courvoisier was brought up in one of Switzerland's French cantons and opinion varies as to his mastery of the English language. According to at least one report, Sarah Mancer told the inquest that Courvoisier 'did not speak English very well'. The cook, Mary Hannell, directly contradicted this claim, saying that he spoke English 'extremely well, although with a slight accent'.[20] When asked at Bow Street whether Courvoisier spoke English sufficiently well to understand the proceedings, Hobler asserted his complete confidence in the valet's grasp of the language: 'Oh yes, he understands English, and can speak it very well'.[21] If fluent in terms of everyday usage, it still seems highly unlikely that Courvoisier would have spoken precisely in the manner of his various post-trial confessions. His final accounts were also written in French and published in translation. Towards the end of Courvoisier's life, for a variety of reasons, words were undoubtedly put into his mouth.

Talking heads: servants and portraiture

Although the murder of William Russell was committed in an era which pre-dates the routine use of photography, the public was nonetheless eager for descriptions of the murderer's physical appearance as well as his speech. Courvoisier, according to the *Morning Chronicle*, exhibited 'neither in his bearing nor appearance the look or demeanour of a foreigner'.[22] 'Appearance', foreign or otherwise, is a tricky matter where any of Russell's servants are concerned. Broadsides and some of the newspapers illustrated the discovery of his body, but the 'housemaid' depicted in them was generic. I have found no illustrations of Hannell, the cook. Courvoisier is the sole of Russell's employees whose physical appearance was documented in any way, and the descriptions and illustrations of the valet were unreliable and often contradictory.[23] Later in the Victorian period group photographs of domestic staff would become common, with servants in uniform and posed with emblems of the work they performed. An 1852 photograph of the servants of the Yorke family in North Wales, for example, shows the cook-housekeeper clutching a brace of fowl, the butler a cork screw and bottle of wine, the head carpenter a saw, the butler a whip. Such props are absent in photos taken later in the century, but the group portraits continued as visible testimony of a family's wealth and status. No such photos are available for Russell's small 'family' – although there is, intriguingly, an undated photograph of an unidentified trio of servants precisely mirroring it, cook with saucepan and maid with iron in the front, standing behind them a young male servant.[24]

In the highly unlikely event that he would have wanted a portrait of this nature, at the time of Russell's murder photography was in its infancy.[25] Nicéphore Niépce and L.J.M. Daguerre had invented the 'daguerreotype' photograph, which used silvered copper plates and iodine vapour to create single images, and Englishman William Henry Fox Talbot patented a process to make copies in the year after Russell's death. By 1843, Talbot's calotype photos had begun to be used for portraiture and photographs of criminals were taken on the Continent in the same year, but routine police 'mug shots' lay in the future.[26] These originated in France, and Alphonse Bertillon's standard two-part photos, side and front head shots, date from 1888. In the absence of photographic evidence, we must rely on written descriptions, courtroom sketches, the untrustworthy illustrations found in broadsides and the newspaper press, a death mask, and a recently rediscovered plaster cast made post-execution, discussed below.

Prior to the invention of photography, portraits of servants were rare. The most famous exception is William Hogarth's composite oil painting, 'Heads of Six of Hogarth's Servants', c. 1750–55. It portrayed three women and three men, of varying ages: a coachman, valet, page, housekeeper, and two housemaids. 'Hogarth's decision to group his own servants together, outside the confines of their daily routine', as the Tate Gallery's picture caption acknowledges, 'is quite unique. Perhaps the most striking aspect of this picture is the collective sense of dignity and humanity displayed by this assemblage of unassuming individuals'. Generally speaking, servants simply weren't deemed sufficiently important as individuals to warrant portraits or to be accorded dignity or humanity. It was much more typical for them to be reduced to stereotypes, robbed of their individuality, and appropriated as targets for either censure or comedy. In the early nineteenth century both cooks and housemaids provided fodder for caricaturists. A 'Paul Pry' cartoon dating from 1829, for instance, captioned 'Do you please to have your bed warm'd Sir', shows a pert and sexualized housemaid carrying candle and bed warmer – and indeed the unfortunate Sarah Mancer would be accused by some of having warmed Russell's bed. (Joseph) Kenny Meadow's portrait of a 'Maid of All Work', part of the c. 1840 'Heads of the People' series and paired with an essay on the subject by Cornelius Webb, depicts something probably closer to the truth: a much plainer girl with a pained expression.[27]

Courvoisier's appearance, by contrast, and for obvious reasons, was commented on endlessly. The *Standard* described the valet as 'having very dark hair and eyes, brown complexion, regular, handsome features, a black, intelligent eye, but downcast'.[28] The *Southern Star*, repeating a description published in *The Times* on 12 May, said he was a 'middle-sized man, rather stoutly made', and guessed him, erroneously, to be about 30 years of age. Like the *Morning Chronicle*, the paper found 'not much of the foreigner in his general appearance'.[29] *The Times* had further described him as 'in stature about the middle height, rather sallow complexion, with full face, the features of which are strongly marked, and dark hair'. It also described his clothing: 'a brown frock coat, slate coloured figured waistcoat, black trousers, and boots'.[30] Russell's valet, Yseult Bridges wrote censoriously in her twentieth-century study of the case, kept himself 'extremely well-groomed' – excessively well groomed for one of his class? – and 'in spite of a low, narrow and receding brow, which bulged curiously on either side, gave the impression of being good-looking'. 'His voice ... was smooth and sleek – indeed everything about him was smooth and sleek, and his movements so sinuous and soundless as to suggest the feline'.[31] No evidence is cited for this highly prejudicial portrait. Bridges was describing not Courvoisier, but 'the criminal'.

Courvoisier was also sketched during the trial. Hobler pasted two pencil portraits into his scrapbook, believing them to be good likenesses. Following the valet's execution, a horribly realistic death mask was made, as well as plaster casts of his head. To my eye, at least, these various 'likenesses' are remarkably unlike. The impression left by the mask is overwhelmingly of youth; the slightly open mouth revealing crooked and possibly chipped front teeth makes the face look vulnerable.[32] Courvoisier's mouth is closed in the plaster cast, which also renders him bald, only recently rediscovered: in February 2017 the head was found, among a total of nine casts of Victorian criminals, in a toolshed near Penrith, Cumbria, by an auctioneer engaged in a routine valuation.[33] At least two of the casts in that collection were made by James De Ville. A keen phrenologist, De Ville began collecting specimens and from the 1820s into the 1840s, he was unrivalled as a maker of phrenological casts. Although unsigned, the cast discovered of Courvoisier may have been his work as well: De Ville was among those permitted to take one following the execution. On 22 July 1840, the *Manchester Guardian* reported that De Ville's cast had been acquired by Swiss sculptor and curator of the Manchester Phrenology Society William Bally, who had been denied permission to make a cast himself:

> The cast ... demonstrates the following to be the relative proportions of the three regions of the brain, in a head of very large size, and manifesting great energy: – the animal propensities, or occipital region, very large; the moral sentiments, or coronal region, retreating and moderate in size; the perceptive faculties large, and the reflective full, giving fair size to the frontal region generally. The region assigned to the animal propensities, measuring from the ridge to which the temporal muscle is attached, upwards to the base of the coronal region ... is larger than that in any other cast in Mr. Bally's collection, which includes the heads of twenty-five notorious criminals, both English and foreign. We mention this because the measurement by callipers from the orifice of the ear is stated to be fallacious, the ear of Courvoisier being placed much lower than in the great mass of men; and, consequently, the head at first sight appears to have a better development of the moral sentiments, than a more minute examination will exhibit. The organs of amativeness, destructiveness, secretiveness, acquisitiveness, constructiveness, firmness, and individuality are all very large; and the only organs that appear to be of the smallest size are conscientiousness and mirthfulness, or wit. There is a remarkable facial resemblance to the cast of Heaton, who was executed for the murder of a man at Buxton Wood with a billhook; and there are also very striking phrenological resemblances between the casts of Heaton, Greenacres [sic], and Courvoisier – especially as to the position of the temporal ridge.[34]

In the present day such artefacts have a certain cachet as macabre souvenirs; in their own time, the plaster impressions were highly prized because the shape of human heads was thought to shed light on character and disposition. There is a tiny snippet from an unspecified newspaper – presumably the *Guardian* again – inviting the public to view Bally's extensive collection of casts, now including Courvoisier's, on loan from De Ville, at the Phrenological Gallery, 54 King Street Manchester. The gallery admission price was one shilling. In London, a full-length model of Russell's murderer was on view at Tussaud's waxworks, for the same price, although 'the lunatic Edward Oxford' received star billing for his attempt to murder the queen.[35] In a brief paragraph titled 'Summary Vengeance', the *Weekly Dispatch* reported on 18 October 1840 that one 'T.S.' took offence to the exhibition of another wax figure of Courvoisier at a fair in Wincanton and knocked its head off, for which he was fined 10/6.[36]

Silence in court: the accused does *not* speak

Even if an accurate visual representation of Courvoisier could be identified, the speech emitted from this particular 'talking head' remains problematic. Prior to his committal to trial the valet was not monosyllabic, but he was certainly circumspect and tight-lipped. Solicitor Thomas Flower became his mouthpiece at Bow Street and their consultations were private. At the end of the first pre-trial hearing magistrate Thomas Hall asked Courvoisier if he 'wished to make any observation'. He replied, 'No, Sir, none at all'.[37] At the conclusion of the third hearing he seemed to be 'more alive to his situation than on previous occasions' and his communications with Flower became more frequent.[38] At the conclusion of the final hearing, immediately prior to his committal to Newgate, Courvoisier was again asked by Hall whether he wished to speak but this time he was under caution: 'whatever you do say will be taken down in writing, and may be produced in evidence either for or against you'.

> Mr Flower looked at the prisoner apparently with a view to ascertain if he wished to say anything. The prisoner, however, shook his head to signify that he had nothing to say, and
> Mr Flower said – he has nothing to say, Sir, at present, but that he is entirely innocent of the murder.[39]

Once formally charged with murder, recent changes to the law allowed Courvoisier to become completely silent after pleading 'not guilty': the most notable forum in which his voice was not heard was the Old Bailey. The older form of felony trial, dubbed by John Langbein as 'the accused speaks' variety, had certainly not disappeared by 1840. Even after the passage of the Prisoner's Counsel Act many defendants appeared in court without counsel, including some charged with murder, being too poor to afford them. Judges in murder trials occasionally assigned counsel in such cases: this practice, which had been rare in the 1820s and 1830s, became more common in the 1840s and 1850s but not until the 1880s did assignment become universal in trials of murder in which the accused appeared unrepresented.[40] In the absence of a barrister, the accused addressed the jury on his own behalf after the evidence had been heard. Most offered little beyond protestations of innocence, although there are a few famous exceptions. The 'school-master murderer' Eugene Aram (1759) was one; John Thurtell was another. Accused, as we have seen, together with Joseph Hunt and William Probert, of the murder of William Weare in 1823, Thurtell was defended in court by Old Bailey barrister Thomas Andrews, Thomas Platt (later Baron Platt), and Joseph Chitty. None of these men were permitted to address the jury, and Thurtell himself spoke long and eloquently, having practised his carefully crafted speech while in prison. In an unusual twist where the issue of voice in the courtroom is concerned, he claimed that he had used the published speeches of Charles Phillips, who would defend Courvoisier, to guide his oration, as well as directly incorporating paragraphs from them. The performance appears to have been impressive. When he rose to address the court Thurtell

> seemed to retire within himself for half a minute, – and then slowly, – the crowd being breathlessly silent and anxious, – drawing in his breath, gathering up his frame, and looking very steadfastly at the jury, he commenced his defence. – He spoke in a deep, measured, and unshaken tone; – accompanying it with a rather studied and theatrical action.

His reading of a written comment on the evidence was less successful. Here, 'he stammered, blundered, and seemed confused throughout' and 'preached some very tedious instances of the fallibility of circumstantial evidence'.[41] But Thurtell returned to form with his final words.

'Was the conclusion', he asked while the jury was deliberating his fate, 'not very fine? I took it principally from Phillips's speeches; it is in the defence he wrote for Turnor, the bank clerk'.[42] What Phillips, who as counsel for Probert would have been in the courtroom, thought of this appropriation has gone unrecorded.

By the time of Courvoisier's trial, the defendant was effectively silenced if he employed a barrister (though it is interesting to speculate on what Courvoisier might have said on his own behalf). Courvoisier did not cross-examine the witnesses who appeared against him, nor did he personally offer a defence. Richard Gould, tried in the same sessions without counsel, did speak on his own behalf.[43] To the great detriment of his professional reputation, Phillips spoke in his client's place. Nor could he call Courvoisier as a witness: defendants were forbidden to testify on oath until 1898 (Criminal Evidence Act). The prohibition was intended to spare them from committing perjury to save themselves from conviction.[44] At trial, Courvoisier spoke through his lawyers and his instructions to them. Until the surprise evidence of Madame Piolaine he appears to have done little but to insist upon his innocence; after his private confession, his instructions amounted to nothing more than a plea to save him from the gallows.

Post-trial confession(s): from anonymity to celebrity

If he had been silent in court, following the conclusion of the trial and his conviction, David Mellinkoff comments, Courvoisier found his tongue, 'anxious to be talking, to have people listen to something different every time. Each day a new confession right down to the night before he was hanged 16 days later...'[45] This is a slight exaggeration, but the convicted murderer did make multiple confessions, and they were contradictory. According to Phillips, the valet's mid-trial concession of guilt consisted simply of acknowledgement that he had committed the murder. That volte face admission, after weeks of asserting his innocence, quickly became public knowledge. The final sentence of *The Times*'s 22 June report of the trial's conclusion and verdict was followed by an article titled 'Courvoisier's Confession of Guilt', reprinted from the *Observer*: 'After the verdict was returned a report was circulated that the prisoner had confessed to the murder, and upon inquiry we found that the rumour was correct'. Of whom they enquired is not specified, but the informant may have been Hobler. The report described the solicitor's discovery of a rust spot on one of the carving knives and Piolaine's identification at Newgate of Courvoisier as the man who had left a parcel containing the missing silverware. The newspaper report claimed Courvoisier had related a version of events subsequently elaborated on to his solicitor, Flower, and William Wadham Cope, the governor of Newgate prison. In this version – later disavowed – the convict said that Russell had come unexpectedly downstairs in the night, discovered him concealing stolen items within the house, and told the valet he would be dismissed in the morning.

Rumours continued to fly and *The Times*'s initial report was followed two days later by one which suggested that Russell had not been Courvoisier's first victim:

> A circumstance has just been communicated to us which, were it not for the confidence which we have every reason to place in our informant, we should consider wholly incredible. He assures us, upon authority which in such a case is unquestionable, that the miscreant who is now in Newgate under sentence of death for the murder of Lord William Russell has confessed that he is also guilty of the murder of Eliza Grimwood, an unfortunate woman, who, as it will be remember, was found about two years since in a house in the Waterloo-road under circumstances which left no doubt that a murder had been committed, although the utmost ingenuity of the police could never discover a clue by which the criminal could be traced.
>
> It appeared at the time, from what meagre evidence could be procured, that the crime had probably been committed by a foreigner ...

The Times continued, indignantly, that it had also been informed that the authorities were attempting to keep the second confession a secret from the public. The next day, however, it admitted that their informant had been deceived: 'we have every reason to believe that we were in error in stating that the confession of a second murder was made by Courvoisier'. This mistake 'possibly arose in consequence of Courvoisier have made a second confession respecting the murder of Lord William Russell'.[46] The *Morning Chronicle* elaborated: Under-sheriff Jackson and Governor Cope, the alleged informant, denied they had ever heard Courvoisier confess to the Grimwood murder and after being questioned by some of the City's aldermen Cope went directly to the convict, in the company of both the Ordinary and Courvoisier's uncle, and heard his refutation of the claim.[47]

Having remained largely silent for almost two months, Courvoisier now wanted to talk and he had many willing listeners, all eager to take down his story and, it seems, in competition to win credit for the correct version. The convicted murderer had become a celebrity. Flower reported that he had been summoned by his client during the time the jury was considering its verdict; 'suspecting that his object was to describe the circumstances connected with the murder ... in more detail', the solicitor advised him to wait until after the verdict had been returned. Cope had promised Flower access, but the sheriffs, who had visited Courvoisier themselves following the verdict, blocked him. Flower returned on Monday, 22 June, with his clerk, Wolff, who, in the presence of Cope, took down a full confession. This confession, which was sent to the Home Office the following day, opened:

> On the Friday before the murder was committed I began two or three times not to like my place. I did not know what to do; I thought if I gave warning, none of my friends would take notice of me again, and I thought by making it appear a kind of robbery he would discharge me; and on the Saturday before I took this plate to Leicester-place. I had a mind to rob the house on Monday, and after I had forced the door down stairs, I thought it was not right, and went to bed: nothing further happened on the Monday.

But on Tuesday Russell gave him further reason to dislike his employment, being 'rather cross' about the carriage not having been sent to pick him up from Brooks's, and again when he gave the valet letters to post. Russell then grumbled that, when he rang from his bedroom, Courvoisier had taken up the warming pan of his own accord rather than waiting to see what his master wanted. At about 20 past 12, the valet was allowed to warm the bed and told, again 'rather crossly', that he should be more attentive. It was now Courvoisier's turn to be 'very cross'. In this version of events Russell later came downstairs to use the water closet on the ground floor and confronted the valet in the dining room: 'What are you doing here? You have no good intentions in doing this; you must quit my service to-morrow morning, and I shall acquaint your friends with it'. From this point, Courvoisier said, 'I thought it was all up with me; my character was gone, and I thought it was the only way I could cover my faults by murdering him'. Then followed a long and unconvincing account of how, while the police were in the house, he managed to secret the locket, watch, seal, and two sovereigns about his person and later hide them where they had been found, without the police noticing. He also claimed that he had not drugged the female servants' ale because the murder had not been planned. In the early evening, he said, he 'had no idea of committing the deed'. He hadn't washed his hands or the knife in Russell's bedroom, but merely wiped them on the towel he placed over the murdered man's face; he had burned nothing. He had not used a pillow to staunch the flow of blood. The confession concluded with an acceptance of sole responsibility for the murder: 'Sarah Mancer knew nothing about it. Neither did the cook, nor any of the other servants. I am the only person who is at all guilty'.[48]

Newgate's governor also recorded this confession and served as a witness for it, but asked Flower for his copy, believing it would be more accurate. Once given, it fell into the hands of the sheriffs, who 'positively refused to deliver it up' to the indignant solicitor. Flower 'supposed the object of the sheriffs was to obtain another confession from Courvoisier, or an amended statement, as they had both visited the convict very frequently since in company with the rev. ordinary'. He also said he thought the convict, having made a detailed confession already, should not be pressed further.[49]

Flower was correct in his assumptions and Sheriff William Evans did secure another confession on the following day, 23 June:

> After I had warmed his Lordship's bed, I went downstairs and waited about an hour, after which time I placed the different articles as they were found by the police. I afterwards went to the dining room, and took one of the knives from the sideboard. I then entered his bed-room and found him asleep. I went to the side of the bed and drew the knife across his throat. He appeared to die instantly.[50]

'This short confession', Hobler wrote in his scrapbook, 'is the only one which can be depended on'. Courvoisier had murdered his master as he slept, using one of the household knives. The solicitor remained convinced, however, that, as the surgeon Elsgood had suggested as a possibility when questioned at Bow Street, Russell's pillow had been used to stem the flow of his blood.[51]

While the signed confession was terse, other details were provided in conversation with the sheriff, who pressed Courvoisier on various issues. The information gleaned was deemed less reliable. Courvoisier 'assured' Evans that Russell had not discovered him in the act of theft or threatened him with dismissal. 'His Lordship had certainly spoken to him in a cross tone, and told him to be more attentive to his business, but that was all. There was no further provocation'. When questioned about the discrepancies in his two confessions, Courvoisier said that his uncle had visited him and urged that he tell the truth. In this version of events the murder had been premeditated, planned, together with the robbery, a week earlier. He denied any involvement in the murder of Eliza Grimwood and, as in the 22 June account, 'expressed much regret that any imputation should, for a moment, have been cast upon either of the poor unoffending female servants, who had been so unfortunate as to have been in the house with him'. He also, 'frequently, too, declared that he was indebted for the idea of committing this atrocious crime to *Jack Sheppard*'.[52]

The press response was scathing. *The Times* reprinted a column from 'an evening paper' which stated in no uncertain terms that 'there was no truth whatever' in the parts of Courvoisier's revised confession relating to what would have amounted to police negligence. Courvoisier had claimed, for example, to have hidden Russell's watch and seal in his pocket prior to concealing them in the house, but the police had searched his clothing carefully, including asking him to turn out his pockets. It might, moreover, 'be sufficient, in order to prove that the confession in those parts is not entitled to the slightest credit', to consider that the valet had also retracted his statement with respect to Russell having come downstairs in the night.

> It is dreadful to reflect that an individual upon the verge of eternity should, from any motives, have made a confession which appears to be totally false, and even contradictory to his own subsequent confessions ...It seems pretty clear that no credit can be given to any statement which has hitherto been made by this wretched culprit, except as regard the fact of the murder itself: but it would be idle to speculate on the motives of a mind so manifestly perverted.[53]

Three days later the paper returned to the subject:

> On Thursday Courvoisier stated to the Sheriffs, that owing to the very careless manner in which he was search by the police after they took him into custody, he contrived to secret ten sovereigns about his person in such a manner as to elude their detection, and that the first day he was taken to Bow-street police court for examination, on his being placed in the lock-up cell adjoining the office, he dug a hole in the floor, and there hid the money. Improbable as the story was, Mr. Cope, the governor of Newgate, by the direction of the Sheriffs, communicated the circumstances to the magistrates. The consequence was, that on Friday the cell was examined, the floor dug up, and everything done that could be, in order to ascertain the truth of the statement. The result was, that no money was found, and that it was quite clear that none had ever been deposited there, as stated by the convict. It is impossible to conjecture what was the wretched man's object in telling such an abominable falsehood. He has told so many palpable lies since his conviction that not the slightest reliance can be placed on anything he states.[54]

Courvoisier had still not finished. Having confessed to his barrister, his solicitor and the governor of Newgate, and Sheriff Evans, he now wrote letters to the Ordinary, prison chaplain James Carver, offering both a brief autobiography and yet another account of why he had committed the murder. Translations of these documents were published in the newspapers after the convict's execution. The confession dated 4 July and published on the 7th, the day after Courvoisier's execution, '[b]eing written when every motive for falsehood must have passed away, ... will probably be considered authentic', commented *The Times*.[55]

> After all the false statements which have been published in the newspapers, I feel constrained to tell you again all things as I related them to you when my uncle was here. If there are any contradictions, it is because I did not rightly understand the persons who questioned me, or because my answers were not rightly understood. It is true that I have not told the truth to Mr Flower, but I have stated the reason why I did not. The public think now I am a liar, and they will not believe me when I say the truth; therefore I pray you will correct all misunderstanding ... The evil dispositions of my heart began by a strong dislike (hatred) of my situation, and by a desire for another situation. My next idea was that I could live at the expense of others. Then I thought that if I could rob my master of 30*l*. or 40*l*. it would be so much gained and I had afterwards the idea that by killing my master the robbery would be better concealed, and that I should have done with him all at once, and be ready for my journey. I took the plate out of the house on Saturday or Sunday evening. I was waiting for a favourable opportunity of accomplishing my design.
>
> Monday evening the 4th of May, I had an evil thought of putting my hand to the work, but, after I had forced the door, a remnant of conscience told me I was doing wrong. I stopped about 10 minutes, without knowing what to do. I vanquished the temptation of the devil, and went to bed, after having put again the door in order. Oh! If I had but determined so on Tuesday night, how happy I should be! I ought, at least, to have prayed to God, and thanked him for having preserved me from that temptation, but I went to bed like a dog, without thinking even that God had seen me. Tuesday evening, the 5th of May, I had some altercation with my master, but it was not worth the while to speak of it.

On the night of the murder, he again heard his conscience telling him, 'Thou art doing wrong', but he didn't listen. The remainder of the confession detailed once more the alleged cat-and-mouse game played with the police in the days that followed, as he secreted various stolen items about the house. The original letter and its translation were reported to have been read over to their writer by Carver and Charles Baup, minister of the French Protestant Church in London, who indicated that the convict had assured them of the truth of this version of events.

In a statement to the Ordinary begun on 3 July and continued on the 5th, Courvoisier elaborated on the biographical sketch of his previous history published in the lead-up to his trial, providing in his words – again in French – 'an account of the short duration of his life' which was to be terminated on the 6th.

> I was born of very pious parents, who have neglected nothing on their part for my education and religious instruction; on the contrary, they have done all in their power; and if I am not so well informed as I should be, it is my own fault. It has been my evil habit to have always a falsehood in my mouth ready to excuse what I did wrong or what I omitted to do I fancied it was more disgraceful to have a bad memory than to be a liar.

A schoolmaster in his early years had proved a good influence, but the schoolmaster had left the village and Courvoisier had reverted to his bad habits. 'Very religious' at the age of 12, by the time of his first communion aged 16, he began to be 'righteous in the sight of men only'. In England, he had 'acted unjustly toward Mrs. Fector at the time of leaving her', acting in a way he would not have dared to 'a year before'; by the time he was employed by Russell he had gained in confidence so that in making plans he never considered whether they would please God. At this point in his confession, Courvoisier's professed motives again diverged from previous statements:

> having heard the other servants speaking of different scenes (towns, villages, country-houses) I began to desire an employment which would enable me to travel throughout England. I afterwards formed an idea that I should be able to travel on foot from city to city for six months, I then intended to endeavour to secure a place or return to Switzerland. I thought I should be able to make my friends believe that I was in place during these six months. This was the beginning of my misfortunes, for I soon began to harbour still worse designs, I thought I could go to a town, take a lodging; and after remaining five or six days I would depart without payment. I thought that 10*l*. or 12*l*. would suffice for this excursion, and began to seek an opportunity for departure, but this was not enough, I began to premeditate the seizure of what this venerable victim had with him in gold, bank notes and his watch; but this did not satisfy me. Satan, who knew that he had my heart in his power, began to persuade me that it was not enough only to rob my master, and that if suspicion rested upon me the world would be ready to believe it; and as during that time I was at Camden Hill I read a book containing the lives of thieves and murderers being under the dominion of Satan (I read it with pleasure), I did not think that it would be a great sin to place myself among them. On the contrary, I admired their skill and their valour. I was particularly struck with the history of a young man who was born of very respectable parents, and who had spent his fortune in gaming and debauchery, and afterwards went from place to place stealing all he could. I admired his

cunning, instead of feeling horrified at it; and now I reap but too well the fruit of those papers and books which I had too long suffered to supplant devotional works, and this book – yes, this book – was read by me with more attention than the Holy Bible. Why so? Because my heart was under the dominion of Satan ...

In this penultimate confession the offending literature is not specified by name. 'Courvoisier', or whoever instructed him, drew upon conventions that simply fleshed out the traditional wording of criminal indictments: he had not had the fear of God before his eyes but was moved and instigated by the devil. The author enumerated his breaking of the various commandments and declared himself 'an abomination in the sight of God'. Continuing his thoughts two days later, on the 5th – this letter thus bookending the confession of 4 July – he reflected on the disgrace he had brought to his (biological) family and friends before returning to the offence he had caused to God: 'Oh wretch that I have been, have I not rebelled against thee?' He nonetheless begged to be washed from his sins by the blood of the Lamb. Interestingly, he also spared a thought, again, for his fellow servants within Russell's 'family' at 14 Norfolk Street:

> I still think of those poor servants whom I have had the heart to treat so cruelly. I doubt not that they will pardon me. I pray to God that he may bless them, and make them prosper in this world, and promote their salvation.

He concluded by saying that the police had treated him 'as a friend', and while in prison both his bodily and spiritual needs had been well attended. This final statement, incorporating as it did acknowledgement of the justice and fairness of the legal system which had condemned him, the last speech recorded prior to the silence impelled by the noose, Baup witnessed as being 'translated from the original French by a competent scholar'.[56]

Capitalized speech and commercialization

Broadside coverage in the 1830s and 1840s

Despite multiple recorded confessions, Courvoisier by no means retained ownership of his story. While the 'respectable classes' as well as those below them were fascinated by tales of murder, there was a noticeable divide in the way in which the same stories were conveyed. The higher classes tended to eschew popular literature; the lower classes embraced cheap broadsides. 'During the first half of the nineteenth century', Rosalind Crone writes, 'the broadside trade dramatically expanded to become a dominant method of crime reporting for the common people and a central feature of life in London'.[57] This particular form of cheap print had firm roots in the plebian culture of previous centuries. Traditionally, such sheets had engaged with a wide variety of subjects, including politics – the newspaper press had its origins in the political crises of the seventeenth century – and scandals of many sorts, but from the 1820s a focus on murder intensified.

The contraction of the capital code, which confined executions to murder and made them much rarer than they had been in the past, may have contributed to the new press focus on murderers. Advances in printing technology also reduced the cost of producing such publications and the dramatic increase in London's population created a growing market. In 1838, 1,650,000 sheets were sold covering Greenacre's murder and dismemberment of Hannah Brown. By this period quarter sheets were issued for early reports of murder; half sheets, using newspaper reports for details, were devoted to developments made in the case; full, decorative sheets were published following a convict's execution. In the early nineteenth century, their contents were sung or recited in the streets by 'patterers', drawing on the older, oral tradition of street ballads. Although single sheets, printed crudely on the cheapest of paper, were unlikely to survive, notorious crimes merited four or perhaps eight pages folded into a miniature 'book', which could be kept as a souvenir. Such publications were highly lucrative. James Catnach, one of the most successful publishers of the genre, made a profit of £500 for the 500,000 copies sold of a report of the trial of John Thurtell for the murder of William Weare in 1823.[58]

The inexpensive broadsheet format would be adopted by religious tract societies, among others, but Catnach and other publishers of the sensational, for all their protestations of moral teaching, primarily provided the poor with entertainment.[59] Publication of such texts would peak in the 1840s, and by the time of Russell's murder, Crone argues, they testified to a particular anxiety about breakdowns in human relationships. In terms of content, broadsides drew on the older tradition of recording a convict's final moments and punishment. The most common illustration was a gallows scene; they might include reference to earlier murders; and they frequently contained letters purportedly written by the convict in the condemned cell. Such letters – again like the earlier tradition of last dying speeches – were highly formulaic, their script including confession, acceptance of guilt and the justice of punishment, and expressions of remorse for what they had done. Illustrations enabled the story to be absorbed by those whose reading skills were limited. Apart from gallows scenes, after 1820 broadsides increasingly included portraits of both murderer and victim, prisoners in condemned cells bidding farewell to family or writing their letters of confession, and the crime scene itself, with 'often ridiculous poses of both felons and victims'. 'Great emphasis' was placed 'on the blood that flowed from the victim's fatal wounds'.[60] Textually, verse narratives, in either the first or third person, were 'perhaps the most important feature' of such broadsides.[61] By 1840 objective, third-person verses had become more common, with demonization of the murderer also increasing. The 'everyman' thought to be capable of criminality unless warned against it was replaced by the criminal as a 'monster'.[62]

186 *Who Speaks?*

Broadside coverage of Russell's murder and the trial and execution of Courvoisier provides a textbook example of what Crone has described, including illustrations of the discovery of the body, blood flowing from its neck, servants and police positioned ludicrously with legs apart and arms flung in the air to indicate horror. Not all were published in London: Bonners in Bristol issued sheets on Courvoisier's execution, just as he had done for the Ratcliffe Highway murders in 1811. So too did George Thomas in Plymouth. In London, Henry Paul, a printer active between 1839 and 1845, published individual sheets spanning Courvoisier's examination at Bow Street through his committal for trial, confessions, and execution. Edward Lloyd published a comprehensive account, covering Courvoisier's trial, confession, and execution on a single page.[63] Some of these broadsides told Courvoisier's story in (execrable) verse. The moral is simple, but arguably these accounts were not far off in assessing the valet's motivation:

> I valet was unto Lord Russell,
> Who lived in Norfolk Street, Park Lane,
> Where I might have lived a life of comfort,
> But for one thing which gives me pain;
> I was not contented in my station,
> My thirst for gold it was too great,
> And now I see how base I have acted,
> But ah, repentance, comes too late.[64]

The convict appropriated: The Newgate novels

Broadside printers happily assumed the role of mouthpiece for Russell's valet, offering their accounts in the first person singular as per long-established tradition. The texts are as generic as the illustrations of the crime scene and the gallows; the poetic lamentations are pure invention. More problematic are the newspaper reports of Courvoisier's 'true' confessions, at least one of which appropriated his voice for a new purpose. The various reports were clearly influenced by and in some regards tailored to particular audiences. The final versions, addressed to Carver, were thus couched in the traditional language of penitence and contrition typical of the older genre of 'last dying speeches'.[65] Such texts served to legitimate the legal processes; they also preached a moral lesson while seeking at the same time to entertain. The convict's fall from grace was framed within the concept of a slippery slope of immoral behaviours: Courvoisier's claim that he had become a liar as a child, and laments that he later became more interested in reading lives of criminals than the Bible, is typical of such accounts. Ironically, Newgate's chaplain had in previous centuries (1676–1772) profited considerably from selling 'accounts' of capital convicts which included short biographies, descriptions of their crimes, final confessions, and behaviour at Tyburn's scaffold, precisely the type of reading which Courvoisier claimed had led him into error.[66]

Last dying speeches and the Ordinary's Account were very much commercial ventures and never particularly noted for veracity. While these forms of criminal biography had declined by 1840, Courvoisier was no doubt coached and led by Carver in their discussions prior to his execution, taught how to frame his story within traditional parameters. Less obvious is who suggested a specific text – William Harrison Ainsworth's *Jack Sheppard* – as the inspiration for Courvoisier's murder of his master. Regardless, this claim reveals public anxiety about early Victorian reading habits and the habits, in particular, of the lower orders.

Servants and reading

In the eighteenth century educating the poor had been seen as dangerous: it might lead them to reject their place in society. Hannah More believed that their reading should be limited to Scripture and the catechisms, and that on no account should the poor be taught to write. Patrick Colquhoun similarly believed it was dangerous to educate people above their station. By the early nineteenth century, opinion had changed. Henry Brougham was convinced that education provided 'the best security for morals'; John Stuart Mill that it would transform the working class into 'rational beings'; Samuel Smiles, that it would increase self-respect and ambition. John Clay, chaplain of the Preston House of Correction, argued that literacy would prevent crime by inculcating religious principles and elevating low tastes.[67] Literacy in servants was certainly desired by the time Courvoisier entered service: 'Hire no servant that cannot Read and Write, and keep a Common Account', wrote Dr William Kitchiner in *The Housekeeper's Oracle; or, art of domestic management* (1827).[68] A literate servant could calculate grocery accounts and follow recipes as well as written instructions from their employers. But Kitchiner also recommended that servants be allowed time to themselves in the evenings 'to improve their Minds by reading instructive Books'.[69] Footman William Tayler, as described in Chapter 2 above, had done just that, reading history.

That servants should read was a given by 1840, but what they were choosing to read became a major cause for concern. A potentially transformative 'wholesome literacy', or 'respectable literacy', was to be encouraged; 'pernicious literacy', by contrast, required 'strategies of containment'.[70] The alarm about 'low tastes' among the working class was not a little hypocritical, given the reading tastes of their superiors. Preparing for his study of Victorian sensational literature, Thomas Boyle went off to the Colindale newspaper library and

> attempted to put myself into the mind of a contemporary reader. I imagined myself encountering one newspaper or the other at my breakfast table ... at my pub or club in a leather chair with a glass by my side; at home by the blazing hearth, in a starched collar and a smoking jacket, reading aloud to my respectfully dutiful and obedient wife and family ...

188 *Who Speaks?*

This was not so easy after I started reading, for I found immediately that the mid-Victorian newspaper was sensational to say the least, certainly not supportive of an image of domestic tranquility.

The Times of January 3, 1857, lay open before me. It featured an account of 'The Double Murder of Children in Newington'; a lead article on 'Robberies and Personal Violence'; an extended rendition of 'A Week of Horror'.[71]

Respectable journalism for the middle classes extended beyond *The Times* to include the London Sunday papers, which offered not merely radical politics but 'Establishment scandal and sidewalk sensation'.[72] Two years after Russell's murder, Herbert Ingram's *Illustrated London News*, a paper which at 6*d* rather than a penny per issue was not aimed at the lower classes, began publication. Rumoured to have originally been conceived as a police gazette, it too devoted considerable coverage to crime.[73]

Boyle should not have been surprised by the content he found, given the nine million words' worth of newspaper clippings loaned to him by his thesis supervisor. 'Various Trials Cut from Newspapers' between 1840 and 1861 and pasted into 1,500 pages (5 volumes) by retired naval surgeon and Scottish laird William Bell Macdonald had been happily indexed under assault, bigamy, criminal conversation, murder.[74] Macdonald's compilation is another example of a criminal scrapbook, although a very different one from Francis Hobler's.

Despite their own very evident taste for lurid tales of crime, real or fictional, the middle classes were united in a belief that such literature would corrupt the lower orders, including the newly literate servant class. The challenge was thus to provide them with wholesome literature. The Religious Tract Society, founded in 1799, constituted a deliberate attempt to counter 'vile publications' that promoted 'moral corruption'. As R.K. Webb writes, 'the tract tradition was a strong one in the nineteenth century. Servants' halls were supplied with them by benevolent or worried masters'. In actual working-class homes, books were not only rare but also dominated by religious works. Yet within any class, being in possession of books or tracts was not necessarily synonymous with reading them. Webb cautions that 'it seems probable' that the success of efforts to constrain and confine servant reading was 'less than has been commonly supposed'. Distribution didn't mean that religious tracts were read, 'and being paper, an immensely large number of tracts must have gone to light fires or to serve base but vital domestic purposes which religious writers would understandably not care to mention'. Webb concluded that while religious publications were definitely 'important as a nineteenth century phenomenon', 'they were apparently read largely by an already pious middle class'.[75] Their tone and style alienated working-class readers; tracts were formulaic and dull and their intended audience craved entertainment and escapism. Jean Fernandez reached the same conclusion: 'Victorian efforts at domesticating working-class literacy ended in failure'. Servants preferred texts which, rather than inculcating virtue, instead offered 'an education in venality and indiscipline'.[76]

Some authors found comedy in servants' reading tastes. Leigh Hunt's 1825 essay on 'The Maid Servant' suggested her personal books might include 'an odd volume of "Pamela," and perhaps a sixpenny play, such as "George Barnwell," or Mrs. Behn's "Oroonoko"';

> two or three song-books, consisting of nineteen for the penny; sundry Tragedies at a halfpenny the sheet; the "Whole Nature of Dreams Laid Open," together with the "Fortune-teller" and the "Account of the Ghost of Mrs. Veal;" the "Story of the Beautiful Zoa" "who was cast away on a desart island, showing how," etc.[77]

The undated *A Mistress' Counsel; or a Few Words to Servants*, clearly published in the late Victorian period and assuming a reasonably high degree of literacy among servants, similarly targeted the reading material of female servants and cautioned, 'Don't read 'silly sensational stories,' published in 'poisonous publications which are brought to the back doors of gentlemen's homes': such tales 'unsettle the weak minds of those who read them'.[78] The unsettling effects on female domestics of reading the wrong sort of material were humorously described by the Mayhew brothers in *The Greatest Plague of Life, or The Adventures of a Lady in Search of a Good Servant* (1847). The worst of the 'delinquent domestics' portrayed is Betsy, addicted to penny dreadfuls and

> always marching about the house with a broom in her hand, either fancying herself "ADA THE BETRAYED" or "AMY" in "LOVE AND MARRIAGE" – or else sitting for hours on the fender, crying her eyes out, over "THE MURDER AT THE OLD SMITHY" or "THE HEADS OF THE HEADLESS"[79]

while saucepans burn and food is ruined. When her exasperated mistress finally burns her servant's books, Betsy retaliates by overfilling the warming pan and drenching the marital bed.

How did servants acquire their reading material? Examining 90 inventories of 'middling-sort Londoners' in the eighteenth century, Abigail Williams found only one that mentioned books as part of the property in a servant's room.[80] Yet, she argues, by the early nineteenth century a few of the grander households contained servants' libraries, although these were more common by the end of that century. The books found within them, which included 'cautionary tales about drinking and gambling', she suggests, were predictably more likely to reflect the interests and concerns of employers rather than those whom they employed.[81] Some literature may have found its way downstairs from the master's study or library. 'If I leave this manuscript open upon my table', said Morgan Pendennis in Thackeray's *Pendennis* (1848–50), 'I have not the slightest doubt that Betty will read it, and they will talk it over in the lower regions to-night'.[82] Literate servants are certainly found in literature: Richardson's Pamela is the most famous eighteenth-century example, and the tradition continued, as did reliance on employers for reading material. In Emily Brontë's *Wuthering Heights*, Nelly Dean tells Lockwood:

> I have read more than you would fancy, Mr Lockwood. You could not open a book in this library that I have not looked into, and got something out of also; unless it be that range of Greek and Latin and that of French; and those I know one from another: it is as much as you can expect from a poor man's daughter ...[83]

Similarly, Catherine Linton bribes Thrushcross Grange's manservant, Michael, to secretly prepare and later restable the pony she rides to the Heights with unspecified 'books and pictures': 'He is fond of reading ... so he offered, if I would lend him books out of the library, to do what I wished: but I preferred giving him my own, and they satisfied him better'.[84] Not all of the literature from above stairs could be guaranteed to be respectable: in 1838 the London Statistical Society tabulated the contents of ten libraries in three Westminster parishes, from which the respectable classes would have borrowed. Its categorizations are interesting: numerically, 'novels of the lowest character ... containing no good, although probably nothing decidedly bad' topped the list, with over a thousand volumes. Ten books, their authors, titles, and subject matter left unspecified, were listed as 'books decidedly bad'. The Newgate Calendar was named in the list but lumped in with 'miscellaneous old books' rather than bad ones.[85]

Apart from borrowing books, some servants may have purchased inexpensive literature themselves. 'It was principally from among the skilled workers, small shopkeepers, clerks, and the better grade of domestic servants', Richard Altick writes, 'that the new mass audience for printed matter was recruited during the first half of the century'.[86] There is no question that some publishers deliberately targeted a working-class readership. Edward Lloyd, publisher of one of the Courvoisier broadsides, was prominent amongst them. The son of a Welsh labourer, Lloyd had been employed in a solicitor's office but by the age of 18 had opened book shops in London selling cheap works and he subsequently became a leading publisher of sensational literature: *The Calendar of Horrors* (1835) was an early foray in this regard.[87]

Jack Sheppard

I have not found an account of the books housed in 14 Norfolk Street, upstairs or down, other than the report that William Russell had been reading a life of Samuel Romilly, the penal reformer who committed suicide, the night he died.[88] The extent of his servant Courvoisier's reading is unknown, and the fact that English was not his first language complicates the matter. But the allegation of the influence of William Ainsworth's *Jack Sheppard* upon Courvoisier's actions is, I suggest, more likely to be another reflection of the anxiety over servants' reading than a creditable explanation for his murder of Russell.

Published in 1839, *Jack Sheppard* belongs to a new incarnation of criminal biography: Ainsworth, like Edward Bulwer-Lytton, reworked the lives of real criminals into fiction.[89] Wildly popular with the public, these novels also attracted considerable criticism for glamorizing crime and criminals. Ainsworth's portrayal of the eighteenth-century thief and gaol-breaker had come under attack prior to Russell's murder, condemned in the *Aethenaeum*, in *Fraser's Magazine*, in the *Examiner*, and by Thackeray in *Catherine*, a short novel first published in instalments (1839–40). Exasperated by the sensational retellings of the stories of eighteenth-century criminals, Thackeray took as his subject Catherine Hayes, burnt at the stake in 1726 for the murder of her husband, and in his tale of 'agreeably low' and 'delightfully disgusting' characters he made great sport of Bulwer's prose style.[90] What he termed his 'Catherine cathartic' has been deemed a failure, if an 'interesting one', 'at the level of parody': 'the targets are too wide and the attack loses focus'.[91] But Thackeray's intention was sincere.

In the *Aethenaeum*, Sydney Owenson, Lady Morgan blamed social change for the emergence of the low literature that Thackeray deplored: 'the demand for books having descended to the masses, has rendered an inferior literature not merely tolerable, but acceptable'. Authors, she claimed, were now forced by the marketplace to subordinate their own tastes to those of a new readership, to 'write down to the mediocrity of the purchasing multitude'.[92] On her view, Ainsworth and others followed their readership, but subsequent critics worried instead about their negative influence on it. The *Standard* certainly concurred in its view of the worth of Ainsworth's novel. In a review of a stage adaptation published three days later, the newspaper dismissed the 'monstrous nonsense of the original' work, which was full of 'blunders and absurdities': 'Most persons have heard of Captain Ainsworth's *Life and Death of Jack Sheppard*, and many there are who have had sufficient pertinacity of purpose to wade through the almost endless rubbish, balderdash, twaddle, and vulgarity of which it consists'.[93] While the *Standard* reviewed the Adelphi's stage adaptation favourably – much of its praise was devoted to technical aspects of the staging – ultimately such transfers raised further cause for alarm and the theatrical versions of *Jack Sheppard* would receive the greatest condemnation:

> In the penny theatres that abound in the poor and populous districts of London, and which are chiefly frequented by striplings of idle and dissolute habits, tales of thieves and murderers are more admired, and draw more crowded audiences, than any other species of representation. ... There, whenever a crime of unusual atrocity is committed, it is brought out afresh, with all its disgusting incidents copied from the life, for the amusement of those who will one day become its imitators.[94]

Both novels and plays alike provoked a moral panic similar to the alarm raised in the late twentieth century by the potentially corrupting influence of 'video nasties' on vulnerable youth. In the nineteenth century, it was the effect of

192 *Who Speaks?*

sensational literature on vulnerable young people of the lower classes that provoked the most concern.

The *Examiner* voiced its fears on 3 November 1839:

> We notice this 'romance' with very great reluctance, because we have thought the author capable of better things. It is however in every sense of the word so bad, and has been recommended to circulation by such disreputable means, that the silence we meant to preserve upon the subject would be almost as great a compromise with truth as the morals of the book or the puffs of the bookseller.
>
> ...
>
> The danger is in the resources that have been called in aid; in the paragraphs that with such nauseous repetition have drugged every town and country paper; and in the adaptations of the 'romance' that are alike rife in the low smoking-rooms, the common barbers' shops, the cheap reading places, the private booksellers, and the minor theatres. Jack Sheppard is the attraction at the *Adelphi*; Jack Sheppard is the bill of fare at the Surrey; Jack Sheppard is the choice example of morals and conduct held forth to the young citizens at the *City of London*; Jack Sheppard reigns over the *Victoria*; Jack Sheppard rejoices crowds at the *Pavilion*; Jack Sheppard is the favourite at the *Queen's*; and at *Sadler's Wells* there is no profit but of Jack Sheppard. In every one of these places the worst passages [of the book] ... are served up in the most attractive form to all the candidates for hulks or rope – *and especially youthful ones* – that infest this vast city.

It was not, Forster, said, the subject of Ainsworth's novel that offended, but the treatment of it. Vice 'from its least beginnings to its grossest ends' could be found in the work of John Gay, Henry Fielding, and William Hogarth, 'but only to pull down the false pretensions of the high':

> *The vulgarity of vice was the object at which they drove, and not its false pretensions to heroism or its vile cravings for sympathy.* It was not so much that they sought to discover the soul of goodness in things evil, as to brand the stamp of evil upon things the world was apt to think good.[95]

Fraser's Magazine made the same point:

> We retain, in 1840, the opinions we expressed in March 1834; and regret to find Ainsworth now doing what we then reprehend – 'pampering the vanity which perpetrates the determination to crime,' by investing the low ruffians of the *Newgate Calendar*, and their profligate companions, with all the interest and the graces of romance ... there is no doubt that the popular exhibition of Jack Sheppard, metamorphosed from a vulgar ruffian to a melodramatic hero, with all the melodramatic virtues and

splendours about him, in Mr Ainsworth's novel, and its manifold theatrical adaptations, will tend to fill many a juvenile aspirant for riot and notoriety with ideas highly conducive to the progress of so ennobling a profession as that of housebreaking ...

It too distinguished between 'Newgate literature' and the works of Gay and Fielding and concluded that it was 'impossible to disagree with the author of "Catherine, a story"'.[96]

Reflecting on Courvoisier's various confessions, some of the newspapers likewise condemned the novel as pernicious in its influence:

> In Courvoisier's second confession, which we are more disposed to believe than the first, he ascribes his crimes to the perusal of that detestable book, 'Jack Sheppard'; and certainly it is a publication calculated to familiarize the mind with cruelties and to serve as the cut-throat's manual, or the midnight assassin's *vade-mecum*, in which character we now expect to see it advertised ... If ever there was a publication that deserved to be burnt by the common hangman it is 'Jack Sheppard'.[97]

Ainsworth, unsurprisingly, was quick to refute accusations that his novel had inspired murder:

> I have taken means to ascertain the correctness of the report, and I find it utterly without foundation. The wretched man declared he had neither read the work in question nor made any such statement. A Collection of Trials of Noted Malefactors (probably 'The Newgate Calendar') had indeed fallen in his way, but the account of Jack Sheppard contained in this series had not particularly attracted his attention. I am the more anxious to contradict this false and injurious statement because a writer in *The Examiner* of Sunday last, without inquiring into the truth of the matter, has made it the groundwork of a most violent and libellous attack on my romance.[98]

Sheriff Evans responded the following day,

> I think it my duty to state distinctly, that Courvoisier did assert to me that "the idea of murdering his master was first suggested to him by a perusal of the book called *Jack Sheppard*, and that the said book was lent to him by a valet of the Duke of Bedford.[99]

But at least some of the papers were sceptical of the claims made.

> The work on an immoral tendency which he stated he had read to Sheriff Evans, was not "Jack Sheppard," but a book called the "History of the successful Progress of Criminals" and he says his attention was much

194   *Who Speaks?*

attracted to the acts of a young gentleman charged with a high offence, the *Morning Chronicle* reported on 6 July, and on the following day,

It may be agreeable to some to state that the work called "Jack Sheppard" has had, in the opinion of those who had opportunities of observing the prisoner, nothing at all to do with the murder. Courvoisier was qualified to perpetrate, without any provocation. He has himself denied that he had ever seen the book, or the dramatic performance of the famous robber, but our opinion is not occasioned by anything that he has declared.[100]

On the evidence of Francis Hobler, accusations that the valet had been led astray by a Newgate novel were indeed untrue. In an annotation beside the copy of Ainsworth's letter to the editor of *The Times* pasted into his scrapbook, Hobler protested that Courvoisier had not read the novel in question but rather a collection of trials, and that even within that collection, Jack Sheppard had not attracted his attention:

The work which was lent to Courvoisier by the Duke of Bedford's Butler while he & Lord Wm were staying at the Duke's at Camden Hill a few days before the murder, was a collection of Trials, as Turpin & others among them was the life & Trial of Jack Sheppard & the frontispiece was a portrait of that fellow – the last time I saw the identical book it was in the possession of Mr Mayne –[101]

The murder of William Russell was not 'murder by the book'. Courvoisier's voice had simply been co-opted to support the moral crusade against Newgate fiction.

Conclusion: 'abominable falsehoods', 'palpable lies', and unreliable narrators

In the days between the discovery of Russell's murder on the morning of 6 May and the execution of his murderer on 6 July, when do we hear François Benjamin Courvoisier speak in his own voice? Arguably, the answer is in part when he was telling lies, in his original protestations of an innocence he knew to be false, and in what amounts to adolescent and easily dismissed boasting of having outwitted the police officers attempting to secure evidence against him. But we should also remember the constants in confessions that diverge on so many other grounds: William Russell had been cross with him on a number of occasions, and the female servants were entirely innocent. Whatever his sins, in none of his various statements did Courvoisier attempt to shift the blame for the theft or murder to other persons.

By contrast, in the confession made to Newgate's chaplain he followed a long-established script, employing – or having dictated to him? – the standard language of penitence and contrition expected for centuries of a convict facing execution, even if in Courvoisier's case 'his' words had to be translated from French to English for domestic consumption in the press. Thackeray commented on this:

> Clergymen are with him ceaselessly; religious tracts are forced into his hands; night and day they ply him with the heinousness of his crime, and exhortations to repentance. Read through that last paper of his; by Heaven, it is pitiful to read it. See the Scripture phrases brought in now and anon; the peculiar terms of tract-phraseology (I do not wish to speak of these often meritorious publications with disrespect); one knows too well how such language is learned, – imitated from the priest at the bedside, eagerly seized and appropriated, and confounded by the poor prisoner.[102]

Who raised the *Jack Sheppard* association is less obvious. That connection first surfaced in reports of Courvoisier's confession to Evans; it may have been prompted by visitors to his cell, or been entirely made up by others. Behind all of the convict's various statements are police officers, legal counsel, and prison officials, among myriad persons, probing for answers and in some cases possibly soliciting them. All were pursuing agendas of their own. Most of these accounts were probably suspect to some degree.

What are we to make of Francis Hobler's narration of events? He too of course had an agenda, one which was avowed in the opening pages of his 'book': to assemble a case for the prosecution and provide documentation of how that case was put together. He worked as a professional and eschewed sensationalism. He also worked from a personal conviction of Courvoisier's guilt but did not concern himself with explanations, nor did he contemplate or speculate on the possibility that the police had the wrong man. I believe his painstaking narration can be accepted as a trustworthy account of the police investigation into Russell's death and the trial of the man accused of the murder. But Hobler could not speak to motivation and Courvoisier's post-trial conflicting narratives serve to obscure rather than reveal the truth of the murder itself. Courvoisier himself was the ultimate 'unreliable narrator', a term coined by Wayne C. Booth in *The Rhetoric of Fiction* (1961). Unreliable narrators have been a trope in fictional tales from the time of Agatha Christie's *Murder of Roger Ackroyd*, but in crime fiction, they are typically used to facilitate a surprise, and unfair, revelation of the truth. In this tale of a true-life crime, there was no such revelation.

Notes

1. See, e.g., *A Taste for Death*, 260.
2. Altick, *Victorian Studies in Scarlet*, 13.
3. *The Servant's Hand*, 2.
4. Repr. in *The Four Georges*, 315.
5. *The Servant's Hand*, 79.
6. Thackeray, 'On a Chalk-Mark on the Door', 507 and 510.

196 *Who Speaks?*

7   Hartley, *Charles Dickens and the House of Fallen Women*, 154.
8   https://www.historyextra.com/period/victorian/charles-dickens-and-the-house-of-fallen-women/.
9   On servant autobiography, see also Fernandez, *Victorian Servants*, chap. 7.
10 On the subject of servants in literature, and servants as narrators, see also Fernandez, *Victorian Servants*, chaps. 2–6.
11 *Master and Servant*, 193.
12 *Master and Servant*, 195.
13 Mowry, Johns, and Ziser, 'Reopening the Question of Class Formation', 517.
14 Statements, 18 May 1840, Item 60 (seq. 211–14 (Baldwin); 214–17 (Rose)).
15 John Tedman statement, 20 May 1840, Item 60 (seq. 217–31 at 219).
16 Copy of Pearce's deposition for the prosecution, n.d., Item 74 (seq. 322–28).
17 Copy of Collier's deposition for the prosecution, n.d., Item 74 (seq. 329).
18 Item 6 (seq. 16–20).
19 Item 10 (seq. 53–4).
20 *The Era*, 10 May 1840.
21 *The Times*, 12 May 1840.
22 7 May 1840.
23 For woodcut portraits (full length, in silhouette, and two busts), see 'Life, trial, confession, execution: F.B. Courvoisier for the murder of Lord William Russell'; 'Trial confession and execution of the valet Courvoisier, for the murder of Lord W. Russell; 'This day's examination of the valet for the murder of Lord William Russell, M.P'; 'This day's proceedings. Copy of a letter committal of the valet charged with the inhuman murder of Lord William Russell, M.P'.
24 'Servants from an Unidentified House in Cheltenham', reproduced in Hamlett, *Material Relations*, Fig. 1.17.
25 In England Thomas Wedgewood had created 'photograms' as early as 1790, placing objects on leather sensitized with silver nitrate; in France in 1826 Nicéphore Niépce succeeded in taking the first photograph, using a pewter plate, a camera obscura – and an exposure time of roughly eight hours.
26 On the history of photography see, among others, Hirsch, *Seizing the Light*; Bajac, *The Invention of Photography*.
27 *Heads of the People*.
28 7 May 1840.
29 17 May 1840.
30 12 May 1840.
31 *Two Studies in Crime*, 16–7.
32 Reproduced in Gatrell, *The Hanging Tree*, 118.
33 The *Daily Mail*, the *Mirror*, and the *Sun*, 9 Feb. 2017. The *Daily Mail* correctly identified Courvoisier as the murderer of Russell; the *Mirror* and the *Sun* both described him as a 'serial killer'; the *Sun*'s headline referring to him as a 'naked serial killer'. The nine plaster heads sold for almost £40,000, Courvoisier's cast accounting for half of that sum.
34 Pasted into Hobler's scrapbook, Item 121 (seq. 447). For De Ville and Bray see Cooter, *Phrenology in the British Isles*.
35 *Morning Chronicle*, 23 Sept. 1840.
36 The report was pasted into Hobler's scrapbook. Item 107 (seq. 409).
37 *The Times*, 12 May 1840.
38 *The Times*, 25 May 1840.
39 *The Times*, 30 May 1840.
40 Bentley, *English Criminal Justice*, 110–15.
41 Herbert, 'Pen and Ink Sketch of a Late Trial for Murder', 179, 182. Herbert reproduced the speech between these two pages and commented on its effect at 182–83.

Who Speaks? 197

42 Egan, *Recollection of John Thurtell*; quoted in Borowitz, *The Thurtell-Hunt Murder Case*, 178. On Thurtell's use of Phillips's speeches, see also, 77, 167, 171.
43 See OBP t18400615-1696.
44 On this act see Bentley, *English Criminal Justice*, chaps. 15–8, and Devereaux, 'Swearing and Feeling'.
45 Mellinkoff, *The Conscience of a Lawyer*, 126.
46 *The Times*, 24 and 25 June 1840.
47 25 June 1840.
48 *The Times*, 26 June 1840.
49 *The Times*, 25 June 1840.
50 *Morning Chronicle*, 25 June 1840.
51 Annotation, Item 100 (seq. 396).
52 *The Times*, 25 June 1840.
53 27 June 1840.
54 *The Times*, 30 June 1840.
55 7 July 1840.
56 *The Times*, 8 July 1840.
57 *Violent Victorians*, 96.
58 See *Violent Victorians*, 96–116.
59 On broadsides, see also Gatrell, *The Hanging Tree*, c. 5; Collison, *The Story of Street Literature*; Neuberg, *Popular Literature*; Shepard, *The Broadside Ballad* and *The History of Street Literature*; and Vincent, *Literacy and Popular Culture*.
60 Crone, *Violent Victorians*, 107.
61 Crone, *Violent Victorians*, 110.
62 Crone, *Violent Victorians*, 115.
63 Copies of various broadsides may be found at https://curiosity.lib.harvard.edu/crime-broadsides/catalog/46-990080975000203941: 'Apprehension & examination of the valet, for the awful murder of Lord Russell, M.P.'; 'This day's examination of the valet for the murder of Lord William Russell, M.P'; 'This day's proceedings. Copy of a letter committal of the valet charged with the inhuman murder of Lord William Russell, M.P'; 'The sorrowful lamentation and last farewell to the world of F.B. Courvoisier, with an account of his attempted self-destruction: with a copy of a letter from Courvoisier to his parents'; 'Trial confession and execution of the valet Courvoisier, for the murder of Lord W. Russell: With a copy of a letter written to his father and mother'; 'Life, trial, confession, execution: F.B. Courvoisier for the murder of Lord William Russell. Farewell letter to his parents, sister; and the rest of the family, with good advice to all persons in trust'; 'Trial, confession, and execution of Courvoisier for the murder of Lord Wm. Russell: Courvoisier's lament'; 'The sorrowful lamentation and last farewell to the world of F.B. Courvoisier: who was found guilty at the Old Bailey, on Saturday, June 20, of the wilful murder of Lord William Russell'; 'The lamentation of Francis B. Courvoisier, for the murder of Lord Wm. Russell'.
64 'The lamentation of Francis B. Courvoisier, for the murder of Lord Wm. Russell'.
65 On this genre see Sharpe, 'Last Dying Speeches'; Mckenzie, 'Martyrs in Low Life?', 'On the "very Brink between Time and Eternity"', and *Tyburn's Martyrs*; and Gladfelder, *Criminality and Narrative in Eighteenth-Century England*.
66 See Linebaugh, 'The Ordinary of Newgate and his Account' and McKenzie, 'Making Crime Pay' and 'From True Confessions to True Reporting?'.
67 See Webb, *The British Working Class Reader*, 14–5.
68 126.
69 126, 141.
70 Fernandez, *Victorian Servants*, 3.
71 Boyle, *Black Swine in the Sewers*, 3.

Who Speaks?

72 Altick, *Victorian Studies in Scarlet*, 58.
73 Altick, *Victorian Studies in Scarlet*, 60–1.
74 The murder of William Russell did not figure in this compilation.
75 Webb, *The British Working Class Reader*, 26–8.
76 *Victorian Servants*, 178, 13.
77 http://essays.quotidiana.org/hunt/maid-servant/ [accessed 19-05-2020].
78 49.
79 192; quoted *Victorian Servants*, 11.
80 *The Social Life of Books*, 53.
81 *The Social Life of Books*, 105.
82 *Complete Works*, 3:431.
83 Brontë, *Wuthering Heights*, 52.
84 Brontë, *Wuthering Heights*, 211.
85 Altick, *The English Common Reader*, 217–18.
86 Altick, *The English Common Reader*, 83.
87 On Lloyd, see *ODNB*.
88 *The Times*, 19 June 1840.
89 Hollingsworth, *The Newgate Novel* remains the best introduction to this genre of fiction; see also Juliet John's introduction to *Cult Criminals*, 1: v–lxii; Phillip Hoare's introduction to the 2002 Penguin edition of *Oliver Twist*, esp. xxx–xxxviii; Kelly, 'General Introduction', *Newgate Narratives*, 1: ix–xciii, and Jacobs and Mourão, 'Newgate Novels'.
90 On *Catherine* see, e.g., Colby, 'Catherine'; McKendy, 'Sources of Parody'; Goldfarb, 'Historical Commentary'. [Sydney Owenson Morgan], *Athenaeum* 626 (26 Oct. 1839): 803–5; [John Forster], *Examiner*, 3 Nov. 1839; *Fraser's Magazine*, 21 (Mar. 1840): 227–45. For Ainsworth, see Ellis, *William Harrison Ainsworth* and Worth, *William Harrison Ainsworth*. There is now a considerable academic literature on *Jack Sheppard*. See, e.g., Buckley, 'Sensations of Celebrity'; Gillingham, 'Ainsworth's "Jack Sheppard"' and 'The Newgate Novel and the Police Casebook'; Schwarzbach, 'Newgate Novel to Detective Fiction'; and Carver, 'Writing the Underworld'.
91 Peters, *Thackeray's Universe*, 86.
92 [Morgan], 804. On Morgan's reviews in this periodical more generally, see Casey, 'Silver-Forks and the Commodity Text'.
93 29 Oct 1839.
94 Mackay, 'Popular Admiration of Great Thieves', 260.
95 Emphasis in the original.
96 21 (March 1840) at 228 and 245. Henry Mayhew levelled similar criticisms at broadsides, which he claimed promoted sympathy and apology for criminals. See Crone, *Violent Victorians*, 161.
97 *Examiner*, 28 June 1840.
98 *The Times*, 7 July 1840.
99 *The Times*, 9 July 1840.
100 *Morning Chronicle*, 7 July 1840.
101 Item 105 (seq. 408).
102 'On Going to See a Man Hanged', 157.

7 Explanations and Consequences

Explanations: 'Disorder and discontent within the domestic space'[1]

From the time of Courvoisier's arrest contemporaries puzzled over his motivation. Prior to his horrific actions on the night of 5 May 1840, the valet had appeared to all who knew him as sane and possessing a good character. In the OBP's report, all of the witnesses called by William Clarkson on the conclusion of Charles Phillips's speech 'deposed to his good character for kindheartedness, humanity, and inoffensiveness of disposition'. The hotel proprietor testified that he had 'often remarked [Courvoisier's] diffidence, modesty, and simplicity. He was a young man of apparent humanity and feeling'. Noble, who had known the accused when he was at Fector's, remembered him as 'harmless, quiet, and inoffensive'. Fector's coachman, James Leach, said that Courvoisier 'was not a man that let us know his affairs' and that 'there was no one in particular he was intimate with' but described him as a 'steady man' and 'very good fellow servant'. Petthaud spoke from his knowledge of Courvoisier when employed by Lady Julia Lockwood. He had found him 'good natured and kind hearted and remarkable for his good conduct'. Lady Julia told the court she had 'believed him to deserve the character of a kind hearted young man'.[2] Courvoisier had demonstrated no tendencies to violence or cruelty, there is no evidence that he was what we would now term a 'psychopath', and the valet's contemptuous remarks about 'Old Billy', if he had not murdered him, differ little from the disrespectful discussion of his employers found in William Tayler's 1837 diary.

From a young man's point of view, William Russell's household must have seemed a soft target; theft from an elderly widower with no other manservant could so easily be accomplished. And what did an old man want with so many gold rings and other ornaments? The murder, too, was easy, a strong young man attacking someone three times his age, and deaf, while he slept. But why? I have argued that this murder might best be described as impersonal and rooted in a sense of social injustice, a sense never articulated in words but very evident in Courvoisier's deeds, in a murder that seems otherwise entirely and grossly disproportionate to any offence Russell might have caused to his servant.

DOI: 10.4324/9781003481638-7

The advice given to those entering service – 'Had God seen that it would have been better for your eternal good that you should be great and rich, He would have made you so; but he gives to all the places and duties best fitted for them'[3] – must have galled and grated on many servants. Courvoisier's dismissal from his previous employment with John Fector, and the reasons for it, may have initiated a sense of resentment. Nationality and height would not today constitute reasonable grounds for dismissal, but in 1840 there was no tribunal to which Courvoisier could have appealed his employer's decision. The centuries-old master and servant law that granted penal sanctions to employers on occasion also provided remedies for workers, but from the late eighteenth century onwards, domestic servants had been excluded from the remit of the legislation in question. The magistrates who administered the law, moreover, were employers of servants themselves and as such unlikely to have found Fector's reasons for letting his footman go unusual or objectionable.[4] In 1801 'A Bill for the Better Settling of Disputes between Masters and Mistresses of Families and their Menial or Domestic Servants', modelled on earlier, eighteenth-century efforts covering other workers, had been introduced, providing for the summary determination of issues including improper dismissal as well as wages, notices, liveries, and servants leaving service. It failed to pass and never became law: 'gentlemen and peers did not want their domestics taking them before magistrates'.[5]

In his closing speech at Courvoisier's trial Charles Phillips had insisted his client had no motive to commit murder; he also refuted John Adolphus's 'monstrous assertion' 'that it was not necessary for a man to have a motive for the commission of crime'. 'He knows', Phillips said, 'that if he were to ransack his ingenuity of thirty or forty years' experience, he could not point out a single case where a man had committed either a murder or a robbery without a motive ...'. Phillips himself was 'convinced' that there were motives for any commission of crime. He proceeded to list them – jealousy, hatred and revenge, avarice, and plunder – and dismissed each possibility where Courvoisier was concerned. What motive had the valet of hatred? 'None whatever. He was living with a master who loved him, and whom he loved'. According to Phillips, Courvoisier had neither reason to be jealous, nor cause for seeking revenge.[6] Yet Courvoisier might easily have been dazzled by the world he found himself in in England, and angered by its disparities in wealth. The bottom 50% of the population possessed 3% of the wealth, the top 1% 60%, and the top 10% almost 90%.[7] It is not unreasonable to suppose that a politics of envy played a part in his dissatisfaction with his place.

Comments made by Lord Campbell, summing up in another famous murder trial, that of 'Palmer the Poisoner' (1856), are of more use where motive is concerned:

> With respect to the alleged motive, it is of great importance to see whether there was a motive for committing such a crime, or whether there was

not, or whether there is an improbability of its having been committed so strong as not to be overpowered by positive evidence. *But, gentlemen, if there be any motive which can be assigned, I am bound to tell you that the adequacy of that motive is of little importance. We know from the experience of criminal courts that atrocious crimes of this sort have been committed from very slight motives;* nor merely from malice and revenge, but to gain a small pecuniary advantage, and to drive off for a time pressing difficulties.[8]

In this case, the action was disproportionate to the cause, and the motive was conceivably slight. Courvoisier had no 'pressing' financial difficulties, although pecuniary advantage must certainly have been the motive for his household theft and he appears to have envied his employer's wealth. With only five weeks' acquaintance it is unlikely that either Russell or Courvoisier 'loved' each other, as Phillips claimed. Yet five weeks is also a perplexingly short time to establish personal hatred on a scale to provoke murder. Russell's irritability during a visit to Richmond may have caused resentment, and his rebuke for the late carriage on the day of his death may have served as a flash point in Courvoisier's (hitherto masked) revolt against his subservient state. Whether termed a 'family' or 'establishment', the relationship between an employer and the servants who lived within it remained social as well as contractual. It involved daily, intimate contact, a physical proximity which might, as Tim Meldrum has commented, seem intolerable today to those of us who don't employ servants.[9] Even in its own time, such proximity was as likely to breed contempt as affection; it could also foster and sustain jealousy and grievances. Although most of Theodore Hook's hypothesizing about who was involved in Russell's murder is groundless nonsense, he made one sensible observation: 'is it creditable that the murder was committed with a view of robbery at all – I think not – a much deeper character seems to attach itself to the whole affair'.[10] That deeper character, I suggest, is rooted in master and servant relations. Phillips, like Hook, was correct in arguing that it made no sense to attribute Russell's murder to a desire for plunder. Russell had not caught Courvoisier in the act; the theft did not require murder. The murder itself, especially given the degree of violence it involved, seems instead a consequence and expression of a profound resentment. As reported in the press, in his final confessions Courvoisier told Newgate's Ordinary that 'The evil dispositions of my heart began by a strong dislike (hatred) of my situation, and by the wish for another situation'.[11] But did he in fact wish for another situation? Russell's young valet clearly fretted under the discipline and boredom inherent in domestic service. He also claimed at various times that he would like to go back to Switzerland or to travel about England on his own. He was of course a fantasist. An attractive, well-groomed young man, careful of his dress and appearance, might, if he had been English, have attempted and possibly succeeded in the short term in passing himself off as belonging to a higher station. But an immigrant, with an accent (to most Englishmen he would probably have sounded French), no matter how slight, would have attracted unwanted attention.

The 'most available form for articulating [the] relationship' between the late eighteenth- and early nineteenth-century master and servant 'was thought by means of things', writes Carolyn Steedman, and she continues to enumerate the types of things that constituted 'the material through which lives were lived, and the furnishings of all the imaginations that reworked and remade a society'. For servants, she argued, were 'in possession of imagination as much as their masters – rather more imagination, in fact'. The things chosen for Steedman's own list included 'laundry and laundry-lists, horses and hay, small coin and candles, manchets and muslin, dripping pans and dusters'. In the case of Courvoisier, envy of other material things – jewellery and plate and candlesticks – would have contributed to a sense of social injustice. What precisely he intended to do or how he planned to use the items he stole from Russell is a matter of conjecture, but his attempts at removing the crests which clearly marked their provenance were unsuccessful. Readily identifiable as Russell's property, the stolen goods would have been impossible to pawn or sell. Such clumsy and reckless appropriation, even if Russell had not been murdered, was doomed to detection and failure. Courvoisier would inevitably have been discovered as a thief. Frustrated he may have been, but his ambitions had no grounding in reality.

As discussed in Chapter 1 above, Courvoisier was not the first servant to murder an employer, nor would he be the last. Richard Altick argues that 'Victorian servant-neurosis' originated in 1840 with the Russell murder, but much more macabre instances of servant violence followed.[12] Seventeen-year-old Sarah Thomas murdered, in Bristol (1849), her 61-year-old mistress, Elizabeth Jeffries. Jeffries was bludgeoned to death with a stone, her dog killed and thrust down the lavatory, and the house robbed and ransacked. 'I never should have committed so desperate a crime', Thomas said in her confession, 'had Miss Jeffries conduct been less provoking'. Jeffries – unlike William Russell – was by all accounts a thoroughly unpleasant and difficult employer. A previous servant had lasted only a week, Jeffries 'considering her to be too dressy ... and to wear too many flounces on her gown'. Thomas was convicted and, despite appeals made on her behalf, executed nonetheless:

> A midnight murder of a sleeping woman, one to whom the murderess stood in a relation of trust and confidence, that murder attended by circumstances showing a most depraved and hardened nature, followed by robbery, and sought to be evaded by fixing the guilt on innocent parties, such an offence certainly presents no redeeming features ...

Elizabeth Laws, who had been pawning various belongings of her mistress, Catherine Bacon, before murdering her (1855) is unique – with the possible exception of Joseph Sellis – in attempting to avoid suspicion with a self-inflicted throat wound.[13] But perhaps the most gruesome case of this type is Kate Webster's murder, in 1879, of her mistress, Mrs Thomas. The victim was another example of an employer easily vexed, but Webster, who had a criminal record for theft and was a careless servant, probably gave considerable cause for complaint. After receiving notice Webster bludgeoned her mistress to death, then mutilated, disembowelled, and dismembered her body, boiling up pieces on the stove and reportedly offering jars of rendered fat about the neighbourhood as dripping. Mrs Thomas's head, wrapped in brown paper, was carried in a black bag while Webster paid social calls and an 'assortment of anatomical odds and ends, unfit for boiling' was placed in a box which was thrown into the Thames at Richmond bridge.[14]

Gory details aside, there are constants running through these domestic murders: peevish employers, servants resenting the subservience required and craving money and possessions of their own, and the freedom to wear as many 'flounces' in their apparel as they liked. Webster briefly impersonated her late mistress, assuming her life. As the nineteenth century wore on, there was an increased recognition of the injustices felt. Wilkie Collins commented, in 1856, that for the domestic servant, 'Life means dirty work, small wages, hard words, no holidays, no social station, no future … No human being ever was created for this'.[15] Four years later, A.J. Munby, famous for his erotic fascination with the female servant class, wrote in a diary entry, after observing a 'pretty but coarsemade rustic and redhanded waiting maid', 'why should she have a life so different? Why should she wear a cotton frock and a cap and hand me dishes …?'[16]

Domestic service, with all of its inherent inequalities, continued. So too did caricature in novelists' representation of the servant class; it certainly did in Dickens's work. 'Dickens' novels "most often" do *not* represent the contradictory position of the mid-Victorian domestic. What they do with servants is for the most part closer to "farce"'.[17] But among the literati, the vitriol expressed by Defoe and Swift in the eighteenth century, and the cheerful mockery typical of Leigh Hunt and William Hazlitt in the early nineteenth, were gradually being replaced by a degree of sympathy. Thackeray, an 'uneasy Victorian', did, like Collins, become acutely aware of the unfairness inherent in any servant's position.[18] In 'On a Chalk-Mark on the Door', the essay in which he referenced 'Jeames's great strength and the tools surrounding his knife-board', Thackeray took for his subject 'a little mark on the doorpost' of his house

> which I hope will relate, not to chalk, nor to any of its special uses or abuses (such as milk, neck-powder, and the like), but to servants. Surely ours might remove that unseemly little mark. Suppose it were on my coat, might I not request its removal? I remember, when I was at school, a little careless boy, upon whose forehead an ink-mark remained, and was perfectly recognizable for three weeks after its first appearance. May

I take any notice of this chalk-stain on the forehead of my house? Whose business is it to wash that forehead? and ought I to fetch a brush and a little hot water, and wash it off myself?

Yes. But that spot removed, why not come down at six, and wash the doorsteps? I dare say the early rising and exercise would do me a great deal of good. The housemaid, in that case, might lie in bed a little later, and have her tea and the morning paper brought to her in bed: then, of course, Thomas would expect to be helped about the boots and knives; cook about the saucepans, dishes, and what not; the lady's-maid would want somebody to take the curl-papers out of her hair, and get her bath ready. You should have a set of servants for the servants, and these under servants should have slaves to wait on them. ... There are orders, gradations, hierarchies, everywhere. In your house and mine there are mysteries unknown to us.[19]

If he could not know the mysteries, Thackeray at least imagined them, as well as the suppression of feelings:

When we were at the seaside, and poor Ellen used to look so pale, and run after the postman's bell, and seize a letter in a great scrawling hand, and read it, and cry in a corner, how should we know that the poor little thing's heart was breaking? She fetched the water, and she smoothed the ribbons, and she laid out the dresses, and brought the early cup of tea in the morning, just as if she had had no cares to keep her awake.[20]

Fear as well as empathy had nonetheless been introduced: as I have argued, Courvoisier's execution may have haunted Thackeray, but so too did his crime. The hands of the servants who 'opened their doors, cooked and served their meals, brought up their children, initiated them into sexuality and closed their eyes when they died' – as Hobler believed Courvoisier to have closed Russell's – might also cause their death.[21] Bruce Robbins comments that three of the 'acknowledged masterpieces of Victorian realism' – *Bleak House*, *Middlemarch*, and *Vanity Fair* – 'all turn on the murder of a character by a servant'.[22] He also uses one of the most disturbing episodes in Dickens's *Great Expectations* (1860–61), the dinner Pip attends at the attorney Jaggers's house, as an epigraph to his opening chapter. Jaggers's housekeeper, the almost silent Molly (Estelle's mother) was once accused of murder. Jaggers was responsible for her acquittal.

'If you talk of strength,' said Mr. Jaggers, 'I'll show you a wrist. Molly, let them see your wrist.' ... 'There's power here,' said Mr. Jaggers, coolly tracing out the sinews with his forefinger. 'Very few men have the power of wrist that this woman has. It's remarkable what mere force of grip there is in these hands. I have had occasion to notice many hands; but I never saw stronger in that respect, man's or woman's, than these'.[23]

Domestic manhood

In considering potential causes of Courvoisier's anger, the issues of masculinity and early Victorian domesticity also deserve consideration, although contemporary discussion of Russell's murder did not voice them. By 1840 the doctrine of 'separate spheres' for men and women had been firmly established, but how did a male servant fit into this ideological segregation? The short answer is, he did not. Bridget Walsh's intriguing study, *Domestic Murder in Nineteenth-Century England*, focuses on physical violence between blood relations, lovers, or rivals in love, but she also highlights the cultural limbo in which a male domestic servant found himself in this age. By the time of the sensation novels of the 1850s and 1860s – the same period in which a degree of sensitivity to the servant's plight becomes discernible – the once-lauded sanctuary of home had, she argues, been problematized.

> The home was no longer a source of purity, and the means by which virtue was restored; instead it was an environment dominated by secrecy, one just as likely to foster violence and unregulated desire as the restoration of social order.

Female characters disruptive of the domestic sphere were 'generally motivated by a financial imperative as opposed to a discontent with the domestic sphere itself'.[24] Male motivation differed:

> When we come to examine the problematic relationship between men and the domestic sphere in the fiction of this period, the focus shifts. Rather than seeking to disrupt the domestic idyll for financial gain, the male characters in the novels ... have a problematic relationship with the domestic space *per se*, questioning their very existence within it.

By the mid-nineteenth century, Walsh argues, 'unstable and contested models of masculinity were refracted through trial transcripts and novels that concern themselves with domestic violence and murder'.[25]

The masculinity of a male domestic servant in the Victorian period must have been particularly problematic. As Walsh notes, the work of John Tosh and others on masculinity and domesticity has revealed the oversimplification of viewing the nineteenth-century home as a feminine or private space, and Herbert Sussman has argued for a new and necessary focus on 'masculinities' rather than the singular version of the noun.[26] The subject of male servitude and masculinity in the Victorian period – or indeed any other – however, is currently understudied. Straub does consider the issue, in the context of mid-eighteenth-century Britain, arguing that

> public-sphere homosociality is anchored in private relations between men within the household. As surely as the modern bourgeois order needs "the domestic woman," *it also needs a construct of domestic manhood ... and the male retainer is a vital part of that construct's historical formation.*[27]

206   *Explanations and Consequences*

Theatrical works of the 1730s and 1740s, in her view

> make strong claims for the manservant's heterosexual magnetism as the basis for inclusion in a trans-class ideal of virility and manly authority. This theatrical sexy footman forms part of a modern version of masculine sexuality that depends more on gender than on class difference, and more on a universal, naturalized heterosexual male desire than on the homoeroticism embedded in hierarchical relations between men.[28]

We do need a 'construct of domestic manhood' that encompasses male servants, but I am not persuaded that 'theatrical sexy footmen' are sufficient evidence, even in the eighteenth century, of a trans-class ideal. Even if it existed, that ideal would be limited to sexuality rather than extending to economic realities. And in the nineteenth century the construct would be challenged by the separate spheres ideology, as well as the increasing numerical preponderance of female rather than male servants. William Russell's 'family', as I described in Chapter 2 above, was anomalous for its age, middle class in terms of physical size and Russell's income, but headed by a male aristocrat so that his small complement of servants included a valet. Courvoisier's position as a male servant in such a tiny household was likewise somewhat exceptional. But in 1840, in any household, large or small, how might a male servant waiting on a male master be situated within contemporary understandings of masculinity? How might he himself construe his masculinity? The male role within the home was typically defined in terms of his being the master, in earlier ages pater familias, head of the household and responsible for dependents. But the male servant was a dependent himself, and possibly an increasingly resentful one. John Tosh has argued that, for the Victorians, 'only at home could a man be truly and authentically himself'.[29] This was not true of the male domestic servant, whose home, in terms of workplace, was not his own, and who may well have had another 'home' – like William Tayler and James Ellis – where his wife and children lodged. In his master or mistress's home, the male servant's private persona and authority were required to be masked. In Tayler and Ellis's cases, this requirement went so far as to include the polite fiction that they were single.

Work of necessity implies 'control – physical and psychological, social and symbolic'.[30] The work of a servant, male or female, demanded that personal identity be subsumed within the larger identity of a household which lay outside their authority or personal control. Servants' lives were not their own. For Courvoisier, Tayler, and others in their situation there was also no 'separate sphere': their homes, which were not their own, were also their workplaces, and spaces in which they were subordinate. How was masculinity acted out within the confines of such a domestic space? Male domestic service required submission rather than agency and its daily tasks might be perceived as innately unmanly as well. And, as Fector's dismissal of Courvoisier reveals – and Brian McCuskey has argued with respect to Thackeray's representation of footmen – male, liveried servants suffered physical objectification in the same way that women experience.[31]

Their daily routine was also dull. Contemporary commentators on male servitude complained that male domestics had too little in the way of active employment and too much time on their hands. From the servant's point of view, however – and especially such a servant as Courvoisier, a young man employed in a tiny household by an old, semi-reclusive individual – tedium must likewise have been a problem. Bridget Walsh's discussion of Jasper, the murderer of Edwin Drood in Charles Dickens's final, unfinished novel, is instructive in this regard. Jasper was a nephew rather than a servant, but his complaints of the 'daily drudging round' of his existence, marked by 'no whirl and uproar around me, no distracting commerce or calculation, no risk, no change of place' must have been experienced by Russell's valet, trapped in an even more dependent position. 'The cramped monotony of my existence', Jasper despaired, 'grinds me away by the grain'. Courvoisier, like Jasper, for all he hid it from his relations and fellow servants, appears to have been 'troubled with some sort of ambition, aspiration, restlessness, dissatisfaction'.[32] The frustrations voiced might equally have been experienced by a middle-class Victorian female in the period, as indeed they were by Charlotte Brontë and others. Male servitude in this age might be thought of as emasculating.

Walsh also writes of Jasper's desire to appropriate Drood's 'particular domestic idyll'.[33] An extreme example of the enactment of such a desire on the part of a servant can be found in the late nineteenth-century case of Hilda Blake, an English orphan from Norfolk. Sent abroad in 1888 to work as a domestic servant in the Canadian province of Manitoba, after restless, unhappy transfers from one household to another this cuckoo in the nest nourished such a resentment of her final mistress, Mary Lane, and such a desire to supplant Lane within the household, that in 1899 she shot and killed her. Like Courvoisier, the 21-year-old Blake found her neck in a noose.[34] Courvoisier could not of course have dreamed of physically replacing William Russell within 14 Norfolk Street. But he could and did appropriate his master's physical possessions. The thefts, like Russell's murder, were irrational acts. But they were, to use Robbins's terminology, the 'consequences of unequal power', embodying a servant's frustration with social inequality, just as the murder revealed disparities in age and physical strength.[35] Courvoisier's resentment of his situation found a focal point in a kind, if occasionally irritable, old man.

Immediate consequences: Russell's household

Regardless of Courvoisier's motivation, the murder of a minor, aged aristocrat, having momentarily caught the public eye, might be expected to have faded quickly from public memory. A man had been killed, his killer apprehended, tried, convicted, and executed. Justice had been done. There were a few short-term ripple effects and *The Times*, in 1841, indicated that the murder had given rise to new slang, a knife attack acquiring the name of a 'Swiss hit'.[36]

Others felt the effects more personally and members of Russell's household suffered intensely. Russell's blood relations may have been shocked and horrified by his end, but it was his 'family' in the older sense of the persons living under his roof who felt keenly the consequences of his demise. Courvoisier was one of five servants. His actions cost him his life as well as Russell's; they also cost Mary Hannell, Sarah Mancer, William York, and George Doubleday their jobs and their homes. In sentencing Courvoisier, Lord Chief Justice Tindall commented,

> You selected the dark hour of the night to deprive an innocent and unoffending nobleman, aged and infirm, of his property and life, and thereby destroyed, for a period, the domestic and social comforts of the members of his noble family, who have sustained a shock almost unparalleled, and which has been communicated to the whole community.[37]

The *Morning Chronicle* had commented in similar language in its original report of the 'calamitous event which has suddenly brought sorrow and mourning upon one of the highest and most distinguished of families in this country'.[38] 'By this melancholy occurrence', reported the *Southern Star*,

> the families of the Duke and Duchess of Bedford, Lord John Russell, Marquis and Marchioness of Abercorn, Earl and Countess of Tankerville, Lord and Lady Wriothesley Russell, Earl and Countess of Jersey, Dowager-Duchess of Bedford, Lord and Lady Charles Russell, and upwards of nine others are placed in mourning.[39]

Russell's 'noble' family, despite demonstrating limited interest in him while he lived, were genuinely shocked by his end, but it was his 'family' in the older sense of the persons living under his roof who suffered the practical consequences of his demise. Their 'domestic and social comforts' were destroyed; the entirely innocent Hannell, Mancer, York, and Doubleday lost their 'places' in every sense of the word. A week after the murder the *Morning Chronicle* reported that

> the housemaid is much depressed in spirits respecting her character, fearing that she will be unable to secure a fresh situation, alleging that no respectable person will engage her when they ascertain she has formed one of his late lordship's establishment.[40]

Sarah Mancer was not the only servant of a murder victim to have suffered a notoriety that threatened her livelihood and thus her very life. Hannah Pritty, the middle-aged servant of Westwood, the Soho watch-maker murdered in 1839, was reported to have called on the Marlborough street magistrate 'in much affliction', to complain of the conduct of the police in coming to her and making incessant inquiries of her, although she had, over and over again, given all the evidence she was in possession of relating to the melancholy event. Owing to the annoyance occasioned by the police, who apparently considered they were privileged to demand answers to their interrogatories, wherever they chose to put them, she had just been dismissed from her situation. Unless she was protected in some way, it was impossible she could keep a place; and as there was an objection to engage her as soon as she mentioned with whom she had formerly lived, she was in danger of starvation.

The magistrate was sympathetic and agreed the situation was 'lamentable', but said there was nothing he could do. Pritty left his office in tears.[41]

Francis Hobler carefully recorded the fates of William Russell's servants as of 1842:

> The final end of this case has been one of total forgetfulness on the part of the Russell family, of those who were the principal actors – Cook Housemaid Coachman & Groom were for a long time out of employ – their wages were paid them & I suppose some little trifle besides – the Cook got employed after a time ...The Coachman afterwards got a situation ... the poor groom was left destitute & often was relieved with food by Inspector Tedman to save him from starvation.[42]

The worst affected was the housemaid. Mancer, as we have seen, had been looking for 'light work' rather than a 'hard place' when she entered Russell's household, and for almost three years her employment was quiet and tranquil. That situation changed dramatically on the morning of 6 May, when she discovered her master's corpse. Her life from that date must have been a living nightmare: despite being quickly eliminated as a suspect by the Metropolitan Police she was hounded by Liverpool's Inspector Dowling and the novelist Theodore Hook. She endured examinations by Hobler and the police, the coroner, Bow Street magistrates, and Old Bailey counsel, all in the full glare of publicity. She, like the cook, coachman, and groom, lost her home and employment, and unlike them, she had had serious aspersions cast on her character.

Mancer, fortunately, also attracted sympathy and gained allies. Francis Hobler was the first. As Thackeray and Wilkie Collins would do, Hobler recognized servants as people, whose cares and concerns merited attention. Convinced of her innocence, he raged against those determined to implicate Mancer in the crime and did his best to defend her reputation. It was most likely Hobler who wrote indignantly as 'Adjuta' to the editor of *The Southern Star and London Patriot* on 2 July 1840. The letter was published on 12 July under the headline, 'The Persecution of Sarah Mancer' (her name spelt, for once, correctly):

We are concerned to hear that this poor woman has not received the generous settlement from the relatives of her master, Lord William Russell. The public are not fully acquainted with all the injustice, and all the severity with which she was visited up to the moment of Courvoisier's conviction; and, if all were to be told, it would make the heart bleed to think that while the actual murderer was receiving the most polite attention, and the utmost assistance that a generous sympathy could afford, this poor unfriended girl was not only subjected to extreme mental torture with a view of wringing from her some admission unfavourable to her spotless reputation, but she was also actually dragged about this country to see if a charge could be preferred against her. Prelates, magistrates, and discharged police officers have been zealous in their exertions to damnify her character, and to shift the suspicion of guilt from the murderer and fix it upon this girl. And is she now to be sent out into the world, without reward or recompense? Good God! Is there no humanity in the hearts of her traducers? Are they devoid of feeling? Are they destitute of every principle of honour? The following letter will inform the public of the actual condition of the poor girl at this moment:–

Sir;– It is a noble task to defend the oppressed and persecuted, and a public journalist cannot be better employed in removing the clouds of error and prejudice from an innocent and much-wronged individual. Sarah Mancer has been cruelly treated, and I do hope that the Russell family will not, now that the truth is made apparent, and the murderer convicted – abandon the poor girl, who has suffered so much, while she remained in their service. But if they do, I trust that the public, who are ever ready to sympathize with the distressed, will not forget her. It will naturally be concluded that something has been done for Sarah Mancer, and the other servants of the late Lord William Russell. But, Sir, absolutely nothing has been done for them, at present. They have been paid their wages and dismissed. They have not received one shilling beyond what was due to them. They have left the house and gone into lodgings, but I can scarcely believe that the Bedford family will part with them shabbily, more especially Sarah Mancer, with the whole of whose unexampled treatment they must be fully acquainted. I will, therefore, wait patiently to see whether any thing will be done for the VICTIM; and should there not be, then I will do my utmost to raise a subscription on her behalf; and I am confident that there are thousands that will contribute their mites. The ENGLISH SERVANTS will not be backward, I think, in this cause, for they must know that the FOREIGN SERVANTS subscribed largely to get THE MONSTER acquitted. And I do hope, Mr. Editor, that you will be kind enough to receive the subscriptions, when the time arrives to do so.

Will it be credited, that <u>Sarah Mancer</u> was DRAGGED ABOUT FOR MANY MILES <u>to see if any person could recognize her as being guilty of felony</u>. Every means that could possibly be thought of was used to trample upon this persecuted woman. It is rumoured that the Duke of Bedford intends to do something for her, and I wish sincerely that it may be true. Sarah Mancer is a very different woman now to what she was previous to the murder of Lord William Russell. She is a mere shadow. But look at her treatment from first to last, where is there a woman in a thousand that could endure the torture that this poor creature has gone through?

'It is our opinion', the *Southern Star*'s editor concluded,

> that a suspected individual in a criminal case be subjected to a close and rigid examination. And we readily admit that at the first discovery of the murder of Lord W. Russell suspicion was as likely to fall upon the servant maids as upon the valet.

But, he continued, 'we do complain ... of the persevering endeavours of certain persons to brand the unhappy Sarah Mancer with the felony, and of their unbecoming ardour to fix upon her the guilt of her master's murder'. Would any of them compensate Mancer for the wrong they had done to her, and to her reputation?

Both Mancer and Mary Hannell received £15 from the reward money offered by the Treasury, and the *Examiner* wrote that it anticipated the same sums to be paid from the reward offered by the Bedford family. Other than that the Russells did nothing for Sarah. A public appeal published in *The Times* on 28 July read as follows:

> Sarah Mancer, the Housemaid to the late Lord William Russell – the persecutions this poor woman underwent, the harassing interrogations to which she was subjected preceding the providential discovery of the Guilt of Courvoisier, have so prostrated her mental faculties and bodily strength as to unfit her for those duties her station in Life has called her to – Some persons have therefore ventured this Appeal to public charity, for the purpose of raising a fund to be applied in alleviation of her present and future wants – The following Gentlemen have kindly consented to receive donations – Mr Evans, 17 Maddox Street
> C Stuart Esq, 36 University Street Torrington Square
> Mr Simpson, 261 Oxford Street
> Mssrs Hallet, 41 Ludgate Hill
> Mr Smith, 25 Edward Street Portman Square
> Mr Marchant, 351 Oxford Street
> Mr Gilliam, 50 Frith Street Soho and
> J. Foster Esq, 36 University Street – who would have much pleasure in answering any Inquiries relative to Sarah Mancer

Despite the subscription the 'thousands of mites' hoped for were not forthcoming and Mancer suffered a breakdown of some sort. 'The horrors of the suspicion directed against her, following the terrors of the scene she had witnessed, had, we have been informed, such an effect on the mind of Sarah Mancell [sic], that she became deranged', reported the *Examiner* many years after the fact. It reproduced the subscription advertisement, noting,

> unhappily no effectual response was made, and … [it] was followed by the announcement, a little later, that Sarah Mancer was the inmate of a pauper lunatic asylum … The persecutions this poor woman underwent, the harassing interrogations to which she was subjected preceding the providential discover of the guilt of Courvoisier, have so prostrated her mental faculties and bodily strength, as to unfit her for those duties her station in life have called her to.[43]

In the newspaper record, the last we hear of Mancer are reports of her entering such an asylum. 'Pauper lunatic asylum', in London in 1840, would have meant the 'lunatic' corner of the local workhouse. Poverty was one of the chief causes of insanity identified by experts in Mancer's time, but the *Examiner* blamed not poverty, Courvoisier's actions, or the Russells' indifference to her fate for Mancer's mental afflictions.

> Even the miscreant murderer himself expressed much regret that any imputation should for a moment have been cast upon either of the poor unoffending female servants who had been so unfortunate as to have been in the house with him.[44]

This is a point worth emphasizing once more: while Courvoisier's original protestations of innocence enabled an attack on Mancer by his counsel, the valet himself made no attempt to falsely accuse others, as he could so easily have done. As we have seen, Inspector Dowling and Theodore Hook were only too happy to implicate Mancer in the murder, and Phillips was certainly expected to play on this possibility. Courvoisier never did. While protesting an innocence he knew to be untrue, he forbore to accuse others of his crime. This forbearance – especially in light of the fact of his short acquaintance with Russell's other servants – is, on my view, the single aspect of his behaviour that does him credit.

In discussing Mancer's distress the *Examiner* chose to focus on the role played by Charles Phillips in the course of its crusade against the 'license of counsel' during the 1840s and to contrast their different post-trial fates. Phillips had 'directed the foul and horrible suspicion against poor Sarah Mancer'; he had placed her life in jeopardy and 'about the same time' he had himself been raised to the bench, Mancer, 'driven mad by the terrors that had successively beset her' entered an asylum.[45] Happily, for Mancer this was not the end. She did not die there. While she disappeared from the print record – in the late

1840s, the *Examiner* was relying on newspaper coverage a decade old – Hobler continued her story in his scrapbook:

> ... when she recovered from the illness which was the natural result of the trials she had endured she went for a short time to a relative [inserted with caret: or friend] who kept a public house in Westminster – after a time Sir George Chetwynd, Baronet, who had paid much attention to the case from the first & who I had met at Bow Street – sent a message to her & offered a situation in his Establishment at Grendon Hall, Warwicks & offered her opportunity to change her name, it was gladly accepted & the poor woman is comfortable in the Establishment of that really affluent & hospitable Baronet –[46]

Sarah Mancer had found another friend.[47] Having been misnamed from the time Russell's murder was discovered, even by those who sought to implicate her in the crime, Sarah Mancell/Mancele/Mansell/Manser now assumed a different name entirely. When Chetwynd died in May 1850, ten years after the murder, his will contained various codicils, including legacies for some of his servants. To one 'Mary Alton' he bequeathed all of his 'favourite cats' plus £10 per annum to feed them and an additional £300 for herself.[48] Was Alton the housemaid formerly known as Sarah Mancer? I hope so.

Long-term consequences

The fate of William Russell and his household only briefly captured attention and the public's imagination was soon distracted by other sensational murders which followed in fairly rapid succession. But this particular crime had broad and long-term consequences extending well beyond the personal, helping to shape the development of detective policing, the criminal trial, and popular fiction. The actions of a single, discontented servant, apart from depriving a man of his life, sent ripple effects into the early Victorian public sphere in a variety of ways.

Courvoisier and the novelists

Among the consequences that could not have been foreseen at the time of the Russell murder was its effect on English literature. An alarmed William Harrison Ainsworth, while legitimately protesting his innocence with respect to the influence of his novel *Jack Sheppard* on Russell's murderer, abandoned 'Newgate' fiction to concentrate on historical romances of a different and less controversial sort: those immediately following included *Guy Fawkes* (1840; self-explanatory), *The Tower of London* (1840; the story of Lady Jane Grey), and *Old Saint Paul's* (a tale of the plague and Great Fire of London, 1841). Future writers who continued to write on crime would increasingly focus on detectives and detection rather than criminal biographies. Wilkie Collins's *The*

Moonstone is commonly cited in this regard, while Dickens contributed Inspector Bucket in *Bleak House*. Police detectives, though, had a limited appeal in the nineteenth century: 'the private detective, whether amateur or professional' outnumbered official police detectives, and the private detective 'also often appears as a more competent and praiseworthy figure'.[49] Given the well-publicized policing failures where detection was concerned, this is hardly surprising.

If novelists became more squeamish and circumspect where crime and criminals were concerned, the Victorians' fascination with murder continued, perhaps intensified, after the Russell case, and was catered to in sensationalized 'true crime' publications such as the *Police Gazette*. In our own time, that fascination continues and is arguably stronger still. Victorian cases are repeatedly resurrected in books: Harriet Monckton's murder, for example, was fictionalized by Elizabeth Haynes in 2018. Kate Summerscale's *The Suspicions of Mr Whicher* (2008), an award-winning retelling of the investigation into Constance Kent's murder of her half-brother (1860), was subsequently adapted for television. Other television dramas based on Victorian murders include *Dark Angel* (2016), in which Joanne Froggatt played Mary Ann Cotton, hanged in 1873 for the arsenical poisoning of her stepson and who may, over a 20-year period, have killed husbands and many of her children for insurance money.

Policing and detection

As the investigation into Russell's murder proceeded, perceived inadequacies in policing increasingly occupied the press, and accusations of incompetence escalated to the more serious charge of outright corruption raised during Courvoisier's trial. Despite contemporary allegations, where the Russell investigation is concerned I think we can safely dismiss police corruption with a view to monetary gain. Six of the officers involved in the case were admittedly financially rewarded, but they could not have been certain of that outcome, and the sums in question were relatively small. On the removal of Edward Oxford – the would-be assassin of the young Queen Victoria – from the bar at the same Old Bailey session in which Courvoisier was tried, prosecuting counsel John Adolphus was careful to inform the court of the rules governing police rewards:

> Mr. Adolphus said that, in consequence of what had been said as to the reward in the case of Courvoisier, he deemed it his duty to read to the court a letter from Colonel Rowan, one of the commissioners of the police, on the subject. The letter stated that the police were in no cases permitted to receive, or consider themselves entitled to receive, any reward, whether offered by the government or by individuals, for the discovery of any crime, or for the apprehension of any offender, without the special permission of the commissioners, and that a previous investigation always took place for the purposes of ascertaining whether any

blame whatever could attach to the conduct of the police; in which case, although the crime might be discovered, and the offender apprehended or convicted, they were not permitted to participate in the offered reward, which was considered in the light of a gratuity only.[50]

Rather than being censured, the conduct of Inspectors Pearce, Beresford, and Tedman, as well as police constables Shaw, Collier, and Cronin, was rewarded on Rowan's recommendation. Of the 'promised bounty' Pearce received £50, Beresford and Tedman £30 each, and the constables £10 each from the government reward, plus equal sums from the funds offered by the Russell family.[51] Of these men, Collier and Cronin were the officers who found the stained handkerchiefs and shirtfront with missing sleeves on the fifth search of Courvoisier's belongings. More troubling is the tacit approval, or at least disregard, of their questionable actions by superiors in the force. That these officers were rewarded rather than sanctioned for their behaviour is astonishing. But I have argued that the almost certain fabrication of physical evidence incriminating Courvoisier owed not to greed but instead to desperation on the part of a force working under high pressure with virtually no forensic methods of investigation available to them.

Today, fingerprint evidence would have incriminated their prime suspect. By virtue of his work in Russell's household, Courvoisier's fingerprints would naturally have been all over the house and his master's personal possessions, including those secreted in the butler's pantry, but the bloody prints on Russell's sheets, as surgeon Robert Blake Overton suggested, would have identified him as the murderer. The four poultry carvers, at least, possibly all of the knives in the house, would have been swabbed, and DNA obtained from the one used to murder Russell compared to the DNA profile of the victim using blood taken at his autopsy. CCTV footage would probably have revealed images of the valet, a brown paper parcel containing Russell's silverware under his arm, entering the Dieppe Hotel. In the absence of such forensic resources, while the actions of the police were reprehensible, the temptation can be understood. What might genuinely be condemned as incompetence or negligence on the part of the police, the most glaring and egregious error in the investigation, is the failure to follow up on all of the hotels frequented by foreigners. Information gathering was the one technique available to early Victorian detectives, as it had been to the Fieldings' runners. Beresford, as Hobler described, enquired into 'a few' hotels in Leicester-place, but overlooked the Dieppe. Establishing Courvoisier's connection with that hotel might have resulted in discovery of the stolen plate that unequivocally implicated him in theft, and prompted a confession before the case came to trial. Ironically, this mistake garnered almost no press attention. The one paper that did see fit to comment on it, the *Southern Star*, reported that 'prevailing opinion of the City aldermen, with whom the reporter has conversed, appears to be that this diabolical murder will lead to the establishment of a detective police'.[52]

In the event, not the Russell murder but the police bungling of the Good case, or 'Roehampton murder', in 1842 was more directly responsible for the creation of a detective division within the Metropolitan Police. The dismembered body of Jane Jones was discovered in a Putney stable on 3 April. She had been murdered by her 'husband' – they were not legally married but living as husband and wife – Daniel Good. Good, who had made plausible excuses for her absence, was not suspected of having killed her; discovery of the murder and his arrest instead flowed from an accusation of shoplifting. Constables pursuing inquiries regarding the theft of a pair of trousers were directed to the stable in which what remained of Jones's corpse (Good had been burning it bit by bit) was hidden. What the constables first mistook for a pig in hay proved to be a human female torso. The murderer managed to lock the officers in the stable and escape, and it took the police ten days to locate and apprehend him in Tonbridge, Kent. The arrest owed little to the formal investigation: a former police constable from Wandsworth recognized Good from his days on the beat and reported his whereabouts to the local force. Like Courvoisier, Daniel Good was convicted and executed, but as in the earlier investigation chance had played a significant role in securing justice for the victim. Jane Jones's body had been discovered by accident; the arrest of her murderer rested on the actions of a civilian.[53] And by 1842 the public had been made aware of previous policing failures and was watching their efforts with a new and keen interest.

That the Detective Department was formed in response to criticisms that the Metropolitan Police were unable to investigate homicide successfully is somewhat surprising. The Fielding brothers' Bow Street runners were created in response to concerns about property crime; so too was Peel's preventive force. The role played by the newspaper press in fanning public anxiety and demanding specialized detective expertise in investigating murder cases is significant, and timing was crucial to the formation of public opinion. Perceived failures in the investigations into a series of murders committed within a six-year period, Russell's among them, were cited as evidence of the need for a dedicated detective force within the Metropolitan Police. Prior to the Russell murder, the press had been relatively supportive of police investigations. But the conduct of the inquest into Russell's death, perceived shortcomings in the search of his house, and suspicions about the 'evidence' found eroded confidence. Editors began to view police efforts with a jaundiced eye. By the time of Jane Jones's murder, the press had serious doubts in the ability of Peel's preventive force to successfully investigate murder, and their conduct in that case confirmed those misgivings.

As Rachael Griffin comments, the cases of Davis, Grimwood, Westwood, and Templeman 'would not have been linked to those of Lord William Russell or Jane Jones had the police not made critical mistakes investigating the latter two'.[54] These mistakes, widely reported and discussed, 'caused the press to glance backwards to find similar cases'.[55] James Greenacre's 1836 murder of Hannah Brown was invoked as another instance of police incompetence: Brown's dismembered body had only been discovered after a reward had been offered, and that 'discovery was due to the brother and other friends of the poor victim, rather than to the Police'.[56] Without the highly publicized

Explanations and Consequences 217

detective failures in the Russell and Good investigations the press might not have looked backwards; now, they were keen to detect incompetence. Before Good had been apprehended, *The Times* was drawing parallels with previous cases:

> The conduct of the metropolitan police in the present case, as in those of the unfortunate Eliza Grimwood, Lord William Russell, and others, is marked with a looseness and want of decision which proves that unless a decided change is made in the present system, it is idle to expect that it can be an efficient detective police, and that the most desperate offender may escape with impunity.[57]

The policing failures evident in the investigation of Russell's death, while not solely responsible for the creation of a detective division within the Metropolitan Police, certainly contributed to a sense that London required a professional detective force. The once despised Bow Street runners were now lauded as a superior force where detection was concerned. This claim exasperated Police Commissioners Rowan and Mayne, but, reversing their earlier opinions, they did reluctantly admit, in a letter to Home Secretary Sir James Grey, that a small detective force might be necessary. On 23 August 1842 they submitted a list of eight men, two inspectors and six sergeants, chosen to serve within it. Highlighting continuities in detective policing as well as change, Griffin notes the irony inherent in this 'reorganization born of public criticism': many of the individuals selected 'had been involved in the very investigations that led to the creation of the Detective Department'; they were, she argues, 'the same men wearing different hats'.[58] Among them were Nicholas Pearce and Frederick Shaw. Detached from their former divisions, they would henceforth work at headquarters based in Scotland Yard.

Pearce was perhaps the most successful of the officers who had attended at 14 Norfolk Street. As an inspector in A Division this former member of the Bow Street Patrol had been involved in the investigation into the murder of Jane Jones that attracted so much negative publicity, but that involvement, like his role in the Russell case, did Pearce no long-term damage. He would continue to be involved in high-profile murder cases, including the protracted investigation into the suspicious death of Harriet Monckton in November 1843: after repeated adjournments, the coroner's inquest finally produced a verdict of wilful murder in May 1846.[59] He subsequently investigated Joseph Connors's murder of Mary Brothers (1845) and the murder of 20-year-old PC George Clark at Dagenham (1846).[60] But police orders reveal that during the 1840s – he was promoted out of the Detective Department in 1844 to become superintendent at Holborn – he supervised plainclothes patrols to observe burglars and felons as well. Pearce was also involved in efforts to keep the peace in London's theatre district and supervised plainclothes men for the detection of crime at the opening of the Crystal Palace on 9 June 1854. When he retired to Cornwall the following year Queen Victoria gave this long-serving officer a

218 *Explanations and Consequences*

silver teapot in recognition of his 'constant zeal, intelligence, and discretion shown by him when in attendance upon her visits to the [Great] Exhibition'.[61]

Frederick Shaw likewise suffered no ill consequences from his role in the Russell investigation; in fact, Constable Shaw was promoted to sergeant a few weeks prior to Courvoisier's trial. Unlike Pearce, once appointed he remained with the Detective Division throughout his career. He served nine years and two months as a detective sergeant, and four and a half years as a detective inspector.[62] Shaw would work again under Pearce's direction on the investigation into painter Richard Dadd's murder of his father in 1843 and the murder of PC Clark, among other cases.[63] And he did not escape murder even in retirement. On leaving the police in 1856 the former detective ran the Golden Anchor Public House in Saffron Hill which, on Boxing Day 1864, became a murder site when a violent affray in the bagatelle room resulted in the death of Michael Harrington.[64]

Other officers involved in the Russell murder investigation, while not formally part of the Detective Department, are similarly found participating in murder cases throughout the 1840s. In the years following Courvoisier's execution Inspector Tedman would be involved in the investigations of the murders of Jones and Brothers as well as John Tawell's murder of Sarah Hart (1845). Inspector Beresford had been involved in the Westwood murder investigation as well as Russell's but subsequently became a regular participant in investigations into the non-violent crimes which more normally occupied police attention. *The Times* reported Beresford's involvement in the investigation of a fraud in the autumn of 1840; in 1842 he went undercover to investigate an illegal gaming house and he was involved in a similar investigation in 1843; in the latter year he also investigated a public house which was remaining open during prohibited hours on Sundays.[65]

Not unnaturally, it was murder investigations that continued to attract public attention, but, despite its origins, once the new department had been created, its detectives would spend the bulk of their time investigating not murder but theft: burglary in the forties, forgery and fraud in the sixties and seventies. The Detective Department would work regularly with the Home Office, in the counties as well as within London, but again not exclusively or even primarily in murder cases. Apart from their investigations into white-collar crimes they were employed in maintaining public order at large-scale events, in monitoring foreign nationals and refugees – foreign language skills were highly prized – and evaluating naturalization applications, and in extraditing criminals to and from Britain. 'The government', Griffin argues, 'allowed detectives a great deal of discretion when it came to surveillance of foreigners and naturalization applications and, by relying heavily on detectives' evaluations, gave Scotland Yard detectives a discretionary part in determining who was allowed to remain on British soil'.[66] Such surveillance, had it existed in 1840, while not preventing Russell's murder, might have uncovered Courvoisier's connection with the Hotel de Dieppe and rendered identification of the murderer less difficult. This work, clandestine in its own time, has to date received less attention from

Explanations and Consequences 219

historians than sensational Victorian murder trials, but is now highly topical and eminently worthy of further investigation.[67]

The criminal trial

Charles Phillips, like the unfortunate members of William Russell's household, can also be regarded as collateral damage in the fallout from Courvoisier's trial. Phillips's professional reputation never recovered from his handling of this particular client's defence and he ended his legal career ingloriously, becoming, in 1842, a judge of the Insolvent Debtors' Court. Phillips's story has been told in a variety of forums and need not be returned to here. What remains to be illuminated in more ordinary cases is the role played by solicitors. Adolphus's courtroom conduct of Courvoisier's prosecution rested entirely on the research done and material assembled by Francis Hobler. It is only reasonable to suppose that Phillips likewise relied heavily on the efforts of Thomas Flower. Courvoisier's trial was exceptional in terms of the public interest generated, but these two men, Hobler and Flower, must routinely have worked, in less dramatic circumstances, in the same way throughout their professional careers. Behind the scenes and out of the public eye, where they were employed, the preparation of solicitors was essential to the early Victorian trial process.

Prosecution also requires further investigation. As I've argued elsewhere, apart from various enquiries into covert public prosecution, the subject has received comparatively little attention in academic studies of the eighteenth- and nineteenth-century criminal trial, which have tended instead to focus on efforts to secure justice for those accused of felonies. This preoccupation is understandable, given the severity of criminal sanction at the time when activities of counsel first become discernible. But it means that William Garrow's prosecutorial work in the early nineteenth century has been represented as something that should be viewed as an abandonment of his 'true principles' as revealed during his years at the Old Bailey, and thus needs not merely to be explained, but to be explained away.[68] This is a mistake. A genuinely just system provides redress for victims of crimes as well as protecting defendants from procedural abuse or injustice, and it is worth emphasizing that leading practitioners in the criminal courts acknowledged this fact. Like that of his predecessor, the Old Bailey practice of Courvoisier's counsel consisted almost entirely of defence work, but Charles Phillips also argued for the necessity of a public prosecutor in that court, especially once the Prisoner's Counsel Act came into effect. 'To render [that] measure not effective, but *practicable*, you must have counsel to prosecute'.[69] Henry Brougham agreed and forwarded copies of extracts from Phillips's letters to Lord John Russell.[70] The suggestion was not taken up.

While Phillips and Brougham understood that adversarial procedure requires counsel on both sides, historians have tended to overlook the issue. In the early 1830s, according to Phillips, 'nineteen out of twenty' cases tried at the Old Bailey had no counsel for the prosecution, for the simple reason that

Middlesex magistrates refused to grant costs for their employment. He believed that the trial process, rather than disadvantaging defendants, was actually skewed in their favour.[71] One of the distinguishing features of the trial of William Russell's murderer is the fact that, with counsel employed for both the prosecution and the defence, it provides a rare instance, in its own time, of full adversarial process.

A few last words

As I commented in the introduction to this study, the significance of 'the Russell murder' lies primarily in the timing of its occurrence. Seismic shifts were taking place in prosecution, policing, and punishment in 1840, and at a time when 'society' was still narrow and overlapped considerably with government. It is thus unsurprising that a murder victim who belonged to the aristocracy had been involved in government personally and that the association continued via family ties after William Russell's own retirement from politics. Both Russell's nephew and a son-in-law were, as members of Parliament, involved in discussion of reform of the criminal justice system. There were certain limits to the reforms they were willing to consider. John Russell continued to believe in the value of public execution and never adopted the abolitionist stance urged by the *Hampshire Independent*. He also enabled Francis Hobler's career as a police solicitor, which suggests that, if unwilling to consider the creation of the office of public prosecutor at the Central Criminal Court, he was nonetheless sensitive to the duty owed by the state to victims of crime. Just as significant is the fact that the investigation into this case can be distinguished via the faint stirrings of what might be characterized as democratic feeling. Class tensions are evident in Hobler's aggrieved conviction, once the case had concluded, that his efforts on the Russell family's behalf had not been appreciated, and his exasperation at the way in which he had had to pursue costs incurred in the course of prosecution, despite the fact that he had asked for expenses only, and from a very wealthy family for whom a few hundred pounds was small change. They are also evident in the solicitor's dogged determination that housemaid Sarah Mancer, innocent of any crime, should not be publicly maligned and vilified. The relatively recent ability to feel empathy across class boundaries is equally evident in Thackeray's response to Courvoisier's execution. The identity and social class of Russell's murderer were not a bar to fellow feeling. Thackeray, however, remained deeply conflicted where servants were concerned, recognizing and troubled by the inequities of treatment they suffered while at the same time frightened of their physical power. Separated by merely 'a carpet and a few planks and beams' were people – good or otherwise – who had 'schemes, passions, longing hopes, tragedies' entirely of their own.[72] All told, in 1840, a carving knife wielded by a manservant and the government noose that awaited him were weighed in a slightly new balance. William Makepeace Thackeray was not the only uneasy Victorian.

Notes

1 Walsh, *Domestic Murder*, 94.
2 OBP t18400615-1696; *The Times*, 22 June 1840.
3 Society for Promoting Christian Knowledge, 'Advice to Young Women on Going to Service' (1835), quoted in Burnett, *Useful Toil*, 174.
4 Hay, 'England, 1562–875: The Law and its Uses', 7, 61.
5 Hay, 'England, 1562–875: The Law and its Uses', 90.
6 *Remarkable Trials*, 190; pasted into Hobler's scrapbook at Item 95 (seq. 389).
7 Piketty, *Capital and Ideology*, 195. I am grateful to Doug Hay for this reference.
8 *The Queen V. Palmer*, 308 (emphasis added).
9 *Domestic Service and Gender 1660–750*, 84.
10 Item 53 (seq. 194–95).
11 *The Times*, 8 July 1840.
12 *Victorian Studies in Scarlet*, 220. See generally chap. 12, 'The Trouble with Servants'.
13 For Sellis, see Chapter 1 above, [00].
14 Altick, *Victorian Studies in Scarlet*, 227. See also Kilday, 'Constructing the Cult of the Criminal', and Knelman, *Twisting in the Wind*, chap. 7.
15 'Laid up in two lodgings', 521.
16 Quoted in Robbins, *The Servant's Hand*, 2.
17 Robbins, *The Servant's Hand*, 40.
18 *An Uneasy Victorian* was the astute title given to Ann Monsarrat's study of Thackeray.
19 'On a Chalk-Mark on the Door', 505.
20 'On a Chalk-Mark on the Door', 510.
21 Robbins, *The Servant's Hand*, xi.
22 Robbins, *The Servant's Hand*, 153.
23 *Great Expectations*, 236.
24 Walsh, *Domestic Murder*, 94.
25 Walsh, *Domestic Murder*, 95.
26 Sussman, *Victorian Masculinities*. See also McLaren, *The Trials of Masculinity*.
27 *Domestic Affairs*, 110–11 (emphasis added).
28 *Domestic Affairs*, 112.
29 *A Man's Place*, 33.
30 S. Wallman, *Social Anthropology of Work* (London, 1979), 1, quoted in Meldrum, *Domestic Service and Gender 1660–1750*, 135; Meldrum, *Domestic Service and Gender 1660–1750*, 146.
31 See 'Fetishizing the Flunkey'.
32 *Domestic Murder*, 19–20.
33 *Domestic Murder*, 105.
34 See Mitchell and Kramer, *Walk Towards the Gallows*.
35 *The Servant's Hand*, ix.
36 7 December 1841.
37 *The Times*, 22 June 1840.
38 7 May 1840.
39 10 May 1840.
40 *Morning Chronicle*, 15 May 1840.
41 *The Champion and Weekly Herald*, 25 August 1839. I am grateful to Rachael Griffin for this reference.
42 Item 110 (seq. 412).
43 24 Nov. 1849.
44 24 Nov. 1849.
45 *Examiner*, 9 Jan. 1847; 3 Nov 1849.
46 Item 110 (seq. 412). Harman overlooks this information in her study of the case. *Murder by the Book*, 151.

222 *Explanations and Consequences*

47 This particular Sir George was the second to hold the title, his father having been knighted in 1787 and created a baronet in 1795, and Grendon Hall had been inherited around the turn of the nineteenth century on the expiry of a distant branch of the Chetwynd family. The first baronet had been an authority on the magistracy, the second, called to the bar in 1813, served as chairman of the Staffordshire quarter sessions. Sir George also entered politics in 1820 by means of the borough of Stafford, which had intermittently returned members of the family since 1661. His politics are best described as old school: he was a benevolent country squire. Where criminal justice was concerned, Chetwynd supported a bill to prohibit stealing in shops; he also believed that England was overrun by work-shy vagrants, 'idle and disorderly persons', 'incorrigible rogues', and vagabonds, and he introduced bills to consolidate the vagrancy laws in 1821 and 1822. He voted against the forgery punishment mitigation bill in 1821; Henry Grey Bennet, William Russell's son-in-law, described Chetwynd in that year as 'a government Member' of a 'conservative Parliament'. Yet, he was not an unkind man: two years earlier his bill to abolish the private whipping of women in workhouses, houses of correction, and lunatic asylums was passed as 1 Geo. IV, c. 57. Following his retirement from politics at the dissolution of Parliament in 1826, Sir George focused his energies on altering and making additions to the Hall and collecting coins and works of art. As a fellow member of Brooks's club, he may have known William Russell; he certainly followed the trial of his murderer closely. http://www.historyofparliamentonline.org/volume/1820-1832/member/chetwynd-george-1783-1850.
48 PROB 11/2116.
49 Shpayer-Makov, *Ascent of the Detective*, 226. For a discussion of the representation of police detectives in fiction, see Shpayer-Makov, *Ascent of the Detective*, chap. 6.
50 *Morning Chronicle*, 23 June 1840.
51 *Examiner*, 23 August 1840.
52 28 June 1840.
53 OBP: t18420509-1705. The police records are at MEPO 3/45. For press coverage see, e.g., *The Times*, 8 April 1842; 11 April 1842; 19 April 1842; 28 April 1842.
54 OBP: t18420509-1705, 81. Investigation into Templeman's murder was still ongoing when Russell was found dead, and press coverage of the two overlapped for a couple of months.
55 'Detective Policing and the State', 82.
56 *Remarks on the Recent Murders in London*, 3.
57 11 April 1842.
58 'Detective Policing and the State', 83.
59 On this case see, e.g., *Morning Chronicle*, 13 Nov. 1845; and *The Times*, 14 and 19 February, 20 March, 23 April, and 8 May 1846. The police records are at MEPO 3/48.
60 MEPO 3/51 and 3/53.
61 See MEPO 7/11, 7/14, 7/15, and 7/16 as well as Pearce's retirement file at MEPO 21/3 (1855). I am grateful to Rachael Griffin for this information. For Pearce's policing career see also Griffin, 'Detective Policing and the State', 88, 110, 238.
62 Shaw's retirement file is at MEPO 21/3. The chief inspector rank had not been created prior to his retirement in 1856, so he could rise no further.
63 Dadd was declared insane and incarcerated at Bethlem and later Broadmoor. See Allderidge, *Richard Dadd*, and Tromans, *Richard Dadd*.
64 *The Times*, 9 February 1865. Seraphini Polioni was sentenced to death for murder in January 1865 but reprieved following the confession of his cousin, Gregorio Mogni. Mogni was convicted of manslaughter and sentenced to five years' penal servitude. OBP: t18650227-333; Polioni was tried again for wounding Alfred Rebbeck and Charles Bannister and acquitted. OBP: t18650410-454; t18650410-455. See Griffin, 'Detective Policing and the State', 132.

65 Re Westwood, see MEPO 3/42 1839; *The Times*, 10 October 1840, 24 February 1842, 26 August and 20 September 1843. I am grateful to Rachael Griffin for this information.
66 'Detective Policing and the State', 42.
67 On this important subject, see 'Detective Policing and the State', chap. 6.
68 See May, 'Garrow for the Prosecution'.
69 UCL Brougham Papers, 26,364.
70 PRO 30/22/2C, Russell Papers, ff. 31–7. I am grateful to Simon Devereaux for this reference.
71 See May, *The Bar and the Old Bailey*, 194–97, and UCL, Brougham Papers, 28,347, 36,815.
72 Thackeray, 'On a Chalk-Mark on the Door', 510.

Bibliography

Primary sources

Manuscript

Francis Hobler Scrapbook, HLS MS 4487 (http://nrs.harvard.edu/urn-3:HLS.Libr:12188023)

Francis Hobler Scrapbook. Scrapbook relating to the visit of Queen Victoria to the City of London and her entertainment at Guildhall on Lord Mayor's Day 1837. Comprising printed reports of the Court of Common Council and its committees, interleaved with illustrations, and printed and manuscript ephemera relating to the visit, including an autograph of the Queen. Compiled by Francis Hobler in 1838. London Metropolitan Archives CLC/521/MS00036

HO 45/4492

MEPO 3 Correspondence and Papers, Special Series, 1830–1974

MEPO 7 Police Orders, 1829–1989

MEPO 21 Records of Police Pensioners, 1852–1993

UCL, Brougham papers

Newspapers and serials

Fraser's Magazine
Punch
The Athenaeum
The Blackburn Standard
The Bristol Mercury
The Daily Mail
The Era
The Evening Chronicle
The Essex Standard
The Examiner
The Freeman's Journal
The Hampshire Independent
The Lancaster Gazette
The Law Times
The Leicester Chronicle
The Liverpool Mercury
The Londonderry Sentinel

The Mirror
The Morning Chronicle
The Morning Post
The Newcastle Courant
The Royal Cornwall Gazette
The Sheffield and Rotherham Independent
The Solicitors' Journal and Reporter
The Southern Star and London and Brighton Patriot
The Standard
The Sun
The Times

Broadsides

'Apprehension & examination of the valet, for the awful murder of Lord Russell, M.P.', Paul & Co., printers, 2, 3, Monmouth Court, Seven Dials, 1 sheet ([1] p.): ill. (wood engravings), 60.4 × 37.4 cm.

'The lamentation of Francis B. Courvoisier, for the murder of Lord Wm. Russell', George Thomas, printer, Plymouth, 1 sheet ([1] p.; 25 × 19 cm.

'Life, trial, confession, execution: F.B. Courvoisier for the murder of Lord William Russell'. Farewell letter to his parents, sister; and the rest of the family, with good advice to all persons in trust', Paul & Co., printers, 2, 3 Monmouth Court, Seven Dials, 1 sheet ([1] p.): ill. (wood engravings), 49.3 × 37.3 cm.

'This day's examination of the valet for the murder of Lord William Russell, M.P.', Paul & Co., printers, 2, 3, Monmouth Court Seven Dials, 1 sheet ([1] p.): ill. (wood engravings), 60.3 × 37.2 cm.

'This day's proceedings. Copy of a letter committal of the valet charged with the inhuman murder of Lord William Russell, M.P', Paul & Co., printers, 2, 3 Monmouth-court, Seven Dials, 1 sheet ([1] p.): ill. (wood engravings), 63 × 39 cm.

'The sorrowful lamentation and last farewell to the world of F.B. Courvoisier, with an account of his attempted self-destruction: with a copy of a letter from Courvoisier to his parents', Paul & Co., printers, 2, 3 Monmouth-court, Seven Dials, 1 sheet ([1] p.): ill. (wood engraving), 38 × 25 cm.

'The sorrowful lamentation and last farewell to the world of F.B. Courvoisier: who was found guilty at the Old Bailey, on Saturday, June 20, of the willful murder of Lord William Russell', Birt, Printer, 39 Great St. Andrew Street, Seven Dials, 1 sheet ([1] p.): ill. (wood engraving), 35.5 × 22.5 cm.

'Trial confession and execution of the valet Courvoisier, for the murder of Lord W. Russell: With a copy of a letter written to his father and mother', H. Paul, printer, 22, Brick Lane, Spitalfields. Shops & hawkers supplied; 1 sheet ([1] p.) ill. (wood engravings), 52 × 37 cm.

'Trial, confession, and execution of Courvoisier for the murder of Lord Wm. Russell: Courvoisier's lament', printed and published by E. Lloyd, 44, Holywell Street, Strand, and at 30, Curtain Road, Shoreditch, 1 sheet ([1] p.): ll. (wood engravings), 75.5 × 51 cm.

Trial reports

The Proceedings of the Old Bailey. https://www.oldbaileyonline.org (OBP).

226   Bibliography

Government documents

Hansard. Parliamentary Debates. Series 1 & 2.
Parliamentary Papers:
   Report on Public Prosecution (1856)
   Report from the Select Committee of the House of Lords Appointed to Consider the Law of Defamation and Libel (1843)
   Report from the Select Committee on the Metropolis Police Office (1837–38)
   Report from the Select Committee on the Office of Coroner for Middlesex (1840)
   Report from the Select Committee on the Petition of Frederick Young and Others (1833)
   Report from the Select Committee on the Police of the Metropolis (1834)

Primary print sources

Adams, Samuel and Sarah. *The Complete Servant; Being a Practical Guide to the Peculiar Duties and Business of All Description of Servants from the Housekeeper to the Servant of All-Work, and from the Land Steward to the Footboy; with Useful Receipts and Tables.* London: Knight and Lacy, 1825.

Allibone, S. Austin. *A Critical Dictionary of English Literature and British and American Authors, Living and Deceased, from the Earliest Accounts to the Latter Half of the Nineteenth Century: Containing Over Forty-Six Thousand Articles (authors), with Forty Indexes of Subjects*, vol. 2, 1581–82. Philadelphia: J.B. Lippincott Company, 1874.

Anon. *Awful Confession of Greenacre to the Murder of Hannah Brown*. London: Smeeton, 1837.

Anon. *Reflections on the Relative Situations of Master and Servant, Historically and Politically Considered; The Irregularities of Servants; The Employment of Foreigners; and The General Inconveniences Resulting from the Want of Proper Regulations.* London: W. Miller, 1800.

Anon. *Remarks on the Recent Murders in London of Hannah Brown, Eliza Davis, Eliza Grimwood, Mr. Westwood, Mr. Templeman, and Lord William Russell, Showing the Present Undefended State of Human Life at Night in the Metropolis.* London: James Pattie, 1840.

Ballantine, William. *Some Experiences of a Barrister's Life*. 8th ed. London: J.M. Stoddart, 1883.

Beeton, Isabella. *Book of Household Management*. London: Ward & Lock, 1861.

Bell, T. *The Beadle's, Headborough's and Constable's Guide as to Their Duty in Respect to Coroners' Inquests; Containing Useful Information to Ministers, Churchwardens, Overseers of the Poor, Guardians and Subordinate Officers 306 Appointed Under the Poor Law Amendment Act, Officers and Constables of the Metropolitan and of the Rural Police*. 2nd ed. London, 1837.

Booth, Charles, and Jesse Argyll. 'Of Domestic Servants'. In *Life and Labour of the People in London*, edited by Charles Booth, vol. 8. London: Macmillan, 1896.

Bristow, W. *The Genuine Account of the Life and Trial of Eugene Aram, School-Master, for the Murder of Daniel Clark*. London, 1759.

Brontë, Emily. *Wuthering Heights*. 1847; rev. 1850; London: Dent, 1975.

Campbell, John. *Life of John, Lord Campbell*. London: John Murray, 1881.

Coleridge, Samuel Taylor. *The Notebooks of Samuel Taylor Coleridge*, edited by Kathleen Coburn and Anthony John Harding, vol. 5, 1827–34. Princeton: Princeton University Press, 2002.

Collins, Wilkie. 'Laid up in Two Lodgings'. *Household Words* (14 June 1856): 517–23.

Conan Doyle, Arthur. *The Adventure of the Crooked Man*. Strand Magazine, 1893.

Conan Doyle, Arthur. *The Sign of the Four*. Ward Lock & Co, 1890.

Conan Doyle, Arthur. *A Study in Scarlet*. Ward Lock & Co, 1887.
De Veil, Thomas. *Memoirs of the Life and Times of Sir Thomas Devil*. London, 1748.
Dickens, Charles. *Great Expectations*. 1861; Harmondsworth: Penguin, 1980.
Dickens, Charles. *Oliver Twist*. 1837–39; Harmondsworth: Penguin, 1985.
Egan, Pierce. *Recollections of John Thurtell*. London: Knight & Lacey, 1824.
Eliot, George. *Middlemarch*. 1871–72; Harmondsworth: Penguin, 1965.
Galton, Francis. *Finger Prints*. London: Macmillan & Co, 1892.
Godwin, William. 'Of Servants'. In *The Enquirer: Reflections on Education, Manners, and Literature. In a Series of Essays*, 201–211. London: G.G. and J. Robinson, 1797.
Greville, Charles Cavendish Fulke. *The Greville Memoirs: A Journal of the Reigns of King George IV, King William IV and Queen Victoria*, edited by Henry Reeves, vol. 4. 1888; Cambridge: Cambridge University Press, 2011.
Harris, Alexandra. 'Moving House'. In *Lives of Houses*, edited by Kate Kennedy and Hermione Lee. Princeton: Princeton University Press, 2020.
Hazlitt, William. 'Footmen'. *The English Comic Writers and Miscellaneous Essays*. 1830; London: Dent, n.d.
Henderson, Emily. *Recollections of the Public Career and Private Life of John Adolphus*. London: T. Cautley Newby, 1871.
Herbert, Edward. 'A Pen and Ink Sketch of a Late Trial for Murder, in a Letter from Hertford'. *London Magazine* 9 (1824): 165–85.
Hunt, Leigh. 'The Maid Servant'. 1854. *Quotidiana*, edited by Patrick Madden. 3 Jun 2015. 17 Feb 2019 http://essays.quotidiana.org/hunt/maid-servant/
Impey, J. *The Office and Duty of Coroner, with an Appendix of Useful Precedents*. London: J. Butterworth, 1800.
Jervis, J. *A Practical Treatise on the Office and Duty of Coroners with an Appendix of Forms and Precedents*. London: S. Sweet, 1829.
Kitchiner, William. *The Housekeeper's Oracle; or, Art of Domestic Management*. London: Whittaker, Treacher & Co, 1829.
Mackay, Charles. 'Popular Admiration of Great Thieves'. In *Memoirs of Extraordinary Popular Delusions and the Madness of Crowds*, 632–46. London: Richard Bentley, 1841.
Mayhew, Henry, and John Binny. *The Criminal Prisons of London, and Scenes of Prison Life*. London: Griffin, Bohn & Co, 1862.
Meadows, Joseph Kenny, William Makepeace Thackeray, and Douglas Jerrold. *Heads of the People*. London: R. Tyas, 1840.
O'Daniel, W. *Ins and Outs of London*. Philadelphia: S.C. Lamb, 1859.
The Queen V. Palmer: Verbatim Report of the Trial of William Palmer at the Central Criminal Court, Old Bailey, London, May 14, and Following Days, 1856, Before Lord Campbell, Mr. Justice Cresswell, and Mr. Baron Alderson. London: J. Allen, 1856.
Shepherd, Lloyd. *The Detective and the Devil*. New York, NY: Simon & Schuster, 2016.
Shepherd, Lloyd. *The English Monster*. New York, NY: Simon & Schuster, 2012.
Shepherd, Lloyd. *Poisoned Island*. New York, NY: Simon & Schuster, 2013.
Shepherd, Lloyd. *Savage Magic*. New York, NY: Simon & Schuster, 2015.
Sheridan, Richard Brinsley. *The Rivals, a Comedy* (1775). In *The Dramatic Works of Richard Brinsley Sheridan*, edited by Cecil Price, 2 vols. Oxford: Clarendon Press, 1973.
Spike, Edward. *The Law of Master and Servant in Regard to Domestic Servants and Clerks, Chiefly Designed for the Use of Families*. London: Shaw, 1839.
Sprigge, S.S. *The Life and Times of Thomas Wakley, Founder and First Editor of the 'Lancet', Member of Parliament for Finsbury, and Coroner for West Middlesex*. London: Longmans Green and Company, 1897a.
Tayler, William. *Diary of William Tayler, Footman 1837*, edited by Dorothy Wise. London: St Marylebone Society Publications Group, 1962.
Thackeray, William Makepeace. *The Book of Snobs*. London: Bradbury and Evans, 1856a.

Thackeray, William Makepeace. *The History of the Next French Revolution*. Punch, 24 Feb.–20 Apr. 1844a.
Thackeray, William Makepeace. *The Irish Sketch Book of 1842*, 1843. New York, NY: Scribners, 1904.
Thackeray, William Makepeace. *The Luck of Barry Lyndon*. London, *Fraser's Magazine*, 1844b.
Thackeray, William Makepeace. *Memoirs of Barry Lyndon*. London: Bradbury and Evans, 1856b.
Thackeray, William Makepeace. 'On a Chalk-Mark on the Door'. *Cornhill Magazine* 3 (April 1861): 504–12.
Thackeray, William Makepeace. 'On Going to See a Man Hanged'. *Fraser's Magazine* 22 (August 1840): 150–58.
Thackeray, William Makepeace. *Pendennis*. London: Bradbury and Evans, 1850.
Thackeray, William Makepeace. 'The Yellowplush Correspondence'. *Fraser's Magazine* xvi (November 1837): 644–49.
Thornbury, Walter. *Old and New London*, vol. 4. London: Cassell, Petter & Galpin, 1878.
The Trial of John Thurtell and Joseph Hunt, for the murder of Mr. William Weare: in Gill's Hill Lane, Herts, before Mr. Justice Park, on Tuesday, the 6th, and Wednesday, the 7th January, 1824; with the prayer, and the condemned sermon, that was preached before the unhappy culprits: also, full particulars of the execution. London: Hodgson & Co, 1824.
The Trial of Richard Patch for the wilful murder of Isaac Blight ... Taken in Shorthand by J. Gurney and W.B. Gurney. London, 1806.
Wellington, Arthur Wellesley, ed. *Wellington and his friends: letters of the First Duke of Wellington to the Rt.Hon. Charles and Mrs. Arbuthnot, the Earl and Countess of Wilton, Princess Lieven, and Miss Burdett-Coutts*. London: Macmillan, 1965.
Woolf, Virginia. *The Diary of Virginia Woolf*, vol. 1. London: Hogarth Press, 1977.
Woolf, Virginia. *Mr. Bennett and Mrs. Brown*. London: Hogarth Press, 1924.

Secondary sources

Allderidge, Patricia. *The late Richard Dadd*. Exh. cat., Tate Gallery, London, 19 June–18 Aug 1974.
Altick, Richard D. *The English Common Reader: A Social History of the Mass Reading Public, 1800–1900*. 2nd ed. Columbus: Ohio State University Press, 1998.
Altick, Richard D. *Victorian Studies in Scarlet: Murders and Manners in the Age of Victoria*. New York: W.W. Norton, 1970.
Armitage, Gilbert. *The History of the Bow Street Runners*. London: Wishart, 1932.
Ascoli, David. *The Queen's Peace: The Origins and Development of the Metropolitan Police 1829–1979*. London: Hamish Hamilton, 1979.
Atkinson, Diane. *Love and Dirt: The Marriage of Arthur Munby and Hannah Cullwick*. New York, NY: Macmillan, 2003.
Babington, Anthony. *A House in Bow Street: Crime and the Magistracy, London 1740–1881*. London: Macdonald, 1969.
Bajac, Quention. *The History of Photography*. London: Thames and Hudson, 2002.
Barham, *The Life and Remains of Theodore Edward Hook*. London: R. Bentley, 1853.
Barker, Hannah. *Newspapers, Politics and English Society 1695–1855*. London: Longman, 2000.
Beattie, J.M. 'Early detection: The Bow Street Runners in late 18th century London'. In *Police Detectives in History, 1750-1950*, edited by Clive Emsley and Haia Shpayer-Makov, 15–32. Aldershot: Ashgate, 2006.
Beattie, J.M. *The First English Detectives: The Bow Street Runners and the Policing of London, 1750–1840*. Oxford: Oxford University Press, 2012.

Beattie, J.M. *Policing and Punishment in London, 1660-1750: Urban Crime and the Limits of Terror*. Oxford: Oxford University Press, 2001.
Beattie, J.M. 'Scales of Justice: Defense Counsel and the English Criminal Trial in the Eighteenth and Nineteenth Centuries'. *Law and History Review* 9 (1991): 221–67.
Beattie, J.M. 'Sir John Fielding and Public Justice: The Bow Street Magistrates' Court, 1754–1780'. *Law and History Review* 25(1) (2007): 61–100.
Begg, Paul, and Keith Skinner. *The Scotland Yard Files: 150 Years of the CID*. London: Headline Publishing, 1992.
Bentley, David. *English Criminal Justice in the Nineteenth Century*. London and Rio Grande: Hambledon Press, 1998.
Blakiston, Georgiana. *Lord William Russell and his Wife, 1815–1846*. London: John Murray, 1972.
Borowitz, Albert. *The Thurtell-Hunt Murder Case: Dark Mirror to Regency England*. Baton Rouge: Louisiana State University Press, 1987.
Borowitz, Albert I. 'Why Thackeray Went to See a Man Hanged'. *Victorian Newsletter* 48 (1975): 15–21.
Boyle, Thomas. *Black Swine in the Sewers of Hampstead: Beneath the Surface of Victorian Sensationalism*. London: Hodder & Stoughton, 1990.
Bridges, Yseult. *Two Studies in Crime: A Reissue of Studies of the Murders of Lord William Russell and Julia Wallace*. 1959; London: Macmillan & Co., 1970.
Brook, Charles Wortham. *Battling Surgeon: A Life of Thomas Wakley*. London: Socialist Medical Association, 1962.
Brown, Lucy. *Victorian News and Newspapers*. Oxford and Toronto: Clarendon Press, 1985.
Browne, Douglas G. *The Rise of Scotland Yard: A History of the Metropolitan Police*. Westport, CT: Greenwood Press, 1956.
Buckley, Matthew. 'Sensations of Celebrity: 'Jack Sheppard' and the Mass Audience'. *Victorian Studies* 44(3) (Spring 2002): 423–63.
Burnett, John. *Useful Toil: Autobiographies of Working People from the 1820s to the 1920s*. 1974; Harmondsworth: Penguin, 1984.
Burney, Ian. *Bodies of Evidence: Medicine and the Politics of the English Inquest 1830–1926*. Baltimore and London: Johns Hopkins University Press, 2000.
Burney, Ian. *Poison, detection, and the Victorian Imagination*. Manchester: Manchester University Press, 2006.
Cairns, David. *Advocacy and the Making of the Adversarial Criminal Trial, 1800–1865*. Oxford: Clarendon Press, 1998.
Carver, Stephen. *The Author Who Outsold Dickens: The Life and Work of W.H. Ainsworth*. Barnsley: Pen and Sword, 2020.
Carver, Stephen. 'Writing the Underworld: Ainsworth's *Jack Sheppard* and the Newgate Controversy'. In *The Life and Works of the Lancashire Novelist William Harrison Ainsworth*. Lewiston, N.J.: Edwin Mellen Press, 2003.
Casey, Ellen Miller. 'Silver-forks and the Commodity Text: Lady Morgan and the Athenaeum'. *Women's Writing: Silver Fork Fiction* 16(2) (2009): 253–62.
Cawthorn, Elizabeth. 'Thomas Wakley and the Medical Coronership – Occupational Death and the Judicial Process'. *Medical History* 30 (1986): 191–202.
Chittick, Kathryn. *Dickens and the 1830s*. Cambridge: Cambridge University Press, 1990.
Cobb, Belton. *The First Detectives and the Early Career of Richard Mayne Commissioner of Police*. London: Faber and Faber Ltd., 1957.
Colby, Robert A. 'Catherine: Thackeray's Credo'. *The Review of English Studies* 15(60) (1964): 381–96.
Collins, Phillip, ed. *Thackeray: Interviews and Recollections*. 2 vols. London: Macmillan, 1983.
Collison, Robert. *The Story of Street Literature*. London: J.M. Dent, 1973.

Bibliography

Cooper, David D. *The Lesson of the Scaffold: The Public Execution Controversy in Victorian England*. Athens: Ohio University Press, 1974.

Cooper, David D. 'Public Executions in Victorian England: A Reform Adrift'. In *Executions and the British Experience from the 17th to the 20th Century: A Collection of Essays*, ed. William B. Thesig. Jefferson: McFarland, 1990.

Cooter, Roger. *Phrenology in the British Isles: An Annotated Historical Biobibliography and Index*. London: Scarecrow Press, 1989.

Cox, David. *A Certain Share of Low Cunning: A History of the Bow Street Runners, 1792–1839*. Cullompton: Willan Publishing, 2010.

Critchley, T.A. *A History of Police in England and Wales, 1900-1966*. London: Constable, 1967.

Critchley, T.A., and P.D. James, *The Maul and the Pear Tree: The Ratcliffe Highway Murders, 1811*. 1971; London: Faber and Faber, 2010.

Crone, Rosalind. *Violent Victorians: Popular Entertainment in Nineteenth-Century London*. Manchester and New York, NY: Manchester University Press, 2012.

Davidoff, Leonore, and Ruth Hawthorn. *A Day in the Life of a Victorian Domestic Servant*. London: George Allen & Unwin, 1976.

Devereaux, Simon. 'England's "Bloody Code" in Crisis and Transition: Executions at the Old Bailey, 1760–1837'. *Journal of the Canadian Historical Association* 24(2) (2013): 71–113.

Devereaux, Simon. *Execution, State and Society in England, 1660–1900*. Cambridge: Cambridge University Press, 2023.

Devereaux, Simon. 'Swearing and Feeling: The Secularisation of Truth-Seeking in the Victorian English Court'. In *Criminal Justice During the Long Eighteenth Century: Theatre, Representation and Emotion*, edited by David Lemmings and Allyson N. May. New York, NY: Routledge, 2019.

Devereaux, Simon. https://hcmc.uvic.ca/project/oldbailey/index.php

Dunn, Bill Newton. *The Man Who Was John Bull*. London: Allendale, 1996.

Edwards, J.L.L.J. *The Law Officers of the Crown*. London: Sweet & Maxwell, 1964.

Ellis, S.M. *William Henry Ainsworth and his Friends*. London, J. Lane, 1911.

Emmerichs, Mary Beth. 'Getting Away with Murder? Homicide and the Coroners in Nineteenth-Century London'. *Social Science History* 25(1) (Spring 2001): 93–100.

Emsley, Clive. *The English Police: A Political and Social History*. 2nd ed. London: Longman, 1996.

Emsley, Clive. *The Great British Bobby: A History of British Policing from the 18th Century to the Present*. London: Quercus, 2009.

Emsley, Clive. 'The Home Office and its Sources of Information 1791-1801'. *English Historical Review* 94 (July 1979): 532–61.

Emsley, Clive. *Policing and its Context 1750–1870*. London and Basingstoke: Macmillan Press Ltd., 1983.

Emsley, Clive, and Haia Shpayer-Makov, eds. *Police Detectives in History 1750–1950*. Aldershot: Ashgate, 2006.

Fernandez, Jean. *Victorian Servants, Class, and the Politics of Literacy*. New York, NY and London: Routledge, 2010.

Fido, Martin, and Keith Skinner. *The Official Encyclopedia of Scotland Yard*. London: Virgin Books, 1999.

Fisher, D.R. *The House of Commons, 1820–1832*. 7 vols. Cambridge: Cambridge University Press, 2009.

Fisher, Pamela Jane. 'The Politics of Sudden Death: The Office and Role of the Coroner in England and Wales, 1726–1888'. Unpublished PhD thesis, University of Leicester, 2007.

Flanders, Judith. *The Invention of Murder: How the Victorians Revelled in Death and Detection and Created Modern Crime*. London: UK General Books, 2011.

Flukinger, Roy. *The Formative Decades: Photography in Great Britain, 1839–1920*. Austin: University of Texas Press, 1985.

Forbes, T.R. 'Coroners' Inquests in the County of Middlesex, England, 1819–42'. *Journal of the History of Medicine and Allied Sciences* 32 (1977): 375–94.

Forbes, T.R. 'Crowner's Quest'. *Transactions of the American Philosophical Society* 68(1) (1978): 1–50.

Gatrell, V.A.C. *The Hanging Tree: Execution and the English People 1770–1868*. Oxford: Oxford University Press, 1994.

George, M. Dorothy. *London Life in the Eighteenth Century*. London: Kegan Paul, 1925.

Gettman, Royal A. *A Victorian Publisher: A Study of the Bentley Papers*. Cambridge: Cambridge University Press, 1960.

Gillingham, Lauren. 'Ainsworth's *Jack Sheppard* and the Crimes of History'. *Studies in English Literature, 1500–1900* 49(4) (Autumn, 2009): 879–906.

Gillingham, Lauren. 'The Newgate Novel and the Police Casebook'. In *A Companion to Crime Fiction*, edited by Charles J. Rzepka and Lee Horsley, 93–104. Oxford: Blackwell, 2010.

Gladfelder, Hal. *Criminality and Narrative in Eighteenth-Century England: Beyond the Law*. Baltimore: Johns Hopkins University Press, 2001.

Goldfarb, Sheldon F. 'Historical Commentary'. In *Catherine: A Story*, edited by Sheldon Goldfarb. Ann Arbor, MI: University of Michigan Press, 1999.

Greenham, G.H. *Scotland Yard Experiences*. London: George Routledge & Sons, 1904.

Gregory, James. *Victorians Against the Gallows: Capital Punishment and the Abolitionist Movement in Nineteenth Century Britain*. London: I.B. Tauris, 2012a.

Littlechild, John George, *The Reminiscences of Chief-Inspector Littlechild*. 2nd ed. London: Leadenhall, Ltd., 1894.

Gregory, James. *Victorians Against the Gallows: Capital Punishment and the Abolitionist Movement in Nineteenth-Century Britain*. London: I.B. Tauris, 2012b.

Griffin, Rachael. 'Detective Policing and the State in Nineteenth-Century England: The Detective Department of the London Metropolitan Police, 1842–1878'. Unpublished PhD thesis, University of Western Ontario, 2016.

Habermas, Jürgen. *The Structural Transformation of the Public Sphere: An Inquiry into a Category of Bourgeois Society*. Translated by Thomas Burger. Cambridge: MIT Press, 1998.

Hamlett, Jane. *Material Relations: Domestic Interiors and Middle-Class Families in England, 1850–1910*. Manchester: Manchester University Press, 2010.

Harman, Claire. *Murder by the Book: A Sensational Chapter in Victorian Crime*. London: Viking, 2018.

Harris, Andrew T. *Policing the City: Crime and Legal Authority in London, 1780–1840*. Columbus: Ohio State University Press, 2004.

Hartley, Jenny. *Charles Dickens and the House of Fallen Women*. York: Methuen, 2008.

Hay, Douglas. 'England, 1562–1875: The Law and its Uses'. In *Masters, Servants, and Magistrates in Britain and the Empire, 1562–1955*, edited by Douglas Hay and Paul Craven, 59–116. Chapel Hill: University of North Carolina Press, 2004.

Hay, Douglas, and Francis Snyder. 'Using the Criminal Law, 1750–1850: Policing, Private Prosecution, and the State'. In *Policing and Prosecution in Britain, 1750–1850*, edited by Hay and Snyder. Oxford: Clarendon Press, 1989.

Hibbert, Christopher. *Queen Victoria: A Personal History*. London: HarperCollins, 2001.

Hirsch, Robert. *Seizing the Light: A Social and Aesthetic History of Photography*. New York, NY: Routledge, 2017.

Hollingsworth, Keith. *The Newgate Novel, 1830–1847*. Detroit: Wayne State University Press, 1963.

Horn, Pamela. *The Rise and Fall of the Victorian Domestic Servant*. Stroud: Alan Sutton, 1990.
Hostettler, J. 'Thomas Wakley – An Enemy of Injustice'. *Journal of Legal History* 5 (1984): 60–75.
Howe, Sir Ronald. *The Story of Scotland Yard: A History of the C.I.D. from the Earliest Times to the Present Day*. London: Arthur Barker Limited, 1965.
Huggett, Frank E. *Life Below Stairs: Domestic Servants in England from Victorian Times*. Norwich: Book Club Associates, 1977.
Jacobs, Edward, and Manuela Mourão. 'Newgate Novels'. In *A Companion to Sensation Fiction*, edited by Pamela K. Gilbert. Chichester: Wiley-Blackwell, 2011.
Jalland, Pat. *Death in the Victorian Family*. Oxford: Oxford University Press, 1996.
James, P.D. *Devices and Desires*. Toronto: Lester & Orpen Dennys, 1990.
James, P.D. *A Taste for Death*. New York, NY: Alfred A. Knopf, 1986.
John, Juliet, ed. *Cult Criminals: The Newgate Novels, 1830–1847*. London: Routledge, 1998.
Kelly, Gary. 'General Introduction'. *Newgate Narratives*, 1:ix-xciii. 5 vols. London: Routledge, 2008.
Kilday, Anne-Marie. 'Constructing the Cult of the Criminal: Kate Webster – Victorian Murderess and Media Sensation'. In *Law, Crime and Deviance Since 1700: Micro-Studies in the History of Crime*, edited by Anne-Marie Kilday and David Nash. London: Bloomsbury Academic, 2017.
Knelman, Judith. *Twisting in the Wind: The Murderess and the English Press*. Toronto: University of Toronto Press, 1998.
Kurland, Philip B., and D.W.M. Waters. 'Public Prosecutions in England, 1854–79: An Essay in English Legislative History'. *Duke Law Journal* (1959): 493–562.
Landsman, Stephan. 'The Rise of the Contentious Spirit: Adversary Procedure in Eighteenth-Century England'. *Cornell Law Review* 75 (1989–90): 591–692.
Langbein, John H. *The Origins of Adversary Criminal Trial*. Oxford: Oxford University Press, 2003.
Light, Alison. *Mrs. Woolf and the Servants*. London: Bloomsbury, 2008.
Linebaugh, Peter. 'The Ordinary of Newgate and his Account'. In *Crime in England*, edited by J.S. Cockburn, 1550–1800. Princeton, NJ: Princeton University Press, 1977.
Lock, Joan. *Dreadful Deeds and Awful Murders: Scotland Yard's First Detectives 1829 1878*. Taunton: Barn Owl Books, 1990.
Lockwood, Matthew. *The Conquest of Death: Violence and the Birth of the Modern English State*. New Haven: Yale University Press, 2017.
May, Allyson N. *The Bar and the Old Bailey, 1750–1850*. Chapel Hill: University of North Carolina Press, 2003a.
May, Allyson N. 'Garrow for the Prosecution'. In *Law, Media, Emotion and the Self: Public Justice in Eighteenth-Century Britain*, edited by Katie Barclay and Amy Milka. New York, NY: Routledge, 2022.
May, Allyson N. 'Irish Sensibilities and the English Bar: The Advocacy of Charles Phillips'. In *Criminal Justice During the Long Eighteenth Century: Theatre, Representation and Emotion*, edited by David Lemmings and Allyson N. May. New York, NY: Routledge, 2019.
May, Trevor. *The Victorian Domestic Servant*. Princes Risborough, Bucks: Shire Publications, 2003b.
McCuskey, Brian. 'Fetishizing the Flunkey: Thackeray and the Uses of Deviance'. *NOVEL: A Forum on Fiction* 32(3) (Summer 1999): 384–400.
McGowen, Randall. 'Civilizing Punishment: The End of Public Execution in England'. *Journal of British Studies* 33(3) (July 1994): 257–82.
McGowen, Randall. 'Doctor Dodd and the Law in the Age of the Sentimental Revolution'. In *Criminal Justice During the Long Eighteenth Century: Theatre,

Representation and Emotion, edited by David Lemmings and Allyson N. May. New York, NY: Routledge, 2019.

McGowen, Randall. 'History, Culture and the Death Penalty: The British Debates, 1840–70'. *Historical Reflections/Réflexions Historiques* 29(2) (Summer 2003): 229–49.

McKendy, Thomas. 'Sources of Parody in Thackeray's "Catherine"'. *Dickens Studies Annual* 23 (1994): 287–302.

McKenzie, Andrea. 'From True Confessions to True Reporting? The Decline and Fall of the Ordinary's Account'. *London Journal* 30(1) (2005): 55–70.

McKenzie, Andrea. 'Making Crime Pay: Motives, Marketing Strategies, and the Printed Literature of Crime in England 1670-1770'. In *Criminal Justice in the Old World and the New: Essays in Honour of J. M. Beattie*, edited by Greg T. Smith, Allyson N. May, and Simon Devereaux, 235–69. Toronto: University of Toronto Centre of Criminology, 1998.

McKenzie, Andrea. 'Martyrs in Low Life? Dying "Game" in Augustan England'. *Journal of British Studies* 42 (April, 2003): 167–205.

McKenzie, Andrea. 'On the "Very Brink Between Time and Eternity": Truth, Charity and Last Dying Words in England, c. 1649–1700'. *Journal of the Canadian Historical Society/Revue de la Société historique du Canada* 24(2) (2013): 33–70.

McKenzie, Andrea. 'The "Real McHeath": Social Satire, Appropriation and Eighteenth-Century English Criminal Biography'. *The Huntington Library Quarterly* 69(4) (2006): 581–605.

McKenzie, Andrea. *Tyburn's Martyrs: Execution in England, 1675–1775*. London and New York, NY: Hambledon Continuum, 2007.

McLaren, Angus. *The Trials of Masculinity: Policing Sexual Boundaries, 1870–1930*. Chicago, IL: University of Chicago Press, 1999.

Meldrum, Tim. *Domestic Service and Gender 1660–1750: Life and Work in the London Household*. London: Routledge, 2014.

Mellinkoff, David. *The Conscience of a Lawyer*. St. Paul, MN: West Publishing Co, 1973.

Miller, Andrew. '*Vanity Fair* through Plate Glass'. *PMLA* 105(5) (October 1990): 1042–54.

Milne-Smith, Amy. *London Clubland: A Cultural History of Gender and Class in Late Victorian Britain*. London: Palgrave Macmillan, 2011.

Mitch, David. *The Rise of Popular Literacy in Victorian England: The Influence of Public Choice and Private Policy*. Philadelphia: University of Pennsylvania Press, 1992.

Mitchell, Tom, and Reinhold Kramer. *Walk Towards the Gallows: The Tragedy of Hilda Blake, Hanged 1899*. Toronto: University of Toronto Press, 2007.

Monsarrat, Ann. *An Uneasy Victorian: Thackeray the Man, 1811–1863*. New York: Dodd, Mead & Company, 1980.

Morris, R.M. '"Crime Does Not Pay": Thinking again about detectives in the first century of the Metropolitan Police'. In *Police Detectives in History, 1750–1950*, edited by Clive Emsley and Haia Shpayer Makov. Aldershot: Ashgate, 2006.

Mowry, Melissa M., Alessa Johns, and Michael Ziser, 'Reopening the Question of Class Formation', *Eighteenth-Century Studies*, 43(4) (Summer 2010): 515–19.

Neuberg, Victor E. *Popular Literature: A History and Guide*. New York, NY: Routledge, 1977.

Paley, Ruth. '"An Imperfect, Inadequate and Wretched System"?: Policing in London before Peel'. *Criminal Justice History* 10 (1989): 95–130.

Palmer, Stanley. *Police and Protest in England and Ireland 1780–1850*. Cambridge: Cambridge University Press, 1988.

Payne, Chris. *The Chieftain: Victorian True Crime through the Eyes of a Scotland Yard Detective*. Stroud: The History Press, 2011.

Peters, Catherine. *Thackeray's Universe: Shifting Worlds of Imagination and Reality*. London: Faber and Faber, 1987.

Philips, David. '"A new engine of power and authority": The Institutionalization of Law Enforcement in England 1780–1830'. In *Crime and the Law: The Social History of Crime in Western Europe since 1500*, edited by V.A.C. Gatrell, Bruce Lenman, and Geoffrey Parker, 155–189. London: Europa Publications Limited, 1980.

Piketty, Thomas. *Capital and Ideology*. Boston: Harvard University Press, 2020.

Ponsonby, Margaret. *Stories from Home: English Domestic Interiors, 1750–1850*. Aldershot: Ashgate, 2007.

Potter, Harry. *Hanging in Judgment: Religion and the Death Penalty in England from the Bloody Code to Abolition*. London: SCM, 1993.

Prest, John. *Lord John Russell*. Columbia: University of South Carolina Press, 1972.

Pringle, Patrick. *Hue and Cry: The History of the Bow Street Runners*. London: Morrow, 1955.

Radzinowicz, Sir Leon. *A History of English Criminal Law and its Administration from 1750*, vol. 4: *Grappling for Control*. London: Stevens & Sons, 1968.

Rawlings, Philip. *Policing: A Short History*. Cullompton, Devon: Willan, 2002.

Reid, J.C. *Bucks and Bruisers: Pierce Egan and Regency England*. London: Routledge, 1971.

Reith, Charles. *The Blind Eye of History: A Study of the Origins of the Present Police Era*. London: Faber and Faber, 1952.

Reynolds, Elaine A. *Before the Bobbies: The Night Watch and Police Reform in Metropolitan London, 1720–1830*. Stanford: Stanford University Press, 1998.

Robbins, Bruce. *The Servant's Hand*. Durham, NC: Duke University Press, 1993.

Sainty, J.C. *Office-Holders in Modern Britain: Volume 1, Treasury Officials 1660–1870*. London: University of London, 1972.

Schramm, Jan-Melissa. '"Anatomy of a Barrister's Tongue": Rhetoric, Satire, and the Victorian Bar in England'. *Victorian Literature and Culture* 32(2) (2004): 285–303.

Schramm, Jan-Melissa. *Testimony and Advocacy in Victorian Law, Literature, and Theology*. Cambridge: Cambridge University Press, 2000.

Schwarzbach, F.S. 'Newgate Novel to Detective Fiction'. In *A Companion to the Victorian Novel*, edited by Patrick Brantlinger and William B. Thesing, 227–78. Oxford: Blackwell, 2002.

Seleski, Patti. 'Domesticity is in the Streets: Eliza Fenning, Public Opinion and the Politics of Private Life'. In *The Politics of the Excluded, c. 1500–1850*, edited by Tim Harris. Hampshire: Palgrave, 2001.

Seleski, Patti. 'A Mistress, a Mother and a Murderess too: Elizabeth Brownrigg and the Social Construction of the Eighteenth-Century Mistress'. In *Lewd and Notorious: Female Transgression in the Eighteenth Century*, edited by Katherine Kitredge. Ann Arbor: University of Michigan Press, 2003.

Sharpe, J.A. '"Last Dying Speeches": Religion, Ideology and Public Execution in Seventeenth-Century England'. *Past & Present* 107 (May, 1985): 144–67.

Shepard, Leslie. *The Broadside Ballad: A Study in Origins and Meaning*. London: H. Jenkins, 1962.

Shepard, Leslie. *The History of Street Literature*. London: David and Charles, 1973.

Sheppard, F.H.W., ed. *Survey of London, Vol. 40: The Grosvenor Estate in Mayfair, Part 2 (The Buildings)*. London, 1980.

Sherrington, 'Thomas Wakley and Reform'. D.Phil. Oxford, 1973.

Shpayer-Makov, Haia. *The Ascent of the Detective: Police Sleuths in Victorian and Edwardian England*. Oxford: Oxford University Press, 2011.

Shpayer-Makov, Haia. *The Making of a Policeman: A Social History of a Labour Force in Metropolitan London, 1829–1914*. London: Ashgate, 2002.

Sim, J., and T. Ward. 'The Magistrate of the Poor? Coroners and Deaths in Custody in Nineteenth Century England'. In *Legal Medicine in History*, edited by M. Clark and C. Crawford, 245–67. Cambridge, 1994.

Simpson, Antony E. 'Thackeray and the Execution of Courvoisier'. In *Witnesses to the Scaffold: English Literary Figures as Observers of Public Executions*, edited by Simpson. Lamberton, NJ: True Bill Press, 2008.
Smith, Bruce P. 'The Emergence of Public Prosecution in London, 1790–1850'. *Yale Journal of Law and the Humanities* 18 (2006): 29–62.
Smith, Phillip Thurmond. *Policing Victorian London: Political Policing, Public Order, and the London Metropolitan Police*. London and Westport: Greenwood Press, 1985.
Sprigge, S. Squire. *The Life and Times of Thomas Wakley*. London: Longmans, Green, 1897.
Steedman, Carolyn. *Labours Lost: Domestic Service and the Making of Modern England*. Cambridge: Cambridge University Press, 2009.
Steedman, Carolyn. *Master and Servant: Love and Labour in the Industrial Age*. Cambridge: Cambridge University Press, 2007.
Straub, Kristina. *Domestic Affairs: Intimacy, Eroticism, and Violence Between Servants and Masters in Eighteenth-Century Britain*. Baltimore, MD: John Hopkins University Press, 2008.
Straub, Kristina. 'The Tortured Apprentice: Sexual Monstrosity and the Suffering of Poor Children in the Brownrigg Murder Case'. In *Monstrous Dreams of Reason*, edited by Laura Rosenthal and Mita Choudhary. London: Associated Universities Presses, 2002.
Summerscale, Kate. *The Suspicious of Mr. Whicher: A Shocking Murder and the Undoing of a Great Victorian Detective*. Vancouver: Raincoast Books, 2008.
Sussman, Herbert. *Victorian Masculinities: Manhood and Masculine Poetics in Early Victorian Literature and Art*. Cambridge: Cambridge University Press, 2008.
Taylor, David. *The New Police in Nineteenth-Century England: Crime, Conflict and Control*. Manchester and New York, NY: Manchester University Press, 1997.
Thomas, Deborah A. 'Thackeray, Capital Punishment, and the Demise of Jos Sedley'. *Victorian Literature and Culture* 33(1) (2005): 1–20.
Thompson, E.P. 'The Crime of Anonymity'. In *Albion's Fatal Tree: Crime and Society in Eighteenth-Century England*, edited by Douglas Hay et al.. New York: Pantheon Books, 1975.
Thomson, Basil. *The Story of Scotland Yard*. New York: The Literary Guild, 1936.
Thorne, R.G. *The House of Commons, 1790–1820*. 5 vols. London: Secker & Warburg, 1986.
Tosh, John. *A Man's Place: Masculinity and the Middle-Class Home*. New Haven: Yale University Press, 1999.
Tromans, Nicholas. *Richard Dadd: The Artist and the Asylum*. London: DAP/Tate, 2011.
Turner, E.S. *What the Butler Saw: Two Hundred and Fifty Years of the Servant Problem*. 1962; London: Penguin, 2001.
van Thal, H. *Ernest Augustus, Duke of Cumberland and King of Hanover*. Arthur Barker, 1936.
Vincent, David. *Literacy and Popular Culture in England, 1750–1914*. Cambridge: Cambridge University Press, 1989.
Walsh, Bridget. *Domestic Murder in Nineteenth-century England: Literary and Cultural Representations*. Farnham: Ashgate, 2014.
Ward, J. 'Origins and Development of Forensic Medicine and Forensic Science in England, 1823–1946'. Unpublished Ph.D. thesis, Open University, 1993.
Ward, Richard, ed. *A Global History of Execution and the Criminal Corpse*. London: Palgrave Macmillan, 2015.
Wardroper, J. *Wicked Ernest*. London: Shelfmark Books, 2002.
Waterson, Merlin. *The Servants Hall: A Domestic History of Erddig*. Routledge and Kegan Paul, 1980.
Watson, E. *Eugene Aram: His Life and Trial*. Edinburgh: W. Hodge & Co, 1913.

Watson, Katherine D. *Forensic Medicine in Western Society: A History*. London and New York, NY: Routledge, 2011.
Webb, R.K. *The British Working Class Reader, 1790–1848: Literary and Social Tension*. 1955, repr. New York, NY: Augustus M Kelley, 1971.
Wentworth, Patricia. *The Clock Strikes Twelve*. 1944; New York: Warner Books, 1984.
Wentworth, Patricia. *Pilgrim's Rest*. 1946; New York, NY: Warner Books, 1985.
White, Edward M. 'Thackeray's Contributions to *Fraser's Magazine*'. *Studies in Bibliography* 19 (1966): 67–84.
Wiener, Martin J. 'Market Culture, Reckless Passion, and the Victorian Reconstruction of Punishment'. In *The Culture of the Market: Historical Essays*, edited by Thomas L. Haskell and Richard F. Teichgraeber III. Cambridge: Cambridge University Press, 1993.
Williams, Abigail. *The Social Life of Books: Reading Together in the Eighteenth-Century Home*. New Haven: Yale University Press, 2017.
Williams, Glanville. 'The Power to Prosecute'. *Criminal Law Review* (1955), pt 1.
Willis, G.M. *Ernest Augustus, Duke of Cumberland and King of Hanover*. London: A. Barker, 1954.
Worth, George J. *William Henry Ainsworth*. New York: Twayne, 1972.
Wrightson, Keith. *Ralph Tailor's Summer: A Scrivener, His City and the Plague*. New Haven: Yale University Press, 2011.

Index

Pages in *italics* refer to figures and pages followed by "n" refer to notes.

Adolphus, John (counsel for the prosecution) 6–7, 22, 28, 98, 106; Convinced of Courvoisier's guilt 119; Dependent on Francis Hobler's research 219; On police rewards 214; Opening speech in Courvoisier trial 14, 107, 123–25, 134; Provides Francis Hobler with notes made for his speech 120–21; Reputation as advocate 118–19, 126; Unhappy with Samuel March Phillipps's brief 119
Ainsworth, William Harrison: *Jack Sheppard* 9, 187, 190–94, 213
Altick, Richard 3, 35, 190, 202
Arabin, William St Julien (deputy recorder of London): charge to grand jury in Courvoisier trial 121
Aram, Eugene 177
Aristocracy: Fear of lower orders 20–1
Aristocratic spectators: At Bow Street 114–15, 117; At Courvoisier's execution 155–56, 159; At 14 Norfolk Street 66; At the Old Bailey 123

Baup, Charles (Swiss cleric) 155, 182, 184
Bayley, Lady Sarah 21, 35, 69, 117
Beattie, J.M. 5, 62, 96, 108–9
Beeton, Isabella: on servants 45–6, 52
Bennet, Henry Grey (Russell's son-in-law) 10, 24–5, 110
Bentley, David 7
Blake, Hilda 207
Bodkin, William (counsel for the prosecution) 118, 125, 128
Booth, Wayne C.: unreliable narrators 195

Borowitz, Albert 3, 164
Boswell, James: on execution 161
Bow Street: magistrates 5, 109; Magistrates' court 113; Runners 1, 5, 95–6, 113, 129, 215–17
Boyle, Thomas 187–88
Bridges, Yseult 10, 21–2, 44, 174–75
Brontë, Emily: *Wuthering Heights* 12, 171, 190
Brownrigg, Eliza 13
Burnett, John 28
Burney, Ian 148

Calcraft, William (executioner) 155
Carr, Henry (suspect) 39–40, 42, 70–1, 76, 85, 93, 172
Carver, James (Ordinary of Newgate) 182, 186–87; condemned sermon 152–53; reads burial service 155
Chambers, Montagu (counsel for the prosecution) 118
Chetwynd, Sir George 222n47; hires Sarah Mancer 213
Circumstantial evidence 5, 77, 98–9, 115–16, 119, 121–22, 124, 134, 152, 177
Clarkson, William (counsel for the defence) 118, 199
Cobb, Belton 68, 98
Collins, Wilkie 10, 16, 203, 209, 213–14
Colquhoun, Patrick 62, 187
Cope, William Wadham (governor of Newgate Prison) 87, 127–28, 154–55, 178–79, 181
Coroner's inquest on Russell 65; Critical press coverage 91–2

238 Index

Coroner's office 4, 62; Contest between legal and medical profession 64; Relationship with the new police 63
Cotton, Mary Ann 214
Courvoisier, François Benjamin: Appearance *145*, 174–75; Behaviour on discovery of the murder 61, 75–6; Broadsheet coverage of case 186; Burial 160; Casts of head 147, 159, 175; Charged and removed to Bow Street 71; Confesses guilt to counsel mid–trial 126; Counsel (Charles Phillips) 6, 8, 126; Employment history 40–1; English language proficiency 173; Envies William Russell's wealth 52–3; Execution *146*, 147, 158–59; Exonerates fellow servants 184, 194, 212; Family background 36–8; Final night 154–55; *Jack Sheppard* (had not read) 190, 194; Motivation for murder 10, 13–5, 186, 195, 199–201; Old Bailey trial 121–33; Post–trial confessions 8–9, 173, 178–84, 193–95; Pre–trial hearings at Bow Street 113–18; Protests innocence 68–9; Resentment at treatment by Russell 52; Russell's valet 29, 41; Silence in court 172, 176–77; Trial as public prosecution 7; Voice 8, 186, 194–95; Wax figures of 147, 176
Criminal biography 8, 187, 191
Criminal Evidence Act, 1898 8
Critchley, T.A., and P.D. James: on the Ratcliffe Highway murders 35, 62, 109–10
Crone, Rosalind 184–86
Cullwick, Hannah 12

Davis, Eliza 2, 90, 92, 216
Defoe, Daniel 11–2, 203
De Quincey, Thomas: 'On Murder, considered as one of the fine arts' 148
De Ville, James 175
Dickens, Charles 70, 170–71; Attends Courvoisier's execution 9, 156; *Bleak House* 214; Despises Charles Phillips 156; *Edwin Drood* 207; *Great Expectations* 3–4, 53, 204; *Oliver Twist* 9, 123, 133, 154; On execution 163; On servants 203; *Sketches by Boz* 9, 153–54
Domestic service 10–3, 29–31, 37–44, 51

Doubleday, George (Russell's groom) 36, 208; Left destitute and fed by Inspector Tedman 209
Dowling, M.M.G (Liverpool police inspector): convinced of Sarah Mancer's guilt 77–9, 82

Ellis, James (footman) 26–7, 34, 39–40, 42, 52, 55n76, 56n112, 66, 69–70, 86, 116–17, 127
Elsgood, Henry (surgeon) 61, 65–7, 86, 116–17, 180
Evans, William (Sheriff) 155, 180, 182, 193, 195

Fector, John (Courvoisier's previous employer) 39–42, 44, 53, 73, 116, 183, 199–200
Fenning, Eliza 14, 165
Fernandez, Jean 188
Fielding, Henry 5, 12, 109, 163, 192–93, 216
Fingerprint evidence 90–1
Flower, Thomas (solicitor for the defence) 8, 80, 113–17, 122, 127–28, 130, 137n31, 137n33, 138n38, 172, 176, 178–80, 182, 219
Forensic methodology 5, 215

Garrow, William 219
Gatrell, V.A.C. 161–62, 164
Godwin, William 10, 48–9, 51, 216
Good, Daniel 3, 216
Gould, Richard 121, 163, 177
Graham, Aaron (Bow Street magistrate): as detective 62, 109–10
Griffin, Rachael 3, 216–18
Grimwood, Eliza 2, 91–2, 95, 178–79, 181, 216–17

Hall, Thomas James (Bow Street magistrate) 83, 87, 114–18, 135, 137n33–n34, 176
Hannell, Mary (Russell's cook) 29, 31, 51; Eliminated from list of suspects 66; Finds employment post–trial 209; Hobler pleased with evidence 70; Name misspelt in press 35, 115; Receives £15 reward money 211
Harman, Clare: *Murder by the Book* 10, 102n66, 221n46
Hay, Douglas, and Francis Snyder 110–11
Hazlitt, William 43, 45–6, 50, 203

Index

Higgs, Thomas (Middlesex deputy coroner) 4, 65, 100n29, 172
Hobler, Francis (solicitor for the prosecution): Bow Street pre–trial examinations 113–18; Convinced of Courvoisier's guilt 112–13; Convinced of innocence of Henry Carr 70; Convinced of innocence of Mary Hannell and Sarah Mancer 113; At 14 Norfolk street 66, 111–12; Police solicitor 6–7, 110; Post–trial relations with Russell family 135–36; Queries Russell's closed eyes 61; Records afterstories of Russell's servants to 1842 209; Scrapbook 6–8, 11, 15–6, 106–7, *141*; Volunteers services in Courvoisier prosecution 111
Hook, Theodore: convinced of Sarah Mancer's guilt 80–2, 201
Hotel de Dieppe, Leicester Square: Courvoisier deposits parcel of stolen silverware 99; Insolvency 139n83; Police neglect to make enquiries about Courvoisier 215, 218; Popular with foreigners 126; Proprietor comes forward with evidence against Courvoisier 126
Hunt, Leigh: 'The Maid Servant' 31, 33, 45, 189

Jack the Ripper murders 5
James, P.D. 169

Kent, Constance 5, 214

Langbein, John 8, 176
Light, Alison 48–9
Lockwood, Lady Julia 40–1, 44, 47, 132, 199

Mancer, Sarah: Cross–examined by Charles Phillips 128–29, 132; Discovers murder 60; Eliminated as suspect by Metropolitan Police 66; Employed by Sir George Chetwynd 213; Examined at Bow Street 114–15, 117; Hobler as ally 209–11, 220; Leaves pauper lunatic asylum 213; Name misspelt in press 35, 115, 117, 213; Receives £15 reward money 211; Reputation 13, 35; Russell's housemaid 29, 33–4, 51; Subscription taken up post–trial 211–12; Suffers post–trial breakdown 212; Suspected by public 76–82; Suspicious of Courvoisier's behaviour 52
Maule, Fox (Undersecretary of State, Home Office) 112
Mayne, Richard (police commissioner) 15, 60–3, 66, 68, 70, 78, 85, 100n15, 106, 111–12, 114–15, 133–34, 194, 217
McCuskey, Bruce 147–48, 206–7
Meldrum, Tim 29, 41–2, 201
Mellinkoff, David 6, 22, 73–4, 178
Metropolitan Police; *see also* Police investigation; Police officers; Detective Department 5, 216–18; As a preventive force 1, 5, 63, 216
Miller, Andrew 166
Milnes, Monckton *146*, 162
Munby, A.J. 203

Newgate novel controversy 9, 147, 186–87, 190–94
Normanby, Lord (Home Secretary) 112, 115, 121, 135
Nussey, John (Russell's apothecary) 27, 61, 65, 86, 90, 116–17

Overton, Robert Blake: suggests use of fingerprint evidence 90–1, *144*, 215
Oxford, Edward 121, 214

Parke, James, Baron 123
Patch, Richard 98, 124
Philips, David 2
Phillips, Charles (counsel for the defence) 6, 52, 125, 128; Christian beliefs 131, 139n86; Controversial closing speech 128–32, 153, 200–1, 212; On the need for a public prosecutor 107, 219–20; Opposition to the Prisoner's Counsel Act 126; Professional reputation 8, 18n34, 106, 118, 125–26, 219; Published speeches used by John Thurtell 177; *Vacation Thoughts on Capital Punishment* 163
Phillipps, Samuel March (Undersecretary of State) 112, 114, 134–35; Redrafts Hobler's original brief 119
Piolaine, Madame: responsible for connecting Courvoisier with theft 99, 122, 126–28, 134, 177
Police investigation: Contamination of crime scene 66–7; Failure in intelligence gathering 99; Home Office supervision 112; Press coverage 93–8; Public correspondence on the case

83–9; Searches of Courvoisier's belongings 66, 69, 72–5; Search of premises for murder weapon and stolen goods 69; Theft discovered 68; Workmen called in to assist 68; Written summary of efforts to 17 May 71–2

Police officers: Baker (superintendent) 61, 66–7, 72, 85, 113–14, 116, 149; Baldwin, John (constable) 61, 66–7, 75, 84, 116, 130, 172; Beresford, Henry (inspector) 61, 65, 70–2, 76–7, 86, 88, 93, 99, 116, 127, 215, 218; Collier, George (constable) 68–70, 73, 116–17, 172, 215; Cronin, Paul (constable) 60, 71, 116, 122, 215; Glew, George (constable) 60, 71, 117; Harriott, John (Master Mariner and magistrate, River Police) 62; Horton, Charles (constable, River Police) 62, 100n11; Humphreys (constable) 73; Jarvis (inspector) 15, 66, 71, 172–73; Lovett (sergeant) 73; Pearce, Nicholas (inspector) 5, 35, 40, 61–2, 68–9, 72, 86, 103n102, 113–14, 116–17, 127, 130, 215, 217; Pullen (sergeant) 68, 122; Rose, William (constable) 35, 61, 67, 75, 116, 172; Shaw, Frederick (constable/sergeant) 68–70, 73, 116, 215, 217–18; Slade, Alfred (constable) 60, 117; Tedman, John (inspector) 35, 61, 65–6, 68, 71–3, 75–6, 84–5, 91–2, 116–17, 122, 129, 150–51, 172, 209, 215, 218

Police solicitors 110
Potter, Harry 164
Prisoner's Counsel Act 6, 106
Pritty, Hannah 208
Public prosecution: Bow Street magistrates 109; City solicitor, City of London 108; Director of Public Prosecutions 1879 107; Home Office involvement 109–10, 133; In the lower courts 109; Role of the police 111; Treasury solicitor 107–8

Radzinowicz, Sir Leon 2, 162
Ratcliffe Highway murders 2, 35, 98, 109–10
Reward money: Offered by the Treasury and the Russell family 74; As possible motivation for tainted evidence 99, 121, 125, 130; Rules governing receipt 214–15

River Police 62
Rivers, C.A.: Courtroom sketches of Courvoisier 133; Makes model of 14 Norfolk Street and draws plan of basement 133
Robbins, Bruce: *The Servant's Hand* 10, 13, 37, 49, 165–66, 170, 204, 207
Rowan, Colonel Charles (police commissioner) 63, 214–15, 217
Russell, Lord John 23–4, 83–4, 87, 90, 110, 125, 135, 151, 163, 167n13, 208, 219–20
Russell, Lord William: Burial 149–51; Children 26; Discovery of his murder 60; Domestic murder 13, 203, 205; Family background 23–5; Health and character 27–8; Home: 14 Norfolk Street 21–3, *142*; Last day 59; Marriage 24; Murder: historical significance 1; public interest in 20–1; Newspaper portraits *141*, *143*; Political career 25–6; Servants 29, 36

Saintsbury, George 164
Sellis, Joseph 14, 203
Servants: Foreign 46; Male domestics 205–7; As murderers 14, 202–3; And portraiture 173–74; And reading 187–89; Relationship with employers 47–53; Russell's neighbours' examined by police 67–8; As source of anxiety 46–7; As storytellers 170–71
Smith, Bruce P. 7, 109
Smollett, Tobias 12
Stafford, John (police solicitor) 7, 110
Steedman, Carolyn 10, 14, 28, 45, 171, 202
Stephen, Leslie: 'The decay of murder' 148
Straub, Kristina 11, 19n47, 205–6
Summerscale, Kate 214
Sussman, Herbert 205
Swift, Jonathan 11–2, 203

Tayler, William (footman diarist) 12, 34, 42–4, 47, 50–1, 166, 171, 187, 199, 206
Templeman, John 3, 91–2, 95–6, 121, 163, 216
Thackeray, William Makepeace: Attends Courvoisier's execution 9, 156–59; *Catherine* 191; 'On a Chalk-Mark on the Door' 13, 148, 203–4; On execution 16, 147–48, 157, 160, 162–64; Fear of servants 13, 20–1,

165–66, 204, 220; 'On Going to See a Man Hanged' 9, 13, 147, 163–65; 'The History of the Next French Revolution' 165; Master and servant relations 44, 170; On Newgate novels 147; *Pendennis* 148, 166, 189; 'The Rose and the Ring' 166; On servants' ambitions 32–3; Servants in novels 12, 148; Sympathy for servants 10, 39, 165, 204, 220; *Vanity Fair* 148, 164, 166, 204; 'The Yellow–Plush Correspondence' 166
Thomas, Deborah A. 163–64
Thurtell, John, and Joseph Hunt 4, 98, 177, 185
Tindal, Nicholas Conyngham (Lord Chief Justice) 123, 125; Sentences Courvoisier 208; Sums up for the jury 132

Tosh, John 205–6
Turner, E.S. 12
Turpin, Dick 3, 194

Wakley, Thomas (Middlesex coroner) 4, 64–5
Walsh, Bridget 205, 207
Webb, R.K. 188
Wentworth, Patricia 75
Wild, Jonathan 3
Williams, Abigail 189
Williams, Glanville 7
Wing, Thomas (Russell family solicitor) 111, 114
Woolf, Virginia 48–50, 57n153
Wrightson, Keith 16

York, William (Russell's coachman) 36, 66, 88, 115, 208–9

Printed in the United States
by Baker & Taylor Publisher Services